To Our Dear Frie... ...nges

From The Jon Welch Family

June 2022

THE LIFE OF MOSES

THE LIFE OF MOSES

GOD'S FIRST DELIVERER OF ISRAEL

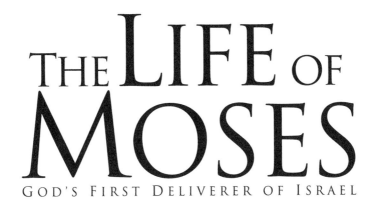

JAMES MONTGOMERY BOICE

P U B L I S H I N G

P.O. BOX 817 • PHILLIPSBURG • NEW JERSEY 08865-0817

Typesetting: Nord Compo

Printed in the United States of America

Library of Congress Cataloging-in-Publication Data
Names: Boice, James Montgomery, 1938-2000, author.
Title: The life of Moses: God's first deliverer of Israel / James Montgomery Boice.
Description: Phillipsburg: P&R Publishing, 2018.
Identifiers: LCCN 2016057994 | ISBN 9781596387539 (hardcover) |
  ISBN 9781596387546 (epub) | ISBN 9781596387553 (mobi)
Subjects: LCSH: Moses (Biblical leader)
Classification: LCC BS580.M6 B635 2017 | DDC 222/.1092—dc23
LC record available at https://lccn.loc.gov/2016057994

CONTENTS

PART 2: MOSES' FINEST HOUR

PART 3: WORSHIPPING IN THE WILDERNESS

Contents

FOREWORD

Introducing this volume is a rare and genuine privilege.

I say "rare" because *The Life of Moses* has never been published. This book thus provides the reading public with completely new material from the exceptional ministry of Dr. James Montgomery Boice, who for more than thirty years served as senior minister of Philadelphia's Tenth Presbyterian Church. To my knowledge, this is the first new expository commentary of Dr. Boice's that has been published since he died in 2000.

I say "genuine" because this new book gives us Boice at his best. Each chapter is based on a sermon that he first preached to his beloved congregation in Center City Philadelphia. Later, some of these messages formed the basis for materials used worldwide by Bible Study Fellowship.

Here we see many hallmarks of Dr. Boice's ministry. First and foremost, we see his absolute commitment to the Bible as the very Word of God. At various points Dr. Boice defends the Bible's historical reliability within the cultural context of Israel and Egypt. He also highlights the human authorship of writings that come to us from the pen of the prophet Moses. But he does all this without ever losing his firm grip on the inspiration of the Holy Spirit.

In effect, *The Life of Moses* completes the exposition of the Pentateuch that Dr. Boice began when he preached his well-known series on the book of Genesis. The exodus is the Old Testament's great story of redemption. Rather than giving a verse-by-verse exposition of this section of the Bible—the kind of approach that he took with the book of Romans, for example—Dr. Boice captures the broad sweep of Israel's captivity, deliverance, and wanderings in the wilderness.

He does this by focusing squarely on the life and ministry of Moses. I am reminded of the advice that he gave me when I decided to preach the book of Jeremiah, which happens to be the longest book in the Bible. For five years I served as Dr. Boice's associate minister for preaching. Frankly, he wasn't sure that preaching the whole book of Jeremiah was a very good idea. But he wisely and kindly suggested that it would be best for me to focus on the dramatic story of the prophet's life and ministry—exactly the approach that he had taken when he preached from Exodus to Deuteronomy and made Moses' ministry come to life.

As we read this big-picture survey, we sense Dr. Boice's obvious love and admiration for Moses as a man of God. The book finds important unity in its thematic focus on Moses as a man of faith and prayer, who led God's people with a rare combination of humility and courage. In many ways, Dr. Boice was a man after Moses' heart—completely committed to communicating the Word of God, totally trusting in God's promises, and faithfully willing to lead the same people of God decade after decade. He, too, combined humility with courage as he fought a series of battles for the Bible and led his congregation out of a denomination that was drifting away from gospel truth.

Much more important than Moses, however, is the God of Moses, who is the real hero of the exodus and everything that happened afterwards. *The Life of Moses* shows God faithfully keeping his covenant promises, graciously rescuing his wayward people, powerfully defeating their enemies, generously providing for their daily needs, and wisely showing them the way of obedience—in short, being everything in a God that they could ever need or desire. *The Life of Moses* is a God-centered book that introduces us to a Savior who comes for his people and delivers them again and again.

It is also a Christ-centered book that gives us a clearer understanding of the person and work of our Lord and Savior Jesus Christ. Dr. Boice had an eye for the many close connections between the Old and New Testaments. With Moses, those connections are especially abundant. The result is an exposition that frequently displays Jesus Christ in his atoning sacrifice and resurrection glory. Moses may have been "God's first deliverer of Israel," but he was only the first: Jesus Christ is God's final Deliverer.

In this study, Dr. Boice supplies sound biblical teaching and wise pastoral advice on a wide range of practical topics—everything from principles for effective leadership to the Christian's relationship to the governing authorities. His constant goal is practical Christianity.

Everyone who reads this life of Moses will have the rare and genuine pleasure of hearing Dr. Boice's strong voice again. By the grace of God, the message in its pages will bring fresh blessing to the church of Jesus Christ. Over the course of a lifetime, God will lead us the way that he led Moses: into a courageous life of faith and prayer.

Philip Graham Ryken
President
Wheaton College

PREFACE

From January 1993 to early February 1994, Jim Boice preached a series of messages on "The Life of Moses" in the Sunday evening services at Tenth Presbyterian Church in Philadelphia, covering four of the five books of the Pentateuch. This was a comprehensive sermon series, but until now it has never appeared in print.

For several reasons, the series differed from Jim's usual approach to preaching through books of the Bible. In the Moses sermons he deliberately presented a more sweeping, introductory series of messages, covering a much greater swath of Scripture than in his usual, often verse-by-verse, exposition. The series also represented an exception to Jim's usual practice of writing out complete manuscripts, which he never failed to do when preparing sermons for the morning services. Sometimes for an evening series, as in the case of these messages on Moses, he made careful notes to guide his preaching but did not prepare complete texts of each sermon. This gave the delivery a kind of freedom, as he was not tied to an edited text. He memorized almost verbatim the written messages after only one or two readings; the more informal delivery seemed to fit the less formal atmosphere of the evening services.

Despite these surface differences, however, Jim did not depart from his deep conviction that the Scriptures are a unity and that all Scripture points to Jesus Christ. Though he focused on the actions and character of Moses, that great deliverer of Israel, and on the many events connected to the exodus and the years of the desert wandering, these messages are much more than an interesting biography and a historical review of Israel's beginnings as a nation, no matter how important or compelling those intertwined narratives might be.

As Jim makes clear in his opening chapter, in studying the deliverance from slavery in Egypt on the night of the Passover, or the great symbolic significance of the rituals performed on the Day of Atonement, or so much other material related to the experiences and struggles of the forty years in the desert wanderings, we see that "all point forward to Jesus Christ"; all "prefigure the coming ministry of Jesus Christ" (p. 8). The discussion of those events leads to an explanation of how they are a "shadow of the things to come, but the substance belongs to Christ" (Col. 2:17). Jesus Christ is present in every chapter. Practical applications flow out of the theological affirmations.

The challenge of turning these "studies," as Jim would have called them, into a published volume has been truly a team effort. These messages, though not written as complete manuscripts, were recorded, and Robert Brady, executive director of the Alliance of Confessing Evangelicals, has had the vision to believe that in book form *The Life of Moses* would provide helpful and readable instruction on four often-neglected books of the Old Testament and would therefore be a blessing to God's people. He persevered, and the editors at P&R Publishing accepted the challenge to put the messages into print.

Transcribing the audio messages was only the beginning of this journey. There has been the need for careful editing, not to alter the content, but to smooth out where needed the transition from verbal to written expression—to make, in other words, the rough places plain. There has also been the need to track down when possible the sources Jim refers to without giving the full publishing data that he would have provided in a more formal manuscript. I became involved in the editing process once the editors at P&R had done much initial work.

I want to express deepest thanks to those whose help, patience, perseverance, and encouragement have brought us to the goal—the publishing of *The Life of Moses.*

Special thanks go to Robert Brady for his gracious perseverance and his involvement at key points—an involvement that has kept the project on course. He has been both a friend and a cheerleader.

I am thankful indeed for an afternoon over tea with Janice and Stan Roberts and for their wisdom and support as we talked over the need for more time to tackle the editing challenges and my possible role in that effort. Their appreciation of the continuing value of Jim's biblical studies has been a great encouragement.

Special thanks are also due to Aaron Gottier, editorial project manager at P&R, who has been endlessly patient as the editing has progressed. He has been a very careful reader and editor, with perceptive questions and gentle nudges in order to improve clarity and, in certain places, nail down specific references when at all possible. He and his team have been immensely supportive.

It has been a great blessing to have Marion Clark, a former pastor of Tenth Presbyterian Church, read through the entire manuscript. He, too, has an eagle eye, as well as sound sense. As one who served with Jim and who knows Jim's work well (having edited *Come to the Waters*, a year's devotional readings gathered from Jim's published and unpublished works), he has been especially helpful in pointing out some statements in the text that needed clarification or revision.

Lydia Brownback, a friend and former editor of Jim's messages for *The Bible Study Hour* radio broadcasts and the monthly magazine *God's Word Today*, has graciously added to her own heavy responsibilities by taking time to tackle the arduous task of preparing the Scripture and topical indexes. I am deeply grateful for her help and expertise.

Deryck Barson, in the midst of his own PhD studies and ministry duties at Tenth Church, has been resourceful and perceptive in tracking down bibliographic data and smoothing out several troublesome places in the text. Faithful friend Bill Edgar, with the help of a research librarian, took time from his busy schedule to find in the recesses of the Westminster Seminary library two volumes needed for documentation. Nancy Hala, for many years a stalwart friend-in-need, dug out from the archives at Tenth Church the preaching schedule for the Moses series. All these efforts have added to the accuracy and helpfulness of the book.

Always, I am thankful for the friendship, wisdom, and guidance of Philip Ryken, once my pastor at Tenth Presbyterian and now president of Wheaton College. His kind introduction to this volume is only one evidence of his gracious spirit. Phil's concern for the continuation of Jim's ministry through the printed word has done much to protect and strengthen that legacy.

Finally, it can truly be said that without the steady, skilled help of Sarah Brubaker, my former student and now my friend and colleague, all the edits of the last year—researched, collated, revised—would be trapped in the ancient technology of pen and paper. Sarah's technology skills, as well as her thoughtful suggestions when a word or phrase just wasn't quite right, have been a vital contribution. Her cheerful, willing spirit has made working together a joy.

May the Lord use these studies of Israel's first deliverer, Moses, to point us to the great Deliverer, the Lord Jesus Christ, and to strengthen the faith and godly walk of all who read these pages.

Linda M. Boice

PART 1

THE BATTLE OF EGYPT

1

ISRAEL IN EGYPT

Exodus 1:1—14

A GREAT MAN IN HISTORY

Apart from Jesus Christ, no person in history has made as deep or lasting an impression on the world as Moses, the "servant of God" (Rev. 15:3). He was the great lawgiver and emancipator of Israel, born to Jewish parents when they were slaves in a land not their own. He was educated in the court of one of the mightiest empires that has ever existed. He was heir to Egypt's wealth, prestige, and legendary pleasures. Yet, when he was forty years old, he elected to identify himself with his own oppressed race. He had to flee the country and live outside Egypt for forty years, until God called him to return and lead the people out. He stood before Pharaoh and demanded in the name of God that Pharaoh let the people go, and God did mighty miracles to deliver his people. Moses then led the Israelites in the wilderness for forty years to the very threshold of the promised land.

His was a remarkable career. The exodus from Egypt alone is one of the great stories in history. The law, which contains the Ten Commandments, is one of the great treasures of the world.

Moses' story is told in Exodus, Leviticus, Numbers, and Deuteronomy, which he authored alongside Genesis. He also wrote at least one psalm—Psalm 90—and is mentioned nearly seven hundred times in Scripture. We find his name on the lips of Jesus Christ. Paul speaks of him often. Obviously he is important.

One English writer says about Moses, "Take him for all in all, regard him not in one but many aspects, Moses is the greatest character in history, sacred or profane."[1] I'm a little leery of that kind of statement. But at the very end of Deuteronomy, after Moses' death, we read God's own evaluation:

> And there has not arisen a prophet since in Israel like Moses, whom the LORD knew face to face, none like him for all the signs and the wonders that the LORD sent him to do in the land of Egypt, to Pharaoh and to all his servants and to all his land, and for all the mighty power and all the great deeds of terror that Moses did in the sight of all Israel. (Deut. 34:10–12)

THE CHARACTER OF MOSES

Important as Moses' achievements are, they are overshadowed by his character. It is Moses' character that brings him down to us and makes this study valuable. If we think only in terms of what Moses achieved, who could ever begin to dream of doing such things? It is almost inconceivable that God would use anybody today in that way. But if we think in terms of those aspects of his personality that God used, this study becomes very practical for us.

Four traits stand out above the others.

His faith. Moses is praised for his faith again and again. He seems to have never taken his eyes off God after God first met him at the burning bush, and so he went from faith to faith and thus from strength to strength. That is the secret of Christian leadership: faith in God. All the great heroes of the Bible—those who are praised by the Scriptures themselves—are praised because of their faith. They were normal people. They had shortcomings and doubts, just as we

1. Thomas Guthrie, *Studies of Character from the Old Testament* (New York: Robert Carter and Brothers, 1872), 107.

do. But because of their faith in God, they became strong and were used by God in great ways. The author of Hebrews says that through faith they "conquered kingdoms, enforced justice, obtained promises" (Heb. 11:33). By faith they "stopped the mouths of lions, quenched the power of fire, escaped the edge of the sword" (vv. 33–34); they "were made strong out of weakness, became mighty in war, put foreign armies to flight" (v. 34). If you feel weak in faith, you have something to learn from Moses.

His dedication to prayer. When God used Moses to lead the people out of Egypt and they were trapped, as it seemed—the water of the Red Sea before them and the pursuing armies of the pharaoh behind—Moses instinctively turned to God in prayer. When the people rebelled in the wilderness, Moses turned to God in prayer. The greatest example of intercessory prayer in the entire Bible—greater even, in my judgment, than Abraham's great plea for Sodom and Gomorrah in Genesis 18—is Moses' prayer for the people when they disobeyed by making the golden calf (Ex. 32). Moses offered to be sent to hell himself if by his sacrifice he could save the people whom he loved. We learn a lot about prayer from Moses.

His meekness. Moses was a meek man. So many people who become great or get into positions of authority lose humility right away. I've not known many of the famous in the world, but I've known some. My experience is that generally they're very much full of themselves; you find yourself thinking that you'd rather go home and be with someone nice instead.

That did not happen to Moses. The greater he became, the more meek, the more humble he became. "Now the man Moses was very meek, more than all people who were on the face of the earth" (Num. 12:3). When you're thinking of leadership qualities, don't forget humility. God puts it right up there at the top.

His courage. Moses excelled in courage. He showed it on many occasions, but if we had no other example, he certainly showed courage in marching up before the mighty pharaoh. A Bedouin shepherd from the desert, Moses stood in the splendor of Egypt and said, "In the name of God Almighty, let my people go." It took courage to do that. He showed that courage throughout his life.

THE DEVELOPMENT OF CHARACTER

In the few incidents we know from Moses' early life, these good qualities do not seem prominent. For example, when Moses decided to quit the court of Pharaoh and identify himself with his people, the first thing we know he did was to kill an Egyptian. He saw oppression taking place, so he killed the oppressor. That's not exactly humility. It may have been courage of a sort, but that courage did not stand him in great stead, because as soon as the murder was found out and he realized that his life was in danger, he fled the country. Then, when he stood before the burning bush and God told him to go back to Egypt, courage was the last thing he showed. He did not want to go. He thought up all kinds of reasons why he couldn't go and why God had to choose somebody else.

You and I can look at characters in the Bible and say, "I wish I had those great traits, but I don't." But it is encouraging to know that *these* people did not always have those traits. They learned them along the way. Moses learned courage and meekness and prayer, and he grew great in faith year by year as he lived with God. If he did it, you can do it, too.

Moses lived to be 120 years old. He had forty years in Egypt in the court, and when he was forty years old, he had to run away. He spent forty years in the desert as a shepherd, and God met him at the burning bush and called him to be the deliverer when he was eighty years old. Then he led the people for forty years. It has been said that Moses spent forty years in Egypt learning *something*, then he spent forty years in the desert learning to be *nothing*, and then spent the last forty years of his life proving God to be *everything*. This is a good way of describing what the Christian life is all about. Some of us do not prove God to be everything because we've never learned that we are nothing. When we come to that point, we are ready to have God work through us as he did with Moses.

MOSES THE AUTHOR

Not only was Moses a great emancipator, but he was also the vehicle by which God gave us the first five books of the Bible: the *Pentateuch* ("five scrolls"). He was the author, humanly speaking, of a large portion of the Scriptures.

Some people once argued that Moses could not have written the Pentateuch because writing was unknown in Moses' day. All that has gone by the boards. Six different written languages from the time of Moses have been discovered in the very area where Moses led the people for forty years. Since Moses was educated in the court of the Egyptians, he certainly knew hieroglyphics; and he probably knew Akkadian, the trade language of the day. He was undoubtedly a highly educated man.

That is not the most important thing that needs to be said, however. Let me give you a basic hermeneutic—some guidelines for how our material in the Pentateuch should be approached. Four important things need to be said about the Bible.

THE BIBLE HAS ONE TRUE AUTHOR: GOD

The Bible comes to us from God. It is more than a merely human book. It contains the characteristics of human books; the various authors put the stamp of their personalities on what they wrote, and their vocabularies differ. But the Bible, having come to us from God, contains the one story that God wants to tell us. One passage, perhaps more than any other in the Bible, makes this point:

> All Scripture is breathed out by God and profitable for teaching, for reproof, for correction, and for training in righteousness, that the man of God may be complete, equipped for every good work. (2 Tim. 3:16–17)

Sometimes we refer to the Bible as being *inspired*. *Inspired* means that God, by his Holy Spirit, *breathed into* human writers so that they wrote what God wanted. That is true, but it is not what this passage says. This passage does not say that the Bible is the result of God's

7

breathing into the human writers, but that the Bible is the result of the *breathing out* of God. It is saying that the Bible is God's Word, "and is therefore perfect and truthful, as God himself is."[2]

Two important principles of interpretation follow from this. First, the Bible is God's book from beginning to end, even though it has come to us through human authors. It is a unity. Second, because the Bible is a unity, it will not contradict itself if rightly understood. Sometimes we read portions of the Bible that seem to contradict. We say, "How can this portion go with this one?" But, if we understand it correctly, we find that the Bible tells a consistent story.

This means that the God we find in the first books of the Old Testament is the same God whom we find in the New Testament. Sometimes people say that the God in the Old Testament is a tribal deity, a God of wrath; they say the descriptions of God in the Old Testament are unworthy of him. We will find as we study that this is not true. The God whom we find at the beginning is exactly the same God who is presented to us by the Lord Jesus Christ—a sovereign, holy, and loving God.

The Bible's unity also means that we are not misinterpreting it but rather interpreting it rightly when we see that the details given for Israel's worship prefigure the coming ministry of Jesus Christ. What we find in the tabernacle, the sacrifices, and the plan of the construction itself—all point forward to Jesus Christ.

THE BIBLE HAS BEEN GIVEN TO US THROUGH HUMAN AUTHORS

Sometimes people argue that to err is human; so, if human beings had anything to do with the Bible, it must contain errors. That is a fallacy of logic. Just because it is natural for me to make mistakes doesn't mean that I have to make mistakes in any given instance. It is possible, for example, even on a human level quite apart from inspiration or anything spiritual, to write an inerrant manual on how to run a dishwasher.

---

2. James Montgomery Boice, *Standing on the Rock: Upholding Biblical Authority in a Secular Age* (Grand Rapids: Kregel, 1998), 39.

Now for human authors to produce an inerrant book covering so many details over such a long period of history would seem an impossibility. But we are not speaking of a book simply put together by human authors. As Paul states so clearly, "this is what we speak, not in words taught us by human wisdom but in words taught by the Spirit" (1 Cor. 2:13 NIV).

And Peter states, "No prophecy of Scripture comes from someone's own interpretation. For no prophecy was ever produced by the will of man, but men spoke from God as they were carried along by the Holy Spirit" (2 Peter 1:20–21). The word translated *carried along* is the same word that Luke, the author of Acts, uses when he describes a ship in the midst of a storm at sea. The sailors cut down the ship's sails to keep them from being torn apart, and the ship was *driven along* before the wind. It was still a ship, but it couldn't control its own destiny; the wind took it wherever it would. That is what Peter says happened to the human authors of Scripture. They were still men; they wrote with their own vocabularies; but the Holy Spirit bore them along. In other words, "What Scripture says, God says—through human agents and without error."[3]

This view of inspiration has an application for interpretation. Interpretation has to do with understanding the author's context, his vocabulary, and the situation out of which he was writing. That means, for example, that when we want to understand these books, we can learn something from secular sources. It is helpful, for example, to know about the religion of Egypt, because the plagues were not a case of God's simply being arbitrary in his choice of scourges. The plagues were all directed against the gods of Egypt. Every single plague showed that the God of the Hebrews—the true God, Jehovah—was more powerful than Apis the bull or Hathor the cow, down through all the gods and goddesses of the Egyptian pantheon.

---

3. This wording, developed by the International Council on Biblical Inerrancy, is taken from James Montgomery Boice, *Does Inerrancy Matter?* (Wheaton: Tyndale House Publishers, 1981), 15, as quoted in Boice, *Standing on the Rock*, 40.

THE BIBLE'S PURPOSE IS TO LEAD US TO FAITH IN JESUS CHRIST

Jesus taught this himself. Talking to the Jewish leaders, he said,

> You search the Scriptures because you think that in them you have eternal life; and it is they that bear witness about me, yet you refuse to come to me that you may have life. (John 5:39–40)

The Scriptures of the Jewish leaders were the Scriptures of the Old Testament. Jesus was saying in very clear language that these Scriptures were given to point to himself.

You couldn't fault the leaders of Jesus' day for failing to study the Scriptures. They did that. They were diligent in their study. They studied individual words when they copied them out. They counted the letters on the page so that they would not make a single mistake in their copying. They were great students of the Scriptures. But Jesus said that they missed the point of it all. The reason God gave the Scriptures was to point to him, and he had come—and they did not understand him and would not come to him to have life.

Do you see what this means? It means that when we study the life of Moses, we are not studying just a great man or even a marvelous story of deliverance for an oppressed people. We are studying things that point to Jesus Christ. If at the end of this book you do not understand Jesus Christ better and are not following him more closely, you have missed the point.

WE NEED THE HOLY SPIRIT TO UNDERSTAND THE BIBLE

Not only was the Holy Spirit active in giving the Bible, but he is also active in opening our minds to understand the Bible when we read it. Theologians refer to this as *illumination*. It is like turning on a light. Paul told the Corinthians, "Now we have received not the spirit of the world, but the Spirit who is from God, that we might understand the things freely given us by God" (1 Cor. 2:12). Without the Spirit, however, spiritual things cannot be understood (see 1 Cor. 2:14). Since the Bible deals with spiritual matters, it requires the ministry of the Holy Spirit for us to understand them.

10

This leads us to a very practical matter: we have to pray as we come to the Bible. You can become very learned in your knowledge of the Bible and not be affected by it in a personal way. You may know all about Pauline theology and even teach it better than many ministers. But for God's Word to have the right impact on you, prayer must precede your study. You have to ask the Holy Spirit for understanding, and, when you study the Bible and understand it, you have to ask the Holy Spirit to give you the grace to actually live by it. The Holy Spirit has to teach us if we are to benefit from this study of Moses' life or any other Bible topic.

IN THE BEGINNING

Moses' story begins in Exodus, and the very first thing we notice is that this second book of the Bible is closely tied to the first. It picks up the story of Abraham's descendants by showing what happened to them in Egypt and how they got out of Egypt.

The tie between Genesis and Exodus is closer than is immediately apparent. For one thing, the Hebrew text of Exodus begins with the word *and*. Exodus 1:1 actually says, "*And* these are the names. . . ." Numbers and Leviticus also begin this way. What Moses is saying, of course, is that the story that is about to begin in Exodus is not a new story. It is a new chapter in the story of redemption and a continuation of what God began when he first called Abraham, the father of the Jewish people, out of Ur of the Chaldeans.

GOD'S PROMISE TO ABRAHAM

God's call to the patriarch Abraham gives us an outline of what is coming. In the next chapter, we will see more of the condition of the people in Egypt. But what we find in Exodus, Leviticus, Numbers, and Deuteronomy was prophesied by God to Abraham and recorded for us in Genesis 15. This chapter in Genesis describes what was probably the most significant day in Abraham's whole life.

God had called Abraham out of Ur when he was seventy years old and had promised him that he would be the father of a great nation. But Abraham had no children. The time came when Abraham started thinking of an alternative. He had a servant in his household named Eliezer, and he thought, *I guess Eliezer is going to be my heir.* Then God intervened.

God took Abraham out at night and told him to look at the stars. "Can you count them?" They were beyond Abraham's ability to count. God told Abraham that his descendants would be like that—innumerable. And Abraham "believed the LORD, and he counted it to him as righteousness" (Gen. 15:6). James and Paul both pick up on believing God as the very essence of the gospel, and Abraham became the first great example of such belief (see Rom. 4:3; Gal. 3:6; James 2:23). Immediately afterward, God gave Abraham a magnificent promise.

He had Abraham make the preparations. In ancient times, when an agreement known as a covenant was enacted between two people, they did it in a solemn way with the shedding of blood. They cut animals in two and put each half of each animal over and against one another on the ground. The two parties to the covenant stood between the two rows of slain animals and the area that had been consecrated by blood, and there they would exchange their promises.

God had Abraham do that. He took a heifer, a goat, a ram, a dove, and a young pigeon, cut each of them except for the birds in half, and arranged them in rows. What happened next, however, differed from the way in which a covenant was normally enacted. Abraham was on the sidelines in a dream or trance, and symbols representing God passed alone between the pieces. In other words, this covenant did not depend on Abraham. Only God participated in the ceremony. The theological term for this is *unilateral.* God's unilateral covenant with Abraham did not depend on Abraham's obedience, faithfulness, understanding, strength, character, courage, or anything else. God said, "This is what I'm going to do" and gave Abraham a great and marvelous promise.

> Know for certain that your offspring will be sojourners in a land that is not theirs and will be servants there, and they will be afflicted for four hundred years. But I will bring judgment on the nation that they serve, and afterward they shall come out with great possessions. . . . And they shall come back here in the fourth generation, for the iniquity of the Amorites is not yet complete. . . .

To your offspring I give this land, from the river of Egypt to the great river, the river Euphrates, the land of the Kenites, the Kenizzites, the Kadmonites, the Hittites, the Perizzites, the Rephaim, the Amorites, the Canaanites, the Girgashites and the Jebusites. (Gen. 15:13–14, 16, 18–21)

A HISTORY OF THE PEOPLE

God's unilateral covenant to bless Abraham contains six great statements, which give us an outline of the subsequent history of the Jewish people.

The Hebrews would be strangers in a land that was not theirs. The Hebrews were from Canaan. How did they end up in Egypt?

The last third of Genesis tells us how this happened. Jacob had twelve sons. One of them, Joseph, was Jacob's favorite, and his brothers hated him because of this and decided to sell him into slavery. A caravan of Midianites came by, so the brothers sold him to the Midianites. The Midianites took Joseph down to Egypt, and he was sold as a slave there.

It was a terrible thing to happen. Joseph was seventeen years old when he was carried away to a foreign land. He did not even know the language. But he was a man of integrity. Remarkably, this young man grew up in a pagan land and kept his faith in God and, furthermore, kept his character. He continued to be a moral man, and God blessed him and protected him, even though he experienced all kinds of terrible things—including lies and jail. And God used the circumstances of his life to bring him to a position of power in Egypt.

On one occasion, while Joseph was still imprisoned, the pharaoh had a dream. He did not know what it meant and was puzzled about it. He couldn't get any help from the wise men in his kingdom, but he had a servant who had been in jail with Joseph some years before, and this servant remembered that Joseph had interpreted one of his dreams, which had come true. He told the pharaoh about Joseph, saying that maybe he could help.

They called Joseph, and Joseph explained the meaning of the pharaoh's dream. There was going to be a period of abundance: seven years of plenty in the land. Then there were going to be seven years of famine. Joseph told them to prepare for these hard years. He conducted himself so wisely that the pharaoh said, "Let's put him in charge of the operation. Let him take charge of saving up the grain for the lean years."

Joseph acquitted himself well and eventually became the second most powerful person in all Egypt. When the famine came, it affected Canaan as well as Egypt. Joseph's brothers and father did not have any food, so they went down to Egypt. Through a chain of events, God not only brought about the repentance of the brothers so that they recognized what they had done and were reconciled with Joseph, but God also saved the family. Under the patronage of Joseph, they came to Egypt, and they and their descendants lived there for 430 years.

The Hebrews would be slaves in the land. Although Joseph was taken to Egypt as a slave, the rest of his family arrived favored by Joseph and with the blessing of the pharaoh. But eventually a new pharaoh arose who had never heard about Joseph (see Ex. 1:8). Under that pharaoh, the people began to experience the oppression that made their lives so bitter.

The Hebrews would be mistreated. Not only would the Hebrews be slaves, but they would also be badly mistreated, relentlessly forced to build for the Egyptians and labor in their fields (see Ex. 1:13–14). At last the oppression reached the point where the pharaoh ordered that all the newborn Hebrew males should be killed. It was a very bitter time.

The nation that mistreated the Hebrews would be punished. The early chapters of Exodus tell us how this happened. God judged the Egyptians by bringing a series of ten plagues on Egypt. The plagues increased in intensity. They began with the judgment on the river, and they ended with the death of all the firstborn. Because of these judgments, in the end Pharaoh was willing to let the people go.

The Hebrews would experience a great deliverance and would leave the land of their oppression with many possessions. Exodus 12 tells how the Israelites left the land of Egypt on the night of the Passover. *Passover* refers to the passing over of the angel of death. The

Israelites were spared on the principle of substitution. The blood they had spread on the lintels of their doors and on their doorposts showed that an innocent victim, a lamb, had died in place of the firstborn of that family. And that very night the Israelites left Egypt.

In the fourth generation, the Hebrews would return to Canaan. It was not an easy return. Their return took a long, long time—forty years passed before they actually entered the land. But this journey is what we read about in the continuation of the story throughout the Pentateuch. The actual entrance into the land happened under Joshua, the successor of Moses, and this story is told in the book of the Bible that bears his name.

LEARNING AS WE GO ALONG

What we will learn in the rest of this study is very practical and can be divided broadly into two areas of application.

THE CHARACTER OF MOSES

Moses was a great leader, and most of us have leadership responsibilities—in the home, in the church, at work, wherever it may be. If you have leadership responsibilities at all, whether you're responsible for a child or for a large group of people, you can learn from Moses and his character.

Do you believe and trust God implicitly in all things, as Moses did? Moses had a great God, and so he learned to obey him. He became great because of the greatness of God. If you do not trust God much now, are you willing to learn to trust him? If you are willing to learn to trust him, God will teach you. Your trust is what God wants more than anything else.

Are you willing to learn about prayer and to pray better than you do now? None of us is very strong in prayer. We need to learn in this area, and Moses is a great example.

Are you humble? If not, are you willing to be made so?

Moses was also courageous. There is a great difference between bravado and real courage, the courage you have when you stand up and do the right thing—even when everything seems to be against you—because you know God. Moses bowed before God alone. He knew the greatness of his God to such a degree that he was able to stand up even before Pharaoh. Are you willing to grow in courage?

THE CHARACTER OF GOD

We have only begun to touch on the character of God. We will see it unfolding here. In the books we will study, God teaches the people of Israel what he is like because, just as with many people today, the Hebrews had no idea. Most people today have a romantic idea of God in their heads that has nothing to do with the true God. In these books, God teaches the people about his character, especially his holiness. Much of Exodus, Leviticus, Numbers, and Deuteronomy has to do with God's people, the Israelites, learning about the holiness of God.

Already we have seen several things about God.

God is faithful. God made promises to Abraham hundreds of years before the exodus. Centuries went by. Many of the people in Egypt who were suffering under the cruel lash of their oppressors thought that God had forgotten them. But God had not forgotten. The four hundred years had not expired. At the end of that time God, who never breaks his word and who always keeps his promises, sent Moses to say to Pharaoh, "Let my people go." By the plagues on Egypt, God brought his people out of bondage.

God is powerful. We've begun to see that God is omnipotent and irresistible. Even Pharaoh, the mightiest monarch of the day, with all the power of the Egyptian armies at his command, was unable to stand against him. The God who delivered the people in that far-off day is the same God who has delivered us from sin through the death of Jesus Christ. He has done it for exactly the same reason: because he is a loving God who is faithful to his promises.

Do you want to know this God in a deeper way? God wants you to know him better. Tell him that, and you will find that he will reveal himself to you as he revealed himself to Moses and the people of Israel.

2

THE KING WHO
KNEW NOT JOSEPH

Exodus 1:15—22

THE GROWTH OF A NATION

Moses' story begins in the book of Exodus. Now *exodus* means "exit" or "going out," and this book is the story of the deliverance, the going out, of the Israelites from Egypt.

Yet it is more than that. What we read in Exodus is the story not only of the deliverance of the nation but of the birth of the nation. When we read the opening verses, we find that the people who initially went to Egypt in the time of Joseph numbered only seventy. They were just a large family.[1] Yet by the time the people left Egypt, the Israelites must have numbered about two million.[2]

That was the problem. As long as the family was just a family, nobody minded. But as the Israelites grew in number, they became a threat to the Egyptians. Exodus 1 tells us that the pharaoh said they were likely to join with Egypt's enemies if war broke out, so he

---

1. The number varies in different places depending on whether Joseph and his wives and their children are counted, so sometimes the number is given as seventy, sometimes as seventy-five.

2. In Exodus 38:26, about two years after the exodus, the number of men over twenty years of age is given as 603,550. When women and children are added to that number, it adds up to at least two million people.

settled on a plan to oppress them, hoping to reduce their numbers by forced labor. When this failed, he gave instructions that all Hebrew males should be put to death when they were born. This also failed, and God greatly blessed the people with abundant offspring.

That is the background of what we want to study.

EGYPT

Egypt is the location for the exodus, so I want to give something of its history as well as some insight into the pharaohs who reigned at the time of Moses' birth and during the exodus of the people from Egypt about eighty years later.

A TIMELINE FOR EGYPT

Egypt is a very ancient land, so old that scholars do not know when its history began. Estimated dates for the first dynasties go back as far as 5500 BC—five and a half millennia before the birth of Christ—and they range forward from that date to perhaps 3100 BC. There is a variation of about two thousand years, which is more or less hazy in the minds of scholars. Even by the latest of those dates, Egypt had been a thriving empire for about a thousand years before the Israelites settled in Goshen under the blessing of the pharaoh of that time.

The United States is only a couple of hundred years old, and we can't remember all the presidents. When there are thousands of years of history, it is hard to remember all the rulers, so scholars generally think in terms of dynasties. A dynasty is a chain of rulers all from one family, until that family ceases to rule and a new family takes over, forming another dynasty. Scholars reckon that there were thirty or thirty-one dynasties in Egypt's history. Even that is hard to keep track of, so they also group these into periods, each period containing a number of dynasties.

If we do that, the history of Egypt goes something like this:

 • *Early Period (Dynasties I–II). c.2950–2575 BC*
 • *Old Kingdom (III–VI). c.2575–2150 BC*

During this period, the great pyramids were built. This means that those pyramids existed for about a thousand years before the time of Moses.

*   *First Intermediate Period (VII–XI).* c.2125–1975 BC
    This was a time of upheaval in Egypt. The land seems to have been taken over by local rulers when the strong rule that had existed in the Old Kingdom broke down.
*   *The Middle Kingdom (XI [cont.]–XIII).* c.1975–1640 BC
    Thieves in Upper Egypt ruled the country during these years.
*   *Second Intermediate Period (XIV–XVII).* c.1630–1520 BC
    This stage becomes interesting from the point of view of Jewish history, because during the Second Intermediate Period an alien people known as the Hyksos ruled Egypt. They were Semitic people, and for a long time scholars thought this was the period when the Israelites were in Egypt. But this view is probably not accurate. During this time the Egyptians realized that they would have to defend their borders, and for the very first time they created a large army and extended their frontiers.
*   *New Kingdom (XVIII–XX).* c.1539–1075 BC
    This period was dominated by the eighteenth dynasty, which marked the peak of Egyptian influence. Under the pharaohs of that dynasty, the kingdom extended as far as the Euphrates River. Raamses II, the most famous pharaoh of the eighteenth dynasty, ruled c.1279–1213 BC
*   *Third Intermediate Period (XXI–XXV).* c.1075–715 BC
*   *Late Period (XXVI–XXXI).* 715–332 BC

In 332 BC Alexander the Great entered Egypt, ending the ancient history of the nation.

THE NATURE OF EGYPT

Egypt is a long country, extending about six hundred miles on either side of the Nile River, from the highlands of Sudan in the south to the Nile delta emptying into the Mediterranean Sea in the north. For thousands of miles to the west there is only desert across North Africa. On the southeast lies the Great Arabian Desert. With almost no annual rainfall, only the Nile River provides the Egyptians enough water to grow crops. So this country developed on each side of the river, extending from one or two miles up to twenty-five or thirty miles to the east and west of the river. The yearly inundations ensured fertility.

Egypt was also wealthy, not only because of the produce that was grown in the river valley but also because the country was rich in natural resources. Fish swarmed in the river. Waterfowl were plentiful along the banks. The land was ideal for raising cattle. Papyrus plants grew in the delta area, and papyrus, from which we get our word *paper*, was used for making paper and matting, baskets, sandals, and even small boats. The Egyptians loved to hunt, and there were lots of wild animals: jackals, foxes, hyenas, lions, lynxes, and leopards. From the banks of the Nile they had plenty of clay for making bricks and pottery. For their more permanent structures, they could carve softer stone like sandstone and limestone from the great cliffs that lined the Nile for much of its length. Mountains to the east, between the Nile and the Red Sea, were mined for alabaster, porphyry, granite, and basalt, for copper and gold. The Egyptians did not have any iron, but it is about the only important metal they lacked.

Egypt was also well protected. It had desert on both the eastern and western borders. There was danger only from the south, and for many thousands of years the Egyptians did not face a threat from that direction. Therefore they did not have to spend a great deal of their natural resources to support and maintain a large army. Only after the Hyksos invaded (1630–1520 BC) were the Egyptians aware that they needed an army, and thus they created a strong military.

Egypt was also sophisticated. Recall that in Acts, when Stephen was rehearsing the history of the Jewish people, he said, "Moses was instructed in all the wisdom of the Egyptians" (Acts 7:22). That is quite a statement, because the Egyptians were known for their learning. They had writing, first of all. The Egyptians wrote by *hieroglyphs*, a "sacred writing" that is pictographic. They kept a great many historical records, as well as wisdom literature, the sayings of the sages, and adventure stories. The Egyptians excelled in art and music. They developed sophisticated forms of medicine, including fillings for decayed teeth, and rudimentary brain surgery. They studied the stars and plotted the seasons, and they excelled in mathematical and engineering skill, as the great pyramids, tombs, and temples demonstrate.

Egypt may have been sophisticated and wealthy, the wonder of the ancient world, but it was also a very pagan land. They had very debased ideas about deity and worshipped animals such as bulls, cows, birds, snakes, and crocodiles. When Paul refers to the depravity of mankind in general, his words certainly could be applied to ancient Egypt.

> For although they knew God, they did not honor him as God or give thanks to him, but they became futile in their thinking, and their foolish hearts were darkened. Claiming to be wise, they became fools, and exchanged the glory of the immortal God for images resembling mortal man and birds and animals and creeping things. (Rom. 1:21–23)

Their great learning and mighty accomplishments did not lead them to worship the Creator and Lord of all nature.

WHAT'S THE DATE?

Who is the king who did not know Joseph? Who is the pharaoh of the exodus? Scholars are divided on this matter because the book of Exodus talks about the pharaoh, the ruler, but does not say who exactly he was. And when we turn to Egyptian records, there is no mention of the Israelites except on a stone monument—a stele—that records a victory by the pharaoh Merneptah over the Israelites in the southern area of Canaan in about 1220 BC, a time clearly after the Israelite invasion and settlement.

Now, this is not surprising. The Israelites came out of Egypt with great power as a result of plagues brought on the country by Jehovah. One would not expect the Egyptians to record defeats of that magnitude. There are perhaps ten references in Egyptian records to a people called the *Habiru.* The word sounds like *Hebrew,* but it refers to Semitic people generally and not necessarily to the Israelites. The stele, however, shows that the Israelites were in Canaan by 1220 BC. The exodus had to have happened before that time.

21

Some scholars give very early dates for the exodus: somewhere between 2000 BC and 1477 BC, a period of about five hundred years. I'm simplifying this, but their reasoning is that there was widespread destruction of the cities of Canaan at about that time. If this destruction resulted from the invasion of the Israelites under Joshua, the exodus would have taken place earlier than other factors indicate.

The difficulty is that these dates do not link up well with the dates given in the Old Testament for various events. In Genesis 15:13, God tells Abraham that the Israelites will be in Egypt for four hundred years; Exodus 12:40 tells us that they were there for 430 years. We do not know exactly when Abraham lived, but that gives us a marker early in the second millennium. Then, in 1 Kings 6:1, we're told that the years between the exodus and the beginning of the construction of the temple under Solomon were 480 years, and the temple was begun around 962 BC. If we take those dates and work them out, they do not fit an early date for the exodus very well.

The second possibility is a very late date: about 1280 BC. Early in Exodus we're told of the people building store cities, called Pithom and Raamses, for the pharaoh (see Ex. 1:11). Now, the great Raamses was Raamses II, who reigned from c.1279–1213 BC. The city of Raamses was named after him. The argument is that, if Raamses was the name for the city at the time it was being built, probably the people of Israel were slaves in Egypt during the reign of King Raamses, and the exodus has to be associated with him. Raamses' father, Seti I, may have been the pharaoh of the oppression; Raamses himself, Raamses II, may have been the pharaoh of the exodus.

A few other factors contribute to that argument. Cuneiform tablets, known as the Amarna letters, found at Tel El Amarna in upper Egypt and dated to about 1400 BC, refer to the Habiru people, who were brickmakers. Of course, brickmaking would have happened whether or not the Habiru were the Israelites. But it is a possibility. Archeology shows that several important cities in Palestine—cities such as Lachish, Bethel, Debir, and Hazor—were destroyed in about 1240 BC. If that matches the invasion under Joshua, that information would fit well with the date of 1280 BC for the exodus.

The third possibility is a date around 1445 BC. I think this one is right, because this is the date we reach when we begin with the biblical data. There are some difficulties: this date does not necessarily fit what we know about the destruction of the cities in Palestine. But here is the argument: The Bible says that the temple was begun in the fourth year of Solomon's reign. We know that this was either 966 or 965 BC. If the exodus took place 480 years before that, it must have happened in 1446 or 1445 BC. If the Israelites were in Egypt for 430 years, they must have entered in the time of Joseph—about 1857 BC.

However, that takes us away from Raamses II. Raamses is popular because we know a great deal about him, but there is another king who fits the bill very well: a king named Thutmose III. He reigned from c. 1483–1450 BC and is known to have been antagonistic to foreigners, because he was the chief king to drive the Hyksos out of Egypt. It is understandable that he'd be critical and oppressive toward foreigners. Amenhotep II (c. 1453–1425) succeeded him and was thus probably the pharaoh of the exodus.[3]

None of this is conclusive. There are attractive arguments for each side, which is why even conservative scholars differ on this dating. People make their decisions based on the evidence that they think is most convincing. If one is most impressed with the archeological evidence, then either the very early or very late dates seem most plausible. But if the years given in the Old Testament have any bearing, then the mid-fifteenth-century dating seems most accurate.

As long as one believes that the exodus took place, whether it happened early or late does not make a lot of difference. But if the exodus took place under Thutmose III or his successor Amenhotep II, then it took place during the eighteenth dynasty, the great period of Egypt's long history. This would mean that God brought the people out of Egypt with a mighty hand when Egypt was at its strongest,

---

3. Scholars and commentators disagree on the exact dating of Thutmose III, Amenhotep II, and Raamses II, but the variations differ by only a few years. Amenhotep II reigned for two or three years with his father Thutmose III (see Howard F. Vos, *Nelson's New Illustrated Bible Manners and Customs: How the People of the Bible Really Lived* [Nashville: Thomas Nelson, 1999], 53–54).

most sophisticated, most powerful—at the very period when it had developed its greatest army. This is a way of saying that God is more powerful than even the most powerful nations of the world, and we need to bow before him, our great God and King of Kings.

CRUELTY IN EGYPT

Even, perhaps especially, at times of great sophistication and power, a nation can be cruel. In Exodus 1 we read about the way in which Pharaoh oppressed the people. He did so in two stages.

SLAVERY

People have estimated that, at any given time in the ancient world, about half the people were enslaved to the other half. Even the Egyptians worked in forced labor gangs at times. But the slavery described in Exodus 1 is different. It involved a whole people. That is, it was ethnic. It was not just a convenient way of getting something built—it was directed against the Israelites as Israelites, and it involved all the people. Furthermore, it was motivated by fear. Pharaoh was concerned that the Hebrews would grow in number and join Egypt's enemies in war against his nation.

We might understand that fear. It was not quite noble, however, because when Pharaoh said, "They might fight against us," he also added, "They might leave the country." The reason that mattered, of course, is because he needed them as slaves to build his storage cities. So he oppressed them. Exodus 1 tells of how he made their lives miserable. The Israelites toiled in the hot sun, and Pharaoh used them ruthlessly, hoping to kill off as many as he could. But, instead of dying, the Israelites multiplied.

GENOCIDE

When slavery failed, Pharaoh made a second attempt to do away with the Israelites. This time he tried genocide: instructing the midwives to kill the male babies. Presumably he planned for the female Israelites to become slave-wives of the Egyptians, until within a generation the people would vanish as an ethnic group.

But this plan did not work. The Hebrew midwives disobeyed the pharaoh. When he called them on it, they gave an explanation that was certainly dubious: "You know, the Hebrew women are very active, and their babies come quickly. By the time we get there, well, the babies are already born. We're not able to do away with them in the birth." Then the pharaoh said, "Just kill them. All the male babies must be killed or thrown into the Nile." This was outright genocide.

This was the first example in history of anti-Semitism—that is, hatred against the Jewish people. It had to do with the rapid, remarkable multiplication of the people. Some have said that the numerical growth of the Jews borders on the miraculous. It certainly seems to have been so. The plans to do away with them backfired; they had increased from seventy people to two million within four centuries. That is remarkable growth.

But this sort of growth has happened throughout history. In 1836, a world census showed that about three million Jews were living in many different countries. The hundred years that followed were a time of great persecution for the Jewish people, particularly in Russia, yet in 1936 another world census showed that the original three million Jewish people had increased to sixteen million. That is an increase of thirteen million in a century, despite persecution. Under Nazi persecution, six million Jews were killed, yet today it is estimated that there are more than fourteen million Jews living around the world.[4]

I think that these figures have to do with God's promise to Abraham. When he put his blessing on the people, he said that he would make Abraham's descendants as many as the stars in heaven or the sand on the seashore (see Gen. 22:17).

That promise also explains the persecution. We have to remember that we are dealing with spiritual realities. This is not just one people hating another people. The Israelites were the people through whom God would send the Messiah. Back in Genesis 3:15, God announced

4. Sergio DellaPergola, "World Jewish Population, 2014," in *The American Jewish Year Book*, vol. 114, ed. Arnold Dashefsky and Iran M. Sheskin (Dordrecht, Netherlands: Springer, 2014), 301–93, cited in "World Jewish Population 2014—DellaPergola (American Jewish Year Book)," Berman Jewish Databank, accessed August 25, 2016, http://www .jewishdatabank.org/studies/details.cfm?StudyID=776.

...can that the seed of the woman would crush Satan's head. We have to see the hand of Satan in anti-Semitism throughout history. He moved the pharaoh to kill the male babies. He did the same thing at the time of the birth of Jesus Christ, working in Herod to kill the babes of Bethlehem. Adolf Hitler is only the most recent example. Yet God has preserved the Jews and kept them and delivered them. History shows that nations that have persecuted the Jews have done so at their peril. The words of God to Abraham still hold true: "I will bless those who bless you, and him who dishonors you I will curse" (Gen. 12:3).

RIGHT CONDUCT IN EGYPT

There is one bright spot in the grim picture in Exodus 1, and that is the conduct of the Hebrew midwives, Shiphrah and Puah. Instead of obeying the king, they allowed the children to live, and God blessed them. He was kind to the midwives and gave them families of their own (see Ex. 1:20–21).

The midwives were sensitive to God. They did the right thing and would not participate in the killing of newborns. We have their names when we are not even told the name of the pharaoh. In those days, who would have paid any attention to these midwives? Yet everybody knew the pharaoh and his father and the pharaoh before him, and their names were written on the monuments. In the book of Exodus, God does not record the pharaohs' names, but he remembers these two women, Shiphrah and Puah, because they did the right thing.

LEARNING FROM EXODUS 1

We are impressed by the world and by those in the world who are powerful, sophisticated, or prosperous. But we have to learn not to think that way. We have to learn to think biblically. Jesus Christ said, "My kingdom is not of this world" (John 18:36). If we really believed that, we would not be so impressed with the world. Jesus told his followers that the world hates them because they have been chosen by God out of the world and do not belong to it (see John 15:19). And John, one of his followers, later wrote to those for whom he had responsibility, "Do not love the world or the things in the world. If anyone loves the world, the love of the Father is not in him" (1 John 2:15). That leads to three points of application.

Neither wealth nor sophistication leads to godliness. For all its sophistication, Egypt was a pagan land. That is true of our culture also. We are impressed by our achievements in technology, but neither technology nor wealth nor sophistication makes a nation godly. As a matter of fact, if we pursue these things apart from God, they do exactly the opposite. Instead of making us godly, they actually make us godless, and we become insensitive and cruel to others as we pursue wealth and technology. What we need is a revival, and revival will not come by our technology. It will come by God. Do you pray for revival? We need to ask God to begin a work of revival in us.

Salvation is from the Lord. Pharaoh would not save the Israelites. That was clear enough. They would not be saved by any other earthly monarch, and neither are we. We have got to get over the idea that we will get salvation from government. Even people who are not Christians are beginning to be sensitive to this. Government does not save. If that is true in such areas as economics, it is above all true spiritually. If we are to be saved, salvation must come from the Lord. We have to ask for it. We have to look for it.

It would be better to be a Hebrew midwife than to be Pharaoh. The world exalts the great and despises the lowly, but in God's way of doing things, usually exalted people are brought low and lowly people are exalted—at least if they do the right thing out of reverence for God. Are you willing to be among the foolish, weak, and despised people of this world? That is what most Christians are. When God works through you, you will not be glorified—the glory will go to God. In order to be lowly, you have to pay a costly price. Sometimes it even brings you into danger, as was the case with the midwives. But if you stand for God, God will notice it. God notices every act of righteousness. Nothing ever escapes him. He writes the names of those people in his Book. Not only that, but God will reward you in his own right time.

3

THE BIRTH OF MOSES

Exodus 2:1–10

THE DRY GROUND

When I think of the period in Jewish history prior to the birth of Moses, a verse from Isaiah 44 comes to mind, in which God says to the people, "I will pour water on the thirsty land, and streams on the dry ground" (Isa. 44:3). It is usually that way with God. When things are grim, when the earth is spiritually barren and dry, *then* the Holy Spirit of God moves, and blessing follows.

Think of the state of Israel at the time of Christ's birth, a time of oppression under the heel of Rome. The Israelites were not faithful in following God. Yet into these conditions God sent Jesus Christ.

Or think of the years preceding the Reformation. Those were dry, barren years in the history of the church. The church was riddled with superstition and immorality, with no vitality left, and yet God poured out the streams of his blessing in Martin Luther's day, and the Reformation followed.

This is what we have at the beginning of Exodus. The ground was both literally and, more significantly, spiritually dry in Egypt in 1445 BC. The Israelites had been in Egypt for 430 years. They had been oppressed for four hundred years; yet, in the midst of their oppression and misery, God sent Moses, the one who was to be their great emancipator and lawgiver by God's hand.

The dryness of the times is not seen merely in such outward things as the Israelites' physical oppression. That was bad enough. Far more significant, though, was the spiritual barrenness of the people themselves. If we look at the Hebrew people of this time not through the rosy eyes of romance but through the sober spectacles of the Word of God, we are forced to conclude that not many in this period had retained the memory of the true God and were faithful to him. The contrary was true.

This is not surprising, in one sense, although it is very sad. The Israelites had no written Scriptures. They had no central place of worship. They did not even have an established priesthood, though probably the fathers functioned as priests within their households. We can understand how, without any of these blessings, they would easily forget the true God. We have these blessings, and *we* still forget the true God. Many areas of the visible church have become spiritually dead or moribund.

We see this spiritual barrenness, first of all, in the conduct of the people. The Israelites were not faithful to God even after the exodus and the great miracles the Lord did on their behalf. The Bible is also very explicit in indicating that the people had fallen into a period of spiritual apostasy and idolatry before Moses came to rescue them.

That idolatry did not end with the exodus. It was still an issue years later. Toward the end of the book of Joshua, when the land is nearly conquered and Joshua has finished his work of leading the people in the conquest, in the midst of his parting sermon to the people, Joshua says, "Put away the gods that your fathers served beyond the River [Euphrates] and in Egypt, and serve the LORD" (Josh. 24:14). That one verse tells us not only that the people had a pagan past, but also that they had hung on to pagan practices for generations. All throughout their four hundred years in Egypt, during the forty years of their wandering in the wilderness, and even during the approximately ten years it took to conquer the promised land, they had clung to their idols.

We find another example in the book of Ezekiel, one of the later prophets. The elders of Israel come to inquire of the Lord, but God refuses to allow it, responding that the Israelites had disobeyed him by not ridding themselves of Egyptian idols even after he brought them out of the land (see Ezek. 20:5–8).

We must conclude from this that the Israelites were not a godly people at this time, if they ever were, but an idolatrous people. That would produce a great many problems, as Moses found out in the years during which he led them.

THE FAITHFUL REMNANT

Yet although the Israelites as a whole departed from the knowledge of the true God, God always has a remnant that is faithful to him, even in dry times.

In Elijah's day, seven thousand had not bowed the knee to Baal. At the time of the birth of Jesus Christ, a faithful few are mentioned in the Gospels—Joseph, Mary, Elizabeth, Simeon, and Anna. When Anna saw the Christ child, she spoke about him to all those who were looking for redemption in Jerusalem (see Luke 2:38). There was a remnant in that time.

In Exodus 2, the remnant that we are told about is one family: Amram and Jochebed, a husband and wife. *Amram* means "exalted people"; his name is supplied not in Exodus 2 but in Old Testament genealogies in Exodus 6, Numbers 3, 1 Chronicles 6, and so on. He was of the tribe of Levi and lived to be 137 years old. *Jochebed* means "the honor of Jehovah." She is mentioned by name only twice in the Bible, in Exodus 6 and in Numbers 26. She too was of the tribe of Levi and was Amram's father's sister—his aunt. Only later are marriages between such close relatives forbidden (see Lev. 18).

Amram and Jochebed had two other children besides Moses: Miriam and Aaron. Aaron was three years older than Moses (see Ex. 7:7). We are not told Miriam's age, but judging by the story she was probably eight to ten years older than Moses.

The most important thing about this family is that it was a believing family. Moreover, it seems to have been a believing family for several generations. Significantly, the names *Amram* and *Jochebed* are religious names. They must have had believing parents who gave them names that would remind them of the God of Israel and the special destiny to which he called the Jewish people. Amram and Jochebed themselves had faith, because they are praised for it in the book of Hebrews. In the midst of a great list of the heroes of the faith, one verse says, "By faith Moses, when he was born, was hidden for three months by his parents, because they saw that the child was beautiful, and they were not afraid of the king's edict" (Heb. 11:23). And their children, Moses, Aaron, and Miriam, were servants of the Lord for a long, long time. At some point, each was guilty of serious sin, and there were very serious consequences. But in Hebrews 11, that great chapter on faith, not just the faith of Moses is commended but also the faith of his parents.

This leads one to observe that faith is normally preserved in families. The pioneer evangelism seen in missions work is absolutely important and the duty of the church. But there is much evidence that most people become Christians within the family in which they grow up. Faith is passed on from generation to generation, as seen in Moses' family. If you are a parent, you have a great responsibility to your children. You need to teach them spiritual truths. Plant the Word of God in their minds, and the Holy Spirit will implant it in their hearts. Children are a treasure and a gift from God. We have a great privilege and responsibility to raise them in the nurture and admonition of the Lord.

AN INAUSPICIOUS TIME AND PLACE

F. B. Meyer wrote a study called *Moses: The Servant of God*. In it he makes four valuable points about the time and conditions of Moses' birth.[1]

Moses belonged to an alien race. It used to be popular among scholars to identify the coming of the people of Israel into Egypt with the age of the Hyksos kings. The Hyksos were an alien, Semitic people, so it was natural to think that Joseph came when the Hyksos were in Egypt and that Joseph was favored because the pharaoh of the time

---

1. F. B. Meyer, *Moses: The Servant of God* (New York: Fleming H. Revell Company, n.d.), 12–14.

was related to him ethnically. As we put those dates together today, it seems that this theory is probably incorrect. The Hyksos period began with the fifteenth dynasty in about 1630 BC. However, Joseph and his father's family must have entered Egypt in 1875 BC if we are right about the time of the exodus, which I suggested was 1445 BC. Therefore, the family of Joseph arrived in Egypt about two hundred years before the time of the Hyksos.

In addition, about 1521 BC, the Egyptian dynasties drove out the Hyksos. Probably the greatest persecution of the Israelites came under the kings who had done this. The Egyptians had been ruled by a foreign people, had succeeded in driving the foreign people out, and now did not want to have any more foreigners—including the Israelites—in any position of power. That would explain, in large measure, the severe persecutions the Israelites experienced toward the end of the period leading up to the exodus.

The Israelites were foreigners in Egypt, an alien presence, and they remained so even after the Hyksos had been driven out.

Moses belonged to an oppressed race. When the Israelites had first come to Egypt, they had been treated well because of Joseph. Joseph had been used by God to deliver the Egyptians, and other nations as well, in a time of great famine, and the pharaoh had favored him. But all that was past. Not only were the Israelites an alien race, but they also became an oppressed race as the pharaohs brought them to a position of abject slavery. They were forced to cut wood and draw water and till the fields of the Egyptians. Eventually they were forced to make bricks and to work as slave laborers on the storage cities of Pithom and Raamses. The oppression may have reached an apex under Thutmose III, the pharaoh probably ruling at the time of Moses' birth.

Moses was born at a time of "unusual trouble." It is unlikely that Pharaoh's decree to kill all the male Hebrew children lasted for a long time. Such a decree would be hard to sustain for generation after generation. Some scholars suggest that it may have existed for only a matter of months. But however long that period, it was the period in which Moses was born.

Moses was born to believing parents. Moses' parents understood the cruel nature of the times. They were well aware of the edict of the pharaoh, but nevertheless, because they believed God, they were willing to defy the pharaoh and do everything in their power to save Moses.

SAVING MOSES

JOCHEBED (EX. 2:1–2)

The Germans have a saying: "Every mother's child is beautiful"—to the mother, if not to everybody else. But there does seem to have been something significant about Moses. In three places in the Bible, he is described as being an extraordinarily beautiful or exceptional child. In Exodus 2:2, he is called a "fine child." In Acts 7:20 and Hebrews 11:23, he is called "beautiful." A fair rendition of these descriptions of Moses would be *exceptional, divinely fair,* and *wellborn.* You do not find this said of other children in the Bible, and that probably means that there was something significant about Moses' appearance. His parents, especially Jochebed, saw this and were hopeful, perhaps believing in faith that this was the one whom God would use to deliver their people.

They did what they could to save him. Jochebed hid him for three months. She kept him quietly in seclusion. But as children begin to grow, they develop lungs that are rather strong; after three months Moses' cry was no newborn whimper. His mother was well aware that one day a soldier or guard would hear her child and throw him in the river.

So Jochebed took a little papyrus basket, covered it with tar and pitch so that it would not leak, put her baby in it, and put it in the reeds by the river. The Hebrew word used for that papyrus basket is *têbâh.* It occurs only one other place in the Bible—as a description for Noah's ark. So Jochebed made a little ark for her child, and just as God used an ark to save Noah, his family, and the animals, so he used that small ark to save Moses.

Jochebed put Miriam, Moses' sister, on the hillside to see what would happen. This indicates that she truly expected God to deliver the baby somehow. She was giving him up, but she did not expect him to die. If she had expected him to be thrown to the crocodiles by some passerby, she would not have put his sister there to watch. She expected him to be delivered.

BABIES IN THE BULRUSHES (EX. 2:3-4)

There is a similar account to the story of Moses in the bulrushes in the story of a great king of antiquity, Sargon of Akkad, who ruled much of western Asia during the twenty-fourth century BC. In the story, Sargon is the son of a princess, who gets rid of him by putting him by the bulrushes. A poor canal worker named Akki finds him there and raises him as his son, and eventually he becomes a great king.

Liberal scholars say that this story was floating around as part of the mythology of the ancient Near East and that the Hebrews picked it up and used it for their great deliverer. The Akkadian story, however, is in certain essentials the exact opposite of Moses' story. Moses was born to poor parents and became the son of Pharaoh's daughter. Sargon was the son of a princess and fell into the hands of the poor.

The similarities do not prove any kind of borrowing, one from the other. All they indicate is that this was a convenient way of getting rid of unwanted children in the ancient world—their equivalent of putting the baby on the courthouse steps or dropping him at the door of a church, knowing that somebody would find and take care of the child. As a matter of fact, the story of Sargon anchors the story of Moses in what was apparently a common practice in antiquity. In other words, it adds authenticity, rather than taking away from its believability.

THE PRINCESS (EX. 2:5-6)

God is the God of providence. He is the God of every circumstance, however great or small. In this case, the God of providence directed the steps of Pharaoh's daughter down to the Nile at exactly the right time and to exactly the right place.

Who was the princess? The early church historian Eusebius calls her Merris; the rabbinic tradition calls her Bithiah; and Josephus calls her Thermutis. We do not have evidence of anybody by those names, so the names do not mean much. Perhaps it is impossible to know who this woman was.

There is a possibility that we do know, however. If the oppression of the Hebrews began under the rule of Thutmose I—one of the strongest and greatest of the pharaohs—and if it continued under the reign of Thutmose III, whose son, Amenhotep II, would have been the pharaoh of the exodus, then the princess may have been somebody whom we know very well—a woman named Hatshepsut, who reigned as queen during the minority of Thutmose III. We know much about her because she built a great mortuary temple near Thebes, a magnificent columned building constructed against a cliff.

At any rate, the princess came down to the water and saw the little ark. She sent her slave girls to fetch it, and when they opened it up, there was the child, crying. The God of providence—who had ordered the steps of the princess to the Nile at the very time that Moses was placed there in the basket by his mother—caused the baby to cry and the tears to touch the woman's heart. Moses' cries softened the heart of this highborn lady. As Proverbs 21:1 says, "The king's heart is in the hand of the LORD; he directs it like a watercourse wherever he pleases" (NIV). Not only is the king's heart in the Lord's hand, but so is the heart of the king's daughter.

For one reason or another, Christian parents have to release their children and entrust them entirely to the Lord—sometimes when their children are young, but always when they become adults. As F. B. Meyer writes regarding this incident involving Jochebed and her baby:

> There is abundant warrant, afforded by this narrative, for Christian parents to cast their children upon God. The mother, whose child goes to earn her living among strangers; the father, whose son must leave the quiet homestead for the great city; the parents, who, as missionaries, are unable to nurture their children on the mission field, because of the pernicious moral climate, more harmful than the heat of the plains of India; or those who on their deathbed must part with their babes to the care of comparative strangers—all these may learn a lesson from the faith that cast the young child on the providence

of God even more absolutely than on the buoyancy of the Nile. God lives, and loves, and cares. More quick and tender than Miriam's, His eye neither slumbers nor sleeps.[2]

THE RETURN (EX. 2:6–9)

We know that the woman was touched by the cries of the baby, because even though she recognized at once that he was a Hebrew child and knew why he had been placed in the basket by the reeds of the river, she decided to save him. Yet she had an immediate problem, because the baby was crying, and usually when babies cry they are hungry.

Miriam, who was watchful and wise, saw the situation at once and said to Pharaoh's daughter, "Would you like me to find a wet nurse for you from among the mothers of the Hebrews?" There were probably a lot of mothers whose babies had been killed, and Pharaoh's daughter understood that it would not be hard to find a woman to nurse the baby. So Miriam trotted off and, not surprisingly, came back with Moses' mother.

We have a wonderful picture here of Moses' mother about to receive her baby back. She is not at all letting on what has happened. Pharaoh's daughter does not understand the full situation, but she needs this woman. She says, "Take this baby and nurse him for me, and I will pay you." Jochebed gets her son back. Even though she gave him up to God, she gets the very thing that she wanted, and God even sees that she is paid for doing what she most wants to do. It is as if she said, "Not my will, but yours be done. Here, I give my child to your hands." And God gave him back, the child she wanted, and paid her for taking him.

More than anything else, Jochebed wanted to raise her son. Circumstances were against her. The will of the pharaoh stood like a rock against her desires. She feared the worst, but she committed the matter to God. So she received Moses back, and God paid her wages.

2. F. B. Meyer, "Devotional Studies in the Sunday School Lessons," in *Record of Christian Work*, vol. 32, edited by William Revell Moody (East Northfield, MA: W. R. Moody, 1913), 394–95.

What a great example of trusting God when our circumstances seem most heartbreaking, and then seeing God work for good beyond our wildest hopes in those very circumstances.

MOSES (EX. 2:10)

There is much controversy about the meaning of Moses' name. On the one hand, in the form we know it today, the name is a Hebrew word: *Moshe*. In that form, it is probably a play on the verb meaning *draw out*. Exodus 2:10 says, "She named him Moses, 'Because,' she said, 'I drew him out of the water.'" *She* could refer to Pharaoh's daughter because she is mentioned immediately before that, but *she* could also be Moses' mother.

On the other hand, the Egyptian words *mes* and *mesu* mean "one born" or "child," and they appear quite often in Egyptian names. For example, the pharaoh Ahmose's name means "the one born of Ah" or "the son of Ah" (Ah being the moon god). The name *Kamose* means "the one born of ka" (*ka* being the deified soul in Egyptian mythology). *Thutmose* means "one who is born of Thoth," another one of the gods. In the Egyptian language, *seh* means "lake" and can also refer to the Nile. *Moses* may be a shortened form of the word *meseh*, which means "one born of the Nile." It is possible that he had a longer name, such as Hopmoseh or Ermoseh, which were common names in Egypt. If that is the case, then when he later refused to be identified as the son of Pharaoh's daughter, he may have rejected the name in its full form, shortening it to *Moses* so he would not be identified with one of the Egyptian gods.

LEARNING FROM EXODUS 2

There are a few applications of this passage that I want to emphasize.

PROVIDENCE

Many miracles take place in Moses' story as God works through him to deliver the people. In fact, more miracles are associated with Moses and his lifetime than with any other biblical figure except Jesus. But it is striking that no miracles take place at the beginning of the story. An unbeliever would call these events *coincidence*; we say *providence*.

Notice what happened. The providence of God ordered the steps of Pharaoh's daughter as she came to the Nile to bathe. The providence of God allowed the baby to cry at just the right time. The providence of God moved the heart of the princess to want to save the baby. Finally, the providence of God arranged for the baby to be raised by his own mother, even though the princess did not suspect it. The point is that God was at work here as much as he was later in Moses' life.

God is at work in the circumstances of your life as well. You may protest that you haven't seen any miracles in your life. There is no reason why you should. God is the God of providence, not just the God of miracles, and that means that he has been operating in all the details in all the circumstances of your life. Shouldn't you recognize this if you believe in a providential God? Shouldn't you thank him for it?

We may not like our circumstances, but, no matter what state we are in, we have to learn to thank God and praise him. This is what the apostle Paul learned to do. Furthermore, we need to trust God in circumstances when things do not seem to be going well. Romans 8:28 says, "We know that for those who love God all things work together for good, for those who are called according to his purpose." Yes, even in sickness, even in joblessness, even in times of sorrow, even in death, God is working for our good.

We focus, as the story itself does, on the providential circumstances surrounding the birth of Moses. But should we think that Amram and Jochebed were the only believing parents in Egypt in that day? There must have been other believing parents, even if most of the people had gotten far from God. Some of the believing parents must have had children too. As far as we know, God did not intervene to save the other children.

Does that mean that God's providence was not at work? No. God was operating in the circumstances of the lives of these other men and women just as much as he was operating in the circumstances of Moses' family's lives. What happened to them is no less dear to God than what happened to Amram and Jochebed. We have to trust God in all circumstances, not just in the pleasant ones. Job the patriarch knew this. He said, "Though he slay me, I will hope in him" (Job 13:15). That is a believing response.

FAITH

It is hard to know the exact content of the faith of Moses' parents, because we are not told much about it in Exodus 2. We know that they had faith because they are praised for their faith in Hebrews 11. The point that seems significant is this: their faith did not lead to inaction but rather to thoughtful action that God blessed. To have faith is not to do nothing, but rather to do much.

People who have faith in God always do much. They do everything that they possibly can. Faith led Amram and Jochebed to defy Pharaoh's order and hide their son for three months. Then, when he could not be hidden any longer, Jochebed made that little papyrus basket, put her baby in it, put him in the reeds by the river, and put Miriam where she could see what would happen. They did all that because they had faith. They could not save their child, but what they could do, they did. William Carey, a man of faith and a great missionary, said that we should expect great things of God and attempt great things for God.[3] He did it himself, and so have all who have achieved great victories of faith.

What could you do for God? You need to ask yourself that. What can you attempt in your circumstances? There are important things to be done.

SMALL BEGINNINGS

Great events come from small beginnings. Nothing could be less portentous than this story of an impoverished, enslaved people and a mother in a poor family giving birth to a child in a time of unusual oppression, perhaps expecting his death at any moment. Yet God intervened. He used a small baby born to a poor family from an oppressed race to be the great emancipator and lawgiver.

---

3. Attributed to William Carey, "The Deathless Sermon" (sermon, Friar Lane Baptist Chapel, Nottingham, UK, May 30, 1792).

There is a great parallel here to Jesus Christ, who was also born to a poor family in a time of oppression, when the Jews were close to being slaves under the heel of the Roman Empire. In that time of national defeat, God sent Jesus to be the great Deliverer—not just of Israel but of all who come to him in faith.

Ours may be a day of small things. As you have tried to do things for God, I am sure you have felt from time to time that they are the smallest things of all. But you and I do not know what God will bring from the small, weak, insignificant beginnings that we make. In the case of Jochebed, God raised up her child to become the greatest leader, other than Jesus Christ, that the world has ever had. Who knows what God will accomplish from your small beginning?

THE REMNANT

On the whole, these were not great days for Israel. In fact, it probably would be hard to find any days in the life of the nation to call great, except perhaps those of David and Solomon. But in spite of the fact that the Jews were often in terrible conditions, God has preserved a remnant in all periods of their history, from the time of Abraham to today—not always many, but nevertheless a remnant. And God has worked through those people to accomplish what he himself has determined to do.

Get in the habit of learning to think like God. If you look for the remnant, you will find it. It will not be the people whom the world generally seeks out to do something important. The Bible says that the people whom God uses are often the foolish, the weak, and the despised. He does that because, through them, he can display his wisdom and reveal his righteousness.

Look for people like that. When you have found them, get alongside them and work with them, and see what God will do.

4

DOING THE RIGHT THING IN THE WRONG WAY

Exodus 2:11—25

FORTY MISSING YEARS

Between Exodus 2:10 and 2:11 there is a gap of approximately forty years. Significantly, we do not learn this from Exodus; Exodus tells us only that Moses was about eighty years old when he appeared before Pharaoh. However, in Acts 7, Stephen says that Moses was about forty years old when his heart was moved to deliver the people (v. 23). We can learn something about Moses' training in those first forty years from an Egyptian called Manetho, from Josephus the Jewish historian, and from Eusebius, a historian of the early church. Nothing that they say carries scriptural weight, and their writings are not authoritative or inerrant. But these men were far closer to the events of the time than we are and have reasonable information to supplement the biblical account.

For example, according to early traditions, Moses was educated in Heliopolis. Many youths from the Egyptian nobility, but also from the noble families of surrounding nations, were educated there. In this way Egypt maintained ties with its neighbors. Joseph married a woman named Asenath, who was the daughter of Potiphera, a priest at Heliopolis (see Gen. 41:45); therefore Joseph, at least, had a connection to the city.

41

What did Moses do as a child? Egyptian children made toys out of sticks and stones and little figures out of mud. Some of these toys have been found. Wealthier families provided toys for their children; these toys were made by hand and would have been expensive luxuries. We have found some of these as well. There is, for example, a toy that has a little row of dwarfs on a stick. They would have jumped up and down when the child pulled a string, although the string decayed long before the toy was found.

Young Egyptian children were taught to swim. It was also very important for them to know how to ride a horse, shoot a bow, and hunt. This would have been Moses' informal experience. His formal training was also important and would have started at a very early age. The Egyptians were well advanced in their writing and mathematics—including geometry, trigonometry, and the ability to measure and partition land. They studied history, medicine, music, and the art of war.

Moses was a linguist. He undoubtedly knew how to read and write in Egyptian hieroglyphs. He would have been taught the trade language of that period, Akkadian, as well; and he would have learned Hebrew from his mother in his home. It is not surprising that he spent a great deal of the forty years in the wilderness writing the Pentateuch.

Moses must have been taught about law—Egyptian law, of course, but also the laws of other nations. One of the most famous law codes of the day was the law code of Hammurabi of Babylon (c.1750 BC). This is set up in a treaty structure, in which the king enters into an agreement with the people to protect them, and they agree to obey his laws. Scholars point out that the Old Testament laws, particularly the Ten Commandments, are based more or less on the same kind of treaty formulations. The people have to obey God because he is the God who brought them out of Egypt. It is not surprising that these parallels to the law codes of the surrounding cultures are reflected in the presentation of the Mosaic law.

Moses was also "mighty in his words and deeds," as Stephen states in Acts 7:22. According to Josephus, Moses was a military commander who captured the cities Hermopolis and Saba. A highborn Egyptian son would have been expected to fight in wars. This would explain

Moses' role as the commanding general over Joshua during the battles in which they were sometimes engaged in the wilderness journey.

God gave Moses his Egyptian background in order to prepare him for the work that lay ahead. Yet, as important as this secular education was during those first forty years, it was overshadowed by the religious education that he received in his early years from his slave mother.

Not all Hebrew families were godly. Much evidence in the Old Testament indicates that many worshipped idols. But some of them, the remnant, remained true to the God of Israel, and apparently that was the case with Moses' family—probably for several generations, and maybe faithfully going all the way back to the days of Joseph.

What would Moses' mother have taught him? She would have taught him about his miraculous deliverance by the hand of God, so that he had not been killed when Pharaoh was killing all the Hebrew boys. In other words, she would have taught him about God's sovereignty and providence. She would have taught him about the patriarchs—Abraham, Isaac, and Jacob—about God's revelation to them, and about the promises that God had made to the people. This believing mother knew that those were the traditions that God had given to the Israelites, and she passed them on to her son. Maybe she even indicated to Moses her hope that, because the four hundred years were nearly ended, this was the time when God would soon provide a deliverer for his people—and that maybe Moses was the one who would one day be that deliverer.

THE TURNING POINT

When Moses was forty years old, a momentous turning point came in his life. We all have turning points in our lives, an event that happens or a decision we make that affects what happens afterward, but it is hard to imagine any turning point in anyone's life more monumental than what happened to Moses when he threw in his lot with his people and turned his back on the pleasures of Egypt.

The book of Exodus does not tell us much about this turning point, but two texts in the New Testament do. We ought to keep them in our minds as the authoritative New Testament interpretation of the Old Testament event.

Consider Stephen's speech, before the Jewish leaders in Jerusalem:

> When he was forty years old, it came into his heart to visit his brothers, the children of Israel. And seeing one of them being wronged, he defended the oppressed man and avenged him by striking down the Egyptian. He supposed that his brothers would understand that God was giving them salvation by his hand, but they did not understand. (Acts 7:23–25)

All the years that Moses had spent in the palace of the pharaoh had not eclipsed his knowledge of his origins. He knew who he was. When he decided to visit his people, he knew that they were his people. Even at this point, he was thinking that maybe God would use him to be their deliverer.

The second passage is Hebrews 11, a great chapter that lists the heroes of the faith and tells us what each did by faith.

> By faith Moses, when he had grown up, refused to be known as the son of Pharaoh's daughter. He chose to be mistreated along with the people of God rather than to enjoy the pleasures of sin for a short time. He regarded disgrace for the sake of Christ as of greater value than the treasures of Egypt, because he was looking ahead to his reward. (Heb. 11:24–26 NIV)

These verses add something that we do not see in Stephen's speech in Acts. They tell us that Moses made a deliberate choice to reject his Egyptian privileges in order to identify with his own people for what he understood to be the purposes of God in history. This was a monumental and noble choice.

What Moses actually *did*, however, did not turn out so well. He got ahead of God. But let's not forget how noble his intention was.

THE SIGNIFICANCE OF MOSES' CHOICE

In *Moses: The Servant of God*, F. B. Meyer gives several reasons for the significance of Moses' choice. Moses' decision was made (1) "in the full maturity of his powers," (2) "when the fortunes of the children of Israel were at their lowest ebb," (3) "when the pleasures of sin seemed most fascinating," and (4) "decisively."[1]

THE MATURITY OF MOSES

At forty years old, Moses was old enough and experienced enough to know what he was doing. A teenager might have felt mistreated by his Egyptian mother, said, "You're not my real mother," and run off to identify with his mother among the slaves. Moses did not do that. Nor did he, as a young man, assess the situation, conclude that he would never get ahead by competing with so many other nobles, and decide to throw in his lot with these Hebrews, lead them out of Egypt, and become king of an entirely new nation. Instead he made his choice as a mature adult. His murder of the Egyptian had a measure of rashness to it, but his basic decision to identify with the Hebrews did not.

THE DEPTH OF ISRAEL'S TROUBLE

During the days of Joseph, the Israelite people had held a favored position in Egypt. But then a pharaoh arose who did not know Joseph. If this took place after the Hyksos period, the new pharaohs would have been on their guard against foreigners. They oppressed and enslaved them. The Hebrews were now at the nadir of their national fortunes; their misery was at its peak.

Yet at this time, Moses identified with them. He chose to go from a palace to a hovel, from privilege to persecution, from luxury to bare subsistence. He seems to have counted this as a small thing in order to be identified with God and God's people. How many of us would pay that price?

1. F. B. Meyer, *Moses: The Servant of God* (New York: Fleming H. Revell Company, n.d.), 21.

THE FASCINATIONS OF SIN

Perhaps in his early childhood Moses had not understood all the privileges and pleasures that Egypt had to offer, but as he got older he certainly came to know them. He was on the inside track. He was part of the establishment. Power, prestige, any kind of sexual experience that he wanted—all were there for the taking. Yet Moses willingly turned his back on all of it.

THE FINAL DECISION

The silence of Moses' first forty years is significant. Moses is the author of Exodus. As he wrote his own story, why did he not tell us about the first third of his life? Why does he not tell us about his Egyptian mother—not even her name? Why does he not tell us about his companions and early childhood? If he was a military man who experienced warfare, why does he not boast about his victories?

The only reasonable explanation is that when Moses turned his back on Egypt, he did so for good. Most of us want to compromise; we want to keep a foot in both camps. We want to be in the world, and we want to be Christians too. Moses could have tried to be both a Hebrew and an Egyptian. But when he turned his back on Egypt, he shut the door and never opened it again. Never once in the Pentateuch does he long for the pleasures of Egypt. The people do. They want to go back to Egypt so that they can eat onions, leeks, and garlic. But Moses left, and he left permanently.

THE RIGHT THING IN THE WRONG WAY

In spite of his training and the nobility of his purpose, Moses' first act of identification with his people ended in failure. He killed an Egyptian and had to run away. Whatever that Egyptian had been doing, he did not deserve to be killed. Even if the deed had merited death, Moses was not called to be the judge or executioner. Yet he gave himself that role.

Surrounded by the world's ideas and ideals, even Christians tend to want to do God's work in the world's way, through power, pressure, and money. We begin to think that we need to collect a war chest to get our programs through and that we need to get our people elected and put them in positions of government so that they can pass laws and force people to do what we think is right. There is a place for just laws; just laws flow from a citizenry that wants to do just things. But the Christian's mode of operating is not by money, power, or politics. We operate by teaching the Word, by the truth, and by prayer, asking God to bless our work. In other words, we do not advance our cause by killing Egyptians. Moses had to learn that the great and needed revolution is a revolution in the hearts and minds of men and women.

It has been pointed out that very different events took place in France and England in the latter decades of the eighteenth century. The French Revolution was a revolution of power. The French citizens drove out the aristocratic rascals and put their own leaders in. But the Age of Reason gave birth to the Reign of Terror and finally led to the tyranny of the Napoleonic era. At about the same time, when England could have fallen into a parallel situation, the Wesleyan and Whitefield revivals took place. As the Word of God had its sway in the hearts of thousands and thousands of people, instead of violence and bloodshed, a moral transformation of the land eventually expressed itself in the laws and culture. But those changes did not happen in the world's way.

What happened when Moses acted in the world's way? Even his own people rejected him. In Acts, Stephen tells us that Moses thought the people would say, "Here's somebody on our side at last" (see 7:25). After Moses killed the Egyptian, he hid the body. He thought nobody knew what he had done, but when he tried to settle a dispute between two Hebrews the next day, one struck out against him by saying, "What are you going to do? Kill me just like you killed the Egyptian?" The word was out. Pharaoh was about to kill him, so Moses fled the land. Only after he had spent another four decades in the desert of Midian did God come to him again, give him the call, bring him to Pharaoh, and enable him to lead the people out of Egypt.

Moses needed to learn three things, and so do we.

We need God in order to accomplish the right thing. Jesus told his disciples, "Apart from me you can do nothing" (John 15:5). No matter how talented we think we are, no matter how great our training or education, no matter how successful we have been in business or politics, and no matter how noble our cause, unless Jesus Christ is working in us spiritually, we are unable to accomplish anything at all for the Lord.

We do not think that way. When we read John 15:5, we say, "What this really means is that without Jesus we can't do very much." We think that if we just put enough energy into a task, we can achieve success, even on our own strength. But Jesus said, "Apart from me you can do *nothing.*" Moses was educated in all the wisdom of the Egyptians, yet he failed utterly. If we think we can do something of spiritual value on our own, or even partially on our own, God will allow us to fail so that we might learn, as Zechariah said, that it is "not by might, nor by power, but by my Spirit" (Zech. 4:6)—the Spirit of the Lord.

We go the wrong way by going our way. Moses started out with a noble purpose, and what was the first thing he did? Commit murder. He killed an Egyptian. There is nothing that anyone before us has done that you and I are not capable of doing if we go our way rather than the way of God. David knew this about himself. He failed, and so he prayed that God would keep him from sinning knowingly (see Ps. 19:13).

God can still use those who do wrong things. The encouraging news is that God is able to work in us in spite of our failures. God will work with us again and again. Sometimes it will take a long while. Forty years passed before God called Moses to lead the people, but at the end of the forty years God did call him—and Moses, now obeying God, was successful. Jonah is another example. He ran away from God, but nonetheless, after the great fish spit him up on the beach, God spoke to Jonah again (Jonah 3:1) and renewed his original commission. The Lord's purpose to use Jonah was not thwarted by Jonah's disobedience.

MOSES IN MIDIAN

Nobody is exactly sure where Midian is. Joseph was sold into slavery to Midianites who came through Canaan, so perhaps the Midianites were a nomadic people who moved up and down the desert ways and trade routes. It does seem that Moses went to an area across the Sinai Desert to the east. Probably at least some of the Midianites lived there during this period.

The Midianites were descended from Abraham through his second wife, Keturah, so they may have preserved some knowledge of the true God. The Midianite Reuel, also known as Jethro, was a priest of God. His name means "friend of God," or maybe even "God is my Shepherd." His name does not necessarily identify God as Jehovah, however.

Moses was sitting by a well when Reuel's daughters came to the well to get water for their animals. The local shepherds drove them away, but Moses jumped up and defended them, driving off the shepherds. He was a warrior, and he was kind. He helped to water the women's flocks, and so their father invited Moses into his desert settlement.

We next learn that Reuel gave Moses his daughter Zipporah to be his wife. Zipporah appears again at the end of Exodus 4 and in Exodus 18. Moses had two sons by this woman by the time he set out for Egypt again, but only the first is mentioned in Exodus 2, probably because of the meaning of his name: Gershom. This is translated in the text as if it is based on the two Hebrew words *ger* and *shom*, meaning a resident alien. Moses calls his son Gershom because he has "become an alien in a foreign land" (Ex. 2:22 NIV).

What picture do we have of Moses? He has settled down in Midian. He is married. He has two children. He has become a shepherd. The decades are going by. What did he think about Egypt during those years? The Bible does not tell us. Did Moses think about Egypt at all? From time to time, maybe, but he had crossed an awfully wide desert and was living a much different life in Midian as a shepherd than he had lived as a prince in the palace of the pharaoh. I suppose there were times—maybe long periods of time, maybe years at a time—when Moses utterly forgot his people and life in Egypt. But God had not forgotten them. The last verses of Exodus 2 say,

> The Israelites groaned in their slavery and cried out, and their cry for help because of their slavery went up to God. God heard their groaning and he remembered his covenant with Abraham, with Isaac and with Jacob. So God looked on the Israelites and was concerned about them. (vv. 23–25 NIV)

The Bible startles us from time to time with understatements. "God was concerned about them." Indeed he was. God was about to shake heaven and earth to get his people out of Egypt and bring them into their own land.

LEARNING FROM EXODUS 2

THE VALUE OF AN EARLY, GODLY EDUCATION

We do not know how long Moses stayed with his mother, Jochebed. I am sure that she stretched out the time as long as she could, but it could not have been more than three or four years before he was weaned. But during those three or four years, she taught him what he needed to know, so that forty years later he remembered who he was, remembered the God of his people, and determined that he would stand with Jehovah God and his people rather than with the Egyptians. She taught him enough.

Students of child development reinforce this concept today. They tell us that the earliest years are the most important—the first three to five years especially. If we have children, we need to remember to put time into our children during their first early years. The Bible says, "Train up a child in the way he should go; even when he is old he will not depart from it" (Prov. 22:6). This does not mean that a child will never sin or never get far away from God. But if biblical truths are planted in a child at an early age, they will stick with the child, and God will use them later to bring the child back to himself. Do not underestimate the importance of godly education in our early years.

RIGHT CHOICE, WRONG CHOICE

We can do something utterly right one moment and something utterly wrong the next. Moses is an example of this. He made a right decision to identify with his people and to turn his back on the luxurious life of Egypt, but in the very next breath, as it were, he murdered an Egyptian.

The apostle Peter gives us another great example of this principle (Matthew 16:15–23). Jesus asks, "Who do you say that I am?" (v. 15) and Peter replies, "You are the Christ, the Son of the living God"

(v. 16). Jesus tells Peter that he is right and that the Holy Spirit has revealed this truth to him. Then Jesus begins to say that it is necessary that he, Jesus, should be arrested and crucified by his enemies. At that point Peter breaks in and says, "Far be it from you, Lord! This shall never happen to you" (v. 22). Jesus has to rebuke him: "Get behind me, Satan! You are a hindrance to me. For you are not setting your mind on the things of God, but on the things of man" (v. 23). So one moment Peter is spokesman for God, empowered by the Holy Spirit, and the next second he is a tool of Satan. The same thing will happen with us unless we keep close to God. We are capable of exactly the same sinful failures.

THE LIMITED POWER OF FAILURE

However, one failure does not necessarily disqualify us from future service. We are often destroyed by personal failure because we have too high an opinion of ourselves. If we did not think we were pretty good, we wouldn't be so distressed when we fail. But if we think we cannot fail, we shut down, embarrassed and overwhelmed, when we do. We want to pull down the blinds, hide in bed, and not come out until people have forgotten who we are—perhaps until we have forgotten as well.

Are you demoralized because of some past failure? Do you find yourself thinking, "God can't use me anymore because I've failed him"? That is what Satan would like you to think, and he will put those thoughts into your mind. But they are not true. Moses certainly failed, but it did not mean that God could not use him. And God used him greatly. God knows you. He knows that you are only dust. He made you. He is not surprised that there is failure in you. He knows what you are like, but he also knows what he is able to do through you by Jesus Christ—and that makes the difference.

THE BLESSING OF SOLITUDE

Moses was inactive for forty years, alone with his thoughts in the Midian wilderness. What was accomplished during those forty years? Moses grew deep in himself, and he grew in his knowledge of God. He settled down.

Have you been set in a solitary place temporarily? Have you been inactive, unable to work, unable to contribute much? Sometimes people are laid up because of sickness. They can't work. That is not necessarily bad. If God has brought solitude into your life, receive it from him and use it to study, think, meditate, and pray. Paul spent three years in Arabia after his conversion before he began his missionary journeys, and those were vitally important years in his life.

THE ACTIVENESS OF GOD

Note that God was active even when Moses was not. When you and I are laid up and unable to be busy, we say, "Well, it's all over. Nothing is happening." We may not be doing anything, but God is constantly at work. At the very end of Exodus 2, we find that he hears his people and is concerned about them. Although Moses did not know it, God was preparing him to be the deliverer of Israel. Maybe God is using your solitude to prepare you for some important work that he has planned for you to do.

GOD REMEMBERS FAITH

When we look at this story in the light of the rest of the Bible, we discover that God remembers our faith, not our failures. In Hebrews 11, that great chapter about the faith of the Old Testament saints, three times Moses is praised for his faith. Most people who are mentioned in that chapter are praised for their faith in one instance. We are given four examples of how Abraham acted by faith and three examples for Moses. The writer does not once bring up his sin of murder.

First, Moses is praised for identifying with his own oppressed people rather than with the Egyptians.

> By faith Moses, when he was grown up, refused to be called the son of Pharaoh's daughter, choosing rather to be mistreated with the people of God than to enjoy the fleeting pleasures of sin. (vv. 24–25)

Second, he is praised for leaving Egypt: "By faith he left Egypt, not being afraid of the anger of the king, for he endured as seeing him who is invisible" (v. 27). We may assume that this is a description of the exodus, but, because of what is mentioned next, I would suggest that he is praised here for his faith in his *first* departure from Egypt, when he left the palace and identified with his people.

Third, he is praised for keeping the Passover. "By faith he kept the Passover and sprinkled the blood, so that the Destroyer of the firstborn might not touch them" (v. 28). In this great summary of Moses' life and faith achievements—those things written down in heaven and written down in Hebrews for our benefit—not once is his failure even mentioned.

That is the way God is with us. He does not remember our failures. We may remember them, but it is sin even to bring them up. We ought to forget about them. God said of Israel that he would forgive them and *forget* their sins (see Jer. 31:34). Hezekiah said of the Lord, "You have cast all my sins behind your back" (Isa. 38:17). Our failures as well as our sins have been forgiven because of the work of Jesus Christ. The real question is, do we believe it? If we do, then we will not let a past sin destroy our faithfulness and our ability to serve God now.

5

THE BURNING BUSH

Exodus 3–4

ENDING THE SILENT YEARS

In Old Testament and New Testament scholarship, *the silent years* refers to the period between the last of the Old Testament prophets, Malachi, and the appearance of Gabriel to Zechariah to announce the birth of John the Baptist. For four silent centuries, no new revelation came from God.

In the early history of Israel, a similar period covers about the same length of time. God appeared to the patriarch Jacob in a vision prior to his going down to Egypt. He told Jacob that it was all right for him to go—God would be with him and his family, and eventually God would bring the people out again. Four centuries went by. At the end of that time, God appeared again with a great revelation.

Moses had acted on God's behalf, as he thought, when he was in Egypt. He had acted rashly with good motives, run away, and gone to the far side of the desert. He had lived in Midian for forty silent years. Moses was about eighty years old when God finally appeared to him; he must have thought that he had blown it.

Exodus 3 tells how Moses—now a shepherd in the service of his father-in-law, Jethro—was driving his flock down into the Sinai when he came to Horeb, which is identified as the mountain of God (although it probably was not known as such at that time). As Moses waters his flock, he notices a bush with fire in it that is not being destroyed. His curiosity gets the better of him, and he goes toward it. As he does, God calls to him out of the bush: "Moses. Moses." He responds, as people do in the Bible when God calls them by name, "Here I am." God tells him to take off his shoes so that he can approach God humbly and in purity. Then God has three things to tell him.

GOD'S IDENTITY (EX. 3:6)

God starts by telling Moses who he is: "I am the God of your father, the God of Abraham, the God of Isaac, and the God of Jacob."

The Egyptians had all kinds of gods, but the God who speaks to Moses is not one of the polytheistic, heathen gods. Nor is he a new god. He is *the* true God, the old God of the fathers, the God who had revealed himself to Abraham, Isaac, and Jacob.

Interestingly, Jesus refers to this verse when he is quizzed about the resurrection.[1] The Sadducees are trying to make fun of anybody who believes in such a preposterous thing, and Jesus says that they err because they do not know the power of God or the Scriptures. Jesus hangs the whole theory and doctrine of the resurrection on the present tense of that verb: "I *am* the God of Abraham, the God of Isaac, and the God of Jacob." The verb *am* is in the present tense. If God had said, "I *was* the God of Abraham," speaking in the past tense, then Abraham would be dead and gone. But instead God reveals himself to Moses as the one who *is* the God of the patriarchs. As Jesus makes clear, this means that they are still living.

GOD'S CONCERN (EX. 3:7–9)

God tells Moses that he is concerned for his people, having seen how they are suffering and having heard their cries to him (3:7). He says that he will bring the people to the promised land, which is currently inhabited by "the Canaanites, the Hittites, the Amorites, the Perizzites, the Hivites, and the Jebusites" (3:8). This passage lists the present inhabitants of the promised land where he will take the Israelites. He's going to drive those pagan peoples out. But the significance

---

1. This incident is described in Matthew 22:23–33; Mark 12:18–27; and Luke 20:27–40.

of verse 8 is that the list contains almost all the same people groups that God mentions in an earlier list, when he enacted the covenant with Abraham (see Gen. 15:20–21). So it is a way of saying that God is remembering his covenant—because he had promised to be with Abraham and to bless his posterity and bring them into their own land—and that he is acting on that promise now.

GOD'S MISSION (EX. 3:10-15)

Finally, God tells Moses that he is sending him to lead the people out of Egypt. Unfortunately, this is not a word that Moses is anxious to hear—and, having been left alone, as it were, for four decades, he begins to object to what God is sending him to do. His first question raises the most important issue: what if the people ask Moses who this God is who has sent him to deliver the people of Israel (see v. 13)?

GOD'S REVELATION OF HIMSELF

In this context God reveals his great name to Moses. But even before he reveals his name, the very form in which he appears to Moses already teaches us important things about him that his name will bear out. The setting becomes important for the revelation of the name.

God appears to Moses in a bush. There is a flame of fire, but the bush is not burning up. On the one hand, fire is an ancient and continuing symbol for God. A bush, on the other hand, is a commonplace thing. There are bushes all over the countryside; they are about as earthy as you can get. When the fire is in the bush and the bush is not consumed, we learn about the *immanence* of God: God is not aloof but is actually here with his people. He sees them. He identifies with them. He is not hard to entreat.

But God is also holy. When Moses approaches the bush, he has to take off his sandals. His sandals have picked up all the dust of the ground, and therefore they become a symbol for defilement or impurity. Putting off his sandals signifies that he must approach God in holiness, aware of his *transcendence*.

HOLINESS

Our idea of holiness usually has to do with righteousness and goodness. We think that good people are particularly righteous and that God is better than they are; he's higher up the scale.

But holiness is much more than that. It involves the glory and majesty of God. It involves his will—that is, the force of his personality, which is sovereign and omnipotent. It also involves the idea of wrath. Wrath is closely associated with holiness because the wrath of God is a characteristic that goes out against anything that would intrude on his holiness or would try to oppose his will.

God's holiness is the quality or characteristic we find most often attributed to him in the Bible. We do not often read of God's sovereign name or his loving name or his wise name, but we do read about his holy name again and again. "Who is like you, O LORD, among the gods? Who is like you, majestic in holiness, awesome in glorious deeds, doing wonders?" (Ex. 15:11). We hear it in the threefold repetition in Isaiah 6:3, when the seraphim say, "Holy, holy, holy is the LORD of hosts; the whole earth is full of his glory!" In Revelation 4:8, the seraphs sing the same song. We are to do likewise.

What is the real meaning of *holy*? The basic idea is separation. When it is used of us, it means being separated from sin (negatively) and separated unto God (positively). We belong to him. That is why Peter refers to Christians as "a holy nation" (1 Peter 2:9). He does not mean that Christians are sinless but that, if they are Christians, by definition they are separated unto God. They have done what Jesus in Luke 9:23 explained they must do to be a disciple. They have denied themselves and taken up their crosses and are following him. People who have done this are a holy people, separated unto God.

TRANSCENDENCE

When we talk about holiness in God's case, we are talking about his *transcendence*. God is separated from us. He is over us, above us, infinitely beyond us, and not like us. We have been made like him, in a certain sense, and that is important. But God is not like us. This is why God reveals himself to us by analogy—in anthropomorphic terms. He reveals himself in words that we can understand and relate to because of our experience, but they are only analogous to what God is like. So, for example, when we say that God is powerful, we have an idea of what that means because we understand something of what power means. But the power of God is infinitely above anything we imagine. A transcendent God is one who is above us in all things.

God's form of revelation to Moses symbolizes all this. God is *transcendent*, infinitely above us and in an absolute sense incomprehensible to us, but at the same time *immanent*—that is, remaining with us in our world. Isn't that strange? The nature of our God is both transcendent and immanent. This is held in a wonderful balance in the Scriptures. If God were not transcendent, he would not be God. He would not be worth worshipping. If he were not immanent, we would not know him as a personal God and could not worship him rightly. But in Scripture we find the wonderful truth that the transcendent God makes himself known, being both far above us and also with us. So Jesus, the incarnate God, would be designated Immanuel, "God with us," in the angel's announcement to Joseph (see Matt. 1:23, quoting Isa. 7:14). Revealing himself as both transcendent and immanent is what God does in Exodus 3.

THE NAME OF GOD

When God commissions Moses to return to Egypt, to bring his people out of that land, Moses has one question—a question he assumes that the Israelites will ask him: who is this God? "What is his name?" (Ex. 3:13). In God's case, names are a vehicle of revelation. There are many names for God in the Bible, and they are very, very important: *Elohim*, which is usually translated "God;" *El Shaddai*—"Almighty God;" *Jehovah Jireh*—"The God Who Will Provide." Among the names that reveal something about God's character, none is more important than this one: "I AM WHO I AM" (Ex. 3:14). The Israelites regarded this as God's name above all other names.

There has been much debate about the name's meaning and even its origins. It is called the *tetragrammaton* ("four letters"), because in the Hebrew text it is the four-letter name for God, the covenant-making God of Israel. The Hebrew consonants are *yodh, he, waw*, and *he*. Originally, written Hebrew did not have vowels, only consonants. So YHWH is the way the name would have appeared in the original Hebrew text.

The Jews considered the name so holy that it was blasphemous to speak it. They probably got this from Exodus 20:7, which forbids taking the name of the Lord in vain. In a characteristically rabbinic approach, they said, "That means that you shouldn't even utter it on your lips, because to utter the name of God on sinful human lips is blasphemy." So they did not speak it but substituted *Adonai* instead, which simply means "Lord." Whenever they came to those four letters in the Hebrew text, they said *Adonai*.

As Hebrew developed, vowel points were added to the written language. These are little points and lines that are placed above and below the consonants to give the vowel sounds. Centuries later, as the Old Testament texts were copied, these vowel points were added. What did copyists do when they came to YHWH? Wanting to remind people not to say the holy name of God, they added in the vowel points for the word *Adonai*. So whenever a Jewish scholar came to the holy name of God, he said *Adonai* instead.

The Septuagint, the Greek translation of the Old Testament, continued this practice. When the Greeks came to the holy name of God, they used the Greek word *Kurios,* which means "Lord"—an exact translation of *Adonai*. So the word *Lord* passed over into the New Testament and was used in the New Testament as a name of God.

We get the word *Jehovah* by reading YHWH the way it appears with the vowel points from the word *Adonai*. That is probably not the way it was pronounced. Most scholars think that it was probably pronounced *Yahweh*. While they do not have any Jewish document to support that pronunciation, the word appears in that form in the later Syriac text, where both consonants and vowels are present. On the basis of the Syriac version of the Old Testament, scholars speculate that it was probably *Yahweh*.

The real issue is the meaning of the name. The four consonants come from the verb *to be*. The common form of the verb is what in

Hebrew is called the *kal* form, and that is simply *to be*. Translated this way, Yahweh could mean "I Am That I Am" or "I Will Be What I Will Be." But introducing a certain set of vowel markings puts the word in a Hebrew-language tense called the *hiphil*, which gives it a causative sense. If the verb *to be* is a *hiphil*, it would be translated as "He Who Causes to Be" or "He Who Brings into Being." That would be a good description of God, wouldn't it? He's the Creator.

How does one decide? In the context of the revelation to Moses, the name is not causative; it refers to God not as the Creator but rather as the eternal, ever-existent One. And in the New Testament Jesus refers to himself in the present-tense "I Am" sayings. Thus it seems that God is saying what is translated as "I Am That I Am." God is the eternal I Am. In himself he encompasses the past, present, and future. God can say, "I always have been, I am, and I always will be; I'm unchanged in my eternal being."

THE IMPLICATIONS OF GOD'S NAME

Now that we have laid the background, we can explore the attributes of God that his name expresses. We've already talked about his transcendence and immanence. Here are other attributes.

GOD IS PERSONAL

God is a personal God. When we use that word *person*, we must realize that we're reasoning by analogy. We are persons, and the reason we are persons is because we are made in the image of God. When we talk about the personality of God, we're talking about something very real, yet the personality of God is far over and above anything we can imagine. God is more than a person, and yet he certainly is not less. When God reveals himself to Moses by saying "I Am," the very fact that he says "I" indicates personality.

This is very important to bear in mind because, when we talk about God, we are not talking about a cosmic force. You can't worship a force any more than you can worship gravity. God reveals himself to be a person who is able to interact on a personal level with Moses, a human being.

GOD IS SELF-EXISTENT

God is self-existent. This is the very essence of God's saying, "I am that I am." He just is. You and I came into being. There was a time when we were not. We are now, but we weren't then; now we are because we were brought into being in a certain way. God simply says, "I am that I am." Matthew Henry says, "The greatest and best man in the world must say, By the grace of God I am what I am; but God says absolutely—and it is more than any creature, man or angel, can say—I am that I am."[2]

Among other things, this means that God is unknowable to us—at least unknowable in an exhaustive sense. When we pursue knowledge, we do so in terms of relationships, and the most basic relationship is cause and effect. When we see something, we say that it is what it is because of something else. A chair is something that somebody has made, and the person who makes a chair determines its object. This means we go back a step in order to explain it. But in the case of God we cannot go back to anything. God just is, and so we cannot explain him. In that ultimate sense we cannot know him.

A. W. Tozer has pointed out that this is one reason why the philosophers have so much trouble with God. They cannot quite get him down to where they can analyze him and explain him. Scientists have exactly the same problem. God is above anything that we can imagine or measure. We can't bring him down to our level. As Tozer states, "To admit that there is One who lies beyond us, who exists outside of all our categories . . . who will not appear before the bar of our reason . . . this requires a great deal of humility, more than most of us possess, so we save face by thinking God down to our level, or at least down to where we can manage Him."[3] This is one reason why even Christian people have so much trouble studying God and coming to know him. It is troublesome to deal with someone who is ultimately so far beyond our comprehension.

2. Matthew Henry, *Complete Commentary on the Whole Bible* (1706), Sacred Texts, accessed June 19, 2014, http://www.sacred-texts.com/bib/cmt/henry/exo003.htm.

3. A. W. Tozer, *The Knowledge of the Holy: The Attributes of God; Their Meaning in the Christian Life* (New York: Harper & Brothers, 1961), 33.

GOD IS SELF-SUFFICIENT

The name also points to God's self-sufficiency. *Self-existent* means that God has no origins. *Self-sufficient* means that God has no needs. "I am that I am." God is telling Moses that he is here and doesn't need anything. God does graciously use us to carry out his plan—he's doing that with Moses, after all. He calls Moses because he will send Moses to Egypt as his agent in bringing the people to their own land. But he doesn't have to use Moses, and he doesn't have to use us either.

God has no needs. He doesn't need any helpers. He can do everything without the help of human agents. He doesn't need us. He doesn't need defenders. He is well able to take care of himself. He doesn't even need worshippers. We do not add anything to God by worshipping him. If God uses us as helpers, that is a privilege. If God uses us to defend the gospel, that is a privilege. If God uses us in worshipping him, the blessing is all ours.

When we begin to understand this, we begin to understand why unbelief is such a serious sin. God presents himself as the all-sufficient one, and he calls on us to trust him, which is what faith is. If we refuse to believe in God, we are saying that some other thing is more trustworthy than God himself. In other words, we are saying that something else is sufficient, that God is not sufficient, and that we cannot trust God. That is slander on the name of God, as well as folly.

GOD IS ETERNAL

The verb *to be* also suggests that God is eternal. It is hard to find one word to describe this attribute. We talk about God being everlasting, and we talk about perpetuity or eternity. This means that God is, has always been, and always will be, and that he is always the same in his eternal being.

This is a comfort to us because, since we are made in the image of God, God has put eternity within our hearts, as Ecclesiastes affirms (see 3:11). In other words, we have been given a sense that we are meant to live beyond this life. To know that God is an eternal being is a comfort for those who come to know him.

GOD IS UNCHANGEABLE

God is also unchangeable. Theologians use the term *immutable*. This means that God never differs from himself. What he is today, he will be tomorrow, and he is today what he was yesterday. This attribute is implied in the divine name and has several important consequences for us.

It means, first of all, that God can be trusted. He can be trusted to remain as he is. If he reveals himself to be one way, we can be sure that tomorrow that is the way he will be, and that he will be that way the day after. The same applies to God as revealed in Jesus Christ. Nothing will ever change God. As the writer of Hebrews states, "Jesus Christ is the same yesterday and today and forever" (13:8).

But, second, God's immutability means that God is inescapable. He is not going to go away. None of his attributes will change. He will not become less holy or less sovereign than he is. This means that we have to come to terms with God as he is. And wise is the person who comes to terms with God early.

MOSES' RESPONSE

After a revelation like that, we could expect that Moses would say, "Well, God, that is a great revelation you gave me. Thank you. I really feel honored by that. What would you have me do?" But that is not what happened.

As a matter of fact, God's giving of his name was an answer to one of Moses' objections. When God first called Moses and said, "I'm going to send you to Egypt, to Pharaoh, to tell him 'Let my people go,'" Moses began to make excuses.

First of all, he asked, "Who am I?" He meant that he was insignificant. "Why send me? I can't do the job."

God answered this question, in effect, by saying, "I don't care who you are. That is not the issue. Of course you're inadequate. I'm the one who is sending you. I'm the one who is adequate."

Then Moses said, "Well, who are you?"

So God gave him his great name to show that he is the sovereign, eternal God.

And then Moses began to make more excuses.

FIRST OBJECTION: "THEY WON'T BELIEVE ME"

The first thing Moses did was to ask a question: "What if they do not believe me or listen to me and say, 'The LORD did not appear to you'?" (Ex. 4:1 NIV). This is reasonable, so God responded by giving him three signs. Sometimes we read more into symbols than we should, but there is much to be said about these signs.

First, Moses was to take his shepherd's staff and throw it on the ground. When he did this, it turned into a snake, and when he grabbed it again at the command of God, it turned back into a rod. We will see later that he did this before Pharaoh and the people.

What is important about this sign? The staff is about the most insignificant thing one can think of—just a stick, a piece of dead wood. Moses' staff was not from the burning bush. That would have had symbolic value; he would have been able to say, "This is part of the very bush in which God appeared to me." But instead Moses had a stick he found or cut himself, and God used it.

In his devotional commentary on Exodus, F. B. Meyer makes a great deal of this incident.[4] He points out that whatever we have in our hand—meaning whatever endowment God has given us, whatever talent we have—if we turn it over to God to be used by him, he will use it in a powerful way. Moses' staff will be used in many of the miracles. It was just a staff of wood, but it became a dramatic revelation of God's power.

Second, God gave Moses the sign of the leprous hand. Moses put his hand inside his cloak, and when he pulled it out, it turned white with leprosy. When he put his hand back in his cloak again, it was cured. The power of this sign came from the fact that the Egyptians were very fastidious about personal cleanliness. They did not want to be defiled, and leprosy was the ultimate defilement. Here God revealed himself as a God who is able to inflict illness and also to cure it. Later, during the plagues, we will find out that the gods of Egypt who were supposed to do this kind of wonder were unable to do so. They were powerless before the true God.

4. F. B. Meyer, *Moses: The Servant of God* (New York: Fleming H. Revell Company, n.d.), 35–36.

Third, God promised a sign of turning water into blood. This would eventually become the first of the ten plagues on Egypt. It was a sign against the gods and goddesses of the Nile, a sign we will explore when we get to that section of Exodus.

So, to Moses' first objection, God said, "I'll give you the signs."

SECOND OBJECTION: "I'M NOT ELOQUENT"

Moses' second objection was this: "Oh, my Lord, I am not eloquent, either in the past or since you have spoken to your servant, but I am slow of speech and of tongue" (4:10). This excuse was similar to the first. His first objection—"Who am I?"—really meant "I am unworthy." When he said, "I speak slowly and I don't have a great deal of eloquence," he meant, "I'm not adequate." Both these objections were irrelevant.

Moses' excuses are beginning to go around full circle. Has this happened to you? You object to something God is telling you to do, and you think up a second objection, and then you think up a third. After a while you begin to run out of objections. Then you go back and use the first one all over again.

This time God answered Moses by telling him that God himself made Moses the way he was. "You're slow of speech?" he asked. "That's the way I made you. Now don't complain to me about it. I knew what I was doing." In the words of our text, God's response is irrefutable. "Who gave man his mouth? Who makes him deaf or mute? Who gives him sight or makes him blind? Is it not I, the LORD?" (v. 11 NIV). At this point the only response for Moses was obedience to God's command and promise: "Now therefore go," says the Lord, "and I will be with your mouth and teach you what you shall speak" (v. 12).

THIRD OBJECTION: "I DON'T WANT TO DO IT"

But Moses had one more thing to say, and he couched his final plea in typical polite Semitic language. He *wanted* to say, "I don't want to do it," but he actually said, "O my LORD, send, I pray thee, by the hand of him whom thou wilt send" (KJV). But the New International Version has the right idea when it translates the verse loosely, not literally: "O Lord, please send someone else to do it" (4:13 NIV).

Have you ever felt like that? Have you ever responded to God that way? "Evangelize the world, God—I'll pray for it—but don't send me. Reach my neighbor with the gospel, but don't send me next door."

AFTER THE BURNING BUSH

At this point God became angry with Moses. "Is there not Aaron, your brother, the Levite? I know that he can speak well" (4:14). Something in the tone of that answer must have gotten through to Moses and convinced him that he had gone just about as far as he dared to go. So Moses shut up, and I suppose—reading a little between the lines—that this eighty-year-old man now turned his back on the burning bush with a heavy heart, dismissed; he gathered up his sheep and made his way back to Jethro his father-in-law to say, "I've got to go back to Egypt." I do not detect anywhere in the writings that Moses did this with a buoyant spirit. Nevertheless, he is the one whom God used.

Three events happened on the way back to Egypt. First, God revealed that the people who were trying to kill Moses earlier were dead. This was meant to encourage him. The old pharaoh had died. Next came an incident regarding the circumcision of Moses' son. Finally, Moses met with his brother Aaron. The fourth chapter ends by describing how Moses and Aaron met together with the elders of the people and obtained their endorsement to go to Pharaoh.

Let's go back to Moses' failure to circumcise his son. This is described only briefly in three verses, which makes it a little hard to interpret. God was about to kill Moses because he had neglected to apply the covenant rite of circumcision to his second and possibly newborn son—perhaps because his wife Zipporah objected to it. Zipporah seemed to be unhappy in the story. She reluctantly did what was necessary, performing the rite of circumcision on her son, but with bitter words for Moses.

This says something about our need to obey God, even if somebody very close to us—even a husband or wife—objects. We have to be very careful at this point, because God is not in the business of dividing families. But nevertheless, Zipporah drops out of the narrative. We're told that she was on her way to Egypt with Moses and the children, but we do not learn anything about her in Egypt. Later, after Moses came out of Egypt, Jethro came to see him with Zipporah and the children. So presumably Moses sent her back to her father at this point. F. B. Meyer, whom I quoted before, strikes a wise balance.

> We are not always to follow this example in ridding ourselves of family ties in order to do God's work. . . . The circumstances must be very exceptional that invade the close ties of the home; but when such circumstances arise, they will be so evidently indicated by God's providence that there will be no reflection cast on the character of his servants.[5]

This episode says something about our need for purification and a right heart with God if we are going to do his work. Moses may have been a great man, and he certainly must have learned a great deal from God during those forty years in the wilderness, not to mention the revelation of God at the burning bush. But, even so, he could not proceed until he was right with God. For Moses this meant identifying his sons as members of the covenant community through the rite of circumcision.

LEARNING FROM EXODUS 3–4

The most important thing in life is to know God. This means knowing God in respect to his attributes—what he is like, what words describe him. Do you know God? Do you really know God in terms of his various attributes? Do you want to know him better? If you do not know him at all, are you willing to seek him? The way to know him is by studying the Bible and hearing it taught.

Note God's timing. Moses was eighty years old when God called him to his life's work. He must have thought he was too old. But this was the right time; he had been wrong when at forty he tried to take the matter into his own hands. We could say, "When you're forty, that's the time to get on with your life work. That's when you're at the peak of your strength and ability." But Moses wasn't ready then, and

5. Ibid., 42–43.

God's timing involved waiting and maturing for another forty years. Be ready to serve God. Be willing. But do not be overly impatient. Wait for God to open doors of service and then show you the way forward.

When you enter upon a work from God, you can be sure that he will supply what you need to complete it. All that you really need is God himself. This is why the last thing we hear Jesus say to his disciples as he sends them out to evangelize a hostile, pagan world is that he will be with them until the day he comes again (see Matt. 28:20). Do you believe that? He is with you. If he gives you a task to do, he will be with you just as he was with Moses, and he'll carry you to completion regardless of how weak you feel or how strong the opposition may seem.

6

The First Meeting with Pharaoh

Exodus 5—6

AN UNEXPECTED TURN

When we become Christians, most of us have a pretty clear idea in our minds of how the Christian life ought to go. We live in a technological age, and we expect things to work well, efficiently, predictably, and on time. We think that this is the way the Christian life should be. It should be like driving a car: when you get in the car, turn the switch, and step on the gas, you ought to move forward.

Well, it doesn't always work that way in the Christian life. We think we are doing the right things, but there seem to be setbacks and discouragements. When those difficulties and discouragements happen—and they happen quite often—we become more discouraged, and many of us wonder what has gone wrong.

The first great incident in Moses' life, when he returned to Egypt and confronted Pharaoh, was like that. Moses had been reluctant to take on this challenge; he pleaded a number of excuses before God. Nevertheless, God told him to go back to Egypt in order to meet with his brother, go before the elders of the people, and describe how God had appeared to him on Mount Horeb, and he had given him instructions about confronting the pharaoh.

Moses did all of that, and he did it exactly. It even seems that, to a certain extent, he was successful. At least the people listened to him. He did the signs that God gave him, the people said, "This is wonderful," and so Moses went to Pharaoh . . . but failed utterly. In fact, the worst possible thing happened: not only did Pharaoh refuse to let the people go, but he actually came down harder on the Hebrew people who were slaves in bondage. Pharaoh made their lives so miserable that they cried out to Moses, who by this time had lost all credibility.

We want to ask an obvious question: "Why in the world did such a thing happen?" Looking back, we can suggest a number of reasons. We might say that it happened so that the people could see how desperate their situation was before God delivered them, so that they would appreciate deliverance. We might suggest it was so that the people, and the leaders too, might learn that their salvation was in God alone. We could argue that the leaders, Moses and Aaron, needed to come to the end of self and be utterly surrendered to God and to whatever it might please God to do for them. All these things would be true, but none of the people were aware of this at the time.

This is why, when the people turned against him, Moses prostrated himself before God and cried out, "O Lord, why have you done evil to this people? Why did you ever send me? For since I came to Pharaoh to speak in your name, he has done evil to this people, and you have not delivered your people at all" (Ex. 5:22–23). Do you ever feel like that? If you have ever gone through this experience, this is a story for you.

THUS SAITH THE LORD

The message for Pharaoh in Exodus 5 began the way that the later messages from Israel's prophets all began: "Thus saith the LORD." This introduction sets the words apart from any words by a mere mortal. Pharaoh did not understand the message that way, and he certainly did not receive it that way, but that was irrelevant: it was the Word of God.

Today we teach the Bible to people who are no more disposed to receive or believe it, or to bow before the God of Scripture, than was Pharaoh. But that doesn't change the message in the slightest. When we teach the Bible, we do not say, "Well, this is what I happen to think," or "I have been reflecting on the situation in the world today, and it seems to me that it might be good if we did such-and-such," or "Here's a bit of advice that you might find helpful this week as you put it into practice." No. We say, "Thus saith the Lord."

Why is this? It is because the Word of God has within it the power to accomplish what God chooses to accomplish. When God brought this universe into being, he did it by the word of his mouth. He said, "Let there be light," and there was light. When he said, "Let the water be divided from the land," that is what happened. In Isaiah 55:11, God tells us that his word will always accomplish whatever he intends. When we speak the Word of God to other people, we need to be encouraged by this truth. The results are always in God's hands. They are not always the results we anticipate, but they are God's work. God's power blesses his Word.

Moses' statements contain the message of God for Pharaoh: that Pharaoh must let the people of Israel go into the desert to hold a religious festival (see Ex. 5:1). Moses elaborates that they will be worshipping God and offering sacrifices. He also describes this as a three-day journey (see v. 3).

Some have understood Moses to be dishonest here; they have said that Moses is implying that the Israelites want to go, have a little religious celebration, and then come back. That, of course, is not the case. He is requesting that they be allowed to go into the desert and worship and would perhaps come back—with the implication, of course, that later on there will be stronger demands. But Pharaoh declines even this reasonable suggestion. It becomes very clear early in the story that Pharaoh is not reasonable in this area, and that therefore there will be a knock-down, drag-out fight between Pharaoh and his gods and Jehovah, the God of Israel.

GOD AND THE GOVERNMENT

When Pharaoh said no, he did so in a very arrogant way. "Who is the LORD, that I should obey his voice and let Israel go? I do not know the LORD, and moreover, I will not let Israel go" (5:2). Remember that the Egyptians, and probably Pharaoh himself, considered Pharaoh to be a god. In that day there was an Egyptian phrase, *neter nefer*, which means "the perfect god." If you are a perfect god, why should you listen to any other god, especially the God of a slave people? This is the way that all totalitarian rulers respond to claims from God. Moreover, this is the way that many governments respond, even if they are not totalitarian.

If we analyze this position, we will see that this is exactly the way the American government responds to any claim that religion might make. This is why the government insists, in our day, on this particular form of what we call the doctrine of the separation of church and state. This doctrine is perfectly valid, rightly understood. It means that the state is not to control the churches; in other words, there is to be freedom of religion, and churches can conduct their business as they think best. At the same time, bishops or other church officials are not to dictate to the government. The government is to operate on its own principles. This doesn't mean, however, that the state is not responsible to God or that government workers never have to answer to divine authority or live according to moral standards. In a democracy, the church has opportunity to speak out in order to remind the government that it is ultimately responsible to God, whether this truth is acknowledged or not.

FOUR VIEWS OF GOD AND THE GOVERNMENT

Four different views try to make sense of the relationship between God and Caesar, the church and the state.

One view maintains that Caesar doesn't have any authority at all; only God does. This is the view of monasticism, and sometimes of an evangelical withdrawal from civic responsibility. Thinking that the country, government, and culture are bad, people decide that they cannot have anything to do with public life, so they move into the desert, join a monastic community, or shut themselves up in churches. Either way, they do not interact with the state at all.

The second view, the view of secularism, is exactly the opposite. It denies God. Secularism says that the only things that exist are the ones we can see and measure. We cannot see or measure God, so there is no God. We do not have to think in religious terms at all. All we have to do is operate in a secular, non-religious manner.

The third view recognizes the authority of God and Caesar both, but it sees the authority of Caesar as dominant. Whenever there is a question, the state rules. This is the view of cowards. It is perfectly evident that if you have God in the picture, God by very definition has to have greater authority than Caesar. The only reason we would ever give greater authority to Caesar is because we are afraid of Caesar.

Three times Pontius Pilate acknowledged in Jesus' trial that Jesus was innocent (see John 18:38; 19:4, 6), indicating that Jesus was guiltless before the bar of Roman justice. Yet in the end Pilate agreed to the crucifixion. Why would he do that if he found Jesus innocent? He was afraid of Caesar. The enemies of Jesus came to him and said, "If you release this man, you are not Caesar's friend" (John 19:12). Ironically, Caesar wasn't his friend anyway. Pilate eventually got in trouble with Caesar and, according to some accounts, died an exile in disgrace in France.

The fourth of these views is the biblical and correct view. It recognizes the authority of God and Caesar but accepts that the authority of God is dominant. Caesar has legitimate authority, but all authority comes from God. Romans 13 states that all authority, including state authority, comes from God, whether or not the authority of the government recognizes the authority of God.

In the contemporary environment, the role of Christians and the church is to remind the state of exactly this. We have to remind government officials that they are responsible to God to do the right thing, and we are to articulate this on the basis of Scripture. Moreover, we are to rebuke the state when it departs from this standard. If a state is engaging in an immoral practice—slavery, for example—Christian people must stand up against that unrighteous government, and Christian people have done just that. There is never any significant moral advance in a culture unless it comes in this way—from God's people taking a stand and working for the cause of righteousness.

A HARDENED HEART

So here we have a great confrontation between God and Caesar. Of course Caesar, in the person of Pharaoh, was going to insist on his own way. Pharaoh would not let the people go, because his heart was hard. You find these words again and again throughout this account, yet we are also told that God hardened Pharaoh's heart.

Was Pharaoh's heart hard because the Lord had hardened it?

Or did God harden Pharaoh's heart as a punishment because he had first hardened his heart himself?

Quite a few commentators are worried about God's reputation at this point. They do not want to suggest that God did anything to make Pharaoh worse. F. B. Meyer, whom I have quoted favorably, is one of these people. In his book on Moses, Meyer has a chapter called "The Love of God in the First Four Plagues." In this he argues that God was not hardening Pharaoh's heart but was trying to do the exact opposite: bring Pharaoh to repentance.[1]

There are a few problems with this view. First, the Bible doesn't say anything about God trying to bring Pharaoh to repentance. We might attempt to read that into the narrative out of sentiment, but it is not there. Second, the first time anything is said about Pharaoh's heart is when God tells Moses, "I will harden his heart, so that he will not let the people go" (Ex. 4:21). This suggests that God hardened Pharaoh's heart in order to demonstrate his power and that it was because of God's prior determination that Pharaoh hardened his heart himself.

Of course, God can harden hearts simply by allowing us to go our own way. He does not have to intervene in a special way; our hearts are hard and get harder by themselves. If God does not work in our lives with softening grace, hardening is the inevitable result. This is what the theological term *reprobation* means. Reprobation is when God allows people to go their own way. God could have let Pharaoh's heart harden on its own, but nevertheless the Scripture says he hardened Pharaoh's heart.

---

1. F. B. Meyer, *Moses: The Servant of God* (New York: Fleming H. Revell Company, n.d.), 51–59.

Third, Exodus 9:16 reports the word of God to Pharaoh in which God said, "But for this purpose I have raised you up, to show you my power, so that my name may be proclaimed in all the earth." This suggests that God had determined to harden Pharaoh's heart not merely when he told Moses as much on the mountain, but before Pharaoh was even born. God brought Pharaoh into existence at that particular time in history in order to demonstrate his power.

Paul picks this up in Romans 9, where he argues about the ways of God. After quoting Exodus 9:16, he concludes, "So then he has mercy on whomever he wills, and he hardens whomever he wills" (Rom. 9:18). God is sovereign in the matter of salvation. If he saves us, that is all of grace, and we thank and praise him—but he doesn't have to save us. If God chooses to pass over people, that is his prerogative. We can't protest, because we have no claim—God doesn't owe us anything.

Moreover, the ultimate purpose in all this is not that good comes to us but that God is glorified. We all think in terms of our own well-being. We want what we want. Of course, Pharaoh was getting what he wanted. He operated exactly how he wanted to operate, and God let him go his own way. But God will be glorified as God. This is why Paul refers to Exodus 9:16 in Romans 9 and says that God is going to be glorified in all his attributes whether we like it or not. His justice and wrath will bring him glory in the way that he judges sin. His mercy and compassion and grace will bring him glory in the way that he redeems sinners.

God demonstrated his power, wrath, and justice in judging Pharaoh, and he demonstrated his mercy in saving Israel. The one is as important as the other.

THE REJECTION OF MOSES, AND GOD'S RESPONSE

Moses' first appearance before Pharaoh ended in disaster—at least in apparent disaster. Instead of letting the people go as Moses demanded in the name of God, Pharaoh made their lives harder. The Israelites had been provided with straw for the bricks they were making, but no longer. They now had to gather it themselves, and because this took time and diffused the labor force they were not able to produce as many bricks as they had before. Yet the quota was the same. Their Egyptian masters beat the Israelite foremen who were immediately responsible for the slave gangs because they had not met the quota. The foremen went to Pharaoh and complained, "This isn't fair; we just can't do it," but this was a useless complaint. The whole point was that this was not fair. Pharaoh was trying to be as unfair as he could, and as a result, Moses and Aaron lost their credibility. At the end of the chapter the foremen turned on them and said, "The LORD look on you and judge, because you have made us stink in the sight of Pharaoh and his servants, and have put a sword in their hand to kill us" (5:21).

The rejection of Moses by the people must have seemed like death. There was no doubt at all that he had failed. God had sent him to Pharaoh, he had gone, and Pharaoh had not responded as he should have. Not only that, but the situation had become much, much worse. Moses must have wished that he had never come; he must have thought it would have been better if he had remained in Midian with the sheep.

Actually he was learning something very important. In our terminology, he was dying to his own self-esteem in order that he might become more useful in God's hands. If there is a lesson in the story, that is it. F. B. Meyer is very valuable here. He says, "[Moses] died to his self-esteem, to his castle-building, to pride in his miracles, to the enthusiasm of his people, to everything that a popular leader loves."[2] (If you've seen political figures running for office, you know exactly what we are talking about.) "As he lay there on the ground alone before God, wishing himself back in Midian, and thinking himself [very badly treated], he was falling as a corn of wheat into the ground to die, no longer to abide alone, but to bear much fruit."[3] As long as we are full of ourselves, even in small things, we are no use to God. When we die to self, we become vessels fit for his service. This is true and a great spiritual lesson.

2. Ibid., 49.
3. Ibid.

Not long after I prepared this study, I came across an article by Elisabeth Elliot. In it she described talking to young people who are considering being missionaries and who ask how she "discovered the will of God."

> The first thing was to settle once and for all the supremacy of Christ in my life, I tell them. I put myself utterly and forever at His disposal, which means turning over *all* the rights: to myself, my body, my self-image, my notions of how I am to serve my Master. . . . I tell these earnest kids that the will of God is always *different* from what they expect, always *bigger*, and, ultimately, infinitely more *glorious* than their wildest imaginings.
>
> But there will be deaths to die.[4]

That is exactly what Moses found out, and it is the great lesson of the story. Here he is: defeated, rejected by his own people, alone, isolated. I imagine that the Israelites aren't even talking to him. He does the only reasonable thing, the only thing that is left. He prays. He throws himself before God. His is a desperate prayer (see 5:22–23), growing out of a great deal of personal pain, but it is honest, and it is accurate. Trouble has come on the people, and it is quite reasonable to ask God why.

God responds reasonably and accurately to Moses' reasonable and accurate prayer. In Exodus 6, he tells Moses seven things.

PHARAOH *WILL* LET THE PEOPLE GO

First, God tells Moses that Pharaoh will let the people go. Just because Pharaoh hasn't done it yet doesn't mean that he won't do it. God's timing is not our timing. When Moses had first told Pharaoh that God said to let the people go, Moses would have preferred for Pharaoh to say, "Okay, they can go," but that wasn't God's timing. God is going to show his glory and power before it is all over. He says, "Now you shall see what I will do to Pharaoh. . . . I am the LORD, and I will bring you out from under the burdens of the Egyptians, and I

---

4. Elisabeth Elliot Gren, "The Supremacy of Christ," *The Elisabeth Elliot Newsletter*, March/April 1993, 1.

will deliver you from slavery to them, and I will redeem you with an outstretched arm and with great acts of judgment" (6:1, 6).

If it had happened the way that Moses wanted, Pharaoh would have said, "I'm a wonderful person to have done what I've done" and glorified himself. But God had announced the liberation, and it would happen in his own time.

GOD IS STILL GOD

Second, God tells Moses that he is still God (see Ex. 6:2)—the same God who revealed himself to the patriarchs Abraham, Isaac, and Jacob (see v. 3). These two verses may seem straightforward on the surface, but they actually raise a couple of interesting discussion points.

One is that verse 2 begins a second, somewhat separate, revelation from the one in verse 1, indicated by the way that it starts with the line, "God spoke to Moses and said to him. . . ." This second section contains items of its own and both begins, here in verse 2, and also ends, in verse 8, with the words "I am the LORD." Bible scholars use the Latin word *inclusio* to describe a situation like this, when there is something stated at the beginning of a section and an identical statement at the end of the section that wraps up the section as a whole.

The other interesting thing to note is in verse 3, where God says that although the patriarchs—Abraham, Isaac, and Jacob—knew him as the true God, they did not know or use *Jehovah* as a name for God:[5]

---

5. In the latter half of the eighteenth century, this became a very important verse for liberal scholars, because it was a verse upon which they hung their theory of literary development. They said that the early patriarchs, being unacquainted with God by the name *Jehovah*, knew him as *Elohim* (a generic name meaning "God") or *El Shaddai* (meaning "the all-powerful God; God Almighty"). Moses, they said, picked up the idea of God being Jehovah from the Kenites. Thus the technical term in biblical scholarship for this theory is the *Kenite Hypothesis*. It is also known by the initials *JEPD*. *J* stands for the Jehovah source—the part of the Old Testament that supposedly came from people who knew God as Jehovah. *E* stands for the Elohim source—the part of the Old Testament contributed by people who knew God as Elohim. Then the priests pulled it all together (*P*), and finally the Deuteronomy school or author (*D*) structured the writings—and, as a result of that four-stage development, we have our Old Testament. Evangelicals rejected that theory, and rightly so. It didn't hold up under serious scholarship, and today even many non-evangelicals reject it.

"I appeared to Abraham, to Isaac, and to Jacob, as God Almighty, but by my name the LORD I did not make myself known to them" (Ex. 6:3) There are three possible ways to understand this.

1. Verse 3 is a question that implies a positive answer: "By my name the Lord, did I not make myself known to them?" The answer would be yes. This is a very attractive suggestion that does away with the problem all at once. The only difficulty is that translators do not think it is a question.
2. The patriarchs knew the name Jehovah but did not understand its significance. This is reasonable; God could reveal the full significance of his name as he went along. Unfortunately, that is not what this verse says. It says that they did not know it.
3. The patriarchs really did not know the name Jehovah, because it had not been revealed to them. It was revealed first to Moses at the burning bush.

I think the third, most obvious answer is correct, and there is good evidence for it. Perhaps the greatest evidence is that in the Old Testament, many names incorporate shortened forms of the name of God (most often *Yah*), but these shortened forms are not found in popular names before the time of Moses. The only possible exception might be Jochebed, Moses' mother.[6] Some would point out that the older portions of the Pentateuch (especially the book of Genesis) often use the name Jehovah, but that is easily explained by Moses' authorship of the book. He used the name that had been given to him as a way of saying that the God of the patriarchs actually was Jehovah, even though the patriarchs did not know him by that name.

One verse is a little more significant as a problem. Genesis 4:26 says that after the birth of Seth, in the earliest days of earth's history, man began to call on the name of Yahweh. Although it sounds as though they knew God by that name, this could simply mean that in those days men began to pray. Certainly it could be another case of Moses' using the later name in an earlier context. It could even be

---

6. *Jo* could be a *very* shortened version of the name of God, but that is not certain.

that, in those early days, Seth and the other antediluvians (those who lived before the flood) did know God by the name *Jehovah*, but that the name had been forgotten by the time of Abraham. This indicates that God gave a new revelation of himself at the burning bush, which makes Exodus 3 extremely important.

GOD MADE A COVENANT WITH ABRAHAM

Third, God reminds Moses that he had a covenant with Abraham. God expressed this covenant in Genesis 15 and elaborated on it in Genesis 17, when he gave circumcision as the sign of the covenant. Why had God promised to bless Abraham, multiply his descendants, and eventually bring him into the promised land? We looked at that in chapter 1 of this book.

GOD HAS NOT FORGOTTEN THE COVENANT

Fourth, God tells Moses that he has not forgotten this covenant. The story of Moses begins with this fact. We are told in Exodus 2:23–24 that the Israelites groaned in their slavery and that God heard their groaning, remembered his covenant with Abraham, Isaac, and Jacob, and was concerned about his people. Exodus 6 deliberately echoes Exodus 2, showing that God does not forget.

Does God have a covenant with you? Indeed he does. If you are a follower of Jesus Christ, he has a covenant with you called the covenant of grace. This great and everlasting covenant was established through the blood of Jesus and has Jesus' blood as its sign. The God who established that covenant with you certainly remembers it. When you find yourself in difficulty, suffering because of sickness, lack of a job, abuse, or misunderstanding, the God of the covenant knows you and hears you. He remembers his covenant, and he remembers just as certainly as he did in the case of Israel.

MOSES MUST REPEAT HIS MESSAGE TO THE PEOPLE

Fifth, God tells Moses to repeat his message to the people. Moses had delivered this message once. The people had received it. Then he had brought the message to Pharaoh. Pharaoh had rejected it. Then, when Pharaoh made their lives hard, the people (who were always fickle) had rejected Moses. But that had not changed the message at all. The message was exactly the same as it had been at the beginning: God would set the people free.

God's Word is unchanging. It doesn't make any difference whether people receive it or not. God will do what he has said he will do. Our task as Christian people is to teach what God has taught us.

Here is an interesting fact. When God says that he is going to redeem the people (see 6:6), that is only the second occurrence of that word for "redeem" (*gaal*) so far in the Bible (the first being in Genesis 48:16). It refers to the way that God will bring the Israelites out of slavery. At the first Passover, the lambs will be killed and the blood spread upon the lintel and the doorposts of the house as evidence that an innocent animal has died in the place of the firstborn of each family. God will set them free from slavery at the cost of blood. This Old Testament picture points forward to the great redemption that has been accomplished for us in Jesus Christ, when he brought us out of slavery to sin with the payment of his shed blood. It is a pattern of that final redemption, which is why it was given.

THE ISRAELITES ARE THE UNIQUE PEOPLE OF GOD

Sixth, the Israelites were to be the unique people of God. This is closely linked to the matter of the covenant, and on this basis God requires that they be a holy nation. Peter undoubtedly had these words in mind when he wrote of the people who had been made partakers of the new covenant (you and me), "You are a chosen race, a royal priesthood, a holy nation, a people for his own possession, that you may proclaim the excellencies of him who called you out of darkness into his marvelous light" (1 Peter 2:9).

The Israelites had a wonderful opportunity after their redemption to say, "We were slaves in Egypt, and God, the great God of our people, has set us free." You and I have exactly the same opportunity and responsibility. We were slaves to sin—a far greater slavery than any physical bondage. And God—the same God, Jehovah, the God of the Israelites, the only God there is—delivered us by the death of Jesus Christ our Savior. We have the opportunity to declare his praises.

GOD WILL BRING THE ISRAELITES INTO THE PROMISED LAND

Seventh and finally, God says he will bring the Israelites into the promised land. That was part of the covenant. He said he was going to do it, and here he says again, "This is exactly what I will do."

After God speaks to Moses, the next three verses of the chapter tell us that when God tells Moses to go to Pharaoh a second time, Moses objects again (see Ex. 6:11–13). His grounds for objecting seem reasonable enough: if even his own people refused to believe him, how can he possibly expect Pharaoh to do so, especially since Moses is such a poor speaker? This was his old objection, the objection he had raised on Mount Horeb, and it does not carry any more weight with God the second time around. Moses is still trying to get out of his job, but God does not pay any attention. The objection is repeated again in Exodus 6:30, after an interruption for the genealogy, but again God says that he will be with him and that eventually Pharaoh will let the people go.

F. B. Meyer describes the central point of this chapter:

> Out of the whole story there comes to us this lesson: we must never suppose that the difficulties which confront us indicate that we are not on God's path, and doing his work. Indeed the contrary is generally the case. If we are willing to walk with God, He will test the sincerity and temper of our soul; He will cause men to ride over our heads. . . .[But] He will bring us into a large room, and give us the very thing on which we have been taught to set our hearts.[7]

The bottom line is perseverance. Keep on—and keep on keeping on, especially when things don't seem to be going very well.

---

7. Meyer, *Moses: The Servant of God*, 50.

7

BATTLE AGAINST THE GODS OF EGYPT

Exodus 7—10

THE GOD ABOVE ALL GODS

When it comes to the battle that freed the Israelites from slavery, an enormous gulf lies between the views of a secular historian and the views of the Bible. Secular historians who are inclined to see history as the acts of great men might say this was a case of a marvelous leader bringing people out of slavery through the force of his personality, integrity, vision, and charismatic ability. Historians more inclined to think in terms of mass movements through the consolidation of the will of a vast number would say that this was a people movement: when the Israelites began to get a taste of freedom, they would not rest until they attained complete liberty.

Both views are very different from the Bible's. The Bible does not give credit to Moses, although he was a great leader; it certainly does not speak of a "people movement," because the people were beaten down and crushed, unable to dream of freedom. Instead, the Bible speaks of the battle as one between the true God and the various gods of Egypt.

Moses' father-in-law, Jethro, understood this. In Exodus 18:11, he says, "Now I know that the LORD is greater than all gods, because in this affair they dealt arrogantly with the people." Isaiah later used similar language, describing the false gods of Egypt as trembling before the approaching Lord (see Isa. 19:1). The text that states this perspective most clearly is Numbers 33:3–4: the Israelites "marched out boldly in full view of all the Egyptians, who were burying all their firstborn, whom the LORD had struck down among them; for the LORD had brought judgment on their gods" (NIV). This passage, which was written by Moses, clearly states that the struggle was between God and the gods of Egypt. Demonic forces that were aligned with Satan undoubtedly backed the polytheism of Egypt. Therefore, this was God's intense battle against the demons and Satan, their leader. In the end the people were set free; the idols and gods of Egypt were revealed to be absolutely nothing; and Jehovah, the God of Israel, was proven to be the one and only God.

THE EGYPTIAN RELIGION

To understand this perspective better, we must understand the Egyptian religion and recognize that it was degenerate. Many anthropologists who study religions tend to see a kind of religious evolution. The first tribes, in their ignorance, were animists. They saw gods in every object around them: a god of the tree, a god of the stream, a god of the sky, a god of the rain, and so forth. Slowly animism developed into polytheism. This is still at times animistic, but it goes beyond that, because polytheistic gods sometimes transcend mere objects. Then polytheism rises to become monotheism—in which one great god stands over all the other gods, or one god alone exists. This eventually becomes a kind of ethical humanism, which is probably the religion held by most of the scholars who trace this upward path. They think of themselves as being at the top.

This is not the picture that the Bible gives. The Bible says that polytheism is actually a declension from an original monotheism. Interestingly, a number of scholars and anthropologists are beginning to agree. For example, the great anthropologist Wilhelm Schmidt said that all the evidence points to the belief in one god, from whom and from which these early tribes had departed.[1] In other words, the

---

1. See Wilhelm Schmidt, *The Origin and Growth of Religion: Facts and Theories*, trans. H. J. Rose (London: Methuen & Company, 1931).

people worshipped the gods of nature because the gods of nature seemed closer to them. Fearing those gods, they ceased to fear the God who stands behind nature. The first chapter of Romans spells this out with great clarity. God has revealed himself clearly in nature so that anyone can know "that he exists and that he rewards those who seek him" (Heb. 11:6). But because we do not like this God, whose "eternal power and divine nature . . . have been clearly perceived" (Rom. 1:20), we turn our faces from him. We turn to worshipping "the creature rather than the Creator" (Rom. 1:25).

The polytheism of Egypt was so deeply entrenched in the common lore and belief of the people that there was only one attempt in all the long history of ancient Egypt to break from polytheism and establish monotheism. This attempt was made by Amenhotep IV (known as Akhenaten) during the eighteenth dynasty and was repudiated immediately after his death. The new rulers even obliterated his name from the monuments that had been carved during his reign.

The Egyptian religion was not only polytheistic but also demonic. The Bible says that behind polytheistic gods stand demons—rebellious angels who fell with Satan. This reality can be seen especially in primitive areas of the world where the gospel has not been preached. Missionaries operating on the front lines of the gospel's advance against paganism often describe the oppressive spirit that is present in such places.

When the apostle Paul wrote to the Ephesians, he said, "Our struggle is not against flesh and blood, but . . . against the spiritual forces of evil in the heavenly realms" (Eph. 6:12 NIV). Although today, in our Western world, we often do not recognize that the forces we struggle against are demonic, nevertheless there are demonic powers at work in our present fallen world, just as they were in ancient Egypt.

THE SECOND ATTEMPT

Moses and his brother Aaron had gone to Pharaoh once before and had failed. At least they seemed to have failed—Pharaoh had said no, and not only had he refused to let the people go, but he had also imposed greater burdens on them. Previously the Israelites had been given straw to help the mud bricks they were making to cohere. Now Pharaoh had told them to gather the straw themselves but to keep producing the same quota of bricks. So life had become even harder for the people, and they had turned against Moses.

Now God told Moses and his brother to demand a second time that Pharaoh let the people go. Exodus 7 tells us that during this appearance before Pharaoh they performed a sign—the same sign God had given to Moses on Horeb on the other side of the Arabian Desert. Moses took the staff in his hand, a shepherd's crook, and threw it on the ground. It became a writhing snake. But Pharaoh was not very impressed; he probably had seen his magicians do similar tricks. So he called over his magicians, they threw down their staffs, and immediately their staffs became snakes. There was one problem, though—the snake that had been Moses' staff ate up the other snakes. Yet Pharaoh still refused to let the people go. Exodus 7:13 states something that will be repeated again and again throughout this struggle: "Still Pharaoh's heart was hardened, and he would not listen to them, as the LORD had said."

At this point, the plagues began.

The ancient Egyptians had about eighty major gods and goddesses. A lot of minor deities clustered around the others, but those eighty gods and goddesses were themselves clustered around the three main forces in Egyptian life: the Nile, the land, and the sun. The ancient historian Herodotus called Egypt "the gift of the Nile." If it weren't for the Nile, Egypt would have been part of the desert that stretches across North Africa to the west and across the Gulf of Suez to the Arabian Desert to the east. In ancient times the Nile overflowed its banks every year, depositing in that river valley the wonderful soil that had been carried down from central Africa and making Egypt one of the most fertile lands of the ancient world. Combined with the rich land and the water, the brilliant sun produced marvelous crops.

The plagues were directed against these three forces and against the gods and goddesses of Egypt that were grouped around them. The first two plagues were directed against the gods and goddesses of the Nile and everything associated with the Nile. Four plagues were directed against the gods and goddesses of the land. The final four plagues were directed against the sky and everything associated with the sky. Even the tenth plague, the death of the firstborn, was against the sky. Pharaoh was considered the earthly incarnation of the sun god Ra, the most powerful force in the sky. His firstborn son would have been the next incarnation.

Let us look more closely at the nature of the plagues.

THE PLAGUES

PLAGUES AGAINST THE RIVER

Plague One: Blood. God's first plague was against the Nile. He sent Moses and Aaron to meet Pharaoh as he was walking by the river, probably engaged in an act of Nile worship. They confronted him, Aaron raised his staff in the presence of Pharaoh and struck the water, and immediately the water was changed to blood. The fish in the Nile died, and the river had such a stench that the Egyptians could not drink its water.

Blood was everywhere in Egypt. Whether or not it was literal blood—it seemed enough like blood to be described as such—this was a terrible experience for the Egyptians. Egypt is strung out for hundreds of miles along the banks of the Nile. At times habitable land is only ten or fifteen miles wide, although it is wider in other places, such as in the Nile Delta. Suddenly the Nile, which had been the source of life for this ancient land, became a source of death. Everything in the Nile, and in every stream and pond, began to die.

The question that would have been raised at once was: Where is the god of the Nile, Osiris, one of the great gods of Egypt? Where was his power? The Egyptians said that the Nile was his bloodstream, yet he appeared to be powerless. Where was Khnum, another of the great Nile gods, the guardian of the Nile sources who made sure the Nile kept flowing? Where was Hapi, the spirit of the Nile in Upper Egypt? Where were the gods and goddesses associated with the fish of the Nile, which were a great source of protein for the people? All these gods were revealed to be powerless.

Surely this catastrophe should have made an impression on Pharaoh, but it did not. Pharaoh's heart remained hard, and he would not let the people go (see Ex. 7:22).

Plague Two: Frogs. God told Pharaoh that if he would not let the people go so that they could worship him, God would cause the whole country to be filled with frogs, from the river to the palace and in every house (see 8:1–4). When Aaron stretched out his rod over the Nile, immediately the frogs began to multiply and spread across the land.

Ancient Egyptian amulets carved in the shape of frogs were supposed to have magical powers and religious significance. One of the great goddesses of Egypt was Heket, who was often pictured with the head (and sometimes the body) of a frog. It is possible that the connection between frogs and the goddess meant that frogs were sacred and could not be killed.

Frogs came up into the houses, the beds, the kitchens, and the ovens, jumping into the flour as the people were trying to make the bread—and because they were considered sacred the people could not kill them. This was a misery that simply had to be endured.

Pharaoh asked his magicians to make frogs too, and they could. However, the difficulty wasn't *making* frogs—they had plenty of frogs! The problem was getting rid of them, and that was what the Egyptian magicians could not do.

There was no change in Pharaoh's heart (see Ex. 8:15).

PLAGUES AGAINST THE LAND

Plague Three: Gnats. God's third plague was against the soil—one of the most fertile soils in the world. From it grew all sorts of nourishing vegetables, plants, fruit, and grain; but now, as part of God's judgment on the land, it began to produce gnats in great abundance. Where was the great god of the earth, Geb? Where was he to protect the land and keep it from producing the insects that brought such trouble for the people?

This marks the first time in the account that the Egyptian magicians were unable to duplicate the feat. They said—wisely, although it does not require great perception—"This is the finger of God" (Ex. 8:19). Indeed, it was.

But despite that realization, and despite the confession of impotence from the magicians, Pharaoh refused to obey God. He would not let the people go.

Plague Four: Insects. Insects have always been a problem in Egypt, but with the fourth plague they became intolerable. A literal translation is that swarms of other insects came up over the land. This was a multiplication of all kinds of insects. Many of these insects were also associated with the gods and goddesses. They could not be killed, only endured.

It was an intolerable situation. Pharaoh called Moses and offered the first two of four compromises. First, he said that he would let the Hebrew people go and worship Jehovah, but they had to do it in Egypt. That was unacceptable. In that case, he said, they could go into the desert, but they had to stay close to Egypt. In other words, Pharaoh wanted to keep an eye on them. That seemed to be acceptable to Moses, so he prayed and God removed all those swarms of insects. But as soon as the insects were gone, once again Pharaoh hardened his heart.

This is the first time that we are told explicitly of the distinction between the land of Egypt and the land of Goshen—the region of the eastern delta where the Israelites were living. The Egyptians and their land were plagued with insects, but the Israelites in Goshen were not. This distinction may have existed earlier, but this is the first time we learn of it.

Plague Five: Diseased Livestock. The fifth plague came against the domesticated animals: horses, donkeys, camels, cattle, sheep, and goats. Although it may sound as though all of them died, later we see that when the Lord said he was going to send the plague of hail and fire, the people who believed him took their remaining livestock and put them in barns to be protected. So, while many died, some remained.

The ancient Egyptians gave great veneration to animals. They were regarded as holy or sacred beings—or at least the incarnation of sacred beings. Probably the most worshipped creature in ancient Egypt was the bull. Bulls were symbols of power and potency. In a myth explaining this belief, Apis, the bull god, was conceived when a flash of sunlight came down from heaven and impregnated a cow.

The bull was very highly regarded, yet the bulls died. Where was the power of great Apis? Not only the bulls died, but the cows as well. Nor could Hathor, the cow goddess, a symbol of fertility, keep her sacred animals alive.

The domesticated animals were of great importance for the people. They, along with the crops, were the wealth of Egypt. As the animals and land were destroyed, it really was the case, as the officials said to Pharaoh later, that Egypt was ruined. But the Lord hardened Pharaoh's heart, and he would not listen to Moses and Aaron (see Ex. 9:12).

Plague Six: Boils. The plagues became more intense, now afflicting the bodies of the people. Aaron took soot from a furnace and threw it up in the air. There it dispersed as a dust that created boils on the bodies of the Egyptians.

This was ironic. In the practice of their religion, the Egyptians took the ashes of an offering and threw the ashes into the air as a means of blessing. If ashes fell on individuals, they considered themselves very fortunate. But what had been considered a blessing suddenly became a curse, causing boils to break out on the people. Even the priests, who normally dispensed the blessings, were affected. Because the Egyptians put a great emphasis on bodily cleanliness, people who were defiled in any way could not perform religious rites. So because of the boils that covered their bodies, the Egyptian priests were unable even to stand before Moses.

Egypt was known in that day, more than any other land, for its medical advances. Where were the healing gods? Where was Imhotep, guardian of the healing sciences? Where was Thoth, ibis-headed god of wisdom and knowledge, who fed that wisdom to Egypt's doctors? Where was Sehkmet, lion-headed goddess with the power to create and remove epidemics? Why didn't she remove this particular plague?

Sadly, in spite of all the suffering of his people, Pharaoh still refused to let the Jewish people go.

PLAGUES AGAINST THE SKY

Plague Seven: Hail and Lightning. It does not hail in Egypt. For that matter, there is almost no rain. Even today, the city of Cairo gets only about two inches of rainfall annually, and some places in southern Egypt get no rain at all in the course of a year. Before this next act of judgment, however, the Lord gave Pharaoh a warning—that all livestock and produce of the fields should be gathered into safe shelters.

And "whoever feared the word of the LORD among the servants of Pharaoh hurried his slaves and his livestock into the houses" (9:20). Then suddenly the people saw what they had never seen before. The skies grew dark, and lightning flashed back and forth. And heavy hail came crashing down, killing all the animals that remained outside and destroying what had not already been destroyed in the fields. But again, the only place the hail did not touch was the land of Goshen, where the Israelites remained safe.

With this destruction came the first break in public opinion. The minds of the Egyptian people turned to revolt. They were realizing that the gods and goddesses who were supposed to protect them and their fields were nothing. Shu, the god of the atmosphere; Nut, the sky goddess; and Horus and Monthu, the bird gods, were all useless, helpless.

At that point Pharaoh seemed to be wavering, because he called in Moses and Aaron. In their presence he confessed three things: (1) he had sinned, (2) the Lord was in the right, and (3) Pharaoh and the Egyptians were in the wrong (see Ex. 9:27). Although this sounds hopeful, we must not read too much into the confession, because as soon as there was some relief, Pharaoh immediately hardened his heart again and refused to let the people go.

Plague Eight: Locusts. Public opinion finally reached the palace of the pharaoh as the nobles pleaded with Pharaoh. "How long shall this man be a snare to us?" they said. "Let the men go, that they may serve the LORD their God. Do you not yet understand that Egypt is ruined?" (Ex. 10:7). Their will was broken, but not Pharaoh's. He did, however, offer the third of his four compromises: the Hebrew men could go, but the women had to stay. Then he proposed one more compromise: he would let the men and women go, but they would have to leave behind their herds and flocks. Both compromises were unacceptable to Moses.

So the next plague came—a terrifying invasion of locusts. In a short while, nothing green remained on a tree or plant in all the land of Egypt.

Most of us have never seen such a plague of locusts. For people who live on the land, however, locusts are a catastrophe. The book of

Joel describes such a plague coming to Judah. Joel calls on the people to weep and mourn because of the massive destruction. A plague of locusts was such a terrible event that it is mentioned in the book of Revelation (9:1–10), becoming a symbol of the final plagues of destruction that will come upon the world in the last days.

Where was Nepit, the goddess of the grain? She was supposed to be protecting the crops. Where was Min, the deity of the harvest? They were wiped out and shown to be nothing.

Pharaoh made another shallow confession: "I have sinned against the LORD your God, and against you" (Ex. 10:16). But when the locusts went away, he still refused to let the people go.

Plague Nine: Darkness. No more warnings. The ninth plague came suddenly, without any announcement whatsoever. Darkness descended on the land, and this lasted for three days.

Here was the most significant judgment of all, in terms of Egyptian religion. The greatest of all the gods was the sun god Ra, and Pharaoh was considered Ra incarnate. Pharaoh Akhenaten's hymn to the sun (*Aten* in the poem) is one of the greatest surviving remnants of Egyptian literature. "Thy rising [is] beautiful in the horizon of heaven, O Aten, ordainer of life. Thou dost shoot up in the horizon of the East, thou fillest every land with thy beneficence."[2]

Suddenly, without any warning, the great god of the sky was blotted out—and not only Ra, but also the stars and the planets, the moon and the lights of the night. Ra was nothing at all. Donald Grey Barnhouse describes this in particularly vivid terms:

> Gross darkness could be a normal thing in the land of the midnight sun, but this was not Norway or Alaska, this was Egypt. This was the land of perpetual sunshine. Three hundred and sixty-five days in the year, the sun shines in Egypt. And three hundred and sixty-five nights in the year, the skies are so alight with moon and stars that

---

2. "A Hymn to Aten by Ai, Overseer of the Horse," in E. A. Wallis Budge, *Tutankhamen: Amenism, Atenism and Egyptian Monotheism* (London: Martin Hopkinson, 1923; repr. Mineola, New York: Dover, 1991), 123.

there is little like it to be seen from earth. The planets seem nearer than the lights of neighbors, and the stars hang in the sky, liquid in their trembling beauty. Through our fogs, the heavens may be millions of light years away, but in Egypt they seem to be just out the window and just beyond the tree tops.

Suddenly the sky and the light were eclipsed by a phenomenon that fell upon the land. The verb is one that denotes swiftness as when a lion falls upon an unsuspecting prey. Life came to a halt. The people were forced to remain in their beds for three days. . . . Provisions are not stored up in hot lands, and there was no refrigeration in those days. The people were without food; they could not see each other; they lived, choking and gasping, in their beds.[3]

Yet even at this point Pharaoh refused to let the people go.

LEARNING FROM EXODUS 7–10

We do not have widespread, overt polytheism in the West. But anything can take the place of God. When we have something in our life that is more important than God is, we have another god. This is why God starts the Ten Commandments with "You shall have no other gods before me" (Ex. 20:3). There is only one true God, and that means that God will not compromise with idolatry: "I am the LORD; that is my name; my glory I give to no other, nor my praise to carved idols" (Isa. 42:8).

We need to oppose anything that sets itself up against God. Patriotism is idolatry if it causes us to say, "My country first, right or wrong," and we need to fight that kind of unbiblical perspective. Secularism is an idolatrous philosophy. Materialism, in all its forms, is idolatry. So is humanism—not the right kind of humanism, which is concern for people, but humanism that exists as an ideology unto itself, in which man is the center of all things. Such humanism must be opposed. And a person can be an idol, when that person becomes more important

---

3. Donald Grey Barnhouse, *The Invisible War: The Panorama of the Continuing Conflict Between Good & Evil* (Grand Rapids: Zondervan, 1965), 210.

to us than loving and serving the living God. We are, as Paul exhorts us, to bring "into captivity every thought to the obedience of Christ" (2 Cor. 10:5 KJV).

We learn from the experience of Pharaoh that we cannot compromise with God. Pharaoh wanted to compromise with God, once he understood that God was more powerful than he was, but that would not do. God has a sovereign will, a will that doesn't compromise. Those who oppose God will be broken ultimately, as Pharaoh was. Are we fighting against God in some area? Do we try to oppose his sovereign will in our lives? This is a very foolish thing to do, because those who oppose God will be broken. We must learn to submit ourselves to him wholly as the wise, sovereign, all-powerful, and exceedingly gracious God, whose will for his people is always "good and acceptable and perfect" (Rom. 12:2).

8

THE DEPARTURE FROM EGYPT

Exodus 11–15:21

DAY OF DAYS AND NIGHT OF NIGHTS

It is true, personally as well as historically, that some days are more significant than other days. Surely of all the days that stand out in Jewish memory, this great day of the Passover and the exodus from Egypt by the Israelites stands out above and beyond all the rest.

The deliverance came about through a series of plagues that God brought on the Egyptians—and particularly on Pharaoh—because he was unwilling to listen to the word of the Lord through Moses and to let the people go. The plagues increased in intensity; they got worse and worse until, near the end, even Pharaoh's own ministers said, "Why don't you let the people go? Don't you understand that all of Egypt is ruined?" Yet in spite of that, Pharaoh would not let the Israelites go.

The last of the ten plagues was the deaths of the firstborn in Egypt. As the angel of death came through the land to slay all the firstborn of the Egyptians, the Hebrew people gathered in their houses, protected by the blood of the lambs that had been killed—blood that they had spread on the lintels and doorposts of the houses. This was the night of nights for Israel. This night witnessed nothing less than the birth of a nation. In the early hours of the next morning, the men, women, and children, and all their possessions, flocks, and herds marched out of Egypt, never to be enslaved there again.

THE HEART OF THE OLD TESTAMENT

Chapters 11–15 are the very heart of Exodus. And because this Passover event is at the heart of Old Testament Christology—at least in the minds of many theologians—this section can be considered the very heart of the Old Testament. Anything of that significance demands careful study. After describing what happened, I will reflect on its theological significance.

THE TENTH PLAGUE

Nine plagues have taken place. Now, in the brief eleventh chapter of Exodus, we are told the nature of the final plague. God reveals this to Moses, and Moses repeats his words to Pharaoh. At midnight the destroyer will pass through the land and kill all the firstborn. The destroyer will strike the court of Pharaoh and his very household—Pharaoh's own firstborn son will die. But the deaths will extend down to the most humble families in the nation. Not only will the firstborn of the families die, but even the firstborn of the animals in their stables.

This is a very terrible judgment. But it is a fitting one. It is fitting first of all in view of the cruelty of the Egyptians toward the Israelites, which included the deaths of male Israelite children who had been killed or thrown into the Nile on Pharaoh's orders. It is also fitting in view of the oppression that the Egyptians had brought on the Israelites for many years. God will judge those who persecute his people.

Having seen the other judgments unfold according to the word of Moses, Pharaoh might be expected to be frightened into repenting, but he was not. At the end of Exodus 11, we find what we have found all along: the Lord hardened Pharaoh's heart, meaning also that Pharaoh hardened his own heart. He would not let the Israelites leave his country.

THE INSTRUCTIONS FOR ISRAEL

Scattered throughout chapter 12 are specific instructions for Israel.[1] The details are these:

1. On the tenth day of the month Abib (later called Nisan), each Hebrew family was to take a firstborn male lamb from the flock. It was to be one year old and without blemish or spot. The lamb was to stay with the family until the fourteenth day of the month.
2. When each lamb was killed in the twilight of that evening, the family was to collect the blood. Using a hyssop brush,[2] they were to spread the blood on both sides of the doorframe and on the lintel at the top of the door. These three separate marks were to be a sign to God, as the destroyer passed over the land, not to strike that household with death. Because the lamb had died as a substitute, the firstborn was spared. There would be death in the Hebrew households, but the death of an animal—not of the eldest child.
3. Each lamb was to be roasted whole, and the people were to eat in haste. Dressed for departure, they were to have sandals on their feet, cloaks on their backs, and staffs in their hands. Any uneaten parts of the lamb were to be burned rather than left behind.
4. Every year the people were to remember this night and observe it throughout all generations, so that when their children asked what the ceremony meant they could explain without hesitation or doubt: "It is the sacrifice of the LORD's Passover, for he passed over the houses of the people of Israel in Egypt, when he struck the Egyptians but spared our houses" (v. 27).
5. This was to be an observance for Israel alone; no foreigner was to partake. This distinction was made not on the basis of ethnicity

1. Three separate sections of Exodus 12 deal with these instructions: verses 1–13, 21–28, and 43–51. Two shorter sections in between deal with the Feast of Unleavened Bread, which is connected to the Passover observance. Then comes the account of the death of Egypt's children.
2. Hyssop, probably like marjoram, was a little plant that often grew out of cracks in the walls and made a good brush.

but on whether the individual had become part of God's people by circumcision. This was a faith ordinance for the covenant people (see v. 48).

THE FEAST OF UNLEAVENED BREAD

Instructions in Exodus 12:14–20 lay out the details of what was to become a weeklong feast linked to Passover: the Feast of Unleavened Bread (leaven being the yeast that makes dough rise). Leavened bread took time to rise, and the Israelites had to leave Egypt in a hurry. Because of their hasty departure, they took the bread with them in kneading troughs, wrapped up in cloth and carried on their backs. This feast would start on the Passover Sabbath (that is, the early hours of the fifteenth of Nisan) and would continue for seven days, until the twenty-first day of the month. When they were settled in the land, they were to purge their houses of leaven before the feast. Leaven is a biblical symbol of sin, and purging it from their houses represented spiritual purification.

THE DEATH OF THE FIRSTBORN

The death of the firstborn is recounted in two verses: "At midnight the LORD struck down all the firstborn in the land of Egypt, from the firstborn of Pharaoh . . ." (Ex. 12:29).

There was a loud wailing in Egypt, because "there was not a house where someone was not dead" (v. 30).

Pause and think about that. Reconstruct it in your imagination. Think what it would have been like for the Hebrew families who were eating the roasted lamb together that evening, having carefully followed all the instructions that had come to them from God through Moses. There must have been a suspenseful silence as they began to eat their meal in the dark, having put blood on the doorposts of their houses and now waiting to see what would happen.

And suddenly the wails began to rise from every corner of the land. And the cries became a great, cacophonous sound. The Hebrew families must have stood in utter silence, terrified, trembling, waiting with quickly beating hearts for the hour of their departure.

Where was the power of Pharaoh? He was the incarnate god, the perfect god, Ra on earth. Where was his power? He had no power against death. His son, the next pharaoh, the next incarnation of Ra, was dead. What about the other gods and goddesses? Where was Isis, the symbol of fecundity? Where was Min, the god of procreation and reproduction? Where was Hathor, the deity who attended childbirth? All were supposedly omnipotent. Some were gods of animals, but even the firstborn of the animals died. Goddess Hathor couldn't keep her cows alive, let alone protect the Egyptians. At this climax of the plagues, everyone must have understood that the gods and goddesses of Egypt were absolutely nothing at all.

THE DEPARTURE FROM EGYPT

While it was still dark, just before dawn, the call went out. All the people came out of their houses and gathered up their possessions and their flocks. Then this great mass of people began to make its way out of the land. It is hard to imagine this mighty movement without finding our hearts and minds stirred, as we enter into the deliverance of this people and the day of their birth as a nation.

A few details deserve consideration. Older translations of the Bible say that the Hebrew people "borrowed" articles of silver and gold and clothing from the Egyptians. This suggests to some people that the Israelites were not honest, because they had no intention of ever giving these things back. Unfortunately, this understanding is based on a wrong translation. The Hebrew word is *shaal*, and in almost every other place in the Old Testament where it is used, *shaal* is translated "ask," not "borrow." The Hebrew people asked for these things from the Egyptians, as was proper to do. Those starting out on a journey, in this culture, would have had the right to ask, and it would be proper to give them gifts. Of course, these were unusual circumstances. How could the Egyptians possibly have given gifts willingly to the Israelites? Exodus 12:36 states that the Lord had given the people favor in the eyes of the Egyptians. In this way the people went out with gold, silver, clothing, and tools, just as, centuries before, God had told Abraham would happen: "They shall come out with great possessions" (Gen. 15:14).

The second matter that has been a problem to some is the statement that 600,000 men left Egypt. There were women and children in addition. A great "mixed multitude also went up with them" (see Ex. 12:38)—that is, people (perhaps slaves from other backgrounds) who weren't Israelites but who saw this as the time of their deliverance as well. We cannot put that information together and suppose that there were fewer than two million people involved, and there were probably more. This is an enormous number of people, and some scholars have said that it is impossible—that you could not handle that many people and still have the other events take place that are related in the exodus narrative. For example, it is said that it would take too long for two million people to get across the Red Sea and that it would be impossible to provide for so many people in the wilderness for all those years.

Some scholars have tried to deal with this problem by saying that the word *thousand* refers only to a family unit. Six hundred family units may approximate 2,500 fighting men and between twelve thousand and twenty-five thousand individuals. The only problem is that if we carry this way of thinking over into other passages—in Joshua, for example, in which thousands fight—and also reduce those numbers to family units, there aren't enough people for the major battles. You cannot have it both ways—reducing the numbers in one situation and increasing them in the other. How one translates the Hebrew word *eleph*—as a "clan" or "fighting unit" or as "thousand"—will determine whether one accepts a smaller number of Israelites (e.g., about six hundred clans) or a much larger number based on 600,000 fighters plus women, children, and aliens. What the Bible unequivocally tells us is that a great multitude left Egypt. As Moses wrote, "on that very day the LORD brought the people of Israel out of the land of Egypt by their hosts" (12:51).

LEARNING FROM EXODUS 11–13

These chapters are meant to teach great spiritual truths, and we cannot understand these truths by simply reading through the chapters. We have to study the passages and allow them to sink into our minds and hearts before we can apply them.

THE GUILT OF ISRAEL

We can hardly miss the first lesson: Israel was also guilty before God. If the blood had not been spread on the doorposts of the Israelite houses, the firstborn of the families in those houses would have died too. Were they a better people, or a holy people, or a special people? They were sinners just as the Egyptians were. If they had not done what God had said, their firstborn also would have perished.

No doubt there were reasons for the people to be tempted to draw the wrong conclusion. Somehow we think we are special—which is especially a temptation for religious people. The Israelites could have thought along those lines for any number of reasons. For example, even in the account of the plagues, we are told that God made a distinction between his people, who lived in the land of Goshen, and the Egyptians in the rest of the land during the fourth through the ninth plagues. When the plagues came on the Egyptians and did not touch the Hebrew communities, the Israelites might have thought that they were special and untouchable and that God would not do anything to judge them.

Some might have been proud of their ancestry. They might have said, "We're not pagans like these Egyptians. We are descendants of Abraham, and Abraham was called by God. We are called by God and are a very special people." Somewhere in Egypt that Passover night, there was a young man named Joshua. He would later become Moses' right-hand man, and then, when Moses did not go into the land, he became Moses' successor. He would be the general who governed the armies during the years of the conquest. About fifty years later, at the very end of his life, Joshua gave a powerful sermon to encourage the people to remain faithful to God. He went back over their history, and at one point he said, "Long ago your forefathers, including Terah the father of Abraham and Nahor, lived beyond the River and worshiped other gods" (Josh. 24:2 NIV). This assertion was very clear; back in their ancestry the people had been idol worshippers, too, just like the Egyptians. There was nothing in their so-called spiritual ancestry to set them apart.

Some others might have said, "But once God called Abraham and we found out who the true God was, at least we worshipped him then." But the reality is that they did not. They had not continued faithfully in the worship of the true God but had worshipped other gods. As a matter of fact, some Israelites continued to worship the Egyptian gods. Not so long after the exodus, when they were camped at Sinai, under Aaron's leadership they made a little calf, a replica of Apis the bull god, and bowed down before it, saying that it had saved them from Egypt (see Ex. 32:8).

There was not anything special about the Israelites—and, to be clear, there is nothing special about us either. We are sinners, and sin brings judgment. If we are going to be saved, it must be by God's grace and God's grace alone. Arthur Pink writes,

> The more clearly we perceive the spiritual wretchedness of Israel at this time, the more shall we recognize the absolute *sovereignty* of that grace which redeemed them. So, too, the more fully we are acquainted with the teaching of Scripture concerning the utter corruption and total depravity of the natural man, the more shall we be made to marvel at the infinite mercy of God toward such worthless creatures, and the more highly shall we value that wondrous love that wrought salvation for us.[3]

THERE IS NO SALVATION WITHOUT THE SHEDDING OF BLOOD

Undoubtedly the most important lesson of all is this: without the shedding of blood, there is no salvation. The details of the Passover were meant to teach that. The lamb had to die. Why? Because sin, which in all its forms is rebellion against the will and person of a holy God, is so serious that it demands the ultimate judgment: the death of the sinner. "The soul who sins shall die" (Ezek. 18:20). However, God provided a way for the sinner to be spared. A substitute could die in the place of the sinner, taking on God's judgment, so that the sinner might live and be restored to fellowship with his Creator and Lord. In other words, the sinner could be saved from the judgment of the holy

---

3. Arthur W. Pink, *Gleanings in Exodus* (repr. Lafayette, IN: Sovereign Grace Publishers, 2002), 80.

God, but only when another had died in the sinner's place. The lamb had to die. The blood had to be shed and put on the doorposts of the house. Leviticus 17:11 spells this out explicitly: "For the life of the flesh is in the blood, and I have given it for you on the altar to make atonement for your souls, for it is the blood that makes atonement by the life." We see this same truth stated in the New Testament: "without the shedding of blood there is no forgiveness of sins" (Heb. 9:22).

People today do not like the idea of blood being shed for salvation. People have said to me, "That is barbaric. I can't possibly believe in a religion like that." Was it any easier for the ancient Israelites? Perhaps in a Hebrew household there was a father who had followed everything that God had said up to this point. He had taken the lamb three days earlier, selecting it from the flock, and had brought it into the house. On the night of the Passover, as he looked at the lamb, he said to himself, "I only have ten lambs in the flock. If I kill one, I reduce my assets by ten percent. I think I'll just hang on to this one; it will be far more valuable to me on the journey than if I kill and eat it tonight." But, as the outcome of that decision, the firstborn of his household would have perished.

Without the shedding of blood, there is no forgiveness, no deliverance, from sin. This points to Jesus Christ. Although we are told that without the shedding of blood at the altar there is no forgiveness of sin, the Bible also says that the blood of sheep and goats cannot take away sin (see Heb. 10:4). This means that these things are a picture, or type, looking forward to the coming of Jesus Christ, who would be the perfect sacrifice. Those who, by the grace of God, understood the meaning of Jesus' death put it into Old Testament terminology so that we, too, can understand. In first Corinthians 5:7, Paul says, "Christ, our Passover lamb, has been sacrificed." First Peter 1:19 declares that we were redeemed "with the precious blood of Christ, like that of a lamb without blemish or spot." Perhaps the most significant words of all were those spoken by John the Baptist. He was sent as the forerunner of Christ, the one to identify him when he came. When Jesus approached John on one occasion, John pointed him out and said in the hearing of his disciples, "Behold, the Lamb of God, who takes away the sin of the world!" (John 1:29).

God had begun to teach and demonstrate the necessity for such a death in the garden of Eden after the fall. God took animals and killed them. Adam and Eve saw that death was the penalty for their sin. They also were given an intimation, or picture, of imputed righteousness, when God clothed them with the skins of the animals. Only the Lord God could provide a covering for their shame and guilt. One animal died for each individual. But when a lamb was killed at Passover, its blood protected a whole family. Later on, the Israelites reached Mount Sinai and God explained what was to happen on the Day of Atonement: the high priest would confess the sins of the entire nation over the animal before it was killed. Finally, at the end of this progression, John the Baptist points to Jesus and says, "The Lamb of God, who takes away the sin of the world!" One animal for one individual, one animal for one family, one animal for one nation—and one lamb, the Lamb of God, for all humanity. Thank God it is so, because most of us are not members of the Jewish nation. It is because Jesus is the Savior of the world that you and I can have salvation.

SALVATION IS THROUGH FAITH

Salvation must be received through the channel of human faith. Hebrews 11:28, a verse in that great chapter about faith, is important for us to understand the Passover: "By faith [Moses] kept the Passover and sprinkled the blood, so that the Destroyer of the firstborn might not touch them." This tells us that faith was involved in the deliverance—in fact, it was the very essence of what was involved.

Why? Think of the spreading of blood on the doorposts. Looked at rationally, there was no understandable connection between spreading blood and being saved. The angel of death was going to cross the land, and the firstborn would be slain—and there they were, spreading blood on the door. What possible good could that do? There was no rational reason for doing that. I am sure they did not even begin to understand that this was a foreshadowing of the coming of Jesus Christ and his death. It was just something they had to do. They did not understand it, but they had to do it. They had to believe that it was the word of God revealing to them how to be spared in the coming judgment. Not only did they have to believe, they also had to act. If they had not acted, every firstborn in every Jewish family would have perished.

It is exactly the same today. The requirement of faith seems absurd to unbelievers. When we talk about salvation through faith in Jesus Christ, it sounds absolutely foolish to people today. How can we be saved from sin and go to heaven because a man hung on a cross two thousand years ago? Yet God tells us that salvation is in Jesus Christ and by him—and by him alone. If we believe in Jesus Christ and his death as our spotless substitute, we are spared; the judgment passes over us. If we do not believe, we perish.

CROSSING THE RED SEA

While the Passover is the very heart of the book of Exodus, there is another event very closely tied to it that is extremely important: the crossing of the Red Sea. God intervened in power, parting the waters so that the people could go across, and after they had crossed over on dry ground, the waters rushed back and drowned the Egyptians.

This crossing is mentioned many times in the Old Testament— even more times than the Passover. The deliverance by the parting of the sea is referred to in the psalms, almost always when the history of the people is given (see Pss. 106:9; 114:3, 5; 136:13). We also find references in Joshua, Isaiah, and Nehemiah. It was known among the heathen. When the Israelites came to conquer the promised land and two Hebrew spies made their way to Jericho, Rahab the prostitute told them, "We have heard how the LORD dried up the water of the Red Sea before you when you came out of Egypt" (Josh. 2:10). So word of this great event spread through the ancient cultures; the pagans were well aware of the powers of Jehovah, the Hebrew God.

There has been a great deal of debate about the location of what Exodus refers to as the "Red Sea." Is it that great section of the Gulf of Aden that runs up to where the Suez Canal is today? There is a marshy area to the north that moves farther up to an area called the Bitter Lakes, and there has been speculation that the crossover took place at any point along that line: the Bitter Lakes, the marshy areas in between, or the actual Red Sea itself. We do not even know for sure the borders of the Red Sea in the ancient world. Many years have gone by; water levels rise and fall; areas get silted in. One thing that we know is this: the Israelites weren't merely wading through a marshy area to get to the other side. The water was so deep that it had to be parted in order to let them pass, and it was deep enough to drown the Egyptians when it rushed back. Wherever the crossing took place, it was a stupendous miracle, and the people understood it as such.

If we follow the details of their march, we find that the Israelites moved more or less toward the east—down toward the Sinai Peninsula—but then, at the direction of God, they moved west into an area that was basically a cul-de-sac. They had sand on one side, the mountains on the other, and the water in front of them. They could not go back, of course, because that meant returning to Egypt.

When the pharaoh saw this, he must have thought that the Israelites were wandering around in the desert aimlessly, not knowing where they were going. He said, "Now they're confused, and this is my opportunity." Unfortunately, it was Pharaoh who was confused. He thought that he could fight God. We know what happened: he blundered by pursuing them—and he found out, as it says, that the Lord was fighting with the Israelites against Egypt (see Ex. 14:25).

There are times when you and I seem hemmed in by circumstances and do not know which way to turn. In a situation like that, we have to hear what God told the Hebrew people to do: "Fear not, stand firm, and see the salvation of the LORD, which he will work for you today. . . . The LORD will fight for you, and you have only to be silent" (Ex. 14:13–14). Sometimes we have to fight, as we will see later in this story. But at other times we have to stand still, and even more so when we are hemmed in by circumstances.

After the crossing of the Red Sea, when the sun rose the next morning, it rose on a new free nation. The people had been slaves, fleeing from their masters. Now they were a free people, standing in a new land with a dramatic destiny before them. They were a picture of those who have been redeemed today. We were enslaved to sin, but we have been made new people in Christ. We have been given a new community, and before us is a new and awesome destiny. Peter knew this. "You are a chosen race," he wrote, using Old Testament terminology to speak of Christians, "a royal priesthood, a holy nation, a people for his own possession, that you may proclaim the excellencies of him who called you out of darkness into his marvelous light" (1 Peter 2:9).

After the trauma of the night of Passover, after the march the next morning, after the great deliverance through the Red Sea, what in the world did the people do? They burst into song, led by Moses and his sister Miriam (see Ex. 15:1–18).

There are almost as many ways of analyzing this song by Moses as there are commentators to analyze it. One thing that emerges most clearly is that this great song of Moses is all about God, glorifying God throughout. Moses had been used by God; it must have taken tremendous faith and courage for him to lead two million people out of a land where there was food and into a barren wilderness, but he did it. Yet there is not a word about Moses in the entire song. The name for God occurs eleven times in the eighteen verses and once more in Miriam's refrain. *God* occurs twice, and the pronouns *he, him, his, you,* and *your*—all referring to God—occur twenty-five times more. In general, the song moves from a celebration of God's past deliverance of the people to the victories that are still to come. This is what good hymnody does and what the hymns of the church should do.

Today our hymnody has fallen on sad times. It has become so man-centered that it does not glorify God anymore. Arthur Pink notes, "The majority of the hymns (if such they are entitled to be called) of the past fifty years are full of maudlin sentimentality, instead of divine adoration. They announce *our* love to God, instead of *His* to us. They recount our experiences instead of His excellencies."[4] This song of Moses is far different; its stated purpose from the beginning is to exalt God (see v. 2). Exodus 15 is the great "Hallelujah" chorus of the Hebrew people, so important that it occurs again in Revelation 15:3–4. In these verses all the redeemed are in heaven; all wickedness is put down; Old Testament and New Testament saints are glorifying God—and how do they do that? They "sing the song of Moses, the servant

---

4. "Spiritual Singing," in Arthur W. Pink, *Studies in the Scriptures: Annual Volume 1947*, vol. 26 (repr. Pensacola, FL: Chapel Library Resources, 2009), 53, available online at http://www.chapellibrary.org/files/7413/7643/3384/si47.pdf.

of God, and the song of the Lamb" (Rev. 15:3). In other words, they picked up on the Old Testament theme, but they saw its fulfillment in what Jesus Christ had done in his work of redemption.

LEARNING FROM EXODUS 14–15

In these chapters we see the hardening effects of sin and the consequences of that hardening. As for the Egyptians, the story of the exodus ends with the deaths of the firstborn and the drowning of Pharaoh's many horsemen and charioteers. These were a bitter result of the hardening of Pharaoh's heart. That is the way it is. Sin hardens hearts, and the end result of a hardened heart is destruction. If you will not repent of your sin, confess it, and come to God for his mercy in Jesus Christ, your ultimate end is eternal judgment—for you and often for others.

We also see the absolute necessity of blood atonement. The death of the lamb points toward the death of Jesus. This is the very heart of the biblical message. Although it is contrary to modern religion, teaching that is true to Scripture always makes central Jesus' death and the necessity of faith in him. To apply this properly, we have to ask a question: am I trusting Jesus for my salvation? Do I know that he died in my place, as my substitute? If I do know and believe that, am I teaching others that essential doctrine as clearly as I know how?

We are also reminded of the victory of faith. In one of the last books of the Bible, John wrote, "This is the victory that has overcome the world—our faith" (1 John 5:4). At the Passover, we see the victory of faith. When the blood was put on the doorposts, the people were demonstrating their faith that the Lord would honor his promise to spare the firstborn in those houses. And when the people stood at the edge of the Red Sea and Moses told them to go forward, we see their faith again. They obeyed. Moses said, "Stand firm and you will see the Lord's deliverance," and that is the challenge to faith today. F. B. Meyer puts it very well:

> Learn what God will do for his own. Dread not any result of implicit
> obedience to his command; fear not the angry waters which, in their

proud insolence, forbid your progress; fear not the turbulent crowds of men who are perpetually compared to waters lifting up their voice and roaring with their waves. Fear none of these things. Above the voices of many waters, the mighty breakers of the sea, the Lord sits as king upon the flood; yea, the Lord sitteth as king for ever. . . . His way lies through, as well as *in* the sea, his path amid mighty waters, and his footsteps are veiled from human reason. Dare to trust Him; dare to follow Him![5]

We also learn the value of God-given ceremonies and services. There is a great danger in substituting man-made ceremonies for those that have been given to us by God. We should not add anything to what God has revealed, but we also should not neglect anything that God has revealed. He gave the Hebrew people the Passover so that they might observe it throughout all their generations.

Finally, after deliverance there should always be a song. As they stood on the banks of the Red Sea, the people burst forth in song. This is what we do when we think of the wonders of redemption; it is why we have such rich hymnody in the church. We have ancient hymns by people such as Ambrose of Milan, and we have hymns from the Reformation composed by Martin Luther, John Calvin, and others. We have hymns by Isaac Watts and Charles Wesley and many others, coming right on down to our own time. Do you love to sing? If so, sing. If you do not, God will teach you. He taught David, you know. David said, "[God] put a new song in my mouth, a song of praise to our God" (Ps. 40:3), who alone is worthy of our praise.

5. F. B. Meyer, *Moses: The Servant of God* (New York: Fleming H. Revell Company, n.d.), 85.

PART 2

MOSES' FINEST HOUR

9

LEARNING TO
WALK WITH GOD

Exodus 15:22–17:16

WHAT NEXT?

The Israelites could have taken one of three main routes out of Egypt to Canaan. The shortest route would have been to go up the coast along the Way of the Philistines. Using this route, a Roman general once marched his troops from Egypt to what we would call the Gaza Strip in southern Palestine in only five days. If the Israelites had gone by that route, however, they would have had to fight at the Egyptian fortifications along the way. God's evaluation was that war might drive them back to Egypt (see Ex. 13:17), so they did not go that way. There were also two ways across the desert, one far to the south, and the other, the Way of Shur,[1] a little closer to the coast. But they did not travel any of these main routes. Instead they went southeast, down into the Sinai Peninsula. And they had many lessons to learn along the way.

When Christians read these narratives in Exodus, they see parallels to the Christian life. We think of Canaan, the land to which they are headed, as representative of heaven; their passage through the wilderness is our pilgrimage through this life. The parallels are not always

---

1. *Shur* means "wall" and probably refers to a walled fortification on the borders of Egypt.

exact, but certainly they are in this respect: the people were not mature. They had to learn to trust the Lord and experience his provision for them in all kinds of circumstances. Thus what God did and how he provided for them during their years of wandering are very instructive for us, as we journey in this life toward our heavenly home.

GOD PROVIDES WATER

It is hard to know exactly where the Israelites went when they left Egypt and headed south. The Bible does not give many place names, and names and geography have changed over the years. There is an oasis associated with the journey, however, that today goes by the name Ayun Musa, meaning "the springs of Moses." The people probably passed that way shortly after they crossed the Red Sea.

The hearts of the Israelites must have been buoyant. They had just seen God's wonderful deliverance. He had overshadowed them with a cloud and protected them. The Egyptians who had pursued them in chariots had been defeated, drowned in the rushing waters. They had sung that great song of Moses and Miriam as they rejoiced over what God had done.

But after Ayun Musa, there was a long march of about forty miles to the next oasis, Marah. For a large company of people driving animals, this would have been about a three-day journey, and the desert way was not an easy one. It is a dry stony plain that runs along the Gulf of Suez and then turns into a glaring stretch of sand without water. As that great company traveled south through the wilderness, they found no wells, no welcoming oases, no source of water for them or their flocks and herds.

Moses had lived on the far side of the desert for forty years, driving the flocks to different watering places. He may well have known this area. If he did, he knew that there was an oasis farther up the road, and he probably encouraged the people about it. "I know this is tough now, but God will provide. We'll reach an oasis soon."

The only problem was that when they reached Marah, its water was so bitter that the people couldn't drink it. This was why the oasis was called *Marah*, which means "bitter" in Hebrew. Naomi uses the same word in the book of Ruth when she tells the women to call her *Mara* because her life has been so bitter (see Ruth 1:20).

Now Moses was in trouble. It had taken much faith to lead two million people out across the desert sands without provisions. He had trusted God to provide, but the oasis water was undrinkable. The people were complaining, forgetting how God had provided for them before (see Ex. 15:24). And their need was genuine.

But Moses had not forgotten the lesson he had learned early: when he was in trouble, he should turn to God. So he prayed, "he cried to the LORD," and God told him to take a piece of wood and throw it into the water (Ex. 15:25). When he did this, the wood made the water sweet.

I am always amused when I read the commentaries on passages like this one, because there is a certain ludicrous disposition of the academic mind. Even the evangelical commentators begin to search around for wood with qualities that could make water sweet. But I have never heard of a piece of wood that could make bitter water sweet for two million people. This is an outright miracle. It cannot be explained by looking for special qualities in the wood.

The lesson of this story is not to search for a kind of wood that will turn bitter water sweet. The lesson is to do what Moses did and present your case before the Lord. God provides, as we will see, sometimes by natural means and sometimes by supernatural means. Whichever means he uses, he is the one who does the providing.

At this point God had words of exhortation and promise: "If you will diligently listen to the voice of the LORD your God, and do that which is right in his eyes, and give ear to his commandments and keep all his statutes, I will put none of the diseases on you that I put on the Egyptians, for I am the LORD, your healer" (15:26). God promises that he will heal his people as he healed the water.

"I am the LORD, your healer" presents a new name for God: *Jehovah Rapha.* This is another example of a progressive, or growing, revelation. The Israelites first learned that God is Jehovah, the great "I AM," the powerful God who conquered the Egyptians and brought them out of Egypt. But in the wilderness they learn that their powerful, delivering God is also the God of healing, the God who will take care of them each step of the wilderness way.

At the end of this passage, after about another day's journey, they came to a place called Elim. The commentator Charles R. Erdman wisely notes that this mention of Elim is to remind us that the Christian life is not entirely a desert journey.[2] It sometimes leads through green pastures and beside the still waters. Elim was not Canaan. The Israelites were not yet in the promised land, and there were many hard times ahead. But nevertheless, Elim was an oasis along the way. God provides arbors on the hills of difficulty, oases of refreshment. Haven't you found this to be true? We journey through a hard time, and then God provides an oasis—a time of refreshment for body and spirit before the journey resumes.

GOD PROVIDES MANNA AND QUAIL

The next incident on the road to Sinai is very important. Not only is the account presented in detail in Exodus 16, but it is also referred to again and again throughout the Bible.[3]

To start with, we see in verse 1 that the Israelites were camping in the desert on the fifteenth day of the second month after they had come out of Egypt. The time reference is not accidental. They had left Egypt on the fifteenth day of Abib, which the Lord had declared was to be the first month of the year (see 12:1). Now it was exactly one month later. Last month they had been miraculously delivered, and this month they have forgotten all about it. They had been given victory over the Egyptians; now they were hungry and complaining again.

This significantly parallels the Christian life: God abundantly provides for us, but we grumble much of the time. We can learn the dangers of grumbling here. One of the first lessons is clear: Moses reminded the people that when they grumbled against himself and Aaron, they were actually grumbling against God (see 16:8). The

---

2. See Charles R. Erdman, *The Book of Exodus: An Exposition* (New York: Fleming H. Revell, 1949), 77.

3. In the Old Testament, it is discussed at some length in Numbers 11, Deuteronomy 8, Joshua 5, Nehemiah 9, and in the Psalms. In the New Testament, it is part of one of the great discourses of our Lord in John 6, and it is also mentioned in Hebrews 9 and the book of Revelation.

same is true of us. As Christians, we know that grumbling against God is not good, so we grumble about our circumstances and think that this is safe. But if we are grumbling against hard circumstances or the difficulties we face, aren't we grumbling against God? Again and again God says that he gives hard circumstances to test and train his people. When hard times come into our lives, this is exactly what God is doing—teaching us to trust him, and his care and protection, rather than focusing on our circumstances.

In this journey, God did two things to provide for the people. He provided quail, which are little birds, and he provided manna, which was a bread-like substance that they found on the ground in the mornings. The manna is an utter miracle—nothing can explain it. But the quail are a natural phenomenon. Great flocks of these small birds come south from the Mediterranean into Africa in the winter, and in the spring they make their way back north. As the quail fly long distances, they become so exhausted that people can almost pick them off the ground. Apparently that is what happened. This was the spring, the Passover time; and as the quail made their journey north, the wind, which was of God, blew them in the Israelites' direction.

The manna was quite different: a white wafer that tasted like honey (see v. 31) and was found every morning on the ground around the camp (see vv. 13–14). The Israelites did not know what it was; they had never seen anything like it. Commentators fall all over themselves trying to explain things naturally. Many have credited this edible wafer to a kind of insect that lives on tamarisk trees and secretes a honey-like substance; they have also suggested that it might have been a kind of lichen that grows on rocks, about the size of a pea.

What matters is that the Israelites had manna to eat wherever they journeyed for forty years, every single day except the Sabbath. It was clearly miraculous. When they first saw it, they did not say, "Isn't it interesting what these little insects have produced?" No, they saw it and said, "*Man hu?*" which means "What is it?" From this we have the word *manna*.[4]

---

4. *Man hu* could also mean "This is manna," but the story makes clear that the Hebrew is supposed to be taken as a question.

INSTRUCTIONS CONCERNING THE MANNA

God gave the people a number of instructions about the manna. Six mornings a week they were to gather enough for each individual. They couldn't keep the manna until the next day because it would spoil. However, on the sixth day they were to gather a double portion, because no manna would be provided on the Sabbath. They were to rest on that day.

One other instruction helps us to understand the significance of the manna. The Israelites were to take an omer of manna, put it in a jar, and put it in front of the ark of the covenant (see 16:34). This is an anachronistic reference, because they had not yet constructed the ark of the covenant or the tabernacle. Nevertheless, when the time came, they were to take the manna and lay it in the holy place of the tabernacle as a reminder of what the Lord had done. In Deuteronomy 8:2–3, when the Israelites gathered to hear Moses' final words to them, he exhorted the people,

> And you shall remember the whole way that the LORD your God has led you these forty years in the wilderness, that he might humble you, testing you to know what was in your heart, whether you would keep his commandments or not. And he humbled you and let you hunger and fed you with manna, which you did not know, nor did your fathers know, that he might make you know that man does not live by bread alone, but man lives by every word that comes from the mouth of the LORD.

The manna was miraculous and necessary for daily nourishment. But more important than this heaven-sent physical bread is every word that comes from the mouth of the Lord.

Now, when we handle biblical material, there is always a great danger of overspiritualizing. A lot of evangelical popular literature does this. To overspiritualize, one takes every biblical incident and draws out of it some spiritual lesson that may or may not be a valid interpretation. This is dangerous because the mind seems to be infinitely inventive, and it is very easy to come up with "lessons"—i.e., meanings or applications—that are not suggested or implied at all by the text.

We do not run any risk of doing that with the manna, however, because passages such as Deuteronomy 8:2–3 direct our understanding. Deuteronomy tells us that we can draw a parallel between God's provision of the manna and the way we are to feed on the Scriptures. Jesus himself quoted this text during his temptation in the wilderness (see Matt. 4:4; Luke 4:4).

Manna was bread from heaven, but that bread from heaven reminds us that we need the *true* bread from heaven. Jesus talked about exactly this in his great discourse in John 6:25–59. He had fed the people by multiplying bread and fish in the wilderness. They wanted physical healing and feeding. Jesus said that what they most needed was not the bread that had come from heaven, provided by Moses—which he was duplicating in some sense—but the true bread. "I am the true bread," he told them. They needed him.

LEARNING FROM THE MANNA

I have one book that finds more than twenty lessons drawn from how the manna was given and how it was to be used![5] Some are a little far-fetched, but not all. I want to give you some, because they tell us something about how we ought to study the Bible.

Manna was a supernatural gift from God. It was not a product of some biological organism, it was not man-made, and it was not something that the Israelites brought with them out of Egypt. God provided the manna, and he provided it directly from heaven.

To make a parallel with the Scriptures as Deuteronomy encourages us to do, we must remind ourselves that the Bible is like this. It is not a man-made book. Oh, it is true that the Bible came to us through human hands and human authors. But Peter made it very clear that the human authors did not just write down whatever came out of their own fertile brains, but were carried along by the Holy Spirit (see 2 Peter 1:21). They wrote what God intended them to write.

This is why we call the Bible the Word of God. In a certain sense, we could also call it the word of man, but that is greatly overshadowed

5. See Pink, *Gleanings in Exodus*, 124–30.

by the fact that it is the Word of God. As the Word of God, it carries with it the characteristics that we associate with God. One is perfection. God is perfect. If the Bible is his book, then it is perfect and exactly what God intended it to be. Because God does not lie, the Bible is truthful and contains no errors. And because God, the sovereign God, is authoritative, the Bible has authority. Above all, the Bible is a supernatural book.

Manna had to be gathered. God gave the manna to the Israelites freely; they did not do anything to earn it. In the same way, we did not earn the Bible; God has given it to us freely. Nevertheless, manna did not fall into the Israelites' mouths. They had to go out in the morning and gather it up. This suggests to us that, if we are to benefit from the Bible, it must require work on our part. We have to gather it up. We have to study it. Nobody ever said that Bible study was easy—it is hard work. All kinds of study are hard, but the Bible is especially hard because God's ways are not our ways, and his thoughts are not our thoughts (see Isa. 55:8). When we come to the Bible, we will always find things that we do not understand. We have to wrestle with the Bible, struggle with it, and sift through our prejudices in order to understand what it really says.

Manna had to be gathered daily. What the Israelites gathered up one day would not do for the next, and people have rightly pointed out that we should study the Bible the same way. This doesn't mean, of course, that we will die if for some reason we miss studying the Bible on a particular day. Do you die if you miss a meal? Do you die if you fast for a day or two or a week? Of course not. But normally we eat every day. This is the way the Israelites were supposed to gather the manna. And for spiritual health and growth this is the way we are to feed on God's Word. We are to read and study the Bible in a regular, disciplined way.

Manna gathered daily had to be eaten. Imagine if the Israelites had appreciated the manna, gone to the work of gathering it up, brought it into the house, and said, "Isn't this a wonderful gift that God has given to us? Look at this manna! Aaron had such a splendid idea to put it in a pot and lay it up in the tabernacle, because we never want to forget that God has given this to us." The purpose of the manna would not have been fulfilled in that way. The Israelites had to eat it if it was to do them any good. In the same way, you and I have to "eat" the Word of God, and we have to do it bit by bit.

You serve a great banquet in courses, and, if you are a civilized person, you talk while you are eating instead of gobbling everything down. We need to study the Bible the same way. In a favorite passage of mine, Isaiah gives the rule by repetition: "Do and do, do and do, rule on rule, rule on rule; a little here, a little there" (Isa. 28:10 NIV). This is the way we master the Word of God: not all at once, but little by little. We have to keep at it.

Manna appeared until they reached Canaan. Although the manna was given while the Israelites were wandering in the wilderness for forty years, it ceased when the people entered the land of Canaan. This does not mean that when we get to heaven, the Bible will be gone. Jesus said, "Heaven and earth will pass away, but my words will not pass away" (Matt. 24:35). God is eternal, and so is his Word. But it does mean that the Word of God will not fail us during our earthly pilgrimage. No matter what we go through—terrible illnesses, job loss, confusion, deteriorating minds in old age, the pain of death— the Bible will not fail us, and the wise Christian recognizes this. God will speak to us and minister to us through his Word. If we study the Scriptures, we will have the words and wisdom of God planted in our minds, souls, and spirits.

Having looked at manna as symbolic of the Bible and at how we should read and study it, we cannot miss that Jesus uses the manna as a symbol of himself. He explains that Moses fed the Israelites with the bread from heaven but what we really need is the bread that came down from heaven—and that bread is Jesus Christ, the Messiah (see John 6:32–33). "I am the bread of life," he says (John 6:35). Jesus tells us, using this simple metaphor, that he is essential. We need natural food to live. In order to have spiritual life, we must have Jesus Christ, who feeds our spirits. Jesus has to become part of us. We have to know Jesus Christ in a personal way.

GOD PROVIDES WATER AGAIN

The people came next to a campsite called Rephidim, the last place of encampment before Mount Sinai. There was no water there, so again they began to quarrel with Moses, just as they had done earlier. They had not learned anything, it seems; but Moses had not forgotten what to do. In desperation he "cried out to the LORD, 'What shall I do with this people? They are almost ready to stone me'" (Ex. 17:4). He feared for his life.

This time God directed him to a rock, telling him to strike it with his staff. This was the same staff that Moses had used to strike the Nile, which had then turned to blood and become undrinkable. With exactly the opposite outcome, Moses struck the rock with his staff and out gushed fresh, thirst-satisfying water.

In 1 Corinthians 10, Paul refers to this rock as a symbol of Jesus Christ. In the wilderness, the Israelites "all ate the same spiritual food, and all drank the same spiritual drink. For they drank from the spiritual Rock that followed them, and the Rock was Christ" (1 Cor. 10:3–4). Just like the manna, the water from the rock is a symbol of Jesus. We have to be refreshed by him, the true living water, the only one able to satisfy our souls' thirst (see John 7:37).

GOD PROVIDES VICTORY
OVER THE AMALEKITES

Before the Israelites reached Mount Sinai, they had to battle the Amalekites, a vicious fighting people who had descended from Esau's grandson Amalek (see Gen. 36:12). While they did not occupy all the territory around Mount Sinai, these fierce nomads roamed widely there, regarded it as theirs, and thought they had to protect the territory against anybody who tried to pass through. As the Israelites continued their march, the Amalekites attacked them. Like cowards they fell on the stragglers at the end of the column—people who were weary, old, and sick (see Deut. 25:18). Moses knew that they had to fight whether they wanted to or not, so he appointed Joshua, a man about half his age, as commander of the troops (see Ex. 17:9).[6]

Joshua knew that the people would be delivered not by the strength of his arm, but by God's might. So Moses sent him out to lead the battle while he, with his brother Aaron, and Hur,[7] a friend, went up a hill that overlooked the battle. There they interceded with God for victory. While they were praying, Moses held up his hands, and in his hands he held the staff that he had used to strike the rock and that God had used in the miracles in Egypt. The staff was a symbol of the Lord's presence and power. As long as Moses kept the staff raised, the Israelite troops prevailed. But when his arms grew tired and he lowered them, and thus lowered the staff, the Amalekites prevailed. So Aaron and Hur, Moses' two companions, stood on either side of him and held up his arms.

This has always been seen as a marvelous picture of friends standing together in intercession for the people of God, and rightly so, because that was exactly what was going on. F. B. Meyer writes, "It is a most beautiful picture. Three old men in prayer! Two staying up the third! . . . In earlier days Moses would never have thought of winning a battle save by fighting. He now learns that he can win it by praying."[8] I have to add the obvious: there also must be fighting. Moses, Aaron, and Hur stood on the mountain—you can almost picture the flowing robes and graying beards of these patriarchs of the tribes—but down on the plain Joshua still led the troops and the young men still fought the Amalekites. Prayer and fighting can go together.

For us, the fighting may not be physical, but there are still battles. Writing to the Ephesians, Paul said, "Our struggle is . . . against the

6. This is the first time in the Bible that we come across this remarkable man. Interestingly, he is not actually called Joshua at this point in the Hebrew text. His name is Hoshea, which means "savior." Only later does he add the J, making his name "Jehovah is the Savior."

7. Here in Exodus 17:10 is the first of two of the Bible's mentions of this particular Hur. There is another Hur (see Num. 31:8), who is not to be confused with the first.

8. F. B. Meyer, *Moses: The Servant of God* (New York: Fleming H. Revell Company, n.d.), 106.

spiritual forces of evil" (Eph. 6:12 NIV). Our battle is against wickedness, against falsehood, against injustice. Sometimes these battles must be fought in an active way, but above all prayer must support them. Without prayer, activity is ineffective or useless.

Following the battle with the Amalekites, God told Moses to write down what had happened (see Ex. 17:14). Scholars passed over this for years, assuming that nobody knew how to write in Moses' day, and therefore Moses could not have known how to write and obviously did not write the account of this battle or any part of the Pentateuch. The Pentateuch must have been written later. But this premise was entirely wrong. As was said earlier, not only did people know how to write in Moses' day, but *lots* of people knew how to write—and in lots of different languages. We now know of about a dozen different written languages from the very area where Moses led the people for forty years. Exodus 17:14 tells us that Moses began to keep a record of these things; mentions of Moses' note-taking also appear in Exodus 24:4; 34:27; Numbers 33:2; and Deuteronomy 31:9. This is why we know these books are accurate.

Then Moses erected an altar (see Ex. 17:15). The name that he gave the altar introduces another name for God: *Jehovah Nissi*, meaning "the LORD is my Banner." The Lord is the banner around which we rally, and the God who gives victory.

LEARNING FROM EXODUS 15:22–17:16

The Christian life is not easy. The Rev. William Taylor, a preacher in New York City at the end of the 1800s, wrote, "We may learn that we are not done with hardship when we have left Egypt."[9] It is just as Jesus said to his disciples: "In the world you will have tribulation" (John 16:33). He warned us in advance that we do not have an easy path to glory.

This is the significance of *Marah*. Have bitter things come into your life? It would be surprising if they haven't. Life is filled with

---

9. William M. Taylor, *Moses the Law-Giver* (New York: Harper & Brothers, 1879), 140–41.

bitter things. But these things come from God, and, even though they are bitter, God has his good purpose in them. Do you ask him for the purpose? Do you seek to learn what God has to teach you in the Marah experiences of your life?

The Christian life is not all hardship. We also have Elims in our lives, places of refreshment, just as we have Marahs. Christians do not escape times of hardship and struggle. These are part of life in a fallen world. But we can also expect the Elims that the Lord provides along our way. Maybe you are in a hard place now; maybe you have been there; maybe you know somebody who is still camped by the bitter springs. Encourage that person. Tell younger Christians that the times of refreshment do come. They will come from the hand of God.

Every true leader encounters opposition. Moses exhibited an enormous level of faith in these four incidents. Imagine leading two million people into the desert with no visible means of support, and with the closest oases very far apart. In spite of his great faith, and probably because of it, Moses suffered constant opposition from the people. We have only begun to see it here; he would be opposed all through this long journey, for forty more years, right up to his death.

This is true for any real leader. By definition, a leader is different; he is a visionary, seeing beyond the immediate challenges and opportunities. The masses will not appreciate that. John Calvin was dismissed from his pulpit in Geneva, and Jonathan Edwards from his charge in North Hampton. As Jesus rode into Jerusalem on Palm Sunday, the people hailed him: "Hosanna to the Son of David! Blessed is he who comes in the name of the LORD!" (Matt. 21:9). But just a few days later, they were crying, "Crucify him! Crucify him!" It is always this way. If you are in a position of leadership, do not be surprised if you face times of severe opposition.

God is sufficient for all our needs. Deuteronomy 8:2–3 reminds us that God led the Israelites all the way in the desert, providing them with everything they needed for forty years. He gave them manna and quail to eat; he provided water from the rock. He protected them from sickness and from enemies. Their clothes and sandals did not wear out. When we walk with God through the wilderness of life, we find him to be exactly as the Israelites in their pilgrimage found him to be: Jehovah Rapha, the God who heals, who takes care of us, who provides for all our needs. We also find him to be Jehovah Nissi, God our Banner, around whom we can rally.

Bible study and prayer are essential to the Christian life. We cannot live without manna; nor can we survive without uplifted hands, interceding for God's blessing. Jesus said, "apart from me you can do nothing" (John 15:5). If we believed that, we would be far more conscientious in our Bible study and far more consistent in our prayer. Our problem is that we think we can do things and do them without God. The world may seem appealing, and a life of prayer and Bible study requires commitment and discipline. But as Meyer says, "Better, ten thousand times over, the liberty wherewith Christ makes us free, though we fare only on manna, than the slavery of Egypt, with its flesh-pots—for there is life in the one, and death in the other."[10] A true Christian knows that.

---

10. F. B. Meyer, *Moses: The Servant of God* (New York: Fleming H. Revell Company, n.d.), 148.

10

DELEGATING AUTHORITY

Exodus 18

THE LONELINESS OF THE LONG-DISTANCE LEADER

I am always intrigued by titles—I suppose because I have to produce so many of them for sermons and books. When I find a good title, I always remember it. There is a movie with the title *The Loneliness of the Long Distance Runner*. Well, this particular chapter of Exodus shows us the loneliness of the long-distance leader—especially a Christian leader, because in Christian circles, leadership is a commitment for the long haul.

A leader walks alone. His task is to set a vision, to plan and motivate; and, by the very nature of the task, he must do this more or less by himself or with a team, not with the support of the masses. His vision must be communicated; it is not initially shared. Plans are often misunderstood; motivators are resisted. Yet the leader must carry on.

Moses must have been a very lonely man. All sorts of friends, peers, and activities had surrounded him when he lived in the royal courts of Egypt. All the pleasures, entertainments, and associations of a high–ranking government official were his. But then he spent forty years on the far side of the desert of Midian, virtually alone. He was a shepherd, and we know from the incident of the burning bush that he took care of the sheep himself, spending many long hours and years alone in the desert.

His marriage must have helped. But at the time of the exodus, Moses' family was apparently no longer with him. Although he had started for Egypt with his wife, Zipporah, and his two children (see Ex. 4:20), Moses had sent them back to Jethro (see 18:2). So, during the year and a half or so that it had taken him to complete the journey, meet with Pharaoh, and lead the people out of Egypt, he had not even had the company and consolation of his family.

Not only that, but when Moses left Egypt, he was in charge of two million people. It is easy to be lonely in a crowd. Moses was lonely here. Nobody understood him, nobody appreciated what he was doing, and the people rebelled again and again. Yet he had to carry on, and he did. He carried on for a very long time.

God understands what his servants go through. In Exodus 18, we see God's twofold provision for Moses. First of all, he received his family back. His father-in-law Jethro brought Zipporah and his two children to him. Second, at the counsel of Jethro, he adopted a program by which certain tasks—particularly those of rendering judgments—were divided among designated leaders of the twelve tribes. Some of Moses' leadership responsibilities were thus delegated so that the nearly intolerable burden was no longer on his shoulders alone.

JETHRO'S SIGNIFICANCE

Long before this, when Moses had fled Egypt after killing the Egyptian foreman, as described in Exodus 2, he had, in crossing the desert, stopped by a well. When Jethro's daughters had come to draw water for their flocks, other shepherds had tried to drive them away, and Moses intervened to protect them. As a result, he was invited to come to the tent of Jethro, who befriended him. Eventually Moses married one of Jethro's daughters.

After Moses' encounter with God on the mountain (Exodus 3–4), he went back to Jethro's tent, presumably to return Jethro's sheep, but also to ask his permission to go to Egypt (see 4:18). This is surprising. After all, if God tells you to do something, you would hardly think you needed to stop and ask permission from a mere human. But Moses was exercising proper deference to Jethro, who was his elder at that time and in that place. Now, in this striking second mention, Jethro emerges as a very significant man.

The only thing we are really told about Jethro, other than that he had daughters and flocks, is that he was a priest of Midian (see 2:16; 18:1). The people of Midian were descendants of Midian, who was a son of Abraham by his second wife, Keturah (see Gen 25:1–2). Presumably he had received from Abraham some knowledge of the true God. This does not mean that Midian's descendants were faithful to this knowledge or understood it; nonetheless, we must remember that knowledge of the true God was dispersed more widely than we might think. Although the narrative in the Old Testament traces the line of Abraham through the Jews toward the coming of Jesus Christ, we have the story of Job, who does not seem to be part of that picture, yet who understood a great deal about the true God and worshipped him. Thus, although Jethro was not necessarily a priest of the true God, he may very well have understood something about this God of his ancestor Abraham. In his prayer, recorded in Exodus 18, Jethro acknowledged God by the name *Jehovah*, so we see that by this point in his life he was worshipping the God of Israel.

The exodus had taken place just a couple of months beforehand, but word had traveled quickly in the desert. Jethro had heard that God, the God of Israel, had brought his people out of Egypt with a mighty hand and that his son-in-law had been successful as a deliverer sent by God. So Jethro went to Moses, bringing Zipporah and Moses' sons.

JETHRO'S PRAISE

What happened next was very touching. In the formal manner of a tribal chieftain, Jethro sent a messenger to announce to Moses, "I, your father-in-law Jethro, am coming to you with your wife and her two sons" (18:6). Moses rose to the occasion with all the courtesy of the desert. Going out to meet Jethro, he bowed down and kissed him in a courteous and proper fashion.

These two old men had a great deal to share. As soon as they were settled in the tent, Moses began to rehearse to Jethro all the things that God had done on behalf of the people. He told of traveling to

Egypt, meeting with the elders, appearing before Pharaoh for the first time—and then of Pharaoh's rejection of God's demands; the plagues, one after the other, with all their significance; and, finally, the night of the Passover, as the angel of death came through the land and killed all the firstborn. Moses told how the Israelites had left Egypt and how God had seen them across the Red Sea, protected them in the desert, and even delivered them from the Amalekites, giving them victory in their first great battle. Hearing all this, Jethro began to praise God: "Now I know that the LORD is greater than all gods, because in this affair they dealt arrogantly with the people" (v. 11).

JETHRO'S ADVICE

The day after Jethro's arrival, Moses went out to judge the people. They began to come to him early in the morning, and Moses pronounced judgments from then until late at night. With two million people, it is not surprising that they got in one another's way from time to time. Perhaps somebody's sheep wandered into someone else's pen, and the first man wanted the wanderer back while the second thought it had been his sheep all along. But there must have been more serious issues as well. The people came with their disputes all day long, and at the end of the day Moses was worn out.

PRIORITIES FOR MOSES AND MINISTERS

Looking on, Jethro took it on himself to give Moses some advice: "You shall represent the people before God and bring their cases to God, and you shall warn them about the statutes and the laws, and make them know the way in which they must walk and what they must do" (Ex.18:19–20). Jethro was concerned for the people, but he was first of all concerned for Moses, and he advised him to restrict himself to what he alone could do well: (1) pray and represent the people's concerns before God, since he was the one to whom God spoke directly, and (2) teach the people the ways of God.

This counsel should sound familiar, in part because the tasks of praying and teaching are exactly those that are given to ministers today. But the apostles also took these tasks on themselves in the early days of the church. Acts 6 describes a dispute about whether the benevolence fund was being administered properly. Some believers of Greek background thought that their widows were not getting a fair share, but when they complained to the apostles, the apostles refused to judge the dispute. They told the people to appoint from their own number men called deacons to take care of the issue. Their reasoning was that it would be wrong for them to prioritize diaconal work over their preaching ministry (see Acts 6:2). Jethro told Moses to have the same priorities—to give himself to prayer and the teaching of God's ordinances to the people.

We all have a responsibility to teach the Word in our own settings. We must witness to Christ wherever we are. Parents must teach their children. Some may have opportunities to teach in Christian schools. However, it is primarily the responsibility of ministers in the church to teach the Bible and to pray. If they do not teach the Bible, they fail in their primary calling.

Of course, there are many things that have to be done in a church. Sometimes a minister has to take on many tasks that he would rather not do, especially at the beginning of his pastorate, and if the church has a small staff. I have done many such tasks myself. Some things, such as climbing on scaffolding to paint the church walls, were a lot of fun. But as a minister moves forward, these other activities will quickly become too much for him. Above all, he must teach, because it is all right if the other things do not get done, but it is not all right if the teaching of God's Word is neglected.

JUDGES AND THEIR QUALIFICATIONS

Jethro's second bit of advice concerned the people. He told Moses to appoint judges to handle all but the most difficult judicial cases. "Select capable men from all the people—men who fear God, trustworthy men who hate dishonest gain—and appoint them as officials over thousands, hundreds, fifties and tens" (Ex. 18:21 NIV).

This too is very similar to what happened in Acts. When the apostles called for deacons to be appointed, they told the people to choose men who were "full of the Spirit and of wisdom" (Acts 6:3). Jethro did not tell Moses to appoint just anybody, but instead he listed four qualifications.

They must be capable. Obviously these men needed to be capable as judges. They needed to be able to think clearly, weigh evidence, and be fair. Not everybody has that gift of logical thinking and moral discernment. But why is this strength listed first? Is it more important to be capable than to be spiritual? No—we will see that piety is important, too. But these men were being chosen to be judges. If a very pious, godly person does not have any gifts suited for the demands of a judge's duties, we do not do anybody favors by appointing him to a role for which he is unqualified.

Sometimes, though, we do this in the church. We elect people because they are nice, pleasant, easy to get along with. It is nice to have nice people, but niceness is not the first thing that matters when we look for leaders. In 1 Timothy 3:1–13 and Titus 1:5–9, Paul urges us to take qualifications seriously when we are electing or appointing people to church office. In the same line of thought, Ray Lanning, a former associate at Tenth Presbyterian Church, used to say that 11 o'clock on Sunday morning is not the amateur hour. He did not mean that we do not think highly of godly attributes. He meant that we expect the leaders of public worship to be the most capable and the most prepared for conducting the congregation in corporate worship, with ability in public speaking and other skills needed for those particular duties. Godly attributes are not a substitute for those skills.

They must be pious. Piety is an important qualification for any religious office, but perhaps especially for those who have to judge. We are told that the fear of the Lord is the beginning of wisdom (see Ps. 111:10; Prov. 9:10); and, in order to judge rightly, judges must exercise wisdom, which rests on godly, spiritual maturity.

When we begin with a proper fear or respect for God, this attitude spills into the way we look at people. We respect them, because we know that they are made in the image of God, as we ourselves are. In our respect for God, we respect the image of God in those to whom we are responsible. Fear of God also enables us to place human demands, needs, and cases in proper perspective. We will answer to God for everything we decide and do. People can come to us with demands that might be entirely selfish. We must see these demands from God's perspective and then respond according to scriptural principles.

They must be trustworthy. It is possible for someone to have ability, piety, and godliness, and yet not be someone who can be trusted to get the job done. Jethro told Moses to get trustworthy men—reliable men whom Moses could count on. He would not have to supervise them all the time. He could give them directions and let them move forward, knowing that they would complete what needed to be done.

They must hate dishonest gain. Jethro knew the importance of integrity. From time to time we hear of scandals in which judges or lawyers have been bribed to shift verdicts from what they should be. This is a problem in our court system today, but it was much worse in the ancient world. No system in the ancient world required judges to render speedy judgment; they could put off a decision as long as they chose to. This is why Jesus sometimes spoke of unjust judges. Luke 18:1–8 records Jesus telling a parable about an importunate widow who kept appealing to a judge for justice. Justice was on her side, but the judge would not pay attention because she did not have any money to bribe him. In the end, he heard her case only because she pestered him and because he wanted to get rid of her so he could enjoy his ill-gotten gain. Jesus used this parable to make a point about persistence in prayer, but a secondary lesson points to the need for righteous judges. Jethro wanted Moses to choose people who were not in it for the money. They needed to judge rightly because it was right, not because they could benefit personally from hearing and settling cases.

Perhaps the most remarkable thing about Jethro's advice was that Moses accepted it. Moses might have said, "You may be my father-in-law, Jethro, but just remember, I'm not the shepherd you knew before. God sent me to Egypt, and now I'm the leader of two million people. How many people do you have at your oasis? A dozen? Fifty? You've never had the responsibility that I have, leading millions." He might have said, "God speaks to me, not you. Who are you to tell me how to do this?" But Moses was not like that. He was a humble and a teachable man. He listened to his father-in-law and acted on his advice. That humility shows how great a leader Moses truly was.

THE ORGANIZATION OF THE CHURCH

Jethro's advice has some bearing on the organization of the church. Although the specific details concerning the need to appoint judges over thousands, hundreds, fifties, and tens does not have direct application, there are principles that can be applied to the functioning of church leadership today. We see that this was sound advice given by Jethro, accepted by Moses, apparently endorsed by God, and perhaps enacted at Sinai, as we read in Deuteronomy 1. Therefore, we can derive some helpful principles from it.

DIVISION OF RESPONSIBILITY

The first principle flows from two realities: (1) no one person in Israel at that time, and no one person in the church today, possesses every gift; and (2) even if one person did have all the gifts, that person would not have the time or strength to do everything that needs to be done. Thus God has given a plurality of gifts to a wide number of people. God's way is to divide responsibilities, and that is what we must do in the church (and elsewhere). D. L. Moody once remarked that it is better to get a hundred men to work than to do all the work oneself.[1] Moody wasn't lazy; he understood.

Moses was an extraordinary man; he had magnificent gifts and unbelievable training. If anyone could have done it all, it would have been Moses. But not even Moses was up to the challenges presented by this two-million-person march through the wilderness. Thus we get the division of leadership. If Moses couldn't do it alone, we cannot do it alone either.

---

1. D. L. Moody, *"To the Work! To the Work!" Exhortations to Christians* (Chicago: Revell, 1884), 3.

PLURALITY OF LEADERSHIP

The second principle follows from the first. When we look at New Testament leadership, we find plurality. When Christ appointed apostles, he appointed twelve. He did not appoint one in charge of the others; there were just twelve. When the apostles appointed the deacons, they selected seven. When Paul traveled around the Roman world and established churches, he always left elders in charge of the new congregations—always elders, never just one. In my denomination, we cannot have a "particular" (or self-governing) church until we have at least two elders. A pastor by himself does not make a church.

By contrast, cults almost always revolve around a single leader. That is where the great danger lies. He becomes a god figure, assuming responsibility and authority that he has no right to claim. A Christian church ought not to be like that. There should be plurality in leadership.

SPIRITUAL QUALIFICATIONS

Jethro listed qualifications, some of which were spiritual and some of which simply had to do with various gifts required for the job. Paul does the same thing in the New Testament. Writing to Timothy, he explains that bishops, elders, or deacons should be, among other qualities, irreproachable and respected, apt to teach,[2] and not greedy, drunken, or violent (see 1 Tim. 3:2–10, 12–13). These are necessary qualities for good leadership, whether within or outside the church, in roles sacred or secular.

CHOICE OF THE PEOPLE

In both the Old and New Testaments, we see that the people chose their leaders. When Jethro spoke to Moses, he said, "Select capable men," (NIV) but in Deuteronomy 1 we find that Moses very wisely had the people select those whom they knew were qualified and able to handle their cases. Moses appointed them once they had been selected.

This works well in the church, too. Most denominations, at least to some degree, allow the congregation to choose its minister.

---

2. This is the one qualification that is not also given to the deacons, but of course many deacons teach very well also.

In a hierarchical church, a bishop makes a suggestion, but generally this candidate is not forced on the local congregation. Presbyterian churches form a committee—the committee listens to candidates preach, examines them, and then invites one back to be presented to the congregation. At this point the congregation, having received background information and heard the candidate preach, votes. Only then does the presbytery, the representative body of local ministers and elders, examine, approve, and install the candidate. This follows the same pattern of the people having a part in choosing their leaders.

LEARNING FROM EXODUS 18

While we have seen principles here related to leadership qualities and church government practices, some further applications make this text more personal.

First, we learn that however great our talents may be, no one person can do everything. As we grow older, we will be wise to focus increasingly on what we are able to do well. I have been very thankful that I have had the freedom to do that in the context of the local church I serve. I started out doing many other things, but now our larger staff has allowed me to focus on teaching, preaching, and the things I do best. We need to work on whatever our area may be, to focus increasingly on that area of ministry and service, and thus to strive to do our best.

Second, God provides the gifts that are necessary for the health of the church body. Although sometimes certain jobs just have to be done, and we don't have anyone else to do them, I think that the main reason we want to do everything ourselves is pride. We think we can do the task better than someone else can. We have to do it ourselves, because if we let others do it, it would not get done properly. And so leaders end up trying to do everything themselves. If we analyze this attitude carefully, doing everything ourselves comes from unbelief— from not trusting that God has provided our church with the gifts necessary to get done the things that *he* wants to get done. We need to get in the habit of looking for the skills possessed by others and of encouraging them to exercise those skills, doing the things that we cannot or should not be doing ourselves.

Third, we must remember that even a prophet should not be indifferent to advice. Moses was the one man in Israel who received revelations directly from God. Yet when his father-in-law—a man not even part of the great company brought out of Egypt—said, "You know, what you're doing is not right; you ought to do it another way," Moses listened to him, and the results were beneficial. Do we listen to others? Have we cultivated friends to whom we can listen and from whose advice we can profit?

EXCURSUS: WHERE DID THIS HAPPEN?

This section may not be of interest to you; in that case skip on to the next chapter. I myself do not want to pass over this issue, because people who *are* interested will say that I am avoiding a difficult problem.

Chapter 17 places the Israelites at Rephidim, so we might assume that the events of Exodus 18 took place at Rephidim as well, long before the Israelites got to Mount Sinai. Exodus 19 begins, "In the third month after the Israelites left Egypt—on the very day—they came to the Desert of Sinai" (v. 1 NIV). Again, it seems as though they were at Rephidim, Jethro met them there, and after Jethro left, they went on to Sinai. But, if we read more carefully, Exodus 18:5 makes it sound as though Moses was already in Sinai: "Jethro . . . came to him in the desert, where he was camped near the mountain of God" (NIV). Deuteronomy 1:6–18 describes the appointing of the officials to judge companies of thousands, hundreds, fifties, and tens—and we are told that this happened at the very base of Sinai.

There are three different positions on this. One answer is that the appointing happened in Rephidim, just as its position in Exodus suggests. Walter C. Kaiser Jr., a very respected Old Testament scholar, holds this view, arguing that Deuteronomy 1:6–18 is loosely written and refers to something that happened earlier.[3] A second possibility is that Moses received Jethro's advice closer to Rephidim but acted

---

3. Walter C. Kaiser Jr., *Exodus*, in *The Expositor's Bible Commentary*, vol. 2, *Genesis, Exodus, Leviticus, Numbers*, ed. Frank E. Gaebelein (Grand Rapids: Zondervan, 1990), 411.

on his suggestions at Sinai. John J. Davis believes that is the solution.[4] The third possibility, suggested by William Taylor, is that everything happened at Sinai.[5]

I think this event probably took place later, simply because it does seem that Deuteronomy 1 places it later, and there is no reason to fit it in earlier. So why does it appear at this point in Exodus? There could be several reasons.

First, the story may have been included here to suggest that not all those outside the twelve tribes of Israel were the enemies of the Chosen People. Jethro is sympathetic and knows the true God. Right from the beginning, we have an idea that the gospel has expanded beyond the families of the descendants of Jacob, the patriarch.

Second, this passage might be here to keep the material on the giving of the law at Sinai intact. Exodus 19 tells of the preparations at Sinai, and Exodus 20 lists the Ten Commandments. Would we want to dump a story about appointing officials into the middle of that? In other words, if we divided the book of Exodus into two parts—the first part dealing with the exodus itself, the second part with the giving of the law—this story fits better in the early section.

Third, the passage might have been placed here out of a desire to keep Jethro's advice separate from the divine commands occupying the rest of the book. Jethro's advice was good, but it was merely human advice. A person sensitive to the nature of the material, as Moses the author certainly was, might want to arrange the material in this way.

---

4. John J. Davis, *Moses and the Gods of Egypt: Studies in Exodus* (Grand Rapids: Baker, 1971), 189.

5. See William M. Taylor, *Moses the Law-Giver* (New York: Harper & Brothers, 1879), 164–68.

11

THE TEN COMMANDMENTS

Exodus 19—20

EXODUS DIVIDED

Exodus falls into two parts. Roughly divided, chapters 1–18 deal with the exodus itself, giving the book its name, and chapters 19–40 deal with the giving of the law. We think of Moses as the great emancipator, but, by the grace of God, he was also the lawgiver. Deliverance from slavery is one thing, but freedom without law leads to license, and license is only another form of slavery. The law was necessary for the Israelites if they were to become a true nation. So the second half of Exodus shows God's work through Moses to provide the people with a law code.

Exodus 19–40 falls into three sections, because there are three different kinds of law. The first (chapters 19–20) is the *moral law*, which is embodied in the Ten Commandments. The second (chapters 21–24, known as the book of the covenant) is the *civil law*—governing laws for how a nation is to be operated and run. The third (chapters 25–40, but particularly 25–31) is the *ceremonial law*. This was the religious law: instructions on how the tabernacle was to be constructed and how various ceremonies were to be performed. The ceremonial law is elaborated in the book of Leviticus, especially concerning the role of the priests who served in the tabernacle. Our focus in this chapter is upon the moral law.

THE TEN COMMANDMENTS

It is impossible to overstate the importance of the moral code. However, this is not because the Ten Commandments are in all respects unique to Judaism or the Old Testament. They flow from the moral character of God, and God has stamped his character on the human heart.

Thus, when we travel, we find laws that are very similar to these. Most cultures know that it is right for human beings to seek out, worship, and praise their Creator. They just do not know who he is, and, to the extent that they are aware of him, they suppress that truth, as Paul describes in Romans 1. Nevertheless, a sense of right and wrong resides, in a very fallen state, in the hearts of men and women. Most people know, although it is hard for us to remember, that we are supposed to honor our fathers and mothers and not murder, commit adultery, steal, give false testimony, or even covet.

THEIR STRUCTURE

What makes the Ten Commandments stand out from other moral codes is that they are communicated in the shortest space and in the most brilliant and flawless language. Moses did not get these laws from the cultures around him, though he may have been aware of the laws that existed in Egypt, for example, or in the well-known Code of Hammurabi, which the Egyptians knew and from which they borrowed. But he got these laws from God. They express, in the purest possible form, things that all of us should know.

In recent years a great deal of study has been done on ancient law codes. Scholars have pointed out that there were two main types of law in the ancient world, expressed in the form of treaties: parity treaties and suzerainty treaties. Parity treaties are treaties between equals—for example, between two kings. Neither claims sovereignty over the other, but they agree to live together as neighbors and to respect one another's territory. They enter into a parity agreement and sign a covenant. Most of our contracts today are like that.

But suzerainty treaties have to do with a sovereign (or *suzerain*) and his subjects. They are the kind of covenant that feudal lords impose on their subjects. Most ancient kings were feudal lords in this sense, and the law codes that they promulgated as treaties were given to the people in a form consisting of about six parts. First came the preface, then a statement in which the ruler introduced himself, then a historical section in which he rehearsed what he had done on behalf of the subjects or vassals. The fourth section described the obligations that he was placing on the subjects. Next the treaty listed the blessings that would follow if the vassals obeyed him, before concluding with the curses and judgments that would come if they did not.

The law in Exodus 20 is somewhat like that. It begins with God introducing himself and explaining, very briefly, what he has done for the people: "I am the LORD your God, who brought you out of the land of Egypt, out of the house of slavery" (v. 2). Then God begins to present to the people the obligations that their relationship with him entails. He does not describe judgments or blessings in every case—those are spelled out in far greater detail in Deuteronomy, as we will see in due course. Seeing the Ten Commandments in the light of suzerainty treaties tells us that, when God gives us the law, it is not something that we are free to accept or reject as God's equals. There is no one like God; he is a Sovereign above all sovereigns and is certainly your Sovereign and mine. God says that because he is the Lord, because he has created us (and, if we are Christians, because he has redeemed us from the hand of the enemy and saved us from our sin), this is the way that we should live.

THEIR NECESSITY

Our society needs nothing so much as it needs the Ten Commandments. In a commencement address at Duke University in 1987, Ted Koppel, the well-known news analyst, reminded the graduating class of the Ten Commandments and the fact that our culture deeply needs these precepts. He delineated each one, relating each to the various moral problems of our time. Nobody liked that address, but he was absolutely right.[1]

---

1. See Ted Koppel's commencement address (Duke University Chapel, Durham, NC, May 10, 1987), available online at https://repository.duke.edu/catalog/duke:320525.

The problem, of course, is that Americans do not want the Ten Commandments. As a matter of fact, they do not even know them. Americans consider themselves to be a very religious people. They claim that they believe in God. But when surveys probe to find out what Americans actually know about the Bible (which they profess to have as the basis of their religion), they can hardly answer any question about its content. Very few Americans can name five of the Ten Commandments. George Gallup calls this *biblical illiteracy*. If we do not know the Ten Commandments, we are not living by the Ten Commandments. So what *are* the commandments by which we are living?

The sad fact is that few people believe the law of God anymore, although many give it lip service. More than half of people who respond to surveys express a willingness to steal, lie, drink and drive, and cheat on their spouses. Sadly, evangelicals who take these surveys do not distinguish themselves noticeably from people with no evangelical convictions. We need the Ten Commandments in our day more than ever.

PREPARING TO RECEIVE THE LAW

Exodus 19 tells of a time of preparation before the people received the law. First there was an exchange in which Moses, as the prophet of God, asked the people if they were willing to enter into a law covenant with the Lord. They responded, "All that the LORD has spoken we will do" (v. 8). They did not, of course. They broke God's law almost immediately. But at any rate, they entered into an agreement. Second, for three days there was a period of ceremonial cleansing and consecration. Third, Moses fenced off the mountain, lest when God came down to meet with his prophet, the people should touch the mountain and die.

These preparations stressed the holiness of God—the very attribute impressed by God on Moses back at the burning bush. God had told Moses to take off his shoes because the ground on which he was standing was holy ground (see 3:5). Everything that so frightened the people—the cloud, the fenced-off mountain—stressed God's holiness, which they needed to recognize.

The preparations also stressed that a holy God requires a holy people. The preparations visibly expressed what we find clearly stated later in the Bible. Four times in the book of Leviticus we find the words, "Be holy, because I am holy" (see Lev. 11:44, 45; 19:2; 20:26 NIV); and Peter quotes this as well (see 1 Peter 1:16 NIV). But what does it mean to be holy—to worship a holy God in a holy way? The answer is given in the Ten Commandments.

DIVIDING THE TEN COMMANDMENTS

The Ten Commandments have many names. The Jews call them the Ten Words, or, in the Greek, *Decalogue*. The Ten Commandments are also called the Law, the Covenant, the Law *and* the Covenant, the Tables of Testimony, or the Law of the Testimony.

The Ten Commandments are also organized in different ways. The Roman Catholic Church and some Lutheran communions treat Exodus 20:3–6 as one commandment (whereas other communions see them as two) and then divide the tenth. Some branches of the church mix the order, putting the seventh commandment before the sixth. As far as the two tables of the law are concerned, some put four commandments on one side (the commandments about worshipping and honoring God) and six on the other (the commandments about honoring and caring for human beings). Some break up the commandments five and five.

Scholars today think that probably all ten commandments were written out on each of the two tablets mentioned (see 31:18). In ancient times, each party involved in a covenant received a tablet with the covenant copied on it. The thinking today is that one of the tablets was for the people and the other was for God, though God gave Moses both tablets to take back to the camp (see Gen. 31:18b).

AN OVERVIEW OF THE COMMANDMENTS

We do not have the space to look at each of the commandments exhaustively, but an overview is helpful.

143

1. YOU SHALL HAVE NO OTHER GODS BEFORE ME (EX. 20:3)

The commandments begin exactly as we would expect—with God and our relationship to him. Everything begins with God, including any right relationship we will have with other people.

What does God require in the first commandment? He demands our exclusive and zealous worship, meaning that the worship of any god other than Jehovah breaks this command. But we do not have to worship Zeus, Minerva, or some other clearly defined pagan deity in order to disobey this commandment. Anything in my life that takes priority over God becomes an idol. If striving to succeed in my job is the most important thing, that has become an idol, and I have broken the commandment. Another person might be my idol—or an idol might be my own conception of myself.

All but two of the Ten Commandments are expressed in negative form, but the negative form implies the positive. When God says, "You shall have no other gods before me," he implies, "You shall exclusively worship only me." Jesus handled the commandment the same way. On one occasion, Pharisees came to Jesus and asked him the question they always asked rabbis: "Teacher, which is the great commandment in the Law?" Jesus replied by quoting from Deuteronomy: "You shall love the Lord your God with all your heart and with all your soul and with all your mind" (Matt. 22:36–37). This is the positive side of what the first commandment requires.

To keep this commandment, we must strive to see everything from God's point of view. We have to think and act biblically. We must make his moral will our guide and his glory our goal. We must put him first in our thoughts, in our relationships, in our work, in our leisure, and in our recreation. This also means exercising responsible stewardship of all the money, time, and talents he has given us.

2. YOU SHALL NOT MAKE FOR YOURSELF A CARVED IMAGE (EX. 20:4–6)

Though some communions of the church link the second commandment with the first, it is better to take the second commandment separately, since it addresses a related but different issue. The first commandment deals with the object of our worship: we are to worship God and God only. The second commandment deals with *how* we worship God. We are not to worship God by images.

This is a very important matter. When people with a smattering of Christianity worship with the aid of images, they do not believe that they are worshipping another god. They say, "We are worshipping God, the God of the Bible, but we're doing it by means of the images. The images help us to worship." Yet this second commandment takes the matter very seriously, going on to explain why we should not worship God by any images. Why is that? Why is this matter so important?

In *Knowing God*,[2] J. I. Packer makes two good suggestions. First, he says that images dishonor God because they obscure his glory. This is not what the worshipper thinks—the worshipper thinks the image brings out some aspect of God's nature. But God is above any material representation; any physical material is less than God. A representation of God is always less than God, and to that extent God is dishonored by bringing his glory down to a greatly inferior level. Which is exactly what happens later in Exodus when Aaron is prevailed on to make a golden calf. Even if he thought he was making a bull that would represent the strength of God, that golden calf did not do anything of the sort. It greatly dishonored God. Second, Packer points out that these images mislead us. Because of that, they are not only inadequate but also harmful. They harm because they introduce distortions. In the minds of the people, the bull god of Egypt suggested sexual matters, since the bull symbolized potency. This confused thinking actually led to an orgy.

When God says, "You shall not worship me by images," he implies, "You shall worship me rightly." How is that? Jesus explained to the Samaritan woman, "God is spirit, and those who worship him must worship in spirit and truth" (John 4:24). Spirit is immaterial. The Holy Spirit is like the wind (see John 3:8). We cannot see the wind—it blows where it will. We cannot control the wind, touch it, or direct it; we want a god whom we can see and hold, measure and manipulate. Knowing this, God commands that we worship him spiritually and in the truth of his Word.

2. J. I. Packer, *Knowing God* (Downers Grove, IL: InterVarsity Press, 1973), 40–41.

3. YOU SHALL NOT TAKE THE NAME OF THE LORD YOUR GOD IN VAIN (EX. 20:7)

Again, Jesus gave us the positive implication of this commandment, this time in the Lord's Prayer. We are to pray, "Our Father in heaven, hallowed be your name" (Matt. 6:9). God's name is to be honored, not misused, because the name of God represents God. It reveals his character. If we misuse his name, we misrepresent his character and we dishonor him.

In this book we have already looked at some of the names of God. We studied the great name Jehovah, revealed at the burning bush to show God's self-existence, self-sufficiency, and eternal nature— he always has been and always will be. All this is wrapped up in the name of Jehovah. But there are other names: Jehovah Rapha, "the LORD who heals," for God heals and sustains his people, healing us from sin and its ravages; Jehovah Nissi, "the LORD my Banner," the standard around which we rally; Adonai, "Lord"; El Elyon, "the Most High God"; El Shaddai, "God Almighty"; and Jehovah Jireh, "the God who provides." We know God as Father, Son, and Holy Spirit, the Alpha and the Omega, the First and the Last, the Ancient of Days, the Almighty King, the Creator. Jesus' names and titles also demand that we honor him as God: he is the Word, the Light of the World, Immanuel, the Suffering Servant, the Lamb of God, the True Bread, the Living Water, the Resurrection and the Life, the Way, the Truth, the Good Shepherd, the Judge of all. The Holy Spirit is the Spirit of Truth, our Advocate, the Comforter.

When we receive the names of God that are given to us in the Bible, begin to understand them, and respond to them appropriately, we honor God and bring to him—Father, Son and Holy Spirit—our acceptable worship, which is worship in spirit and in truth.

4. REMEMBER THE SABBATH DAY, TO KEEP IT HOLY (EX. 20:8-11)

Christians generally agree on what the first three commandments require, although we fail to keep them. But there is no longer full agreement on what the fourth commandment actually requires. Here the seventh day is prescribed as a day of Sabbath rest, yet the majority of Christians do not observe that seventh-day Sabbath. We worship on the first day of the week instead, and we worship differently—not the way that is prescribed in other places in the law.

Christians hold three different views of the Sabbath. Seventh-day Adventists, and some others, believe that we are to do exactly what the fourth commandment says: worship on Saturday, the Sabbath day. A second view, one held by the Puritans and stated in the Westminster Confession of Faith, considers Sunday the New Testament counterpart to the Old Testament Sabbath. According to this view, we should observe Sunday as the Lord's Day, but in the same way that the Jews observed Saturday—that is, with no work.

The third view, which I believe is correct, is that the Christian Sabbath (Sunday) is a new day given to us in a new dispensation under the new covenant, to be observed in a new and different way. This was the view of John Calvin. If we turn to the New Testament to see how the Lord's Day was observed, we find that it was not observed with the keeping of the Old Testament regulations. Instead the Lord's Day was a day of joyous activity for the Christians, a day for worship and spiritual refreshment, for witness, and for activities of service and ministry to others.

We cannot treat this issue lightly, because in the Ten Command-ments the Sabbath day prescription is not just declared, but is also elaborated in several verses, similar to the extended treatment of the second commandment. This is also the first commandment stated positively. Obviously God thinks that this issue is important. However we regard the Sabbath, do we observe it in a serious way? Going to church is a good starting point. But do we actually use the Sabbath in a way that glorifies God? Do we put aside the activities which take up the other six days in order to worship God and serve his people? If God takes the Sabbath seriously—and he does—we should as well.

5. HONOR YOUR FATHER AND YOUR MOTHER (EX. 20:12)

As mentioned, the second table of the law has to do with how we respect and treat other people. When Jesus was asked to name the great-est commandment, he gave the Pharisees a second great commandment as well: "You shall love your neighbor as yourself" (Matt. 22:39).

He said that, together, these commandments sum up the Law and the Prophets. The first four commandments tell us how to love God with all our hearts, souls, and minds. Beginning with the fifth commandment, we are told how to love our neighbors as ourselves—and this starts with the family, with honoring our fathers and our mothers. The family is the smallest but most important unit in society. Where the family stands, the culture stands; where the family breaks down, the culture breaks down.

This is also the second of the two positively expressed commands, and, as Paul reminds us in Ephesians 6:2, it is also the first commandment with a promise: "Honor your father and your mother, that your days may be long in the land that the LORD your God is giving you" (20:12). God takes this command seriously enough to affix a promise to it.

6. YOU SHALL NOT MURDER (EX. 20:13)

As the result of an unfortunate translation, many people have understood this commandment to forbid killing in any form. It is obvious, however, that the Israelites themselves did not think they were prohibited from killing: they went to war at God's command and killed their enemies, had capital punishment for a large variety of offenses, and killed animals in sacrifices. So although the Hebrew verb is translated as "kill" in many English translations, it actually means "murder" and is also translated as "assassinate" or "slay." Thus the NIV was correct in translating the command, "You shall not murder."

If you are thinking, "I haven't murdered anybody," remember that Jesus tells us that murder involves the attitude of the heart as well. In the Sermon on the Mount, Jesus said that anyone who uses a term of contempt for his brother has committed a serious crime (see Matt. 5:22). Calling your brother a fool, slandering his name and character, is murder in the eyes of God.

When we understand the sixth commandment, we understand that God regards the way in which we act and think about other people as of the greatest importance. We murder others when we gossip, bear grudges, slander, lose our temper, neglect those whom we ought to honor, show spite, exhibit jealousy. Each of these attitudes or acts breaks the law of God.

7. YOU SHALL NOT COMMIT ADULTERY (EX. 20:14)

In his Sermon on the Mount, Jesus touched on the seventh commandment as well, saying that even a lustful look amounts to adultery in one's heart (see Matt. 5:27–28). There is probably no point at which the Ten Commandments come into more direct opposition to the values of our culture than here. Many people steal. A lot of people dishonor their fathers and mothers. Other people lie. These sins are quite common, but we do not say that such behaviors are excusable or right. But our Western culture has decided that any restrictions on any kind of sexual conduct are unjust, harmful to our psychological health, and evidence of a desire to interfere with another's personal freedom and civil rights. The results of the abandonment of the biblical standard for sexual expression are all too obvious. Sexual license is reaping tragic consequences for individuals and for our culture.

8. YOU SHALL NOT STEAL (EX. 20:15)

Almost any law code tells us not to steal; the Bible tells us why. God has given us everything that we have, and he has given our neighbors everything that they have. Therefore, to steal from our neighbors is to doubt God's ability to provide what we need and to resent his provision for our neighbor. We are saying that we know better than God how he should provide and distribute his gifts.

How do we steal? We steal when we take what is not lawfully or ethically ours to take, not just by breaking into someone's house to take his or her possessions. We steal from an employer when we waste time or do not produce the best work of which we are capable. We steal when we waste our employer's raw products. If we run a business, we steal when we overcharge for our products just because the market will bear it, or if we sell an inferior product at normal cost. We steal when we do not repay a loan, or when we repay it late. We steal from the government when we cheat on our taxes. We steal from God when we fail to worship him as we ought, robbing him of the honor and the glory which belongs to him alone.

What is the positive side of this commandment? We ought to do everything that we can to help other people and to protect their possessions. Jesus expressed it in the Golden Rule: "In everything, do to others what you would have them do to you" (Matt. 7:12 NIV).

9. YOU SHALL NOT BEAR FALSE WITNESS AGAINST YOUR NEIGHBOR (EX. 20:16)

The ninth commandment uses legal language having to do with testimony in a court of law. But it goes beyond that. The ninth commandment requires us to tell the truth at all times. Jesus said we are to let our "yes" be "yes" and our "no" be "no" (see Matt. 5:37). The ninth commandment forbids all forms of slander, gossip, idle talk, and deliberate exaggerations or distortions of the truth.

The Bible tells us to put off lies and to be truthful instead (see Eph. 4:25). That is not easy. In fact, this is one of the hardest of all the commandments. Some of the others are clear: we know what we should and should not do. But telling the truth is hard for several reasons. In some situations, telling a lie or at least modifying the truth seems almost necessary—the truth might hurt another person. In other situations, telling the truth seems almost impossible. Corrie ten Boom, in her account of life in Holland and then in a concentration camp during World War II, describes how the Nazis were forcefully conscripting young Dutchmen into the German army. When Nazi soldiers began scouring their neighborhood in Haarlem, searching for anyone they might have missed, Corrie and several cousins quickly got two young men through a trap door into an enlarged potato cellar, covered the trap door with a rug, and pulled the dining table onto the rug. The Nazis stormed into the house, demanding to know the location of any young men in the family. Corrie's niece, taught from the Bible to always tell the truth, blurted out, "They are under the table!" In the mercy of God, the Nazi officer did not believe this seemingly too honest admission, barely looked under the low-hanging tablecloth, and soon left the house with his men. For the moment the young men were safe—though Corrie and her family debated hotly that evening the principle of "always telling the truth."[3] Most of us, however, do

---

3. See Corrie ten Boom, with John and Elizabeth Sherrill, *The Hiding Place* (Carmel, NY: Guidepost Associates: 1971), 86–88.

not have to face such wrenching and difficult decisions in the area of maintaining truthfulness. "Speaking the truth in love" should be the guide to our speech (Eph. 4:15).

There is also the problem of knowing how to separate truth from falsehood in many "gray situations." We have whole systems of law to sift out the truth from conflicting evidence given in court, where we are admonished to tell the truth, the whole truth, and nothing but the truth. Often cross-examination is required to bring the truth into the light.

How are we to tell the truth? We have to fill our heads with the Bible's teaching, because the Bible is the only source of absolute truth. We must focus our hearts and minds on God and his glory, and we must love Jesus Christ, because that is the antidote to selfishness, which is the very heart of sin. If your mind is focused on yourself, you are going to distort the truth to your own advantage. But if your mind is focused on Jesus Christ, if your goal is the glory of God, and if you are feeding on the Scriptures, then you will be growing in this difficult area, learning to speak and act according to the truth as Jesus Christ himself did.

10. YOU SHALL NOT COVET (EX. 20:17)

The tenth commandment is perhaps the most revealing and most devastating of all the commandments, because it has to do with the inner attitude of the heart. As we have seen, Jesus took commandments that on the surface seemed to deal with concrete actions and related them to the underlying attitude of the heart. Coveting is about attitude from the beginning.

This commandment strikes at the heart of our materialist Western culture. Mass marketing today is meant to make us dissatisfied with what we have and covetous of what we do not have. We should understand that when God tells us not to covet, he does not mean that we are not to improve our lot in life. He does not mean that we are not to work hard or enjoy the things and relationships we have. We covet when we are dissatisfied with what we have because somebody else has more. We covet when we want what another person has, including another person's husband or wife, and are willing to do whatever it takes to get that object, position, honor, or person. We are not to do this, but instead are to set our minds "on things that are above, not on things that are on earth" (Col. 3:2).

LEARNING FROM EXODUS 19–20

We cannot study the moral law without being awakened to our sin. We cannot read one commandment and say, "Well, I kept that one," because we have broken each and every one of them.

But as well as revealing to us the extent and seriousness of our failure, the law also points us to Jesus Christ the Savior. At the same time that God gave the moral law on Mount Sinai, he also gave the ceremonial law, which centered on instructions for building the tabernacle. Everything in the tabernacle pointed to what Jesus Christ would do when he came to be our Savior. God was saying, "This is the law. You have to live by this. But if you do not live by it—and I know you won't—what you need is a Savior."

The law sets forth the perfect standard of holiness, revealed by our righteous God. But the law was only kept perfectly by Jesus Christ. If we try to keep the law in our own strength, we can only fail. The law is powerless to make us righteous. In Romans 8 Paul states emphatically what the law does do, which is to convince us beyond argument of our desperate need of a Savior: "For God has done what the law, weakened by the flesh, could not do. By sending his own Son in the likeness of sinful flesh and for sin, he condemned sin in the flesh, in order that the righteous requirement of the law might be fulfilled in us" (Rom. 8:3–4).

Ask yourself, "What has this study revealed to me about my sin? Has it pointed me to Jesus Christ? Am I looking to him as the one who has fulfilled all the righteous requirements of the law in my place? Am I trusting in him as my Savior? Am I looking to him for forgiveness and cleansing? Is it my desire to be holy even as God is holy? Are there changes in my life that I need to make?"

12

THE CIVIL LAW OF ISRAEL

Exodus 21–24

DOING JUSTICE TO EXODUS

Quite a few years ago, when I had finished preaching on Genesis for about eight years, I thought it might be good to continue on to the book of Exodus. I did not do that, however, because of the chapters we have now reached. The first half of Exodus is a story, and it is always easy to teach stories. We know about the exodus and God's power, the plagues, the destruction of the Egyptians, God's leading the people through the wilderness—and we even know something of the giving of the law at Sinai, which begins with the giving of the Ten Commandments.

But when we move on from there, we begin to deal with the civil law, and then the ceremonial law, of Israel. From most people's point of view, things bog down at that point. But unless we intend to act with a complete lack of integrity and just pull out the story part of Exodus, we have to deal with the law. And in dealing with it, we will find this part of the book of Exodus helpful and worth meditating on today.

HOW MUCH OF THE LAW DO WE OBSERVE TODAY?

The laws following the Ten Commandments, recorded in Exodus 21–23, have to do with the new nation of Israel and how it was to be administered, as well as with criminal acts and how they were to be punished. For this reason, we call these statutes the civil law, but we see that the Israelites called these chapters—including Exodus 20:1–17 (the Ten Commandments)—the Book of the Covenant (see 24:7). This section concludes with the confirmation of the covenant.

The three types of law—moral, civil, and ceremonial—are found throughout the Old Testament, and this raises a question: How much of the Old Testament law is to be observed today?

Some of us do not take the law seriously at all. That is not to our credit. On the one hand, if we begin to think seriously about the law, we do see some difficulties. Much of the Old Testament law has to do with sacrifices; we cannot imagine ourselves offering sacrifices today. Much of it has to do with penalties for crimes; we cannot imagine capital punishment for sorcery, blasphemy, homosexuality, and so on. But on the other hand, this is the law of God—given on Sinai by God himself. Who are we to obey some of the laws and ignore others? There are, generally speaking, three different responses to this problem.

THE TRADITIONAL VIEW

The traditional view of the law distinguishes between the three categories of law, giving a different answer for each case.

Moral law. Because the moral law flows from the character of God, the traditional view states that the moral law is binding on us. After all, the character of God never changes. Since we are made in the image of God, we should obey a law consistent with his character.

It has also been pointed out—I think rightly—that the moral law is the very basis for civilization. If the moral law is disregarded, civilization breaks down. Incidentally, this is why law codes that are not necessarily connected with the Judeo-Christian tradition often include the same respect for life, property, truthfulness, and so on.

Civil law. The traditional view holds that we are not to apply the civil law today, because it was given to Israel, and Israel was a unique state—a *theocracy*, a state ruled by God. There has never been another such theocracy. No other nation in earth's history can claim to be ruled directly by God. There is nothing wrong with each country establishing its own laws; that is exactly the way in which civil government should function.

Ceremonial law. The traditional view says that the ceremonial law was meant to point forward to Jesus Christ, and he has now fulfilled it completely. Thus it would be ludicrous to perform sacrifices and build a tabernacle, and so we do not keep the ceremonial law today.

DISPENSATIONALISM

Dispensationalists make a strong contrast between a dispensation of law (the Old Testament) and a dispensation of grace (the New Testament). The argument goes like this: Today we live under grace, not under law (see Rom. 6:15). We have been freed from the law, and therefore we are not required to obey the moral, civil, or ceremonial law. We are not even bound by the Ten Commandments. A classic text of dispensationalism is Galatians 5:1: "For freedom Christ has set us free; stand firm therefore, and do not submit again to a yoke of slavery."

We must question whether the dispensationalist interpretation is what Paul meant in this verse. We must ask dispensationalists, "Does this mean that Christians are free to steal, lie, commit adultery, and do all the terrible things that are forbidden by the law?" Paul himself asked and answered this very question: "Are we to continue in sin that grace may abound? By no means! How can we who died to sin still live in it?" (Rom. 6:1–2).

Dispensationalists agree that Christians are not to do these things. They argue that when people become Christians, passing from being under the law to being under grace, they are given the character of Jesus Christ and have the life of Jesus Christ within them. This means that they will begin to live like Jesus Christ—not because of a principle of law, but because they want to behave like Jesus.

Dispensationalists also point out that, although we are not under the Old Testament law, the moral laws of the Old Testament are all repeated in one form or another in the New Testament. The one exception is the law of the Sabbath, and they say there is a good reason for that: we are given the Lord's Day instead.

RECONSTRUCTIONISM

A new movement has arisen that is the exact opposite of dispensationalism. While dispensationalists stress that Christians are free from all three types of Old Testament law, except for the moral law reiterated in the New Testament, the reconstruction, or theonomy,[1] movement insists that the entire law is binding—and not only on Christians. Reconstructionists believe that the law is binding on all people and secular governments, simply because it is the law of God. So the government of the United States is morally obligated—whether it understands it or not—to uphold the civil laws that we will discuss in this chapter.

The father of this movement was Rousas Rushdoony, who wrote the important reconstructionist text, *Institutes of Biblical Law* (1973). Men such as Greg Bahnsen and Gary North became his disciples. Although all three were Calvinists, the vast majority of Calvinists do not agree with their view. Strikingly, however, reconstructionism struck a chord with some evangelicals and even leading charismatics such as television host Pat Robertson. Reconstructionism intrigues these people because they are concerned with recapturing American culture and returning it to a moral base.

Implications. In his book *Theonomy in Christian Ethics*, Bahnsen wrote, "*Every* single stroke of the law must be seen by the Christian as applicable to *this* very age between the advents of Christ."[2] Reconstructionists want to reconstruct society according to the law—hence the name of their movement.

This would mean doing away with democracy. Theocracy is not a democracy—it is rule by God, not by the people. Reconstruction would also mean reinstituting the death penalty for a long list of

---

1. Which literally means "the law of God."
2. Greg L. Bahnsen, *Theonomy in Christian Ethics* (Nutley, NJ: The Craig Press, 1979), 82. By "advents of Christ," Bahnsen means Jesus' first and second coming.

crimes, including witchcraft, Sabbath breaking, apostasy, blasphemy, adultery, homosexuality, rape, incest, and even cases of proven, persistent incorrigibility in children. Reconstructionists say that it is the state's duty to enforce these punishments.

Reconstructionists do not propose overthrowing secular governments in order to establish a Christian state by force; they are not revolutionaries. Instead, they expect that as the gospel is preached, this change will happen eventually by choice. In terms of eschatology, they are postmillennialists. They believe that the millennium, the golden age of Christ's rule on earth, will come gradually through the proclamation of the gospel until the world is Christianized. When that happens, secular states will become Christian states that observe these laws. At the end of the millennium, the Lord Jesus Christ will return.

WHAT THE THREE VIEWS HAVE IN COMMON

When I consider the three views, I believe that the traditional view—the oldest of the three—remains the best way to understand the place of the law for Christians. It recognizes the continuance of the covenant in both the Old and New Testaments, while at the same time marks the distinctions that came with Christ's sacrificial work. Can there still be some agreement among the three views? We see a measure of agreement on two points. First, all agree that the ceremonial law has been fulfilled in Jesus Christ. Second, all agree that the moral law applies today in some way, although each view has a different interpretation of how.

But what about the civil law?

THE BOOK OF THE COVENANT

The civil law is the real area of difficulty for us, but it is not hopeless. Whether or not the civil law applies to secular governments,[3] this group of statutes contains within it principles for recognizing basic human rights and for justice based on those rights. This particular category

---

3. I for one do not believe that it does. I think it is not only foolish and impossible but also unbiblical to treat governments today as though they are like ancient Israel.

of the law has principles that we can indeed apply today. Perhaps we can even urge the practice of some of these principles on our secular government. And even if we cannot promote these commands in civil practice, what do they have to say about the way we conduct the affairs of the church? After all, the church is where we are to model righteousness and correct relationships with one another. This is how we need to approach the laws that we find in the Book of the Covenant.

HEBREW SLAVES[4]

It bothers some people that the Bible does not denounce slavery as a terrible evil. Slavery was a fact of life in ancient times; it was the way that economies operated.[5] We should remember that principles in the Old Testament law and particularly in New Testament Christianity eventually led to the abolition of slavery. Exodus lays the basis for radical social reform.

As we look at what Exodus says, one thing we notice is that there was no such thing as the permanent, involuntary servitude of one Israelite to another. A person could become a slave in various ways, mostly through debt, but the period of slavery was not to continue indefinitely. The very first law decreed that a Hebrew slave was to serve for six years and then go free in the seventh (see 21:2). If we inquire into Deuteronomy on the same subject, we find that the master of the freed slave was to provide him with a share of the flock and with some of the produce of the threshing floor and the winepress (see Deut. 15:12–15). In other words, the servant was not to go out empty handed. He was provided for so that he would not fall back into slavery once again.

We also notice that respect is given to the family, even to the family of a slave (see Ex. 21:3–4). If a slave had a wife when he entered the service of his master, he had the right to take her with him when he was set free. If he had been given a wife by his master, the wife

---

4. The people whom the NIV calls "Hebrew servants" were literally "Hebrew slaves."

5. We should keep two points in mind lest we get self-righteous about slavery. First, the United States ended legal slavery less than two hundred years ago. Second, the ancient economy ran on a slave base, while our economy runs on the borrowing and loaning of money and interest—which was forbidden in the Old Testament (see, for instance, Lev. 25:35–37; Deut. 23:19–20).

remained the owner's but had to be set free when her time of servitude was completed. This was far different from the cruel and unjust way that slave families were treated in our own country, where they were broken up at random. Here we see a more humane practice.

A striking element in this set of laws is that the slave had the right to choose permanent slavery if he wished (see 21:5–6). This suggests that, in that economy, slavery was not the worst of all possible options. At any rate, this law preserves the right of the slave to determine his own destiny.

Another provision protects the rights of a daughter who is sold as a servant—particularly her rights to a husband and a home (see 21:7–11). She could not be trifled with. If she had been purchased to be the wife of the master's son, she was to be given the rights that she would have had if she were the master's own daughter.

The Israelites had to deal with the reality of slavery. These laws recognized that slaves were people made in God's image and, therefore, ought to be treated with dignity and respect. This was an enormous step forward from anything that had transpired in the laws of other nations at the time.

PERSONAL INJURY

The next section of the law deals with personal injuries: homicide; physical injuries such as being kidnapped, maimed, or even hurt by words; and injuries caused by animals.

The first part of this section makes a distinction between murder, which is intentional, and manslaughter, which is accidental killing without malice or premeditation (see 21:12–14). According to the Old Testament, murderers were to be put to death. This is not because the Bible treats life lightly. Quite the opposite—*we* treat life lightly. The Bible treats life with deep respect because people are made in the image of God. If someone killed another, he must be killed. Murder, taking the life of a human being, is destroying what the Creator has made in his own image. It is an act deserving the most serious consequence, which is death.

Although no specific legal penalty is given in cases of manslaughter, a person who killed another by accident was still subject to the law of retaliation. In the ancient Near East, it seems it was commonly the duty of a relative to kill the one who had killed a member of his family. The Old Testament provides asylum for people who found themselves in that situation. When the Israelites entered the promised land, they set aside six cities called cities of refuge, three on one side of the Jordan and three on the other. Anyone who committed manslaughter, accidentally killing another, could run to one of those cities and be safe. Once he was there, the elders of that city would conduct a trial. If, after proper inquiry, the death was discovered to be intentional, the murderer was to be put to death, no longer protected in the city of refuge.

The second section deals with physical injuries (see 21:15–27). Significantly, there is no distinction between the various classes of society. Unlike other ancient law codes, this code called for everybody to be treated alike. Individuals were protected, and the rights of individuals were acknowledged, even if the individuals were slaves.

A third section covers injuries caused by animals (see 21:28–36). Here negligence plays an important part. If an animal killed somebody, it made all the difference whether that animal had been known to be dangerous and thus whether anything had been done to protect others. If an animal was cantankerous and killed someone, the animal would be put to death. If the owner had known that there was a problem and been negligent in letting the animal out of the pen, then the owner could be put to death. However, the owner could redeem his life back. For example, the owner of an ox who had killed someone could redeem his own life by paying an agreed upon sum of money. This was a way of paying indemnity.

PERSONAL PROPERTY

The third section of the civil law relates to theft, dishonesty, and damage to personal property (see 22:1–15), and it develops the principle of restitution even more strongly. We find that property damage is never considered a crime against the state but instead against the individual whose property is damaged.[6] The principle is that nonviolent

---

6. We have turned this around in our system of government. Today, if you commit a crime, the state prosecutes you as a criminal against the state, leaving the victim out of the picture. There is no restitution; instead, the state puts you in jail. When we put people

offenders should make restitution directly to the victim. If negligence or guilt was involved in property damage, then, depending on the degree of guilt, the person was to repay the victim one for one, two for one, or five to one.

This section distinguishes between losses that occur through negligence and losses that occur by acts of God (as we call them). If you lend someone something, he is obliged to take care of that item. However, if his house was hit by lightning and your property was destroyed inside his house, that would not be the borrower's fault, and he would bear no guilt.

SEXUAL AND CIVIC MORALITY

The fourth section concerns sexual and civic morality (22:16–31) and covers a range of crimes: seduction; sorcery; sexual relations with an animal; worship of a god other than Jehovah; taking advantage of foreigners, widows, orphans, or the poor; blasphemy; and offerings, particularly offerings of the firstborn.

What holds these regulations together? The principle that our behavior toward others is to mirror the treatment we have received from God. For example, the Israelites were not to mistreat foreigners (see 22:21). Why not? Because they themselves had been foreigners in Egypt, mistreated and oppressed, and God had delivered them and treated them well; they had been blessed, so they were to bless other people. They were also to help the poor (see vv. 22–24), because God had delivered them from their poverty and enriched them. They were to offer the firstfruits of their fields and their firstborn sons and animals to God (see vv. 29–30), because God had spared their firstborn when he had struck down the firstborn of the Egyptians.

---

in jail, they don't earn any money, they don't repay their victims, and we have to pay an average of more than thirty thousand dollars a year to keep each one confined.

Chuck Colson traveled around the country as part of his plan for prison reform, speaking in state legislatures about restitution. After addressing the Texas legislature, lawmakers gathered around him to say things like, "That's a tremendous idea. Why hasn't anyone thought of that?" Then he would have the privilege of saying to them, "Read Exodus 22. It is only what God said to Moses on Mount Sinai . . ." (see Charles Colson, "The Kingdom of God and Human Kingdoms," in *Transforming our World: A Call to Action*, ed. James M. Boice [Portland: Multnomah, 1988], 154–55).

When we think of how we ought to act toward other people, we first have to ask ourselves: How has God acted toward me? Has God been good to me? Yes, he has. Has he retaliated against me? Has he returned tit for tat? Has he been unmerciful? No, he hasn't. We were nothing, and he was merciful. We were poor, and he made us rich in Jesus Christ. That is the way we should treat other people. As Jesus urged his followers, "Be merciful, even as your Father is merciful" (Luke 6:36).

The important last verse—"You are to be my holy people" (22:31 NIV)—is repeated four times in Leviticus and also in 1 Peter 1:16, and affirms the ultimate standard for our public and private interactions: "Be holy, because I am holy" (NIV).

SABBATHS AND FESTIVALS

Chapter 23:1–9 outlines laws concerning justice in the courts. Bribes were common in the ancient Near East; these pervert justice and should be rejected. All the other statements in Exodus 23 have to do with laws concerning the Sabbath and Jewish festivals.

The Sabbath laws and festivals described in Exodus 23:10–19 might seem to belong with the ceremonial law. They do, and accordingly they are repeated later. However, they are also included here because they concern justice for the land, for animals, and even for God.

When it came to the Sabbath rest, God was not just concerned about the people. The weekly Sabbath allowed their oxen and donkeys to rest as well. And the Sabbath wasn't just for the Israelites; under these prescriptions, the slaves and aliens were also to rest and be refreshed.

And just as a slave was not to be worked without any hope of eventual release, so the land was not to be worked without a break. It was to be given a yearlong sabbath rest every seven years in order to recover its vitality. This is a good way to farm, but people did not follow it. They milked the land for all it was worth and impoverished it. Second Chronicles 36:21 implies that the seventy years of the Babylonian captivity were to make up for the sabbath years that the people had not given their land. God took this command seriously.

These laws looked ahead to the later possession of the land. When they were given to Moses, the people were still in the wilderness. They did not have land to let rest for a sabbath year. These laws were for the future, which is why they also include the Feast of Unleavened Bread, the Feast of Harvest, and the Feast of Ingathering.

The very last of these laws is the most puzzling: "You shall not boil a young goat in its mother's milk" (23:19). Scholars have many opinions about the reason for this prohibition. The general wisdom today is that boiling sacrificial goats in their mothers' milk was a common ritualistic practice of the Canaanites. Its religious function meant that the Israelites were not to repeat that practice, and thus participate in a pagan ritual. Today Orthodox Jews do not serve meat and milk-based dishes at the same meal, being careful to maintain that Old Testament mandated separation.

CONFIRMING THE COVENANT

Chapter 24 presents God's promise to be with the people in the conquest yet to come. It also reports how the offering of sacrifices and the sprinkling of blood ratified the covenant between God and the people. During this occasion, Moses read the law, which he had written down overnight. And the people said that they would obey in everything (see v. 7). At the time they meant it, but too soon they failed. We are the same way. You and I say that we will obey, but we do not. Knowing the law does not enable us to keep the law. That is why we need the grace of God.

Then Moses, Aaron, the two sons of Aaron—Nadab and Abihu—and seventy elders of Israel went up into the mountain. There "they saw the God of Israel" (24:10). In a glorious vision, they saw a sea of glass like sapphire, clear as the sky. It must have been an amazing moment for them. They had been given the law, although they did not understand it very well. That would take years of putting it into practice. But on this day they might have said to themselves, "We have had this marvelous vision of the glory of God, and that's going to keep us going all our lives."

Actually it didn't. It didn't at all.

They did not see the face of God, and neither did Moses. But that is what we will do one day, when "we shall be like him, because we shall see him as he is" (1 John 3:2).

13

THE CEREMONIAL LAW

Exodus 25—31

THE GREAT LAWGIVER

The book of Exodus falls into two main parts. The first part—chapters 1–15—which gives the book its name, has to do with the exodus itself. The second part—chapters 16–40—deals with the early months of the people's desert wandering, during which God gave them three types of law: the moral law, embodied in the Ten Commandments; the civil law, having to do with their civil government; and the ceremonial law. The presentation of each of these three areas gets progressively longer. The Ten Commandments themselves occupy only a chapter; even adding the introductory and concluding material only expands this section to two chapters (19 and 20). The civil law, as it appears in Exodus, takes four chapters; it is also developed in Leviticus at greater length. The details of the ceremonial law begin in chapter 25 and continue to the end of the book (chapter 40).

The ceremonial law falls into two parts. Much of it consists of instructions for building the tabernacle—the wilderness worship center of the people—and providing its furnishings. But even this part falls into two sub-sections. The first tells the people what they are to do, and the second simply says that they did it. After a section explaining how the tabernacle is to be built and the furnishings arranged, there are three chapters relating the incident of the golden calf and Moses' intercession for the people. Finally, a second section tells how the people built the tabernacle and its furnishings. In Exodus 40, the last chapter of the book, there is an account of the people's setting up the tabernacle and dedicating it. If we look at commentaries, we will find that they deal extensively with Exodus up to chapter 34, but quickly pass over the remainder, where the material is mostly repetitive.

An outline of the latter half of Exodus looks like this:

+ Instructions for constructing the tabernacle (chapters 25–31)
+ The story of the incident involving the golden calf and the intercession of Moses afterward (chapters 32–34)
+ An account of the actual making of the tabernacle (chapters 35–39)
+ An account of the setting up of the tabernacle and God's approval (chapter 40)

In this chapter, we will study the nature and appearance of the tabernacle itself. There are four different names used to identify the tabernacle in Scripture. Each teaches something important about its function.

1. *Sanctuary* (see Ex. 25:8). A sanctuary is a holy place. What made the tabernacle holy? The presence of God. The tabernacle was sanctified by God's presence.
2. *Tabernacle* (see Ex. 25:9; 26:1). A tabernacle is a dwelling place or a place of settling down, and this refers to the fact that God settled down among his people. We will see how the apostle John references this aspect of the tabernacle in his gospel (see John 1:14).
3. *Tent of Meeting* (see Ex. 29:42). The tabernacle was the place where the people presented themselves before God and where God met with them. (This tent of meeting is not to be confused with the earlier Tent of Meeting set up outside the camp where Moses met with God before the tabernacle had been constructed [see 33:7–11])
4. *Tent (or Tabernacle) of the Testimony* (see Num. 9:15). *The Testimony* refers to the stone tables of the law. The tabernacle was the place where the tables of the law were kept, the law

which made clear the righteous standard required for those who would come into God's presence in worship.

In studying the Bible, we have to be very careful about giving symbolic meanings to objects or events, because it is easy to get carried away. Especially in devotional books or commentaries from a generation or two ago, we see that people found all kinds of secret meanings. That may be an interesting exercise, but whenever we read interpretations into a passage without any biblical verification, we are prone to error.

In the case of the tabernacle, however, we have a great deal of guidance. This portable structure was obviously symbolic and pointed forward to the coming of Jesus Christ, and therefore we are not surprised that when we come to the New Testament we find each aspect interpreted, especially in the book of Hebrews. There we learn what the sacrifices were all about, and we understand how the ark was to function and how its functioning pointed forward to the coming of Jesus Christ. When we look at the tabernacle and its furnishings within that context, it is easy to see that every object in one way or another was meant to point forward to the coming of Jesus Christ and the work he would do for our salvation. Along with that, of course, goes our relationship to him in the way we approach him through his sacrifice and through the confession of sin and prayer. So this tabernacle, which was given to the people with its furnishings, actually illustrates the most profound spiritual truths. We must be careful not to read in more than is justified by the Bible, but the Bible tells us again and again that the whole and the parts of the tabernacle and the instructions for right worship all point to Jesus Christ.

THE ARK OF THE COVENANT

In chapter 25 God commands the people to bring offerings of gold, silver, bronze, and other materials, out of which they will make the frame and appointments for the tabernacle. Next, there are instructions on how to make the *ark*—a golden chest that was the sole piece of furniture within the tabernacle's Most Holy Place.

Now that is not where we would start, is it? We would describe the tabernacle the way it would appear to those approaching it: "The tabernacle is a great big enclosure sitting in the desert, closed off by curtains. You go inside the curtains, and there is a building within the enclosure. That tent-like structure has two parts; in the outer part there is some furniture, and when you go into the inner part, that is where the ark is." The ark, placed in the innermost chamber, would be the very last thing to mention. Yet in Exodus, the ark is the first thing to be described, and for a perfectly good reason: the ark symbolized the presence of God, so by very definition it was at the heart of the tabernacle. Everything else was built around the ark. The building that surrounded the ark was there to house the ark, and the curtains that surrounded the building were to encircle the building that housed the ark, and so on. This immediately brings to our attention that the order in these chapters of Exodus is a theological order.

The ark was made of acacia wood—a hard, dense wood that was well suited to resist the rigors of the desert. It was about four feet long and about two feet wide and deep. We cannot be more precise because the measurement is given in cubits, and cubits differed in length, depending on whether they were Egyptian cubits or Babylonian cubits. The best guess is given in both the New International Version and the English Standard Version, which give the ark's dimensions as three and three-quarters feet long and two and one-quarter feet wide and deep. It had rings at each corner, with long poles to put through the rings. The priests carried the ark by means of these poles when the people were on the march. (They covered the ark so it could not be seen.)

The wood of the ark was covered with gold inside and out, and it had a lid made out of pure gold. There were two figures of cherubim—a kind of angel—one on each end of the lid, also made out of gold and facing inward. They had wings that came together over the top of the ark, almost touching. In the space between their outstretched wings, God promised that the glory of his presence would dwell, and there he would meet with the representative of his people (see Ex. 25:22).

The ark contained a number of items. First and most important, it contained the stone tablets on which God had inscribed the Ten Commandments. But it also held a gold jar that contained a sample of the manna the people had collected during their years in the wilderness.

It also contained Aaron's rod that had budded, as we learn in Hebrews (see Heb. 9:1–5 for a description of the temple furniture).

Because it contained the law, the ark was given different names. It was called the *ark of the testimony*, referring to the law; the *ark of the covenant*, meaning the covenant that God had established on the basis of the law; or simply the *ark of God* or the *ark of the Lord Jehovah*.

In order to understand how the ark functioned and what it was meant to teach, we must understand two important things. The first I have already mentioned: namely, that God was understood to dwell between the wings of the cherubim. This does not mean that the Hebrew people thought God could be confined within a little space between the wings of the angels. They knew perfectly well that God is immaterial, a spirit, and that they were to worship him in spirit and in truth. Furthermore, God is omnipresent and not to be confined in any one place. He is the Lord, the Creator and Sustainer of the entire universe. Nevertheless, God taught by this ark and his immanent presence there that he—the great transcendent, immaterial God of the universe—condescended to dwell among his people. So when the ark was consecrated, the *shekinah*, a glorious cloud that represented the presence of God, came over the tabernacle and descended upon it (see Exodus 40). God was hidden in the cloud yet present with his people.

Second, we need to understand that the gold lid, which was called the mercy seat, was the place where the high priest brought the blood of the animal that had been killed in the courtyard once a year on the Day of Atonement. First, the priest had to make an offering for his own sin; then he brought the blood from the sacrificed animal and sprinkled it on the mercy seat. The blood attested to the death of the animal in the place of the death of the guilty. On the Day of Atonement the blood covered the sins of the entire nation.

Imagine the ark, containing the law. Above its lid is the manifestation of the presence of the holy God. God is looking down, and as he looks down, what does he see? He sees the law that everyone has broken. Thus the ark is a great illustration of the necessity of divine judgment on human sin. If we understand this picture at all, we know that we are to be judged for our sin. The holy God of the universe cannot overlook that we have broken his holy law. But once a year, on the Day of Atonement, when the sacrificial animal has been killed and its blood, shed for the people, has been brought into the Most Holy Place and sprinkled upon the mercy seat, God looks down and sees the *testimonium*. He sees the evidence that an innocent life has been taken in the place of the ones who were guilty. Punishment has been meted out on the innocent victim. A substitute has atoned, or borne the punishment, for sin, and the guilty can be declared not guilty. And so the ark teaches the great principle of *substitutionary atonement*, the very essence of the work of Jesus Christ on the cross. When God looks down, he sees that a sacrifice has been made, and he is able justly to be merciful. That is why the ark had a mercy seat. It taught the people again and again that though the broken law requires judgment, God has provided, by the blood of the innocent sacrifice, a way to show his mercy to the guilty sinner.

THE TABLE AND SHOWBREAD

The tabernacle itself was divided into two parts. The smaller of the two rooms was the Holy of Holies or the Most Holy Place, where the ark was kept. The outer room was the Holy Place, and it contained three objects: a table of showbread, a golden lampstand, and an altar of incense. The table and lampstand are described in sequence after the ark. A description of the altar of incense is held for later, for reasons I will explain.

This table of showbread was only slightly smaller than the ark. It was about three feet long, one-and-a-half feet wide, about two-and-one-fourth feet high. At about thirty inches high, it was a little lower than modern tables, probably because the people were shorter than we are today. A gold molding surrounded it, and it was always to hold twelve loaves of bread, as well as golden plates for the bread and golden ladles, bowls, and pitchers for handling the incense and drink offerings.

The loaves of bread were twelve in number because they represented the twelve tribes of Israel, and they were what the Bible calls a *thank offering*. They were a way of saying to God, "We are grateful for your provision for us. You provide us with the bread we eat that sustains our lives. You keep us going. Day by day you give us health. We return this in order to say that we are thankful."

It is hard to think about the showbread without realizing that the bread, too, points to Jesus Christ, who described himself as the Bread of Life. He must have done so on many occasions and perhaps with variety, but he does so most clearly in John 6:32–33: "I say to you, it was not Moses who gave you the bread from heaven, but my Father gives you the true bread from heaven. For the bread of God is he who comes down from heaven and gives life to the world." In that context, when he speaks of himself as the Bread of Life, he is comparing himself to the manna, which was perishable bread that nourished only the physical body. He is claiming that he gives spiritual food, which is imperishable and provides eternal life for the believer.

When we think of the communion bread and compare it to the Old Testament table of showbread and the loaves placed there, we understand that the showbread was not just a thank offering, but pointed forward to Jesus Christ, teaching that we cannot live spiritually, or thrive spiritually, apart from feeding on him, who is the true Bread of Life.

THE GOLDEN LAMPSTAND

The golden lampstand was a beautiful example of a well-known Hebrew religious object: the seven-branched candlestick known as a *menorah*. After the Roman armies overthrew Jerusalem in AD 70, they carried off many sacred objects from the temple. The Arch of Titus in Rome has bas reliefs of what they found—including a carving of a menorah, a later copy of the item used in the tabernacle. It had seven separate lamps, which were to be supplied with olive oil. The priest was to trim these every morning and evening, and they were never allowed to go out.

The obvious practical purpose of the lampstand was to give light to the priests when they went about their work. But it also had a symbolic purpose, and that was to point forward to Jesus Christ, who also described himself in John's gospel as the Light of the World (see John 8:12; 9:5). John himself develops the theme. In the prologue to his gospel, John says, "The true light, which gives light to everyone, was coming into the world" (John 1:9). He may very well have been thinking about the menorah in the Holy Place of the tabernacle, because shortly after that John writes, "And the Word became flesh and dwelt among us" (John 1:14). He is literally saying, "tabernacled among us." Just as the glory of God came down and dwelt within the Most Holy Place in the Hebrew tabernacle, so the Lord Jesus Christ is God coming down—literally but temporarily—to dwell among us in human form. He is the Light of the World.

This imagery appears later in the Bible. At the beginning of the book of Revelation, Jesus appears in a vision to John, and he is standing in the midst of the seven golden lampstands (see Rev. 1:12–13). Here they symbolize the church. Jesus stands in the midst of his church. How can the lampstand symbolize both Jesus and the church? Because when Jesus was on earth, he was the Light of the World. But now we have to be the light of the world. We become the light by reflecting his light to those around us.

THE COURTYARD

The entirety of Exodus 26 is given over to instructions for making the tabernacle itself—that is, the enclosure for the objects—and the largest part of chapter 27 concerns the making of the outer curtains that defined the courtyard in which the tabernacle stood (see vv. 9–19). The outer courtyard was rectangular, measuring approximately a hundred and fifty feet by seventy-five feet—about a quarter of the size of a football field. The curtains that surrounded it were made of finely twisted linen, supported by posts seven-and-a-half feet high. There was one entrance, on the east side.

When you went in that entrance, you came to the tabernacle itself. It too was rectangular, made up of two rooms—the Most Holy Place and the Holy Place. The Most Holy Place was a perfect cube: fifteen feet by fifteen feet by fifteen feet. The outer room was twice as long: thirty feet long, fifteen feet wide, and fifteen feet high. The whole tabernacle was forty-five feet long.

One item here is particularly interesting, and that is the curtain that divided the outer room (the Holy Place) from the inner room (the Most Holy Place) which held the ark where God's presence was understood to dwell. The curtain between the two rooms was made of blue, purple, and scarlet yarn and fine linen and had figures of cherubim worked into it. It shielded the visible presence of God from human eyes and could be passed through only once a year, and even then only by the high priest on the Day of Atonement.

The tabernacle as a whole teaches us that the great, holy, almighty, immaterial, omnipresent God is willing to dwell with his people. But the curtain teaches us that this does not mean that we can treat God with familiar contempt and simply barge in upon his presence. He is the holy God. So the veil shielded his actual presence. Nobody was allowed to pass that veil; if anybody did, he was struck dead immediately.

Now, at the moment when the Lord Jesus Christ died on the cross, the Bible tells us that the veil in the temple was torn in two from top to bottom (see Matt. 27:51, Mark 15:38; Luke 23:45). Only God could have done this. In our sinful state, we are unable to barge in upon God, but now those who have faith in Jesus have found the way into God's presence opened by his death. God is not veiled from us now. He is approachable. We cannot see him, but one day we will. On the basis of Christ's atoning death for us, we can come into his presence. He accepts our worship and hears and answers our prayers.

THE ALTAR FOR BURNT OFFERINGS

Having dealt with most of the furniture within the tabernacle, the description now moves to what was outside in the courtyard, beginning with the altar for burnt offerings (see Ex. 27:1–8). This altar was very large—seven-and-a-half feet long and wide, approximately four-and-a-half feet high—and made of bronze. If it had been made entirely of bronze, they couldn't have carried it. Bronze is heavy. It was probably a shell of bronze filled with earth, and we can speculate that sacrifices would have been made on the earthen part.

When we get into Leviticus, we will talk more about the burnt offerings. Here we need only note that the altar stood immediately inside the single entrance to the tabernacle. If you were approaching the tabernacle and wanted to go inside as the priests could, and approach the Holy Place and the Most Holy Place as the high priest did on the Day of Atonement, the first thing you would come to was the altar. This teaches that the only way any sinful human being can approach Almighty God is by a sacrifice. God takes sin seriously. We deserve to die for our sin (see Rom. 6:23). The only way that we can approach a holy God is by a sacrifice, a death in our place. This is the most important thing that we learn from the altar.

THE PRIESTLY GARMENTS

In Exodus 28 the description of the furniture breaks off, and we have a description of the garments to be worn by the Israelite priests, followed by an account of their consecration. This may seem misplaced. I wrote earlier about another thing that might seem out of order to us— the description of the ark—but we could understand the reasoning for this. Yet we have not heard about the altar of incense or the basin used for purification. Why doesn't Exodus finish up describing the furniture inside the tabernacle before describing the priests and their garments?

There is a perfectly good reason. We just read about the altar of burnt offerings. The priests' chief responsibility was to perform the sacrifices and make the offerings. Moses does not want us to think that all he is doing is reeling off the various items of furniture, things that were found in the courtyard. No, he is saying, "Look, this is important. Stop here and pay attention. This is what the priests did."

The priests, especially the high priest, in order to perform their duties correctly, wore a number of objects, and it is worth looking at them briefly and noting their significance.

First was the *ephod* (see Ex. 28:6–14). It was a two-piece outer vest joined over the shoulders by gold clasps. On these two clasps were two onyx stones, one on each shoulder, and the names of the tribes were inscribed on the stones. Shoulders bear the weight when we carry something. As the high priest interceded for the people, he carried them, or bore them up, before the Lord.

Second was the *breastpiece*. Instead of being armor, which we might think of, this was a folded pouch of cloth attached to the ephod. On it were twelve stones engraved with the names of Israel's tribes. So the priest had two onyx stones on his shoulders, with six names on one stone and six names on the other, and he had twelve stones on his breastpiece, each representing one tribe, with the names inscribed on the stones. In this way the high priest made a double representation for the people. Not only did he bear them up in his prayers before the Lord, but he kept them close to his heart.

This understanding is echoed in Malachi 3:17, where those who fear the Lord are described as the "treasured possession" of God. We are close to the heart of God. Jesus holds us close to his heart, and when we intercede for other people, we do so in both ways. We bear people up before the Lord. We carry their concerns to God. And we bear them up because they are close to our hearts. We care for them, and so we pray in a caring way.

Third are the *Urim* and *Thummim*. Nobody knows exactly what these were or how they were used, because there are very few references to them in the Old Testament. They were contained in a pouch, and they seem to have been used in some way to discern the will of God. Some people think this means they were like lots or dice and that the priest took them out and threw them and got his signal depending on how they landed. Some think they were supernatural and that they began to glow—one if the answer was yes, the other one if the answer was no. But this is all speculation. We do not know how they were used, but we do know that the priest used them to determine the will of God for a particular situation.

Fourth is the *robe* (see Ex. 28:31–35). Although its shape and colors were probably important, its most interesting feature is that it had bells attached to the hem. We do not know of anything else like this in the Old Testament. The bells would have been heard as the priest performed his duties, especially as he went into the Holy Place and the Most Holy Place and as he returned.

One of our great hymns alludes to this feature as it looks forward to the return of Jesus Christ. If you've sung the hymn, you may not have thought of this. Jesus is returning, and the lines read as follows:

Coming! in the opening east
Herald brightness slowly swells;
Coming! O my glorious Priest,
Hear we not thy golden bells?[1]

1. Frances R. Havergal, "Thou Art Coming, O My Savior," 1872.

174

The hymn uses the imagery of the bells, the robe, and Aaron the great high priest to describe the work of Jesus Christ. Jesus has gone ahead of us into the Most Holy Place, bearing the sacrifice of his blood to make full atonement for our sins and to intercede for us before God the Father. When he comes to take us to himself, once again we hear his bells and know that the work of atonement and intercession is completed.

Fifth is the *turban* and its *gold plate*, which bore the engraved words, "Holy to the Lord" (see Ex. 28:36–38). Here is the very essence of Israel's worship. Because God is holy, those who approach him must be holy too. Only "he who has clean hands and a pure heart" may come before God (Ps. 24:4 NKJV), for "without holiness no one will see the Lord" (Heb. 12:14 NIV).

Now none of us is holy in himself or herself, of course. That is why we need atonement. But once the atonement is made for us, we are cleansed by Jesus Christ. There is a wonderful picture of this reality in Zechariah 3. A man named Joshua, the high priest at the time (not to be confused with the second-in-command to Moses), stood in the temple going about his duties, but Satan was there to accuse him. The high priest was supposed to minister, but he had dirty robes and a dirty turban. Satan pointed out that he was a sinful man, and indeed he was. All of us are—ministers and everyone else besides. But God commanded that Joshua's filthy garments be removed, that he be given new rich garments, and that a clean turban be placed on his head. In other words, Joshua was made holy in order to serve the holy God.

Exodus 29 deals with the consecration of the priests in great detail. There was ritual washing, anointing with oil, several sacrifices, and the eating of a sacrificial meal. It took seven days for the priests to be prepared for service before the Lord.

THE ALTAR OF INCENSE

At this point Exodus goes back to describing the furniture, starting with the altar of incense (see Ex. 30:1–10). This may seem misplaced. After all, the description of the furniture was broken by discussion of the priests. Now we have gone back to talking about the furniture. Not only that, but the altar of incense was in the outermost room, the Holy Place. It seems that it should have been discussed when Moses was talking about the table of showbread and the menorah.

Once again, the explanation is that the order is theological. Incense symbolizes the prayers of the saints (see Rev. 5:8). The incense arises to heaven, as our prayers do, and it smells sweet. Our prayers are sweet to God. He wants to hear our prayers. Our prayers are pleasing to him. Even when we stumble around, not quite knowing what to pray about, God desires to hear us pray.

But this order suggests that before we can pray to God and be heard by him, we have to come to him by the way of the sacrifice of the burnt offering. We have to come through faith in Jesus Christ, the perfect sacrifice for sin. This is the meaning of the altar and the sacrifices. God hears us on the basis of the death of Jesus Christ—but not if we come in our own self-righteousness, spurning Jesus Christ. Jesus is God's very Son given for our salvation; he died in our place. If we do not have any use for that, God does not have any use for our prayers. But when we come to God through the way that God himself opened into his presence by the blood of the cross, then God, who is a gracious God, will hear our prayers and answer them as well.

THE WASHBASIN

The final object is the basin for washing. Again, there is a theological order. The symbolism is beautiful. The guilt of the priest was already atoned for by the offering made on the altar for burnt sacrifices, but the problem with sin is that it doesn't bring only guilt. It also brings defilement. Having presented the sacrifices by which their guilt was atoned for or expiated, the priests had to be ceremonially washed so that they might be clean to do their work.

We need this daily cleansing. This is why John the apostle wrote, "If we say that we have no sin, we deceive ourselves, and the truth is not in us" (1 John 1:8 KJV). We all have sin. But John goes on to say, "If we confess our sins, he is faithful and just to forgive us our sins, and to cleanse us from all unrighteousness" (v. 9 KJV). Confession is the Christian way of daily cleansing, symbolized in the Old Testament.

The washbasin concludes the objects.

THE POSTSCRIPT

Exodus 31 gives an interesting postscript to the description of the objects in the tabernacle. It tells us how God provided not only all the instructions for the building of the tabernacle but how he also provided the workmen. Two of the workmen are mentioned here—Bezalel, who seemed to be in charge, and a man named Oholiab, who was his chief assistant. A very important statement is connected with Bezalel. God says, "I have filled him with the Spirit of God, with ability and intelligence, with knowledge and all craftsmanship" (v. 3). What this teaches is that God is concerned with beauty. Artistic talent is from God and can be used in his service and for his glory. God gave Bezalel, with and by the power of the Holy Spirit, the skill, ability, and knowledge to create something not just useful, but beautiful.

This is true of whatever task God puts into our hands. God will give us the Holy Spirit to help us do it well. And he is as ready to help and bless the work of his most obscure and faithful servant as he is to empower and bless those who are in places of prominence. This is the way God works with his people.

LEARNING FROM EXODUS 25–31

Let me summarize by making a couple of points.

GOD IS HOLY

First of all, everything about the structure of the tabernacle was meant to teach the people about the holiness of God. It taught that God, in his mercy, condescends to be with his people and dwell among them. That is important. But above all, it taught the holiness of God. No one could barge into the tabernacle. The people as a whole had to stay outside. The priests could go inside the courtyard, but only certain priests could go inside the Holy Place. And only the high priest could go inside the Most Holy Place, and only once a year on the Day of Atonement (see Heb. 9:6–8). The veils and altars and lavers for washing all taught that God is holy.

"Holy to the Lord" is something that people need to learn today. We have changed, and we do not live in an age that is concerned about holiness. But God has not changed. God is still a holy God.

THERE IS ONLY ONE WAY TO GOD

Second, there is no way to God except by the shed blood of Jesus Christ. All these objects were symbolic, pointing forward to Jesus Christ. He is the Bread of Life. He is the Light of the World. He is the one in whose name we can pray and by whom we have cleansing. But above all, he is the one who gave his life to be our Mediator, our intermediary, pleading for us before the Father.

We need a mediator. We cannot approach God on our own. Jesus Christ is that Mediator, and he is the only Mediator. Paul said this when he wrote to Timothy,

> For there is one God, and there is one mediator between God and men, the man Christ Jesus, who gave himself as a ransom for all, which is the testimony given at the proper time. (1 Tim. 2:5–6)

Jesus used a short parable to teach the only correct way to approach God. The parable is about two men who came to the temple to pray: a Pharisee and a tax collector. The Pharisee was the kind of man of whom everybody would think very highly. He was pious. He was rich. He was influential. When he prayed he thanked God that he was a superior person: "God, I thank you that I am not like other men, extortioners, unjust, adulterers, or even like this tax collector" (Luke 18:11), and everybody agreed with him. He *wasn't* like other men. He was better.

But in Jesus' parable, the tax collector stands at a distance. The story rings true because everybody would say that that was exactly where he should have been—at a distance. Nobody wanted to have any tax collectors around. A lot of Jews would not even stand on the same side of the street with such a man. If they saw a tax collector coming, they crossed over to the other side. "Sinner! Sinner! Don't have anything to do with him."

The tax collector did not pray like the Pharisee. When he prayed, he used a term referring to the mercy seat on the ark of the covenant: "God, be merciful to me, a sinner" (Luke 18:13). The word used for *mercy* is the very Greek word used to describe the covering lid of the ark—*hilaskomai*. Literally, he was pleading, "God, be mercy-seated to me." He was saying, "God I know that you are holy. And I am a sinner, but you have made a way be which even a sinner like me can come into your presence, and that way is by the blood that is placed on the mercy seat. It testifies to the death of an innocent substitute. Another died in my place, and it is because of that substitute's death that I come. That is the way I come."

You know what Jesus said of that man. He said that the tax collector, rather than the self-righteous man who prayed about himself, went home justified before God (see v. 14). Jesus was saying that if you are going to be justified before God, it can only be in the same way as the tax collector.

As long as you come to God saying, "Look at all I've accomplished. I'm a good person. Everybody looks up to me. Besides, I do good deeds and give money to the church," God will not have any use for that at all. As a matter of fact, you will perish in your sin and self-righteousness. But if you come like the tax collector and say, "God, have mercy on me, a sinner," God will receive you. Not only will he receive you, but you will dwell with him forever and ever in glory. God has established it all, done it all, and provided it all through the work of Jesus Christ, so that the people who by the power of the Holy Spirit hear the message and believe in him might have eternal life.

14

MOSES' FINEST HOUR

Exodus 32

SEIZING THE OPPORTUNITY
FOR GREATNESS

There are moments in the life of any individual or nation that provide opportunities for greatness. If they are seized, they lead to great things. If the person or nation fails to seize them, they lead to defeat and discouragement. Exodus 32 describes a moment like this, which I call the finest hour in the life of this most outstanding man, Moses.

The phrase "their finest hour" comes from Winston Churchill, and I'm sure you are familiar with it. In the early days of the Second World War, the Germans had overrun France and trapped the British and French armies of about 350,000 men at Dunkirk on the coast of France across the Channel from England. From May 26 to June 4, 1940, the British were able to get many of the troops back across the Channel almost miraculously, but without any of their arms or equipment. It was a very discouraging time for the British, who knew that Hitler's direct onslaught against Britain would come next.

Two weeks later, on June 18, Churchill gave a great speech before the House of Commons, in which he sought to rally the British people. Pointing to the terrible struggle that was to come, he concluded the speech with these stirring words: "Let us therefore brace ourselves to our duties, and so bear ourselves that, if the British Empire and its Commonwealth last for a thousand years, men will still say, 'This was their finest hour.'"[1]

When it comes to the life of Moses, his finest hour was when he pleaded for the people of Israel before God on Mount Sinai and was heard by God, and the people were spared.

PROBLEMS AT THE FOOT OF MOUNT SINAI

We have seen that the ceremonial law extends to the very end of the book of Exodus. Yet here is interjected the incident of the golden calf and Moses' intercession for the people.

The story begins in Exodus 24, before the giving of the ceremonial law. That chapter tells us that Moses and Aaron, Aaron's two sons, and the seventy elders of Israel had gone up into the mountain, and that these men had an extraordinary experience. "They beheld God, and ate and drank," (Ex. 24:11) and yet God did not strike them down. No more details are given, except that "there was under his feet as it were a pavement of sapphire stone, like the very heaven for clearness" (Ex. 24:10) indicating that their vision of God was limited and not a full manifestation of his splendor and glory. When it was over, the rest went back to the camp, but Moses went up the mountain with his aide Joshua to meet with God.

Moses was on the mountain for a long time—forty days. As the days stretched into weeks, the people down in the valley grew restless. They began to say to one another, "Whatever has happened to Moses? He went up into the mountain, but we haven't heard from him for weeks. Maybe he has fallen into a hole. Maybe the God he came to worship has consumed him. At any rate, we can't go on like this. We need a God of some sort to guide us if we're going to get through this wilderness."

So they turned to Aaron and said, "Aaron, make us a god."

---

1. Winston Churchill, "Their Finest Hour" (speech given at the House of Commons, London, June 18, 1940), available online at http://www.winstonchurchill.org/resources /speeches/233-1940-the-finest-hour/122-their-finest-hour.

This could have been Aaron's great moment. If Aaron had remained strong, as a leader should, he would have said, "Jehovah is our God. He brought us out of Egypt, and he is conferring with Moses on the mountain and giving Moses the law. We are going to wait right here until Moses comes back down with the law of God." But Aaron was weak, and so he compromised. He asked the people to give him their gold, and they did, and out of the gold, softened in the fire, he made a little calf (see Ex. 32:1–4).

That word *calf* is interesting. The Hebrew word is *êgel*, and some commentators suggest that it doesn't mean what the word *calf* means to us. We think of a small, young animal. Commentator Alan Cole argues that the word really means a young bull in his full strength.[2] This would suggest that the "calf" was in fact a representation of Apis, the Egyptian bull god. The people were returning to the idolatry of Egypt.

When they saw this calf, the Israelites said, "These are your gods, O Israel, who brought you up out of the land of Egypt!" (Ex. 32:4). Then they began to worship the calf, and it turned very quickly into an orgy. The words used in the NIV are "revelry" (v. 6) and "running wild" (v. 25), both suggesting sexual immorality. Or, as the *New Geneva Study Bible* states, the people were showing a "shameful lack of restraint"[3]—probably engaging in practices linked to fertility cults.

LEARNING FROM EXODUS 32: PART 1

Each stage of this story has much to teach us. I want to discuss these applications as we go along.

NO GUARANTEE IN MIRACLES

The first great lesson of the story is that miracles do not guarantee faith or faithfulness to God. Many people say, "If God would only do a miracle in my life, then I could believe in him," or "If he would

---

2. R. Alan Cole, *Exodus*, Tyndale Old Testament Commentaries (Downers Grove, IL: IVP Academic, 1973), 214.

3. See the note on Exodus 32:6 in the *New Geneva Study Bible* (Nashville: Thomas Nelson, 1995).

do a miracle now, my faith would be a lot stronger than it is." It is not that way, of course. Miracles do not guarantee anything. In the 1980s and '90s, a certain movement presented evangelism as spiritual warfare, which of course it is. But there was an emphasis on miracles as a way to catch people's attention and show that the God of the Bible is more powerful than the demon gods. People in this movement were eager to identify miracles and cast out demons.

This episode involving the golden calf ought to teach us that miracles do not guarantee a thing. There has never been a time in all history when any people has seen more miracles of greater scope in a shorter space of time than the Israelites did in their deliverance from Egypt. They saw the devastation of the plagues. They experienced God's provision for them in the wilderness. At the very moment when they began to worship the golden calf, God was on the mountain in an awe-inspiring demonstration of cloud and thunder and lightning—so much so, we are told in other places, that the people trembled when they heard the sound (see Ex. 20:18, 19; Heb. 12:18–21). Yet it did not mean a thing. They turned away from these signs very easily and quickly.

THE PROBLEM WITH IMAGES

A second lesson shows us the problem with images. God had given Moses the Ten Commandments, and the second commandment says, "You shall not make for yourself a carved image, or any likeness of anything that is in heaven above, or that is in the earth beneath, or that is in the water under the earth. You shall not bow down to them or serve them" (Ex. 20:4–5). The commandment goes on to explain how the punishments of God will come on those who make images, even to multiple generations.

Reading that, we say, "What's so important about not making an image?" We can understand God's saying "You shall have no other gods before me." But why can't we worship the true God by means of images?

That is what Aaron thought he was doing. After the idol was made and they had placed an altar in front of it, Aaron said, "Tomorrow shall be a feast to the LORD" (Ex. 32:5). The word that he actually used was *Jehovah*. He thought they were going to worship God. Probably he reasoned that the bull god represented the great strength of the true God. But of course it couldn't begin to represent the strength of the true God, the God who had brought them out of Egypt. This golden statue misled the worshippers, because instead of thinking of the strength of God in the sense of deliverance, of his mighty power to save and sustain, they began to think of his strength only in terms of sexual potency. The pagan concept of strength distorted and perverted the revelation of God's strength that they had just experienced. This led to the orgy that followed and was a disgrace on their name.

SIN ESTABLISHES A HOLD

Third, we see that sin establishes a hold on the one who is sinning. It is hard to shake off its power and influence. That is illustrated years later in the history of Israel during the time of King Jeroboam. Jeroboam was the first ruler of the northern kingdom after civil war split Judah and Benjamin off from the ten northern tribes. After the split, Jeroboam was afraid that those in the northern kingdom would be loyal to the southern kingdom because Jerusalem and the temple were located in the south; so he set up two rival worship centers—one at Bethel in the south of his kingdom, and one at Dan in the north. In each worship center he set up a golden calf. As he did so, in a direct but almost incredible reference to the incident in Exodus 32, he told the people, "Behold your gods, O Israel, who brought you up out of the land of Egypt" (1 Kings 12:28). Incredibly, the same sin was hanging on among the people many generations later.

IRONIC SITUATIONS

Moses was on the mountain and did not know what was going on in the valley. God did. God is omniscient and omnipresent, and he was well aware of the situation. So God interrupted the giving of the law to tell Moses what was happening. "Go down, for your people, whom you brought up out of the land of Egypt, have corrupted themselves. They have turned aside quickly out of the way that I commanded them. They have made for themselves a golden calf and have worshiped it and sacrificed to it and said, 'These are your gods, O Israel, who brought you up out of the land of Egypt'" (Ex. 32:7–8).

This was a painfully ironic situation. God had been giving Moses the law and telling the Israelites that they were not to worship him by means of idols, and at that very moment, the people down in the valley were breaking that commandment.

At this point God made an offer to Moses that would have greatly tempted a lesser man: he would judge the Israelites for their sin by wiping them out, and then he would begin again with Moses and make him a great nation in his own right (see v. 10). Moses would become a new Abraham, a patriarch, the father of his people.

This was undoubtedly meant to test Moses, because God knew perfectly well what he was going to do. God knows the end from the beginning. This offer was meant to draw Moses deeper into his practice of intercession for the people. The offer was not a temptation to Moses. Immediately he pleaded on behalf of the people, "O Lord, why does your wrath burn hot against your people, whom you have brought out of the land of Egypt with great power and with a mighty hand?" (v. 11).

The second great irony of this story lies in the exchange between God and Moses. When God first spoke to Moses, he said, "Go down, for *your* people, whom *you* brought up out of the land of Egypt, have corrupted themselves" (32:7). When Moses began to respond to God, he said, "Why does *your* wrath burn hot against *your* people, whom *you* have brought out of the land of Egypt . . . ?" (32:11). In the Israelites' present disobedient state, neither God nor Moses wanted to acknowledge them. This is the same as when a child misbehaves; the father says to the mother, "I think you'd better discipline your son," and the mother replies, "What do you mean, *my* son? He's *your* son. He takes after you. You discipline him." At that moment, neither parent wants anything to do with the disobedient offspring.

THE INTERCESSION OF MOSES

Moses pleaded for the people with two very impressive arguments. He began by asking what the Egyptians would say if God destroyed his people. "They'll say it was with evil intent that you brought them out, to kill them in the mountains and to wipe them off the face of your earth. Therefore turn from your fierce anger and relent and do not bring disaster on the people" (see 32:12 NIV). If God destroyed the Israelites, the Egyptians would win after all. No one wanted the Egyptians to win.

Moses also asked if God had forgotten his covenant with Abraham. "Remember Abraham, Isaac, and Israel, your servants, to whom you swore by your own self, and said to them, 'I will multiply your offspring as the stars of heaven, and all this land that I have promised I will give to your offspring, and they shall inherit it forever'" (v. 13). This was powerful reasoning. If we think through these words and analyze them carefully, we will see that Moses was being very, very thoughtful in what he said.

First, when Moses named the patriarchs, he said, "Abraham, Isaac, and *Israel*"—not *Jacob*, which is what we usually say. Moses used Jacob's new name *Israel*, because that was the covenant name of the people for whom Moses was pleading. The Israelites were descendants of the covenant family, not just of Jacob the man. Moses was pointing out that God was about to destroy a people with whom God had made the covenant.

Second, Moses reminded God of the several promises he had made to the patriarchs. God had promised to multiply them so they would become a great nation. That promise had been fulfilled. But God had also promised to lead them into a new land and give them that land, and that promise had not been fulfilled. Moses was reminding God, "Remember that promise you made. You haven't fulfilled it yet." That was powerful reasoning.

Third and finally, by using the word *forever*, Moses reminded God that the covenants of God are everlasting covenants, not temporal ones that God can break.

This prayer is similar to the great intercessory prayer of Abraham when he pleaded for Sodom and Gomorrah in Genesis 18. Here, in Exodus 32, we are told that God listened to Moses. The judgment was restrained, at least temporarily: "And the LORD relented from the disaster that he had spoken of bringing on his people" (Ex. 32:14).

186

MOSES DEALS WITH THE PEOPLE

Moses' intercession happened on the mountain, but the sin was still going on in the valley. So Moses came down the mountain and dealt with the people as best he knew how. On the mountain he had only been hearing about their sin. As he made his way down the mountain and saw what was actually going on, he was so overcome with anger that he threw down the stone tables of the law and broke them. The symbolic significance of this act is striking. The people have been breaking the law of God, so Moses breaks the tables of the law as a visual demonstration of their rebellion against God's holy law.

Moses' job was to reclaim the people. But how was he to go about that? Well, he did everything he knew to do.

DESTROY THE IDOL

First of all, Moses took the idol, ground it up into small pieces, burned it, and mixed the ashes with water, which he made the people drink. Scholars think this means that the idol was not made entirely of gold, because gold cannot be burned, but was instead made of wood covered with gold. I don't think it makes any difference. The point is that he destroyed the idol.

By destroying the idol, Moses showed that it was impotent. The people had been worshipping it as a symbol of great sexual potency, praising it as the god who had powerfully brought them out of Egypt. But this idol couldn't even defend itself. When Moses mixed the remains with water and made them drink it, it passed first into, and then out of, their bodies. This was a way of saying that the idol was refuse. It was as worthless as dung.

REBUKE AARON

Second, Moses rebuked Aaron publicly. That was the most he could do, since Aaron had been appointed by God and was the anointed of the Lord. Later in the Old Testament, David would not destroy Saul because Saul was the anointed of the Lord. Neither would Moses lay his hands on Aaron. If Aaron was going to be removed, God had to remove him. But Moses did rebuke Aaron publicly and appropriately, just as Paul rebuked Peter when Peter began to waver on the matter of the purity of the gospel (see Gal. 2:11–14).

And Aaron gave a terribly self-serving, blame-passing, lame excuse. He blamed the people. He blamed Moses indirectly, because the real problem was that Moses had stayed so long on the mountain. If Moses had only come down a little sooner, this would not have happened. Aaron even blamed God when he claimed that he had thrown gold into the fire and the calf had come out fully formed on its own (see Ex. 32:24). It had not happened that way at all, of course; Aaron was guilty, as the text clearly shows us.

The best we can say about Aaron is that he was weak rather than strong; pliant, impressionable, and compromising when he should have been resolute. He was more anxious to please the people than to please God. These sometimes seem like mild faults, but they are not mild in a leader, especially in a Christian leader. Weak leadership probably does more damage in the church of Jesus Christ today than outright opposition by enemies of the gospel. Weakness from within destroyed the Roman Empire, not the barbarians without. And weakness within the church is more harmful than the church's enemies.

EXECUTE LIMITED JUDGMENT ON THE PEOPLE

Third, Moses called those who had remained faithful to God and commissioned them to execute a limited judgment on the people. He asked who was on the Lord's side, and the tribe of Levi came forward (see 32:26). He told the tribe of Levi to arm themselves and kill (see v. 27). It does not say it in so many words, but he must have meant for them to kill the leaders. The people probably numbered several million. They did not kill that many. What is stressed is that the Levites were to execute judgment even on those who were members of their own families, on their friends, and their neighbors. And the Levites did it. They showed that faithfulness to God was more important than the closest human ties.

We are told that three thousand people were killed that day—about one-half of one percent of the 600,000 men who had gone out from Egypt. Proportionately, that was not a large number, but it is a lot of people to kill. And the Levites killed them, even when it affected members of their own households. They were men of integrity, who feared God more than they feared men.

We remember this integrity in connection with what Jesus said when he was speaking about what it means to follow him. He said, "Whoever loves father or mother more than me is not worthy of me; whoever loves son or daughter more than me is not worthy of me" (Matt. 10:37). Both Moses and Jesus were saying that, in the service of God, all other loyalties have to be secondary. If you are going to serve the God of the universe, you have to serve him above all other allegiances and loyalties.

A SECOND INTERCESSION

From a human point of view, Moses had dealt with the sin. He had done everything that he could. He had reclaimed the loyalty of the people. But God still remained in wrath on the mountain.

For armchair theologians reflecting on this incident or on the attributes of God, the wrath of God might not seem like a very compelling quality. After all, we read that it is an outmoded concept. People today do not want to believe in the wrath of God. But God's wrath was not an outmoded concept to Moses. He had been on the mountain. He knew the terror of the holy God of Israel. He had heard God say that he would punish the children for their fathers' sin "to the third and the fourth generation of those who hate me" (Ex. 20:5). The judgment of God was not something to be taken lightly. What in the world was Moses to do? He had done everything that he could do humanly, but he still had to go back up the mountain and face God.

The night passed, and the morning came for Moses to ascend the mountain.

During the night, though, Moses had had an idea. He had remembered that when the people were leaving Egypt, God had told them that they could take an animal, kill it, and put the blood on the doorposts and lintels of their houses, demonstrating that an innocent victim had died in the place of the guilty people who lived within. And that night the angel of death had passed by. God had also given Moses instructions for the Day of Atonement: how the high priest on the Day of Atonement was to take an animal, kill it for the sins of the people, and sprinkle the blood on the mercy seat. Mercy could be found if atonement for sin was made. Moses must have thought about that, and the next day, when he went up the mountain, he must have been saying to himself, "Maybe, *maybe* God will accept . . ."

He reached the top of the mountain. He began to speak to God. The Hebrew text is uneven. Verse 32 breaks off with a dash, right in the middle, indicating that Moses was speaking with great emotion: "Moses returned to the LORD and said, 'Alas, this people has sinned a great sin. They have made for themselves gods of gold. But now, if you will forgive their sin—'" (vv. 31–32). That is where it breaks off. Moses did not have any idea how God, the holy God of the universe, could simply forgive sin just like that, willy-nilly. The holy God of the universe, the just God of the universe, has to do the right thing. Moses paused. Then he continued, "but if not, please blot me out of your book that you have written" (v. 32).

This could mean one of two things. Moses could be referring to the book of eternal life that is mentioned in Revelation in several places (see, for instance, Rev. 3:5; 13:8). In that case, Moses meant that he was willing to be sent to hell if that would mean the salvation of the people. That sounds extreme to some scholars, so they argue that the book could be a "book of the living"—a record of all the living souls in the nation. The problem is that such a book is not mentioned anywhere and does not do justice to the gravity of the situation. God's blotting out the people would not be a temporal judgment but a spiritual judgment. So when Moses offered himself as a substitute, he was offering himself not as a temporal substitute but as a spiritual substitute. He was willing to go to hell if it meant the salvation of the people.

Earlier I mentioned the ironies of the story. On the preceding day, God had made a great offer to Moses. He had said that he would destroy the people but would save Moses and make him the father of a new nation. Moses had gone down the mountain, met with the people, and realized that he loved them in spite of their sin. Back on the mountain, Moses now made a counteroffer. God had said, "I'll destroy them and save you." Moses said, "Save them and destroy me." That is powerful intercession. As far as you and I know, never has a greater offer been made by any human being in all of the course of history.

There is something similar in the writings of the apostle Paul, but it cannot match Moses' offer. Talking about his love for Israel, Paul says,

> I have great sorrow and unceasing anguish in my heart. For I could wish that I myself were accursed and cut off from Christ for the sake of my brothers, my kinsmen according to the flesh. (Rom. 9:2–4)

This is the same kind of offer, but it is not as great as Moses' offer, because Paul knew it was impossible for any human to be a substitute, to sacrifice himself for the sins of others. Moses stood early in the history of revelation. He did not understand all that Paul understood—that Jesus is the only one able to make such an atonement, to be that substitute. While Paul made the offer hypothetically and theoretically, Moses really meant it literally. He was willing to be sent to hell if the people could be saved.

THE ONLY ADEQUATE SACRIFICE

The problem, of course, was that Moses could not save the people. He did not know that. He was offering what he could. But Moses could not die even for his own sin, let alone for the sin of the nation.

But there was one who could, which is why Paul writes in Galatians 4,

> But when the fullness of time had come, God sent forth his Son, born of woman, born under the law, to redeem those who were under the law, so that we might receive adoption as sons. (vv. 4–5)

When we study the Bible, we find that the same themes repeat themselves, because God does not change, we do not change, and the way of salvation does not change. The situation in Exodus is our situation exactly. God is on his holy mountain, and he has given forth his law. People do not pay any more attention to his law today than did the people in the valley in Moses' day. As they turn to all the gods of this world, people say, "Come, let's worship the gods that delivered us from Egypt." We worship political power or money, thinking that they bring liberation. We break all the laws of God. And while we break the laws of God and bring ourselves under God's judgment—a wrath that is sure to fall—Jesus Christ, the Son of God, says to God the Father, "I want to go down there and give my life for those stiff-necked, sinful, arrogant, obnoxious, rebellious people, whom I nevertheless love." God the Father replies, "I accept that offer, because it is a real atonement for sin," and so Jesus Christ goes to the cross and dies for sinners.

Jesus is the only adequate substitute for sinners. There is salvation in none other. There is no other way that you or I or the people of Israel or anyone else on the face of this planet can be saved.

In theology, there are two views regarding the necessity of the atonement. One view speaks of the *absolute necessity* of the atonement. The other speaks of a *circumstantial necessity* of the atonement. A circumstantial necessity is this: God, being infinite, must have had before him an infinite number of ways that he could save us, but as he looked the situation over, he saw that the best possible way was by sending Jesus Christ to die. Those who hold to a better theology say, "No, no. Not like that." Jesus' atonement is an absolute necessity, because even for God Almighty there was no way other than by Christ's atoning death that sinners could be saved. There is a hymn that expresses this in words that are absolutely true:

> There was no other good enough
> To pay the price of sin;
> He only could unlock the gate
> Of heav'n, and let us in.[4]

Moses could not save us. Paul could not save us. No great religious leader on the face of the earth, however much we admire that person, could ever save us. Only Jesus Christ can do so, because he is the sinless Son of God, the perfect sacrifice, the one to whom all of the

---

4. Cecil Frances Alexander, "There Is a Green Hill Far Away," 1848.

other sacrifices pointed. God says, "Whoever has sinned against me, I will blot out of my book" (Ex. 32:33). But in virtue of the mercy seat and the love that took Christ to the cross, forgiveness was granted. Anticipating the death of Christ, Moses was given the command to take the people into the promised land, which he did.

LEARNING FROM EXODUS 32: PART 2

THE IMPORTANCE OF INTERCESSION

Is it very important that we intercede for other people? We sometimes say, in our theological pride, "What point is there in prayer? God's going to do what God's going to do. God is sovereign." But notice that in this chapter, although God is sovereign, he did, as it were, put himself in the hands of Moses. He told Moses that he was going to destroy the people and save him alone. And then God permitted Moses to debate with him and to plead for the people's salvation.

Do not ever say that prayer is unimportant. God works through prayer. He answers prayer. Your challenge is to pray and intercede for other people. The prayers of righteous people are strong and effective (see James 5:16).

THE SOLE MEDIATOR

Finally, "there is one God, and there is one mediator between God and men, the man Christ Jesus" (1 Tim. 2:5). Moses offered to die as a substitute for the people, but no mere human being could do that. We have to have a divine Savior, and that is what we have in Jesus Christ. This is the greatest and most important fact that any person can ever know, and to believe it and trust Jesus Christ as his or her own Savior is the greatest thing that any person can ever do. Do not let the world draw you away with lesser things that promise fulfillment now and end with the loss of your soul. Come to Jesus and trust him. The Bible shouts this from beginning to end.

15

SHOW ME YOUR GLORY

Exodus 33—34

THE SETUP

In the last chapter we saw that the people had sinned in making the golden calf. Moses had intervened on their behalf, and God had postponed judgment. God had even promised to go with the people and not abandon them. Moses had based his plea partly on the fact that God had made an eternal covenant with his people through the covenant made to Abraham, Isaac, and Jacob, and that he ought to keep it. God had said he would. He would bring the people into his land. Furthermore, he would send his presence before them. He was referring, perhaps, to the cloud or an angel or something of that nature, because he added, "I will not go up among you, lest I consume you on the way, for you are a stiff-necked people" (Ex. 33:3).

Moses wasn't satisfied with that. To have any presence, however wonderful, or any angelic power, however great, go with the people rather than God himself was less than he wanted. So Exodus 33 gives us Moses' continuing intercession for the people in order that God himself might go with him and that he himself, as a servant of God, might see God's glory.[1]

---

1. In the NIV there is no heading to break up Exodus 32 and 33. The intercession that Moses began to bring to God in chapter 32 continues into this chapter without interruption.

This is one of the great examples of intercession in the Bible. Arthur W. Pink writes, "Here we behold the typical mediator prevailing in his intercession for a sinful people, not only in averting the wrath of God"—which is what we saw him do in the last chapter—"but in securing His continued presence in their midst."[2]

THE SETTING

Early in the chapter we are told that Moses went outside of the camp to the Tent of Meeting. There is not a great deal of description here, but Moses seems to have constructed a simple tent or tabernacle and pitched it outside the camp. Three times we are told it was "outside the camp" or "far from the camp." This surely symbolized that God was a holy God, and that the Israelites remained a sinful people; God must remain separate and distant from the people of Israel. But when Moses entered the Tent of Meeting, the pillar of cloud came down before the tent door, and God, veiled by the awe-inspiring cloud, spoke to Moses there.

Later on, after the Israelites built the tabernacle, they set it up in the very midst of their encampment. Then, when the pillar of fire and cloud came down upon it, God was in their very midst. In chapter 33, however, Moses is still interceding for them, and God's anger against their great sin has not abated.

THE FIRST REQUEST

Moses' concern is that God had said he would send his angel with the people but not go with them himself. Moses is not satisfied with that arrangement, but it is not the first concern he raises with God. Instead, Moses prays for himself. Then he requests that God go with them instead of sending the angel, and after that he makes the most daring request at all.

But Moses' first request is that God teach him his—God's—ways

---

2. Arthur W. Pink, *Gleanings in Exodus* (repr. Lafayette, IN: Sovereign Grace Publishers, 2002), 338.

so that Moses will know him: "Now therefore, if I have found favor in your sight, please show me now your ways, that I may know you" (Ex. 33:13).

Didn't Moses know God? Yes, he did. God had appeared to Moses in the burning bush and had revealed himself to Moses as Jehovah—as Yahweh, the great eternal God—and Moses had come to know something of God then. But Moses still wanted to know God and to know him more deeply. Think of the apostle Paul in the New Testament, who probably knew more about God than anybody but Moses, but who prayed, just as Moses prayed, "that I may know him [Christ] and the power of his resurrection" (Phil. 3:10). The more these men knew of God, the more they wanted to know God. If you and I have begun to know God, that should be our desire as well. Each one of us needs to know God better, in a deeper, more personal way.

WHAT DOES IT MEAN TO KNOW GOD?

What does this request even mean? That is not a simple question. In his book *Knowing God*, J. I. Packer spends some time analyzing what we mean when we use the word *know*.[3] We use the word in a number of different ways.

First, we use the word *know* to mean that we have a simple awareness, such as the awareness of a fact. "I know where so-and-so lives." That awareness doesn't touch us very deeply. It means that at one point we heard the person give his or her address and so we remembered it. If somebody asks, "Where does so-and-so live?" we can say, "On Pine Street."

This is the simplest kind of knowledge. If we carry it over into the knowledge of God, it corresponds with the awareness that all people have that there is a God. Paul uses this awareness in Romans 1 to say that we are all guilty before God because, although we do not know God in a personal or saving way, we know that he exists. Paul says we are guilty if we do not allow that rudimentary knowledge, that awareness of the being of God, to cause us to seek him out, worship him, and thank him for the many things he has given us, including life itself.

3. J. I. Packer, *Knowing God* (Downers Grove, IL: InterVarsity Press, 1973), 20–37.

The second kind of knowledge is what we would call *knowledge by description*. For example, we could say, "I've lived in Philadelphia for a long time, and I really know Philadelphia." This means that if somebody asks us about Philadelphia, we can tell him or her about the city and explain how the streets run and where Independence Hall is located. We can describe where the art museum is and can add that those are the steps that Rocky Balboa ran up in the first *Rocky* movie. We can talk about the city because we know many facts about it. But it would be possible to do that without having actually lived there; we could accomplish this just by studying a good map or reading a good book about Philadelphia.

There are many theologians in that category. Not necessarily saved men or women, they can study the Bible like anybody else. If we ask them, "What is God like?" they can give theological answers. God is sovereign. God is holy. God is powerful. They can describe the characteristics of the Divine Being, but that is not what the Bible means when it speaks about knowing God in the fullest sense.

Third, we use the word *know* to refer to knowledge by experience. "I really know Philadelphia because I've lived there all my life." We can talk about a person that way. "I really know so-and-so. We've worked together for thirty years, and I know how she functions." That is knowledge by experience, and it is a far greater and far more important knowledge. Whenever we talk about knowing God, that is what we want to achieve—not merely to know that there is a God; not merely able to describe the chief characteristics of God, however accurate we may be; but actually to know God by experience, that is, to experience God for ourselves.

As important as that is, that is still not quite what the Bible means when it talks about knowing God. When the Bible talks about knowing God, this knowledge always involves the *change* that we experience when we come to know him. To come to know God means that we can never really be what we were before. Packer writes,

> Knowing God involves, first, listening to God's Word and receiving it as the Holy Spirit interprets it, in application to oneself; second, noting God's nature and character, as his Word and works reveal it; third,

197

accepting his invitations and doing what he commands; fourth, recognizing and rejoicing in the love that he has shown in thus approaching you and drawing you into this divine fellowship.[4]

This was what Moses wanted. Moses knew much about God. He could have explained what God was like. On the mountain with God, Moses even had an experience of God that was perhaps greater, in some ways, than anything you and I experience. When he entreats God, "Teach me your ways so I may know you," he means that he wants to know God in a way that will change who he is and transform what he does, a knowledge that will enter into every aspect of his life and being.

This takes work. We do not get to know God this way by being lazy.

There is another great book that every Christian should read called *The Pursuit of God*, by A. W. Tozer, a writer and pastor of the mid-twentieth century. The weaknesses of the church which Tozer wrote about in his day are even more characteristic of our own time. Tozer states that we have a shallow, empty form of worship in our evangelical churches. Activities and programs have replaced worship and a true reverence for God and a desire for him. "Spiritual worship [is] at a [low] ebb. . . . Religion, so as far as it is genuine, is in essence the response of created personalities to the Creating Personality."[5] Therefore, "If we would find God amid all the religious externals we must first determine to find Him, and then proceed in the way of simplicity. . . . We must put away all efforts to impress, and come with the guileless candor of childhood."[6]

That is what Moses is doing in chapter 33. He is interceding for the people, because he wants God himself to go with them, not merely an angel. But whatever else he is doing, he is approaching God simply, personally, and very fervently. "Show me now your ways, that I may know you" (Ex. 33:13).

There are more lessons here. First, we are unable to come to know God by ourselves—at least in the way that Packer describes. Moses did

---

4. Ibid., 32.

5. A. W. Tozer, *The Pursuit of God* (Harrisburg: Christian Publications, 1948; repr., Chicago: WingSpread Publishers, 2006), 9, 13.

6. Ibid., 18.

not say, "I'm the leader. I've got a good mind. I can figure out what God is like." He knew he couldn't achieve the kind of knowledge of God that he longed for, and so he came recognizing his own inabilities. He asked God to teach him.

Second, the only person who can ever show us what God is like is God. Nobody else can do that, because our ways are not God's ways. His thoughts are not our thoughts. If we are ever going to come to know God, he himself will have to teach us. We cannot do it by ourselves, so we need to come to God and ask him to do it, as Moses did.

The remainder of chapter 33 is a great revelation of who God really is.

THE SECOND REQUEST

Moses' second petition is, "If your presence will not go with me, do not bring us up from here" (Ex. 33:15). This is a negative petition. Moses pleaded "If you're not going to go with us, do not send us away from here, because I do not want to go without you." Here is a veiled way of asking God to reconsider, and the Lord heard this request and answered it in the way Moses desired: "This very thing that you have spoken I will do, for you have found favor in my sight, and I know you by name" (v. 17).

Think about what Moses was saying. Where were the people? They were camped in a barren desert valley at the foot of Mount Sinai. They had the promised land before them—the very thing that God had promised to the patriarchs more than four centuries earlier. God had said he was taking them to a land flowing with milk and honey, but Moses said, "I'd rather stay right here in the desert for the rest of my life than go to Canaan if you do not go with us."

You and I launch off into so many things by ourselves because we are not really concerned about the presence of God. We think it is far better to have Canaan, with its milk and honey, than to have God. God can come later. Sometimes we say, "I think it's important that we do this project. I don't know whether God is in it, but it's an important thing that we should do." Normally we baptize our projects with the name of God and say that we're ministering in God's name, but we, especially leaders, should be careful never to want to take a step in any direction unless we are sure that God is with us. Moses had been with God long enough to know how important this was, and he had been with the people long enough to know how necessary it was. If God was not going with them, they were in trouble.

Not only should we be afraid to take a step forward unless we know that God is with us, but we should also be bold to move forward when we do know that God is with us. Think of the great missionary hymn by Edith G. Cherry, a favorite hymn of the missionaries who were killed in Ecuador by the Auca Indians in the 1950s.

"We rest on thee"—our shield and our defender!
We go not forth alone against the foe;
Strong in thy strength, safe in thy keeping tender,
"We rest on thee, and in thy name we go."[7]

That was the way that Moses wanted to go forward. If you and I are sure that God is with us, leading and directing, we can go forward with the same confidence.

THE THIRD REQUEST

Before Moses reached his third request, he had already achieved what he wanted. As the leader of the people, he was very concerned that God go with them. Now God declared that he would, but Moses was not quite satisfied. Moses was a remarkable man, and one of his remarkable characteristics is now apparent. Although God had promised to bless him and to teach him his ways, it was not quite enough. A hymn says, "Thou art coming to a King, large petitions with thee bring."[8] Knowing something about the greatness of the God he serves, Moses comes with the greatest request of all: "Please show me your glory" (33:18).

God's answer makes clear that this was nothing less than a request to see God face-to-face in all his splendor, unobscured by the cloud

7. Edith G. Cherry, "We Rest on Thee," c. 1895.
8. John Newton, "Come, My Soul, Thy Suit Prepare," 1779.

that was over the mountain. Moses must have communed with God in what we would call "the dark" or by a burning bush. He did not want that obscurity. He wanted to see God face-to-face.

God told Moses that he would not be able to show his face to Moses, because no human being can see the face of God and live. But God did say that he would reveal his goodness and proclaim his name to Moses and that he would do so by putting Moses in the cleft of a rock, covering the opening with his hand, and then causing his goodness to pass before his servant.

TO SEE GOD AND LIVE

There is a small apparent contradiction here. When God says, "No one may see me and live," perhaps we remember Exodus 24:9–10, where the elders are said to have seen the God of Israel. However, if we read the description of what they actually did see, it is something like a pavement made of sapphire under God's feet. In other words, some of the cloud was removed. They looked up. They saw the floor of heaven. They did not actually see God face-to-face. What God says to Moses is consistent. When Jacob wrestled with God, he did not wrestle with the undisclosed, glorious God of heaven. He probably encountered a pre-incarnate form of Jesus Christ—Godhead veiled in human flesh. When Isaiah had his great vision of God, with God's glory filling the temple, he did not see God face-to-face but saw the revelation of God's glory.

Although God told Moses that he could not grant his request literally and fully, because no one could see him and live, he did nevertheless grant it in substance by giving Moses one of the greatest revelations of himself found anywhere in the Bible.

God began by announcing what he would do: "I will make all my goodness pass before you and will proclaim before you my name 'The LORD.' And I will be gracious to whom I will be gracious, and will show mercy on whom I will show mercy" (Ex. 33:19). Then he told Moses that he would put him in a cleft of rock, probably on Mount Sinai, and cover him with his hand until he had passed by (see Ex. 33:21–23).

The LORD descended in the cloud and stood with him there, and proclaimed the name of the LORD. The LORD passed before him and proclaimed, "The LORD, the LORD, a God merciful and gracious, slow to anger, and abounding in steadfast love and faithfulness, keeping steadfast love for thousands, forgiving iniquity and transgression and sin, but who will by no means clear the guilty, visiting the iniquity of the fathers on the children and the children's children, to the third and the fourth generation." (Ex. 34:5–7)

THE MEANING OF GOD'S NAME

God's revelation to Moses unfolds the meaning of his name: Jehovah, or *Yahweh*. This revelation is so important that verse 6—"The LORD, the LORD, a God merciful and gracious, slow to anger"—is quoted again and again throughout the Old Testament (see, for example, Neh. 9:17; Ps. 86:15; 103:8; 145:8; Joel 2:13; Jonah 4:2). It sums up the essence of God's name, and, since the name of God sums up the character of God, it tells us that knowing who God is and what God is like is far more important for us than seeing God physically.

Today, how do we find out what God is like? We study the Bible, where God has revealed himself. In fact, right now we are studying this revelation to Moses, which comes to us in writing in the Old Testament. This is how we learn about the character of God.

God's revelation to Moses vividly shows that is it far more important to study the Bible than to have visions. Moses thought that he wanted a vision; he wanted to see the face of God. God said he could not have that, but he let Moses hear the voice of God—God speaking. We must study the Bible to hear God speak and thus to find out what God is like.

GOD'S COMMUNICABLE ATTRIBUTES

Moses had already had a similar revelation. When God appeared to him the first time in the burning bush, he revealed his name: "I AM WHO I AM" (Ex. 3:14). In chapter 5 of this book, we saw that the burning bush revelation revealed something of what theologians call God's *incommunicable attributes*, such as self-existence, self-sufficiency, and eternity; these are so much a part of God being uniquely God that he cannot communicate—that is, share—these attributes with us. None of us has those characteristics, nor can we. Yes, God gives us eternal life, but we are not eternal beings because there was a time before we existed. We certainly are not able to sustain ourselves. We are not self-existent nor self-sufficient. We need God and his provision at every single moment. If God ceased to provide we would all be gone in an instant.

But in this revelation to Moses, God explains the meaning of his name more fully; he communicates what we call his *communicable attributes*. These are attributes, or characteristics, that God can communicate or share with us because he has made us in his image—attributes like compassion, grace, slowness to anger, love, and faithfulness (see Ex. 34:6), as well as goodness and mercy (see Ex. 33:19). These are attributes that God not only *can* communicate to us, but *does* communicate to us if we are Christians, and we must possess them if we are Christians. The Holy Spirit has made Christians spiritually alive. We are new creatures in Christ, with the life of God within us. Therefore, if we are Christians, we should show his goodness in our lives; we should be merciful, compassionate, gracious, slow to anger, and so on. We do not receive all these qualities immediately, and we certainly do not receive them in their fullness. The Christian life is a life of growth. But the essence of these qualities has to be there, and it has to begin to grow and blossom as the Holy Spirit works in the believer.

GOD'S MERCY

In the midst of this revelation is a verse that Paul picks up and uses in Romans 9 about reprobation: "'I will be gracious to whom I will be gracious, and will show mercy on whom I will show mercy'" (Ex. 33:19; see also Rom. 9:15). We need to understand how Paul develops this verse, because otherwise we will have a distorted idea of mercy.

If we talk about the sovereignty of God in election or discuss reprobation (condemnation to eternal judgment) with somebody, the objection we hear is this: God owes everybody a chance. Such an objection is a contradiction in terms, because the very essence of mercy is that it cannot be owed. What God owes us is damnation. Because of our sin and rebellion, he owes us wrath and judgment. That is what we deserve. Mercy is quite different—it is undeserved. By the very nature of mercy, God shows it to those on whom he will have mercy, and he passes by those whom he will pass by. Without reprobation, there is no mercy. If God is obliged to save everybody, then that obligation is not mercy at all.

When Paul develops the idea of God's sovereign, or electing, mercy in Romans 9, it is so troubling to commentators that they find all kinds of ways to explain it as something else. They say, for example, that Paul misunderstood what God was saying in Exodus—that the verse refers to God's mercy to Moses only in the sense of granting him a theophany, an appearance of God himself. God was not going to grant that to other people. Or they say that this refers to God's showing mercy to Israel by renewing the covenant and forgiving their sin. Even this answer can't escape his electing mercy, however. It is obvious that God showed mercy to Israel that he did not show to the Egyptians.

This is exactly what Paul talks about in Romans 9. Using Pharaoh as an example, he quotes another text (Ex. 9:16) in which God says that he raised Pharaoh up for this very purpose, that he might display his wrath and judgment in him (see Rom. 9:17). In the case of Israel, God showed his mercy; in the case of Pharaoh, God showed his judgment. The judgment on Pharaoh is necessary in order to preserve the mercy for Israel.

I do not know if Moses fully understood what he was asking when he said to God, "Show me your glory." But seeing his glory means seeing God as he really is. This is profoundly disturbing to sinful people like you and me. We wouldn't mind having God reveal his glory to us if it were all love or mercy or grace; but Paul reminds us that God is also a God of justice and wrath, and the revelation of his glory involves these things as well. The wonder of the revelation is not that God is just, but that God is merciful. The wonder is also that in these words to Moses, God emphasizes his mercy so strongly.

GOD'S INSPIRATION

Immediately after this extraordinary encounter on the mountain come displays of God's mercy. In Exodus 32, Moses had come down the mountain, seen the people sinning, and broken the tablets. God could have said that that was the end of it. But Moses cut out some stone and went back up the mountain (see Ex. 34:4).

Earlier, God had written on the tablets himself; after saying in verse 1 that he would write on them as he had the first time, here God tells Moses to write on them (see Ex. 34:27). Is this a contradiction? It is probably a way of saying that whatever Moses wrote, God wrote. In other words, God wrote through Moses.

This is what we mean when we talk about *inspiration*. The human writers of the Bible wrote with their own vocabulary and with their own limitations, experience, and knowledge. But God superintended what they wrote, so it is true to say that what they wrote is God's writing. When I worked with the International Council on Biblical Inerrancy, we wrestled from time to time with ways to express this. On one occasion we said that "what Scripture says, God says—through human agents and without error."[9] When Moses wrote down the words, he wrote what God had him write. God again gave the law.

MOSES' RADIANT FACE

Then comes the strange incident of Moses' glowing face. When Moses came down from the mountain, his face was radiant with a transferred glory (see Ex. 34:29). It was so bright that the people couldn't look at him, so Moses wore a veil over his face until the glory faded away.

This is an instance in which there was an amusing mistranslation of the Bible. The translators of the Latin Vulgate misread the Hebrew here. In Hebrew, the verb for "he radiated" is *karon*, but a similar word, *karan*, has just slightly different vowel pointings. *Karan* means "horn." So the translators translated the verse to say that Moses had

---

9. Quoted in James Montgomery Boice, *Does Inerrancy Matter?* (Wheaton: Tyndale House Publishers, 1981), 15.

horns coming out of his head. This explains some of the medieval and Renaissance art, such as *Moses*, one of Michelangelo's best-known sculptures. This figure of Moses has horns because Michelangelo thought that was what Scripture said. But this was an error. Moses was radiating light.

In 2 Corinthians 3, Paul refers to this incident with a threefold illustration.

First, in verses 7–13, he uses Moses' radiant face to illustrate the veiled and fading glory of the old covenant in contrast with the unveiled and abiding glory of the new covenant. Old things are passing away; all things are becoming new. The glory of the fullness of the covenant in Jesus Christ overcomes that of the limited revelation in the old, and will not fade as did the radiance from Moses' face.

Second, in verses 14–16, Paul uses the incident to illustrate the veil that seemed to be over the hearts and minds of many Jews, so that they couldn't understand or believe the gospel. Preaching the gospel to Jews today is still very difficult. Paul experienced this difficulty and said there was a veil over their hearts.

Third, in verse 18, Paul uses the incident to illustrate how believers today have been given an unveiled view of Jesus and, as a result, are being transformed into his likeness by the Holy Spirit's work. The people in Exodus could not look on the face of Moses, but we can look on the face of Jesus Christ. How can that be? By the Holy Spirit giving us an unveiled view of God in Scripture, just as he gives us an unveiled view of Jesus. If we study the Bible, we will find out what Jesus Christ is like. And, as the Holy Spirit blesses this discovery, opening our minds and hearts to understand it, we become increasingly like him, and more and more reflect his glory.

LEARNING FROM EXODUS 33–34

We need mercy. We need mercy if we are to be saved. We have to remind ourselves constantly of this truth, because we do not naturally think this way. We think in terms of justice, and we suppose that we want justice because we consider ourselves to be deserving. But justice will send us to hell. We need mercy, not justice from God, in order to be saved. Israel needed mercy, Moses needed mercy, and we need mercy. Apart from God's mercy we will perish.

God is merciful. The good news is that God is a God of mercy. Now, it is true that he is also a God of justice and wrath, which is all that we have any right to expect from him. If we stop thinking about ourselves for a moment and look around at the evil in the world, we might say that what this world most deserves is annihilation. With all the evil out there, the hand of God should blot it out.

But the very essence of God's nature is his mercy. In order to find his mercy, we must come to him through the way he has provided: the death of his Son Jesus Christ.

This is how God puts together his justice and mercy. He has to punish sin, but he punishes our sin in Jesus Christ, if we will have it so. If we come to him on the basis of the death of Jesus Christ, the wrath that we deserve has already been poured out. God doesn't turn his back on that aspect of his nature. He is glorified in his wrath in the punishment of Jesus Christ his Son. At the same time, in the most marvelous way, God's mercy is revealed in the death of Jesus Christ. There wrath and mercy come together and join hands.

We can appeal to God's mercy. The mercy of God is not compelled in any way. God does not owe us mercy. He does not owe us anything but judgment and damnation. But this does not mean that we can't appeal to God on the basis of his mercy. God says that he is a merciful God—slow to anger, compassionate, and of great mercy. We can appeal to this aspect of his nature.

Remember the Pharisee in Jesus' story, a very self-righteous man who stood up and prayed about himself. He said, "God, I thank you that I am not like other men" (Luke 18:11)—not like adulterers, sinners, murderers, and thieves. The Pharisee said he lived a pious life, even tithing everything that he had. Yet God said that this man did not find mercy. He was pleading his works, and his works, as righteous as they seemed to him, deserved only God's judgment. He wasn't a perfect, sinless man. He was self-righteous, proud and utterly self-sufficient. He thought he did not need God's mercy.

Then there was the tax collector. He was a scoundrel. Everybody looked down on him. Upright, moral, pious Jews would not have anything to do with a man like that. They would cross the road to avoid contamination. But he prayed, "God, be merciful to me, a sinner" (Luke 18:13). He appealed to the mercy of God. He did not say he was righteous, because he wasn't. The tax collector said, "I'm a sinner," because he was. He appealed to God on the basis of God's mercy, and he found mercy because God has provided it for us in Jesus Christ. And Jesus said that the tax collector was the man who went home justified, not the Pharisee.

Who are those who receive mercy? Those who ask for it. The elect of God are those who turn from their own self-sufficiency and trust Jesus. They are those who find God to be a God of mercy.

We can proclaim God's mercy to others. God is sovereign in his salvation. He has mercy on whom he wills to have mercy and has compassion on whom he wills to have compassion; but since he is a merciful God, nothing in the Bible hinders us from telling people that God is merciful and from encouraging them to call out to God for mercy, that they may find it in the day of his grace.

> Come, ev'ry soul by sin oppressed,
> There's mercy with the Lord,
> And he will surely give you rest,
> By trusting in his Word.
>
> Only trust him, only trust him,
> Only trust him now;
> He will save you, he will save you,
> He will save you now.[10]

If you come to God on the basis of his mercy, you will find that he is the one who was merciful enough to cause you to call on him. You will find mercy, and you will be saved.

10. John H. Stockton, "Only Trust Him," 1874.

16

THE SHEKINAH GLORY

Exodus 39–40

THE CLOUD AT THE CLIMAX OF EXODUS

There are not many studies of the great cloud that protected the Hebrew people during the years of their desert wanderings. This surprises me for two reasons. The cloud was a striking phenomenon—there has never been anything else like it in history before or since. And it not only was striking, but also is mentioned many times in the Bible. Fifty-eight mentions of the cloud are scattered across ten different books of the Bible. It appears more often than place names like Bethlehem and Nazareth or the names of Herod, Joseph, Mary, Cain, Abel, and Satan.

This great pillar appeared for the very first time when the people left Egypt. As a cloud it went before them in the daytime to direct them in the way they should go. It turned into a pillar of fire by night, as we first learn in Exodus 13:21–22. In the very next chapter, when the people were being pursued by the Egyptians and seemed to be trapped between the Red Sea and the pursuing armies of Pharaoh, the cloud went behind them and protected them from attack by the Egyptians. We are told that it was light toward the camp of the Israelites and darkness toward the Egyptians (see Ex. 14:19–20).

After that, the cloud appears many more times. We can track it throughout the Pentateuch. It appears, too, at the dedication of Solomon's temple. According to 1 Kings 8:10, it descended on the temple

209

as God's way of indicating his blessing on the work and his intention to dwell among his people. It appeared on the Mount of Transfiguration when Jesus was changed before his disciples. "A bright cloud overshadowed them, and a voice from the cloud said, 'This is my beloved Son, with whom I am well pleased'" (Matt. 17:5). God the Father spoke from the cloud to declare the identity and authority of his Son. It may have been present at the ascension, when Jesus was taken up from earth and a cloud received him and he disappeared from their sight (see Acts 1:9).

The climax of the book of Exodus occurs when the cloud "covered the tent of meeting, and the glory of the LORD filled the tabernacle" (40:34). It was so glorious and overwhelming that Moses himself "was not able to enter the tent of meeting" (v. 35).

We have been studying the remarkable story of Moses—the deliverance from the armies of Pharaoh, the plagues on Egypt, the giving of the law. Yet, at the very end of the book, the climax of it all is the descent of the cloud on the tabernacle.

PREPARING FOR THE END

In previous chapters I have pointed out that virtually the same material is given three times in the final section of Exodus. In the first presentation (see Ex. 25–31), God tells the people what to do, and in the second presentation (see Ex. 35–39:31), we are told in almost the same words that this is what they did. This brings us to the middle of Exodus 39. Here the same material is summarized again, in a certain way. We are told that the people did everything just as God had commanded that it be done (see Ex. 39:32, 43), and we are given a description of all the things they had made.

Now there were plenty of times in their history when the people did not do what the Lord had commanded. We saw one example in the making of the golden calf, and we will see many examples later. But as far as building the tabernacle was concerned, they did just as God had commanded, and as a result he blessed them through Moses (see Ex. 39:43). Blessing always follows obedience. It would be wonderful if this statement could be written over the lives of Christian people today: "He" or "she" or "you"—whoever it may be—"did according to all that the LORD had commanded" (v. 32; see also v. 42), and thus received the Lord's blessing.

So, in chapter 39, they completed the work. The first half of Exodus 40 contains the words of the Lord to Moses telling him to set up the tabernacle and exactly how to do it (see vv. 1–15). Then, beginning in verse 16, we're told that he did it exactly as God said. The theme phrase appears again: "according to all that the LORD commanded him" (v. 16), "as the LORD had commanded Moses" (v. 19), "as the LORD had commanded Moses" (v. 21), "as the LORD had commanded Moses" (v. 23), "as the LORD had commanded Moses" (v. 25), and so on (see also vv. 27, 29, 32). All these things were done exactly as the Lord had commanded. We have it declared three times in these two chapters: the people made the tabernacle, God told Moses to set it up, and Moses set it up.

At the very end, the cloud descended on the Tent of Meeting, which was placed at the heart of the tabernacle and included the Holy Place and the Most Holy Place.

> Then the cloud covered the tent of meeting, and the glory of the LORD filled the tabernacle. And Moses was not able to enter the tent of meeting because the cloud settled on it, and the glory of the LORD filled the tabernacle. (Ex. 40:34–35)

Thus God showed that he was pleased with the work, and content to dwell with his people.

WHAT WAS THE CLOUD?

Here we must try to figure out what the cloud was. The people called it a cloud, but only because they had no word in their vocabulary to describe it.

We have something analogous to this in our own recent history. When atomic blasts were set off near the end of World War II, the observers saw an immensely destructive force that rose up into the sky and spread out in a flash with great power. When reporters wrote for the newspapers, they called what they saw a "mushroom cloud." It wasn't really a cloud—not in the sense that we use the word to describe clouds—and it certainly wasn't a mushroom, although it was shaped something like a mushroom. The point is that they did not have any word to describe the appearance of an atomic blast.

This happened to the Israelites as well. An enormous thing came and led them and spread out over the camp, and they looked up at it and said, "What in the world is it?" Then they did just what we would do: they said that it was a cloud. Sometimes they called it a pillar of cloud or a pillar of fire. Sometimes they called it "the pillar of the Lord," and sometimes "the glory" or "the radiance." The Hebrew word for "radiance" is *shekinah*. Usually today when we refer to it, we call it the *Shekinah glory*—the blazing, luminescent glory of the Lord our God displayed in that particular phenomenon.

Anything that immense was certainly of great importance to the people, which is why it is mentioned so many times in the Pentateuch though not as often in the New Testament. We have passed beyond it and do not think much about it today, but it was enormously important to the Israelites.

A MANIFESTATION OF GOD'S PRESENCE

As I have mentioned, the cloud was a manifestation of God's presence. When that cloud came down upon the tabernacle at the end of Exodus, it showed that God had come down on the tabernacle to dwell with his people. As the text makes clear, Moses was unable to enter the tabernacle because God was there, and "the glory of the LORD filled the tabernacle" (Ex. 40:34, 35). Not even Moses could come into the very presence of the most holy God. And the cloud testified to the presence of God.

Earlier, referring to the little Tent of Meeting that Moses had set up outside the camp, Exodus 33:9–10 says,

> When Moses entered the tent, the pillar of cloud would descend and stand at the entrance of the tent, and the LORD would speak with Moses. And when all the people saw the pillar of cloud standing at the entrance of the tent, all the people would rise up and worship, each at his tent door.

The appearance of the cloud announced the presence of God, and the people responded in worship. Psalm 99:7 says, "He spoke to them from the pillar of cloud" (NIV). But, in an even more remarkable passage, Moses actually calls the cloud *the* LORD.

> The cloud of the LORD was over them by day when they set out from the camp.
> Whenever the ark set out, Moses said,
>
> "Rise up, O LORD [referring to the cloud]!
> May your enemies be scattered;
> may your foes flee before you."
>
> Whenever it came to rest, he said,
>
> "Return, O LORD,
> to the countless thousands of Israel." (Num. 10:34–36 NIV)

This is remarkable. Think about what we have learned of God and the nature of God from his revelation of himself to Moses, first at the burning bush and then on Mount Sinai. If anything, we have learned that God is immaterial and transcendent and dwells in unapproachable glory. Yet strikingly, here God indicates that he is willing to dwell among his people. How do we reconcile that? How can God be transcendent, immaterial, and unapproachable and at the same time dwell among his people?

The Bible teaches that God is both transcendent *and* immanent at the same time. We cannot see him. He is infinitely above and beyond us, so much so that we cannot even begin to comprehend what he is like in and of himself. Yet at the same time he is content to dwell among us—and in us—and to be our God.

God's revelation of himself in the cloud culminates in the coming of Jesus Christ. John uses language that harks back to Exodus to talk about the incarnation: "The Word [that is, Jesus] became flesh and dwelt among us, and we have seen his glory, glory as of the only Son from the Father, full of grace and truth" (John 1:14). The Greek word translated as "dwelt" is *eskenosen* and can be translated "tented" or "tabernacled." It is the same word used in Revelation 21:3 where John writes, speaking of the fulfillment of the promise of God's abiding presence, "And I heard a loud voice from the throne saying, 'Behold, the *dwelling place* of God is with man. He will *dwell* with them, and they will be his people, and God himself will be with them as their God.'"[1]

With the presence of the cloud, God taught the reality of his continuing presence in a preliminary, rudimentary, visible, and dramatic way to the people of Israel.

A METHOD OF GOD'S PROTECTION

God did not just appear to the people in the cloud. He also protected the people of Israel by the cloud. He protected them first of all from their enemies, the Egyptians: "Then the angel of God who was going before the host of Israel moved and went behind them, and the pillar of cloud moved from before them and stood behind them, coming between the host of Egypt and the host of Israel. And there was the cloud and the darkness. And it lit up the night without one coming near the other all night" (Ex. 14:19–20). From the very beginning, the people learned that the God who was with them was with them as their protector.

Remember, the number of people who went out from Egypt was very large. In the book of Numbers, the figure is given as 603,550 men, in addition to women, children, and other non-Hebrew people who accompanied them. This is at least two million people total, and probably more. It is very hard to imagine even a million. The Rose Bowl in California, one of the largest athletic stadiums in the world, holds close to a hundred thousand people. The number that went out of Egypt with Moses was at least twenty times that.

God led this large group of people out into one of the most inhospitable environments on earth. The temperature in the daytime goes

---

1. Compare this to the wording in the KJV: "Behold, the *tabernacle* of God is with men, and he will dwell with them, and they shall be his people, and God himself shall be with them, and be their God."

well above a hundred degrees when the sun beats down out of the cloudless sky, and they did not have air conditioning. When I was in Egypt years ago, we went down to Luxor, which is not as far out into the desert as the people were in Sinai, and the temperature in the daytime was 140 degrees. We couldn't go out in the daytime. We had come to tour, so we would get up at about 4 a.m., go out, and come back by 8 a.m. Then we would sit in a bathtub full of water all day long, and at about 8 or 9 at night we would go out and do more sightseeing. And if that weren't enough, because the air is so thin in the desert, when the sun goes down the temperatures drop precipitously. Sometimes temperatures over 100 degrees in the daytime fall below freezing at night. Water left outside the tent freezes.

God's cloud spread out over the people, providing shelter from the sun in the daytime and a certain degree of warmth at night, when it turned into a pillar of fire. Psalm 105:39 describes it this way: "He spread a cloud for a covering, and fire to give light by night." One of our great hymns picks up that idea.

> Round each habitation hov'ring,
> See the cloud and fire appear
> For a glory and a cov'ring,
> Showing that the Lord is near:
> Thus deriving from their banner
> Light by night and shade by day,
> Safe they feed upon the manna
> Which he gives them when they pray.[2]

Thus we see that the cloud was not only a manifestation of God's presence, which was glorious in itself, but also a pledge that God would stand by his people to protect them from any and all circumstances.

A MEANS FOR GOD'S GUIDANCE

The cloud was also God's means for guidance. When that cloud rose up from over the tabernacle and began to move, the people were

2. John Newton, "Glorious Things of Thee Are Spoken," 1779.

215

supposed to move too. When the cloud stopped, the people were to stop. Nehemiah says, "By day the pillar of cloud did not cease to guide them on their path, nor the pillar of fire by night to shine on the way they were to take" (Neh. 9:19 NIV). A more extended passage, in Numbers 9:15–23, gives greater detail, describing how the cloud would remain in one place, sometimes for a few days and sometimes for much longer.

Do you wish that God would lead you with such explicit and unmistakable directions? That the cloud would set out, and you would know where you were to go, and when the cloud stopped you would know you were to stop? I wonder if you would like that. I ask because I do not think that the Israelites liked it one bit.

Imagine a Hebrew family traveling along with all the other families, following the cloud in the heat of the summer in the Sinai Peninsula. The cloud is shading them, but it is hot. They've been walking for five or six hours, and they're uncomfortable and tired. Finally, at the end of the afternoon, the cloud stops. Somebody notices—"I think the cloud has stopped." And they all stop. They look up and say, "Yes. I think the cloud has stopped." That is the signal for them to stop too. They think, *Thank goodness it's the end of the afternoon. It's time to quit.*

The family has a little donkey with them that is carrying their things. They take their tent off the donkey and set it up. They get out a few other household objects and arrange them. Then they get out what they need to cook their supper, and they do so. Having finished their supper, they're ready to stretch out under their tent and sleep until morning.

Then somebody out on the very edge of the camp calls out in a loud voice, "I think the cloud is moving again." They look up. Sure enough, the cloud is moving again. They've just gotten settled, but they have to get going. So they fold up all their stuff and get it back on the donkey, and they start out after the cloud.

The cloud moves for about an hour and a half, from the little valley where they just were to a little farther up, and it stops again. "Well," they say, "it's not going to catch us this time. We'll leave everything packed." So they sit on the sand. Nothing happens. It gets dark, so finally they lie down and fall asleep.

They wake up in the morning. They look up. Cloud's still there. Well, they just make do, getting through the day as best they can. Nighttime. The cloud is still there. They lie down again. In the morning, they get up. Still there. About a week goes by, and finally the mother, who is more sensible in these matters, says to the father, "I think we might as well get it over with and set up camp." The father says, "I guess you're right. We ought to do it."

So they take the tent down and set it up. They get the household items and arrange them inside the tent. And no sooner do they get everything unpacked than somebody calls out, "The cloud is moving again!" and they have to do it all again.

Something of this is conveyed in Numbers 9:15–23. Sometimes the cloud stayed only from the evening to the morning. Sometimes it stayed for three days. Sometimes it stayed for a week, sometimes a month, and sometimes a year, and God did not tell the people in advance what he was doing. I think they must have hated it, because I know that I would have hated it, and you probably would have hated it too. We like regularity. Change is one of the hardest things we face. If we do have to change, we want to be told about it in advance. We want all the options to be laid out. We want to give our input. When we get all the details settled, then we will decide how we are going to go.[3]

Unfortunately, God does not lead his people that way. God does not often take us into his confidence while planning out our lives. He simply does, and you and I have to go along with it. We have to. If one of those stiff-necked people had said, "I don't care if the cloud is moving. I hate that cloud. I'm just going to get by on my own," in a very few minutes he would have been stuck in the desert under the blazing sun. He would have died, either from the heat of the sun in the daytime or from the cold temperatures at night.

---

3. This is an imaginative interpretation first presented in the preaching of Dr. Donald Grey Barnhouse, pastor of Tenth Presbyterian Church in Philadelphia, Pennsylvania, from 1927–1960.

LEARNING FROM EXODUS 39–40

The point is not that God is arbitrary. He was taking a nation of slaves with no discipline, no law, and no religion, and he was giving them all three of those things. He was beginning to train a rabble to become a nation, as well as the kind of fighting force that would one day be able to conquer the land of promise.

If God is guiding us, which he has promised to do for those trusting in the salvation Jesus has provided, there is a goal, a destination, for us, too. That goal is to be "conformed to the image of his Son," as Paul states in Romans 8:29. And God has determined that his children will reach that goal. The Lord will see to it that all the circumstances of our lives, including the hard experiences and disappointments, will work to change us into the image of Jesus. However, unlike many of the Israelites, who through unbelief and disobedience did not reach the land of promise, all the redeemed in Christ, in his perfect timing, will enter the presence of the Lord. As Alan Cole writes, "To speak of a journey is to look for an arrival: He who has begun a work of salvation for Israel will complete it (Phil. 1:6)."[4]

We may think at this point that Israel had an advantage that we do not have. After all, the cloud was visible and unmistakable. The Israelites just had to follow it. We may wish that we had something that visible to guide us. But are we really to suppose that today, in the age of the church, we are in an inferior position to those who were God's people under the old covenant? Are we to think that the new covenant is not better in this respect, as in all other respects? Of course not. What we have today must be better. And it is—because God has given us the Holy Spirit, God himself, the third person of the Trinity. The Holy Spirit is not merely dwelling over us. He is actually dwelling *within* us, and he protects and guides us as he enables us to understand the Bible and obey it. Jesus spoke about this in the upper room when he told his disciples, "When the Spirit of truth comes, he will guide you into all the truth" (John 16:13). Paul, writing in his

---

4. R. Alan Cole, *Exodus*, Tyndale Old Testament Commentaries (Downers Grove, IL: IVP Academic, 1973), 239.

letter to the Galatians, said, "walk by the Spirit, and you will not gratify the desires of the flesh" (Gal. 5:16).

If the Holy Spirit does for us today what the cloud did for Israel in the Old Testament, then the New Testament equivalent of the event at the very end of Exodus is Pentecost, when the Holy Spirit came on the disciples in visible manifestations and empowered them for witness and for service.

> Suddenly a sound like the blowing of a violent wind came from heaven and filled the whole house where they were sitting. They saw what seemed to be tongues of fire that separated and came to rest on each of them. All of them were filled with the Holy Spirit and began to speak in other tongues as the Spirit enabled them. (Acts 2:2–4 NIV)

If you are a Christian, God has already set his mark on you by giving you the Holy Spirit. You would not be a Christian if he had not. But because God, by the presence and power of his Holy Spirit, regenerates you, making you alive in Christ, then the very fact that you are a Christian is evidence that God has set his protecting hand on you—as he did on the people of Israel and their work when he came down in the form of the cloud on the tabernacle. If that great gift of the Holy Spirit has been given to us, then we should aim at God's approval in our lives through our service even more than did those who were under the old covenant.

The Holy Spirit is given to enable us to follow as God leads and as we follow, to know that we are protected from all enemies. Nothing will ever happen to us that does not first pass through the will of God. Nothing will ever happen that is not ultimately for our good: "And we know that for those who love God all things work together for good, for those who are called according to his purpose" (Rom. 8:28).

The way through the desert was not always an easy way, but never did the cloud and pillar of fire, evidence of God's continuing presence, fail to give guidance and protection.

William Williams, in his well-loved hymn "Guide Me, O Thou Great Jehovah," expresses the reality of the Israelites' experience of God's care in the desert and uses the imagery of the desert journey to help Christians pray for that same guidance and protection on our own earthly pilgrimage.

Guide me, O thou great Jehovah,
Pilgrim through this barren land;
I am weak, but thou art mighty;
Hold me with thy pow'rful hand;
Bread of heaven, Bread of heaven,
Feed me till I want no more,
Feed me till I want no more.

Open now the crystal fountain,
Whence the healing stream doth flow;
Let the fire and cloudy pillar
Lead me all my journey through;
Strong Deliverer, strong Deliverer,
Be thou still my Strength and Shield,
Be thou still my Strength and Shield.

When I tread the verge of Jordan,
Bid my anxious fears subside;
Death of death, and hell's Destruction,
Land me safe on Canaan's side;
Songs of praises, songs of praises
I will ever give to thee,
I will ever give to thee.[5]

5. William Williams, "Guide Me, O Thou Great Jehovah," 1745.

PART 3

WORSHIPPING IN THE WILDERNESS

17

LEVITICUS: AN OVERVIEW

Leviticus 1—27

INTRODUCTION TO LEVITICUS

On one occasion, the great Samuel Johnson was talking about *Paradise Lost*, that great classic of the English language. He knew many people who had read it, he said, but he did not know many who had read it *through*.[1] That is true of a lot of classics, and I think it is true of Leviticus. This is a difficult book. I once told the Old Testament scholar Walt Kaiser, "I can't imagine anybody making a real study of Leviticus," and he replied that he'd just written a commentary on it. That put me in my place.

I do not often do surveys of books. (In fact, I incline the other way—I once spent four separate weeks on the shortest verse in the entire Bible: "Jesus wept" [John 11:35].) Yet I will survey Leviticus, because we are studying the life of Moses. We want to concentrate on what Moses did and analyze him in terms of his character and accomplishments. But at the same time we can't *avoid* studying Leviticus, even though we are merely giving it a survey here, because it is one of the books that Moses gave us as he himself was given it by God the Holy Spirit.

Leviticus is the third of the five books of Moses, standing in the very middle of the Pentateuch. Though it contains many prescriptions for

1. See Samuel Johnson, *The Lives of the English Poets* (repr., London, 1826), 1:119–20.

223

holy living, the book has to do primarily with sacrifices and offerings, so placing it in the center of the five books of Moses may be a way of emphasizing that the sacrifices stand at the very heart of the Old Testament religion. They also point to the very heart of Christianity, because all the sacrifices are fulfilled and brought to completion by Jesus Christ. And his death on the cross stands at the very heart of Christianity. So as we come to Leviticus, we come to the very heart of the meaning of the Christian faith.

The book of Leviticus is referred to frequently in the New Testament. It may be a difficult book, but the New Testament writers meditated on this book. They came to understand that the sacrifices described in Leviticus pointed to and explained the necessity for Jesus' death on the cross. As the writer of Hebrews states, "Indeed, under the law almost everything is purified with blood, and without the shedding of blood there is no forgiveness of sins" (Hebrews 9:22). Here is a clear reference to Leviticus 17:11, the verse which sums up the reason for the sacrifices: "For the life of the flesh is in the blood . . . for it is the blood that makes atonement by the life."

Moreover, in Matthew 22:39, Jesus quotes Leviticus 19:18 as a statement of the second greatest commandment: "You shall love your neighbor as yourself." Paul quotes Leviticus 18:5 in Romans 10:5 and Galatians 3:12, and quotes Leviticus 26:12 to support his argument in 2 Corinthians 6:16. The words and the theology of Leviticus undergird the teachings of the New Testament authors.

AN OUTLINE OF LEVITICUS

Leviticus was a handbook for the priests of Israel, who were Levites; so *Leviticus* actually means "Pertaining to the Priests." Jews call this book the Book of the Priests, or the Law of the Offerings. Its Hebrew name is *Vayikra*, which is the opening Hebrew word: "and he called." (The Hebrew books are often known by their opening Hebrew word.) The "and" is left out of the NIV and ESV translations because that is an awkward way to begin a book in English, but it is significant in Hebrew because it ties Leviticus to Exodus, the book preceding it. Exodus itself begins the same way, tying it to Genesis.

224

The books of Moses are one continuous story. Thus, Leviticus is not a radically different book but a continuation—an unfolding of what we already read in Exodus. This is part of the law that was given to the Israelites when they were at Mount Sinai.

Because Leviticus is a handbook for the priests on how to perform the sacrifices and the offerings, as well as a book of instructions for holy living, it does not contain much historical material. In fact, of all Moses' five books, Leviticus contains the fewest narrative portions. One describes the ordination and installation of the priests in their office, followed by the sin and deaths of the two sons of Aaron, Nadab and Abihu. The second episode, recorded in chapter 24, gives a short account of an Israelite found guilty of blasphemy.

The outline is easy for the first half of the book, though scholars differ somewhat on how to divide the last eleven chapters into subtopics. We can see that chapters 1–7 describe the rules for the sacrifices and offerings. Chapters 8–10 contain the first narrative section; Moses could have merely proscribed how the priests were to be installed, but instead he tells how it actually happened. He then gives an account of the failure of Aaron's two sons to fulfill their holy obligations as members of the new priesthood. The next section, chapters 11–15, has to do with uncleanness and purification. This is probably where most readers get bogged down. We can understand the offerings because they are fulfilled in Jesus Christ, but today the purification rituals sound strange to us.

Chapter 16, giving instructions for the Day of Atonement, stands alone. We will look at chapter 16, placed almost in the very center of Leviticus, in more detail in chapter 19 of this commentary, because Jesus fulfilled the sacrifices of the Day of Atonement in a final way as he suffered and died at Calvary.

A collection of material in chapters 17–24 presents detailed directions and instructions for living the holy life, including a repeat of the description of Israel's holy days and feasts, and instructions about the care of items within the tabernacle. Chapter 25 gives instructions about the Sabbath year and the Year of Jubilee, and also the procedures for the redemption of property and of people sold into slavery. Finally, chapters 26 and 27 list the curses which will follow disobedience, the blessings following obedience, and instructions about vows and tithes. Altogether this gives us seven sections. Although I won't go into great detail, I will cover the three major parts of Leviticus in this chapter: offerings, purification, and the holy life.

OFFERINGS (LEV. 1–7)

The sacrifices described in chapters 1–7 are discussed twice— first from the perspective of the worshippers (Lev. 1–6:7), then (with the order changed very slightly) from the perspective of the priests (Lev. 6:8–7:38). It is easy to understand the two sections. The section beginning the book tells the worshipper how to bring his sacrifice and what to do with it, and the second section tells the priest what to do with the sacrifice that he receives.

THE BURNT OFFERING (LEV. 1; 6:8–13)

The burnt offering is mentioned first because it was the most important. Leviticus doesn't tell us what it was for because the answer is so obvious. All the sacrifices on the altar are for sin.

The text focuses on how the animals are to be handled. Notice two matters here. First, the worshipper was to lay his hand on the head of the burnt offering that was going to be accepted on his behalf (see Lev. 1:4). This is critical and pertains to all the sacrifices. When the worshipper put his hand on the sacrifice, he symbolically transferred his sin or guilt to the sacrifice. It was a kind of confession of sin, through which the sin passed in a symbolic way to the animal. Then, when the animal was killed, it was killed in place of the worshipper.

Second, when the animal was killed, the blood of the sacrifice had to be sprinkled on the altar. This was done in different ways with different sacrifices, but in every sacrifice for sin the blood had to be sprinkled on the altar. The blood testified to the death of the substitute. This too is critical. Throughout the Bible we are told that "without the shedding of blood there is no forgiveness of sins" (Heb. 9:22) and that "the wages of sin is death" (Rom. 6:23). My sin requires death. The just God of the universe must punish my sin with death—not just with physical death, which we will all experience, but with spiritual death as well. The only way we can be saved is by an innocent substitute dying in our place. The blood of sheep and goats did not take away sin (see Heb. 10:4). It was only a type that pointed forward to Jesus Christ. When he came and died, those types were fulfilled in him, and his shed blood took away our sin. If we do not have faith in Jesus Christ, we do not have salvation.

THE GRAIN OFFERING (LEV. 2; 6:14–23)

The grain offering was also called the "meal offering"—an older word for grain. This was the only offering that was not for sin, since no blood was shed. It was usually offered at the same time as the animal sacrifices. The offering consisted of finely ground flour that was mixed with oil, incense, and salt—all of which had symbolic meanings—and then, after it was baked or prepared on a griddle, it was given to the priest. The priest took a crumbled handful and offered it on the altar as a memorial, and the rest was kept in order to be eaten—in this case, primarily by the priests.

The grain offering was what we would call an offering of thanksgiving. It was a kind of gift to God, in the same way that as Christians we now give our offerings. We do not atone for sin in any way through anything that we give, but we give because we're thankful to God for what he has done and because we want to see his work go forward.

THE FELLOWSHIP OR PEACE OFFERING
(LEV. 3; 7:11–21)

The third offering was the fellowship offering. Now, the Hebrew word for "fellowship" is a form of the word *shalom*, that well-known Jewish greeting that means "peace" or "well-being." For that reason, this offering is also sometimes called the peace offering.

The fellowship offering was for sin. When the worshipper brought his offering, several of the actions associated with the burnt offering were done in this case as well. The worshipper put his hand on the animal, and the animal was killed. But in this case not all of the animal was burnt—only the interior portions of the animal. The rest was eaten as food—partly by the priests, since they were sustained this way, but mostly by the worshipper, his family, and his friends. This is why it was called a fellowship meal.

Fellowship offerings sometimes involved a great number of animals. For example, when Solomon dedicated the temple (see 1 Kings 8), he offered 22,000 cows and 120,000 sheep, which were afterward used to feed the people. This was a celebration—a great outdoor barbecue that took place at the dedication of the temple—but the slain animals were first presented to the Lord as a fellowship offering.

Although it was a sin offering, the emphasis of the fellowship offering was not on the burning up of the sin or the passing of the sin to the animal. Rather, the focus was on the fellowship, or peace, that was reestablished between the worshipper and God. Having made peace through the offering, the worshipper could sit down in peace, knowing that things were right between himself and God, and thus he could also enjoy a time of true fellowship with his family and friends.

We must remember that this is one aspect of what Jesus Christ accomplished for us by his death. Colossians 1:19–20 says that, "in him all the fullness of God was pleased to dwell, and through him to reconcile to himself all things, whether on earth or in heaven, making peace by the blood of his cross." Peace, or *shalom*, is one thing that our Lord has accomplished for us.

THE SIN OFFERING (LEV. 4:1–5:13; 6:24–30)

The sin offering is given the longest description of any of the five offerings, which leads us to think that it was probably the kind of offering that was offered most often. It was for what we would call *unintentional sin*. Some examples are given in chapter 5. One such sin is failing to speak in another's defense. If you heard someone being accused of some misdeed, knew a mitigating factor that could excuse the accused, and yet did not say anything, that was an offense. You didn't intend to do it; you just let the opportunity slip. Other examples include taking a wrong or meaningless oath or unintentionally touching something ceremonially unclean. There were probably dozens, maybe hundreds, of unintentional transgressions like this. The sin offering atoned for them.

THE GUILT OFFERING (LEV. 5:14–6:7; 7:1–10)

The last offering, the guilt offering, was for damage that was done to another person or to his property. This doesn't mean that if a person damaged somebody's property—either deliberately or by negligence—then all he had to do was go to the tabernacle and present an offering. That would be an easy way to get off the hook. No, Leviticus describes very carefully what the offender had to do. He had to repay the damages, add another twenty percent, i.e. a fifth of its value, and then give this payment to the person who had been defrauded on the very day he went to present his guilt offering.

This was an admission that, yes, the offender had offended God and had to make it right with him—but, even before he made it right with God, the offender had to make it right with the person whom he had hurt as well. Remember what Jesus said in the Sermon on the Mount: "If you are offering your gift at the altar and there remember that your brother has something against you, leave your gift there before the altar and go. First be reconciled to your brother, and then come and offer your gift" (Matt. 5:23–24). Making things right with God does not excuse our responsibility to make them right with other people.

LEARNING FROM LEVITICUS 1–7

Even though Leviticus is hard to wade through or summarize, it nevertheless contains principles that have very practical bearing on our Christian lives.

Anyone could bring an offering. When I studied commentaries on Leviticus and the commentators were discussing the details of the offering, it was not often mentioned that anyone could bring an offering to be sacrificed. It is easy to overlook that fact. Yet this is true egalitarianism, and that is the case with Christianity. Anybody can come—not just the high and the mighty, not just the lonely or the lowly. Jesus said, "Come." Anybody who is hungry and thirsty can come. Whatever your need may be, you can come to Jesus Christ. After all, Jesus said, "Whoever comes to me I will never cast out" (John 6:37).

Every offering cost the worshipper. In one incident in David's life, a friend offered him animals for sacrifice, and David said, "I will not sacrifice to the LORD my God burnt offerings that cost me nothing" (2 Sam. 24:24 NIV). Each of the offerings in Leviticus cost the worshipper something.

Now when it comes to our salvation, it is free for us—although it cost God the death of his Son. It cost Jesus Christ everything. But when we find salvation in Jesus Christ, we come to him with our offerings of thanksgiving and praise, and these too should be costly. We are to offer God our all: everything we are, everything we have, everything we can accomplish. All of this has to be given up to Jesus Christ. He demands no less. He said, "If anyone would come after me, let him deny himself and take up his cross and follow me" (Matt. 16:24; cf. Luke 14:25–33).

Only the best could be offered. As we read through the instructions for the offerings, we find that the people could not bring maimed or bruised animals. A sacrifice had to be a perfect sample from the flock. As a matter of fact, the worshipper had to examine the animal before he brought it to make sure that it was the best he had to offer.

You and I also have to offer our best to God. We're told in Romans 12:1 that we are to offer our bodies as "a living sacrifice, holy and acceptable to God." We can only present ourselves as "holy and acceptable" sacrifices if we understand that we "have been crucified with Christ," as Paul states in Galatians 2:20, and that it is "Christ who lives in me," whose Spirit makes possible such a holy and pleasing life.

PURIFICATIONS (LEV. 11–15)

Following the brief historical section is a second main block of material which has to do with the ceremonial laws of purification. This is the strangest part of the book. As we look at it, we wonder why the people were given such instructions. It is very hard for us to figure out the purpose, and of course it bothers us when we can't figure out the purpose of something. (This is one reason why following the Lord is sometimes so difficult: he doesn't always explain his purposes.)

APPROACHES TO UNDERSTANDING THE
PURIFICATION LAWS

People have taken three general approaches to this part of Leviticus. Some commentators have understood these purification laws to be intended to separate the religious practices of the Israelites from those of the surrounding heathen nations. In other words, the Israelites were given laws that made them different so that they would not get mixed up in the pagan religious practices of their neighbors.

Others believe that these laws were an outward way of reminding the people that they had to be separated from the world to God. So, for example, if one went through a ceremonial washing, he would have shown that he was separating from sin and standing in a holy relationship with the Lord God.

A popular view today is that many of these laws involve matters of health—protecting Israel from a bad diet, dangerous vermin, infectious diseases, and so on. For example, they were not supposed to eat pigs, which spread trichinosis if their flesh is not cooked well enough; rabbits, which carry tularemia; and unclean fish such as eels, which tend to carry more parasites than free-swimming fish with scales. Commentators love pursuing these explanations. They go into great detail about what kinds of problems may have been avoided when the people followed these laws.

Initially I thought that the third explanation had the most to commend it. But then, I live in a very health-conscious environment and culture. Being separated from the religious practices of one's neighbors would have been God's concern for his covenant people, as well as going through a ceremony that reminds you that you are not your own, but that you belong to God and have to be holy unto him. We Christians have something like this in the sacraments. When we baptize people, we are setting them apart to God, identifying them with Jesus Christ. Taking part in the communion service reminds us that we are to have fellowship with Jesus Christ and not continue in sin in the ways of the non-Christian world. Still, it is possible that all three explanations of the purification laws are valid.

THE LAWS OF PURIFICATION

The headings in the New International Version probably give us the best outline for this section. The editors divide it into seven parts: five different sections, plus two repeats.

Clean and unclean food (Lev. 11). The distinction between clean and unclean animals goes all the way back to the flood, because the animals that came on board were identified as either clean or unclean; but at that point we weren't told how such animals were distinguished. Now we are. We can see how these laws served health reasons, but in particular is the second reason noted above—to be separated from the world to God.

When we study Leviticus, we read through verses that do not seem to mean much to us, and then suddenly a key verse jumps out. This happens in Leviticus 11:44–45: "For I am the LORD your God. Consecrate yourselves therefore, and be holy, for I am holy. . . . You shall therefore be holy, for I am holy." This very sentence, or variations of it, occurs again and again throughout Leviticus, and Peter quotes it in the New Testament: "since it is written, 'You shall be holy, for I am holy'" (1 Peter 1:16). Here, in the middle of the book of Leviticus, the theme is stated clearly. The way we relate to some of these purification requirements has changed, but the purpose behind them has not: we are to be holy, for our God is holy. Or, as Paul instructs believers, "do not be conformed to this world, but be transformed . . ." (Rom. 12:2).

Purification after childbirth (Lev. 12). These regulations have puzzled many who suppose they are teaching that sex or childbirth is sinful or unclean. That is not true. The Israelites regarded neither of these things as sinful. God created sex for pleasure and procreation. Children are called a gift from God. A woman who was able to bear many children was considered particularly blessed.

What makes the woman unclean in childbirth are the secretions that accompany and follow the birth, just as secretions of a different nature also defile the man (see Lev. 15). Thus women were supposed to perform purification rites, and in this case it was a very healthy precaution. Before modern medicine, women who did not die in childbirth often died from what was then called *childbirth fever*, an infection that followed the birth. A time of isolation, rest and cleansing was a wise precaution.

Regulations about infectious skin diseases (Lev. 13:1–46; 14:1–32). The word that the NIV renders as "skin diseases" (or "leprous disease" in the ESV) is simply "leprosy" in the Hebrew. The Israelites did not distinguish between different kinds of severe skin diseases.

What is interesting in this section is that the priests apparently functioned as public health officers. They were responsible for the overall health of the community, and one thing they did was to isolate people (quarantine them) when they had skin diseases. We do not quarantine people much today because we have other ways of dealing with infectious illnesses. But in the past, if someone had an infectious disease that was spreading, the best thing to do was to quarantine those who were sick.[2] That is what the people were told to do in Leviticus. God's revelation gave the people a way to contain skin diseases, many spread by contact.

Mildew (Lev. 13:47–59; 14:33–57). The word that many Bible versions translate here as "mildew" is the same word used for infectious skin diseases. I do not know whether the people could distinguish one from the other. Mildew on the wall of a building or on clothing looks like something one might see on the skin. The Israelites treated them similarly. They did not have penicillin or other antibiotics, but they did what they could. If mildew did not clear up by itself when placed in isolation, the object was burned and people were quarantined.

Discharges that cause uncleanness (Lev. 15). Two kinds of discharges are discussed at some length. One is pathological—the passage doesn't describe the specific diseases involved, but it might be venereal disease—and required a sin offering. The second type of discharge is sexual and doesn't require a sin offering. Sex was not regarded as sinful, though there had to be purification.

---

2. And, even in recent times, quarantine has sometimes been used to prevent the spread of such virulent diseases as Ebola.

This chapter gives us the background we need to understand the story about the hemorrhaging woman in Mark 5:25–34. It explains her fear in the situation and the magnitude of her faith.

The woman described in Mark 5 had an emission of blood. This was one of the things that produced uncleanness. It meant that nobody could touch the woman and that she couldn't touch anybody else. She had been unable to be cured of her malady for a long time. When she saw Jesus going along through the crowd, she thought that reaching out and touching him would produce cleansing. She couldn't stop him to ask him to pay attention to her, but she reached out and touched the hem of his garment. She must have done so with fear and trepidation, because by touching even his garment she was breaking the law of Moses, making him unclean.

When Jesus stopped dead in his tracks, turned around, and said, "Who touched me?" she must have been scared to death. She had broken the law—and he was a rabbi, a teacher of the law. He was going to condemn her, an unclean woman, for touching him. This explains her fear, and, at the same time, it explains her faith. She perceived what all who understand who the Lord Jesus Christ is must perceive: when you come to Jesus Christ with your sin, your sin doesn't make him sinful—rather, his holiness purifies you. She thought to herself, "If I can just make contact with Jesus, the power will go from him to me, not the contamination from me to him."

Jesus said that the woman had great faith, and she was healed from that very hour (see Mark 5:34). No one who reaches out to Jesus Christ in faith ever fails to receive healing for his or her sin, his or her moral uncleanness.

LEARNING FROM LEVITICUS 11–15

Jesus gives the best commentary of what the purification laws were meant to do, which is to teach the uncleanness that resides in the heart. The outer uncleanness is meant to shine a light on the inner uncleanness.

Don't you see that whatever enters the mouth goes into the stomach and then out of the body? But the things that come out of the mouth come from the heart, and these make a man "unclean." For out of the heart come evil thoughts, murder, adultery, sexual immorality, theft, false testimony, slander. These are what make a man "unclean"; but eating with unwashed hands does not make him "unclean." (Matt. 15:17–20 NIV)

Jesus' teaching is that it is not what comes into you or touches you that makes you unclean, it is what comes out of you. The problem is not external; the problem is within you, in your heart.

Something like this might tempt us to say, "In that case, I don't have to worry about the law." This is true—of that particular part of the law. But whenever Jesus sets aside something from the Old Testament, he does so in order to establish something even more important. Jesus calls us to a higher standard. If it is not a matter of washing our hands, what is it? It is cleanliness of the heart. That is what matters. If we understand this, we should be even more concerned about the state of our hearts, out of which come impurities that contaminate the world in which we live. This should concern us much more than the Israelites were concerned about their ceremonial purifications—and we know how concerned they were about those.

Jeremiah said, "The heart is deceitful above all things, and desperately wicked: who can know it?" (Jer. 17:9 KJV). He might just as well have said, "Who can cure it?" The answer is "no human." Yet with God all things are possible. Jesus is able to cleanse your heart, however impure it may be, just as he healed the woman who had the issue of blood. He will do it if you ask him.

THE HOLY LIFE (LEV. 17–24)

The third section of Leviticus deals with the holy life. There are prohibitions against eating blood in chapter 17. Chapter 18 designates unlawful sexual relationships: the Israelites were not allowed to marry close family members. This makes good genetic sense. Chapter 19 collects various laws, most of which were already given in Exodus. In chapter 20, punishments are given for various sins, starting with those that required the death penalty. Leviticus 21–22:16 gives rules for the personal lives of the priests, with a description of unacceptable sacrifices taking up the remainder of the chapter. In chapter 23 we find a repetition of the description of Israel's seven annual holy days and feasts.

The section ends with the second historical incident: the man who blasphemed against God (Lev. 24:10–23). At the time, the Israelites did not know how to deal with this grave sin. They put him outside the camp until word came from God that he was to be killed for his blasphemy.

THE THEME OF LEVITICUS

In Leviticus 11:44–45, God says, "Be holy, for I am holy." This is the theme of Leviticus—and, in a certain sense, the theme of the entire Word of God. A holy God demands a holy people. Thus, a study of Leviticus should be a sobering experience. Do we take holiness seriously? Probably we do not. But God does. Do we realize that, because God is holy, we must be holy too? This is not optional. God tells us that we *must* be holy. As we answer these questions honestly, we need to ask what changes we must make to live a holy life.

Holiness is the destiny of God's people. In the great closing section of the book of Zechariah, the prophet envisioned a future day of great blessing for the Jews. On that day, not only will the people be holy, but everything about them will be holy to the Lord. "On that day HOLY TO THE LORD will be inscribed" not just on the high priest's turban but "on the bells of the horses, and the cooking pots in the LORD's house will be like the sacred bowls in front of the altar. Every pot in Jerusalem and Judah will be holy to the LORD Almighty" (Zech. 14:20–21 NIV). What is Zechariah talking about? Holy bells and holy cooking pots? Zechariah means that the people are going to be so holy that everything about them will be holy: people and objects set apart and belonging completely to the Lord.

But holiness is not just the destiny of the Jews. If you belong to Jesus Christ, holiness is your destiny as well. Have you ever thought about heaven as a place where you will be holy like Jesus Christ? Most of us do not. We think of love: Heaven is where we're going to love God perfectly, and he's going to love us, and we're all going to swim around in a wonderful sea of love. I do not doubt that this is true. But the Bible characterizes our destiny as holiness. In that day we will be holy, even as God is holy.

In John's first letter, he wrote, "we know that when he appears we shall be like [Jesus], because we shall see him as he is" (1 John 3:2). We are not holy now, but we will be one day. We will be like Jesus, because we will see him as he is: the holy Son of God. The next verse in 1 John immediately builds on this: "Everyone who thus hopes in him purifies himself as he is pure" (v. 3). If we really believe that one day we will be holy, then we will work at holiness now. We will take seriously the admonition and warning of the writer of Hebrews: "Strive for peace with everyone, and for the holiness without which no one will see the Lord" (12:14).

18

THE PRIESTS AND
THEIR MINISTRY

Leviticus 8—10

THE CALL TO HOLINESS

In the last chapter we saw that if we want to understand Leviticus, we have to understand holiness, since the theme, "You shall be holy, for I the LORD your God am holy" (19:2), is repeated again and again throughout the book. But what *is* holiness? Many of us mistakenly think of holiness in exclusively ethical terms. Because we think of ethics as a scale from 0 (very, very bad) to 100 (very, very good), we think of holiness as moving up the scale.

It is true that holiness involves ethical matters. Holy people will behave in a holy manner. But this is not the chief idea behind the word *holy*. The word has to do with consecration or separation. A good translation of *holy* is "set apart," which is why the word can be used for objects. Remember that Zechariah said that in the day of God's blessing on Israel, even the bells on the horses and the pots in the temple of the Lord will be holy. Pots and bells do not have ethical values, but they can be set apart. In that day, the people will be so set apart for God that everything they have will be set apart for him.

If we want to be holy, this is how: belong to God; be set apart to God; live for God so that everything we have belongs to God. Your bank account ought to be holy, because it ought to be set apart to

God. Your time ought to be holy because it is set apart for God. That is the idea of holiness in Leviticus.

In this chapter we will focus on the priests, for the priests were to be holy, set apart to serve God. We will look at their installation and ordination, their function, and finally the deaths of two of them. As we do so, we will remember that according to the New Testament, all of God's people are priests (see 1 Peter 2:9). Although certain things pertain particularly to the Old Testament priests—the offering of literal sacrifices, for example—the principles in Leviticus 8–10 apply to every single Christian.

ORDINATION OF THE PRIESTS (LEV. 8)

Leviticus 8 describes the public ordination of the priests. First they were purified by washing with water. Then they were clothed. The items of clothing were described in great detail in Exodus 28, as we saw in chapter 13 of this study. In Leviticus the vestments are described in the order in which Aaron and his sons put them on. Next, the tabernacle and the priests were consecrated—anointed with special oil prepared according to the instructions in Exodus 31.

In the Bible, oil is frequently used as a symbol of the Holy Spirit. When an individual was anointed with oil, it signified that the Holy Spirit was coming on him to bless him for the particular office to which he was being consecrated. In the Old Testament, we see people being anointed for three different offices: prophet (as when Elijah anointed his successor, Elisha), priest (as we see in this chapter), and king (when Samuel anointed both Saul and David). This anointing showed that these men were set apart by that special ritual to their unique office and function.

In the Old Testament period, a prophet could not be a priest, a priest could not be a king, a king could not be a prophet, and so on. Yet in Jesus' case, all three offices are combined in his one person.

+ *Prophet.* Jesus speaks the words of God. In the book of Deuteronomy, God says to Moses, "I will raise up for them a prophet like you from among their brothers. And I will put my words in his mouth, and he shall speak to them all that I command him" (Deut. 18:18). Jesus Christ is that prophet. He spoke the words of God. As the author of Hebrews states, "in these last days [God] has spoken to us by his Son" (1:2). This is the prophetic function.

♦ *Priest.* The book of Hebrews also declares that Jesus is a priest, and a priest forever (see Heb. 7:17). In the Old Testament, priests succeeded priests, one after the other; furthermore, they never finished their work but had to keep offering sacrifices again and again. The writer of Hebrews says that this is symbolized by the absence of chairs in the tabernacle and later in the temple (see Heb. 10:11). The priest's work was never done, so he could never sit down. Jesus Christ, however, is an eternal priest. He offered himself as a sacrifice once for all and, having done that, sat down at the right hand of God the Father (see Heb. 10:12). Our Great High Priest had made the atonement; his work as Savior was finished.

♦ *King.* The great prophecy in Isaiah 9:6 speaks about the one who would be called "Wonderful Counselor, Mighty God, Everlasting Father, Prince of Peace." The prophecy continues, stating that he will reign on David's throne and over his kingdom, establishing it with justice forever. This is exactly what Jesus Christ came to do, to reign as an eternal king. In the book of Revelation, we read that he is given the title King of Kings and Lord of Lords (see Rev. 19:16).

Jesus Christ is the perfect prophet, the perfect priest, and the perfect king. Does this have any application to us? Yes, in this sense: the New Testament tells us that although we do not serve as Jesus Christ did, and does, because we belong to Christ we have roles that are analogous to his.

♦ *As prophets.* Jesus is the prophet above all prophets, but we ourselves have a prophetic role because we are to speak the words of God. We do not have any authority in ourselves, but the Word of God has been given to us in the Bible, and our task is to make it known to others.

240

♦ *As priests.* We do not, and cannot, offer ourselves up as sacrifices for sin. Only Jesus could do that. But we are called to offer our bodies as living sacrifices to God (see Rom. 12:1–2), giving ourselves to him in service. We are called "a royal priesthood" (1 Peter 2:9), and one role of the priests was to offer intercession for the people. When people are resistant to the gospel, our prophetic and priestly task is to intercede for them, speaking the Word of God, and to pray that God will open their hearts and minds so they will understand the gospel and have faith in Jesus Christ.

♦ *As kings.* The Bible tells us that we will reign with Jesus Christ. We are called to suffer with him now, but one day we will reign with him in his kingdom (see II Tim. 2:12 and Rev. 20:4–6).

Most of the verses in Leviticus 8 are given over to the next and most important part of the ordination: the offerings (vv. 14–36). Aaron and his sons were to offer a bull as a sin offering, then a ram as a burnt offering, and finally a second ram as a special ordination offering. Here there are two important things to notice.

First, Aaron and his sons laid their hands on the animals' heads. As we have already seen, this was a way of symbolically transferring the sins of the worshipper to the innocent victim, which was then sacrificed in place of the one who deserved to die. The wages of sin was still the death of the sinner (see Rom. 6:23), but an animal died instead. This illustrates the concept of *substitutionary atonement*, pointing forward to Jesus Christ and to what he did for us. But notice that while Aaron and the priests were being set apart to God—they were holy unto the Lord, anointed with oil, blessed by the Holy Spirit for their function— the very first sacrifices they made were for themselves. Although they had been set apart for the Lord, they were nevertheless sinful people like anybody else. This is true of everyone who has ever served in the whole history of the people of God. Ministers, elders, and deacons are sinful, just like anybody else; their sins must be atoned for by Jesus' death before they can offer the grace and mercy of God to others.

Second, the blood from the sacrificed ram was applied to Aaron's right ear, the thumb of his right hand, and the big toe of his right foot. This was also done for his sons. The meaning is self-evident.

Anointing the priest's ear with blood meant that his ear was dedicated to God—he had to hear the word of God and proclaim it faithfully to the people. Anointing the thumb of his right hand meant that his hands were dedicated to God—what he did with his hands was to be in God's service. Anointing the toe of his right foot meant that his feet were dedicated to God—he had to walk in God's way. It is true that these men were sinners like everyone else, but they had been called to serve the living God, and were to live up to that high calling.

Today Christians have no lesser a calling. We too are to hear the Word of God as he speaks to us in Scripture. Every Christian is a priest of God, called to give our hands and feet to his service, offering up our members to God that they might be used by him, and going where he would have us go. We are not our own. We are bought with a price. We belong to Jesus Christ. Therefore all we are, all we have, all we can hope to be must belong to him.

THE FIRST WORSHIP SERVICE (LEV. 9)

The next chapter in Leviticus is extremely important because it gives us the first ever example of formal Hebrew worship. Individuals certainly worshipped God before this—building altars, offering sacrifices, and praying—but this is the first organized worship of the people of God recorded in the Bible.

What is worship, anyway? We can better understand it if we understand the root meaning of the word. Back in the days of Geoffrey Chaucer (late 1300s), when the English language was being shaped more or less into what we know it as today, they did not use the word "worship." They spoke, instead, of *worthship*: ascribing to God his true worth according to his attributes. In the ceremonies that take place in Leviticus 9, we are not told a whole lot about God's attributes, but the chapter does tell us that the Israelites did everything in obedience to the word of the Lord, stressing that everything they did (primarily sacrifices) was in response to God's teaching. The sacrifices, above all, testified to God's holiness.

All God's attributes are great, but the Bible most emphasizes his attribute of holiness. Today we emphasize his love: "God so loved the world that he gave his one and only Son" (John 3:16 NIV). It is true that God's love is a very great thing, but the emphasis of the Bible is on his holiness. Because God is holy, he had to send his Son to be the Savior. He could not save people just by loving them; Jesus had to die so that God's demand for holiness might be met.

The sacrifices offered in Leviticus 9 as part of worship were first for Aaron and his sons—that is, for the priests—and second, for the people. There is a difference between the animals offered at the ordination of the priests in chapter 8—a bull calf, a ram, and a second ram—and the ones that are offered for the people in the service described in chapter 9. Also, although the priests again offer a bull calf and a ram for themselves, as in the ordination service, in chapter 9 no second ram is mentioned being offered for the priests. The animals sacrificed for the people are a male goat (the sin offering), a calf and a lamb (the burnt offerings), and an ox and a ram (the peace/fellowship offerings). Without doubt, the order or sequence of the sacrifices is purposely the same for the priests and the people: the sin offering is first, followed by the burnt offering, and then finally the fellowship offering. What was being taught by the repeated enactment of this sequence of sacrifices?

As we approach God, our big problem is that we are sinners, and sin has to be dealt with. When we come to God, we must recognize that Jesus Christ is our *sin offering*. Because he died for you and me, we also must give ourselves to God completely, as signified by the *burnt offering*. Unlike some other sacrifices, the burnt offering was consumed completely on the altar. Jesus told us, "if you want to be my disciple you have to deny yourself, take up your cross, and follow me" (see Luke 9:23). Discipleship requires a complete giving of oneself. Then we will have peace with God through Jesus' sacrifice, as the *fellowship offering* symbolized. Our experience follows the sequence of the offerings that we see here: forgiveness of sins, the dedication of ourselves to God, and peace with God.[1]

The communion service is a reminder of and a memorial to the sacrificial death of Jesus Christ. The bread and wine signify that he gave

---

1. See Oswald T. Allis, "Leviticus," in *The New Bible Commentary*, ed. F. Davidson (repr., Grand Rapids: Erdmans, 1960), 141.

his life as an offering for our sin. Sharing in this holy meal requires us to search our hearts as we present ourselves to God, confessing our sin when we come to the communion table, in order that no barrier might break our fellowship with the Lord. It also signifies fellowship, as we eat together with fellow believers, and in the presence of the God who has bought us and saved us through Jesus Christ.

Following the worship service described in Leviticus 9, we are told twice that Aaron offered his blessing. First, Aaron "lifted up his hands toward the people and blessed them" (v. 22). Then Moses and Aaron both blessed the people (see v. 23). While we are not told what form the blessing took, Jewish commentators assume it was a blessing known as the "Aaronic blessing," since, where that blessing is found in Numbers 6, it is introduced with "This is how you are to bless the Israelites" (v. 23 NIV):

> The LORD bless you and keep you;
> the LORD make his face to shine upon you and be gracious to you;
> the Lord lift up his countenance upon you and give you peace. (vv. 24–26)

Nothing is more important in life than to have the face of God turned toward us in blessing. We experience this by pursuing the holiness that everything in these chapters describes.

In the end, God accepted the people's worship, revealing his shekinah glory (vv. 23–24). He came down on the tabernacle, and, in a special demonstration of his blessing, a fire went out from the presence of the Lord and consumed what was left on the altar. At the very end of Exodus we were told that the same thing also happened after the people had constructed and erected the tabernacle: God came down in the shekinah glory.

A REBUKE FOR US TODAY

What were the characteristics of this worship that we've seen so far?

- It was dignified and formal.
- It was orderly. Every step had monumental, eternal significance.
- It was serious. Nobody laughed or joked as they worshipped God.

244

♦ It took time. This was the work of an entire day—preparing and offering the sacrifices for Aaron and his sons and then for the people—a task that could not be rushed.

This is a rebuke to us if we compare these characteristics to what so often passes for Christian worship today, especially in evangelical churches. Is our worship dignified? How much goes on in our services that is not dignified at all? Is our worship orderly? *Chaotic* would better describe what happens in many churches. Serious? No—preachers are trying to be funny, to make people feel good so that they come back. Time-consuming? Nobody wants to take time. Services are getting shorter and shorter. Sermons are getting shorter and shorter. Prayers are getting shorter and shorter. Sometimes there are no public prayers at all. Some people even want to squeeze in the service on Friday or Saturday night, so that they do not have to go to church on the Lord's Day but can instead sleep in, watch football, or do whatever else is more important and pleasurable.

What a difference it would make if we truly hungered after God, if we were truly in awe of God, if the holiness of God truly meant something to us. We would begin preparing for worship on Saturday night. We would ask God to bless the Lord's Day and to prepare our hearts and minds to receive whatever he had for us when we came to church the next morning. We would come early—instead of dashing in at the last minute, we would be at church ahead of time, thinking about what was happening and praying for those who were taking part in the service. Assuming that we knew in advance the Scripture that would be explored, we would have studied it ourselves ahead of time. When we sang, we would sing knowledgeably, not anxious to get through the verses quickly and move on to something else. We would think about what the song or hymn had to say about God. When led in prayer, we would pray along with those who were praying, letting their prayer be our prayer and echoing in our hearts what was being said from the pulpit. When the service ended, we would leave with a certain degree of solemnity. I do not mean that we would not talk to one another and enjoy one another's company, but we would go out realizing that we are the people of God, that we have been with

God, and that we are being sent out into the world to represent him, to serve him, and to tell others about him. What a difference it would make if Christian people really participated in worship in that way.

THE DEATHS OF NADAB AND ABIHU (LEV. 10)

The end of chapter 9 is the highest peak to be found in the entire book of Leviticus. The priests have been consecrated and ordained. They have offered sacrifices during the first formal worship of the people, and God has come down upon the tabernacle to bless it in the visible presence of his shekinah glory.

Yet an enormous change comes in chapter 10. Suddenly we're in a different world, where instead of blessing we find death.

What's the difference? Previously everything was done exactly "as the LORD commanded" (see Lev. 8:4), and the result was God's blessing. In chapter 10, "Nadab and Abihu . . . offered unauthorized fire before the LORD, which he had not commanded them" (v. 1), and the result is God's breaking out in sudden judgment on them.

The account is brief. I suppose that reflects something of the pain that everybody must have experienced when these two men were struck down. It had been a glorious day: the first formal worship of the people. They had been doing everything correctly, as far as they knew. God had blessed them. Now, suddenly, tragedy strikes Aaron's family as his two oldest sons are killed.

What did they do that was so serious? What does it mean that they "offered unauthorized fire before the Lord"? The reason is not explicitly stated, and whenever anything is not explained in detail in the Scriptures, the commentaries have all kinds of plausible suggestions. There are many possibilities, and I've read many of them. Here are five:

1. Coals to be placed in the censers were to be taken only from the great altar of burnt sacrifices, which the Lord himself had set on fire. There is no indication that Nadab and Abihu did that.
2. No one other than the high priest was told to put incense on a censer of coals and offer it to God. Nadab and Abihu were

not the high priests, yet did that, assuming a prerogative that belonged only to their father.

3. No record indicates that Nadab and Abihu consulted with either Moses or Aaron prior to this act, evidence that they may have intruded upon an office that was not theirs.

4. The incense may not have been properly prepared. Great detail had been given by God on how this was to be done (see Ex. 30:34–38).

5. Nadab and Abihu may have used their own censers rather than the censer that was specifically consecrated for this function.

When I read the text, which refers to "unauthorized fire," I suspect that the first theory is the answer: Nadab and Abihu did not take the fire from the altar that had been kindled by God, and they were judged for it—with death.

It is such a little thing, we think, and yet causes such a great punishment. But this reminds us that with God nothing is little. What seems to us like small acts of disobedience are not a light thing to our holy God.

Two factors make this sin particularly offensive: who did it and when it was done.

First, it was two priests, the sons of Aaron, the high priest, who made an offering before the Lord with "unauthorized," or strange, fire. The priests had been set aside to represent the Lord before the people, and to mediate between the sinful people and their holy God. After the death of the two men, Moses reminds Aaron of the high standard to which the Lord had called his servants: "This is what the LORD has said: 'Among those who are near me I will be sanctified, and before all the people I will be glorified'" (Lev. 10:3). Those set aside as priests to represent God before the people were called to be holy, not picking and choosing which of God's ordinances and instructions they were going to follow. The same standard for Christian service is set forth in the New Testament, where in several places Paul exhorts those in Christian service to be "above reproach" (see 1 Tim. 3:2).

Secondly, this was a very significant time for the Israelites—the very beginning of the people's participation in public worship. In the

New Testament, there is an account of a parallel situation. In the earliest days of the church Ananias and Sapphira too were struck down by God (see Acts 5:1–11). What had they done? They had noticed that people were selling their possessions and donating the proceeds to the church—a very noble thing. Ananias and Sapphira wanted to be praised as well. They sold their field, but they kept back part of the proceeds, pretending that what they had offered to God was the whole amount. Now, they did not have to give all the money; they could have kept some or part of it. It had been their field, after all. Peter recognized this when he revealed their sin. But they sinned by lying to the Holy Spirit. We say, "Yes, but everybody lies." That is true. But at the beginning of the life of the church, lies were not to be tolerated, and God judged Ananias and Sapphira to show how seriously he takes sin.

Does this mean that, in the long history of Israel, no other priest ever violated the laws that had been laid down in the book of Leviticus? No, of course not. Many did that. The minor prophets, especially Malachi, denounced the priests because they were very unrighteous. They were offering blemished animals before the Lord. They would take the animals that nobody else wanted, make the sacrifices with them, and sell the other ones for a lot of money. And they weren't struck down. In today's church, certainly there are many, many Christians who lie about their spiritual lives and who are not struck down for it. But in these two instances, occurring at the beginning of the worship life of the nation of Israel, and at the beginning of the church, God indicates by his severity that he is doing something new. What were to be the standards of service for priests serving before the Most High God? One commentator answers the question this way: "This whole tragic incident may properly be regarded as intended to impress on Israel, both priests and people, the holiness of their God and to warn them against any presumption or laxity in performance of the law of sacrifice which is so carefully stated in chapters 1–7."[2]

Moses understood the message, and explained the death of the two sons to the people in this way: "This is what the LORD has said:

---

2. Ibid., 144.

'Among those who are near me I will be sanctified, and before all the people I will be glorified'" (Lev. 10:3).

The remainder of chapter 10 has a few details for the people. Priests were not to drink alcohol when they were conducting the service (see v. 9). Although it doesn't say so in as many words, because of where this is placed in the narrative, the suggestion is that Nadab and Abihu were intoxicated when they sinned. While alcohol is not forbidden in the Scriptures, we are warned about the dangers of intoxication. The priests were forbidden to drink alcohol while serving in the tabernacle.

The next section shows how much Aaron was affected by the death of his sons. The death of Aaron's sons was a judgment from God. It would seem that demonstrations of mourning would indicate dissatisfaction or even rebellion against the judgment of God. So Moses told Aaron and his two living sons to refrain from all actions related to public mourning, including the tearing of garments, "lest you die, and wrath come upon all the congregation" (Lev. 10:6). Instead, his relatives could bury the bodies, and they and fellow Israelites could mourn.

The high priest could not touch a dead body, as that would defile him and disqualify him for service before the Lord. Aaron had to both accept God's judgment on his sinful sons and continue to carry out his responsibilities as the mediator between his people and the Lord. His private grief was to be borne quietly. Aaron accepted the Lord's admonitions as Moses relayed them; we read in verse 3 "and Aaron held his peace."

Later, he revealed the depth of his grief when he was chastised by Moses because he and his two remaining sons had failed to eat the meat of the sin offering, as required by the ordinances for the sacrifices. Aaron explained to Moses that "today they have offered their sin offering and their burnt offering before the LORD, and yet such things as these have happened to me! If I had eaten the sin offering today, would the LORD have approved?' And when Moses heard that, he approved" (v. 19). In spite of the fact that these chapters insist that everything was to be done exactly according to the commandments of the Lord, the important thing was the attitude of the heart. Moses was satisfied when he saw that the attitude of Aaron's heart was contrite and broken, not rebellious.

OUR HIGH CALLING

At the beginning of this chapter I wrote that all Christians today are priests. Therefore, what we learn in these chapters is to be applied to us. The apostle Peter makes a great deal of this connection, using Old Testament language to describe New Testament believers: "You are a chosen race, a royal priesthood, a holy nation, a people for his own possession, that you may proclaim the excellencies of him who called you out of darkness into his marvelous light" (1 Peter 2:9). In the Old Testament, the people had a high priest, under-priests, and eventually the tribe of Levi, all of whom were priests—but not all the people of Israel were priests. Yet Peter says that in the church today, all believers are priests. We are a holy nation called and drawn to God in order that we might show forth his glory to a world that is perishing without him, and that we might exercise the function of priestly intercessors by praying for those who are lost.

Do you do that? Do you recognize your high calling? We say, "Look at how important Aaron was." And he was important, right up there next to Moses. But our responsibility is no less great. All the challenges given in Leviticus 8–10 are for us as well. Jesus Christ was accounted a faithful priest before God (see Heb. 2:17). May we who follow him be accounted faithful as well, so that one day, when we stand before him, we will hear him say, "Well done, good and faithful servant. Enter into the joy of your Lord."

19

THE DAY OF ATONEMENT

Leviticus 16

THE MOST IMPORTANT HOLY DAY

It is impossible to overestimate the importance of Leviticus 16 and the Day of Atonement in the religion of the Old Testament. The Day of Atonement took place halfway through the month that was halfway through the year. It is central to the book of Leviticus as well. Because Leviticus contains the instructions for the priests and the sacrifices—and because the sacrifices are the very heart of how one becomes right before God, prefiguring the coming of the Lord Jesus Christ—this chapter is more important than anything we have studied thus far.

Unlike the other holy days, or, "holy convocations" (KJV and ESV),[1] most of which were joyful celebrations, the Day of Atonement was a time of great solemnity. It was the one such holy day in the year for which the people were commanded to fast. It was also the only time in the year when the high priest was allowed to go into the Most Holy Place of the tabernacle. Nobody was allowed to go in there at any other time, and on the Day of Atonement only the high priest was allowed to enter. The people did not go up to Jerusalem for this holy day. They

---

1. These are also called "holy convocations" (Lev. 23:2–4 ESV and KJV) or "sacred assemblies" (ibid. NIV).

251

stayed home, where they were to spend the day in self-examination, reflecting on themselves and their sin and confessing their sin while the sacrifices were being made.

All these sacrifices point forward to the coming of Jesus Christ. That is basic to the relationship between the Old Testament and the New Testament. This chapter is critical to the understanding of Old Testament religion, and thus it is the most important chapter in the Old Testament for helping us to understand what Jesus Christ did on the cross when he fulfilled these Old Testament types.

THE FEASTS OF ISRAEL

I'd like to put the Day of Atonement in the context of the six great holy days or feasts of Israel listed in Leviticus 23. This is the only chapter in the Bible that lists all six, although shorter lists occur in several other places (for example, Ex. 23:14–17; 34:18–22; Deut. 16). You will see that I have not mentioned Purim or Hanukkah; these are not mentioned in the first five books of the Bible because they came later historically. Purim dates from the time of Esther and finds its origin in that book, and Hanukkah is post-Old Testament, having to do with the rededication of the temple in the year 165 BC. The Jews observe those two holidays today, and rightly so, but they are not found in the book of Leviticus.

PASSOVER AND THE FEAST OF UNLEAVENED BREAD

The very first feast of the calendar year was the Passover and the Feast of Unleavened Bread. This was the most joyful of all the feasts because it was a memorial to the deliverance of the people from their bondage in Egypt. Like the Fourth of July for Americans or Bastille Day for the French, it was a celebration of freedom and independence.

The feast was held in the first month of the year, beginning on the fourteenth of Nisan, and it lasted for seven days. Passover itself was the first day, and technically the Feast of Unleavened Bread began after that, although the Feast of Unleavened Bread is sometimes described as being seven days long and including the Passover. At any rate, the two came together. The Feast of Unleavened Bread had its name because, at the time of the Passover, the Israelites had left Egypt in such a hurry that they hadn't had the time or opportunity to put yeast in the dough so that the bread would rise.

The New Testament writers, guided by the Holy Spirit, saw that each of the four main Old Testament holy days prefigured what was fulfilled in Jesus' work of redemption.[2] John, in the first chapter of his gospel, records John the Baptist's pointing out Jesus as "the Lamb of God who takes away the sin of the world" (John 1:29 NKJV). The Baptist was proclaiming to his disciples that Jesus, the sacrificial Lamb, had come to fulfill once and for all the promises of the repeated Passover sacrifices. Three years later Jesus entered Jerusalem—the triumphal entry—as thousands of lambs were being brought into the city in preparation for the Passover, and strong evidence points to the crucifixion of Jesus taking place at the same time the Passover lambs were being killed for the next day's Passover observance.[3] The apostle Paul states clearly, "for Christ, our Passover lamb, has been sacrificed" (I Cor. 5:7).

The Feast of Unleavened Bread followed directly after the Passover celebration, is more fully described in Numbers 28:16–25, and can be considered a continuation of the Passover observance.

THE FEAST OF FIRSTFRUITS

The next feast, the Feast of Firstfruits, occurred in the springtime, near the time of Passover. The warm climate of the Holy Land provided for a long growing season, so the Israelites planted several crops during the course of the year. When the first produce of the field was ripe, the people were instructed to bring a bundle of grain to the priest, who waved it before the Lord as a way of dedicating the entire harvest to him.

The idea of the firstfruits is also found in the New Testament. In 1 Corinthians 15 the apostle Paul identifies Jesus as the firstfruits

---

2. Only the Feast of Trumpets, which heralded the later feasts in the seventh month, and the Feast of Tabernacles, with its specific reference to the years in the wilderness, are not explicitly referred to in the New Testament.

3. See my discussion of this dating in James Montgomery Boice, *The Gospel of John* (repr., Grand Rapids: Baker, 1999), 3:929–32.

because he is the first of the resurrected ones (see 1 Cor. 15:20). Jesus' resurrection becomes the promise of the full harvest—the resurrection of all his people at the last day. In Romans 8:23 Paul calls our possession of the Holy Spirit the firstfruits, meaning that the Spirit is a pledge of everything we will have one day when we are fully sanctified and in heaven with the Lord Jesus Christ.

THE FEAST OF WEEKS

The third feast, the Feast of Weeks, commemorated the wheat harvest. It is also called the Feast of Harvest (see Ex. 23:16), and it was celebrated with the firstfruits of the wheat harvest (see Ex. 34:22). It was observed seven weeks and one day (that is, fifty days) after the Sabbath that followed the Passover. It was later called Pentecost, after the Greek word meaning "fiftieth."

You will recall that in the New Testament the Holy Spirit came on the believers at Pentecost with great signs to inaugurate the church age (see Acts 2:1–4). In other words, the Holy Spirit came during the harvest festival to indwell the earliest believers, his presence pointing to the great harvest of salvation among Jews and Gentiles that would take place in the church age.

THE FEAST OF TRUMPETS

The fourth feast, the Feast of Trumpets, was a special day of rest that was held on the first day of the seventh month, Tishri, exactly halfway through the Jewish calendar. It doesn't seem to have any particular religious significance—that is, no special sacrifices are connected with it and it's not tied to any special historical event. The people were to gather for a holy convocation and to present a food offering to the Lord. It inaugurated a number of other feasts or festivals that took place during that same month, including the Day of Atonement and the Feast of Tabernacles. This holy day is now known as *Rosh Hashanah*, the beginning of the civil year.[4]

---

4. See Oswald T. Allis, "Leviticus," in *The New Bible Commentary*, ed. F. Davidson (repr., Grand Rapids: Erdmans, 1960), 156.

THE DAY OF ATONEMENT

The Day of Atonement, occurring ten days after the Feast of Trumpets during the seventh month, was a time of self-examination and repentance. Because of the nature of this day, the people did not travel to Jerusalem. Doing so would turn it into a celebration and a festival, and it was not that kind of event. Rather, it was to be "a Sabbath of solemn rest" (Lev. 23:32). The Israelites stayed home while the sacrifices described in detail in Leviticus 16 were performed.

In Leviticus 23, where all the holy days are listed, the Day of Atonement is described from the viewpoint of the Jewish worshipper: the chapter stresses fasting and cessation from work, because the day was a holy Sabbath to the Lord, the holiest day of the Jewish year. In Leviticus 16 the same day is described from the point of view of the priest, telling the priest what to do and what kind of sacrifices he was to offer. The Day of Atonement, *Yom Kippur*, remains the holiest day of the Jewish calendar.

THE FEAST OF TABERNACLES

The final feast was the Feast of Tabernacles, also called the Feast of Booths. It took place in the fall of the year, at the very end of the growing season. People built small booths outside the houses and stayed in them for the seven days of the festival.

There were two important purposes for this feast. First, living in booths—flimsy, temporary shelters—was to remind the people of those years of the wilderness wandering when the Lord had provided for them and protected them. As the Lord instructed Moses to explain, "You shall dwell in booths for seven days . . . that your generations may know that I made the people of Israel dwell in booths when I brought them out of the land of Egypt: I am the LORD your God" (Lev 23:42–43).

Secondly, this was the end of the harvest, so the feast became what we might call a kind of Thanksgiving festival.

My comparison of this feast to Thanksgiving is not accidental. When the Puritans in New England celebrated the first Thanksgiving, they did so in conscious recognition of this feast of Israel. They said that God gave that feast to the Jewish people as a time to thank him for the harvest, and the Puritans wanted to thank him for his provision for them in that first harvest in the new land. Jewish families and synagogues still maintain this tradition of celebrating the Feast of Booths (*Sukkot)* by building small booths on their properties.

THE PROGRESSION OF SACRIFICES

What sets the Day of Atonement apart from the other holy days? The key difference is that on this day sacrifices were made for the entire nation. All the other sacrifices we've studied (and we've studied many of them) were individual sacrifices, with one worshipper making a sacrifice—sometimes a burnt offering, sometimes a sin offering, sometimes a peace offering—for his sin or the sins of his family. The Day of Atonement was the only time in the year when sacrifices were made for the sins of the entire nation. As we examine the pattern of sacrifices, we see that this is an important step forward in God's revelation of the doctrine of salvation in the Old Testament.

When Adam and Eve sinned in the garden of Eden, God taught them the way of salvation through sacrifice. They had sinned. God had said that they would die on the day they ate of the fruit of the tree (see Gen. 2:17). The "wages of sin is death" (Rom. 6:23), but they did not die. Instead, God offered animal sacrifices in their place. For the very first time they saw what death truly was, and they understood that the animals were dying in their place. This demonstrated the principle of *substitution,* which pointed forward to the coming of Jesus Christ. But at that stage of the revelation, the substitution was one animal for Adam and one animal for Eve, and they were clothed with the skins of the animals.

Years later, at the time of the Passover, God commanded Moses to have each Israelite family take a lamb and examine it for three days. Then, on the night of the Passover, they were to kill the lamb and spread its blood on the doorposts and lintel of the house, so that the angel of death would pass over and the firstborn would not die. One lamb was substituted for a family.

Then, in Leviticus 16, on the Day of Atonement, we have one sacrificial animal which dies for the nation.

256

It's a great progression: one lamb for an individual, one lamb for a family, and one lamb for a nation.

The climax comes when John the Baptist points to the Lord Jesus Christ and says, "Behold, the Lamb of God, who takes away the sin of the world!" (John 1:29). Jesus Christ is the culmination of the revelation—the one who embodies all that the sacrifices symbolized, the one to whom all the sacrifices pointed.

THE PATTERN OF THE DAY OF ATONEMENT

In the Hebrew text, the name for this feast is actually plural—the Day of Atonements, or the Day of Sacrifices—because there were several sacrifices. But before I go into detail about the significance of these sacrifices, let's get an idea of the day's pattern of events.

As a sinful man, Aaron could not handle the sacrifice that would represent the sin of the nation until he had first offered a sacrifice for himself: a bull, a very large animal. He was to sprinkle the blood of the bull on the mercy seat within the Most Holy Place.

Before Aaron could do this, however, he had to take a censer and put incense on it, which would burn and produce clouds of smoke. He was to pass through the curtain that separated the Holy Place from the Most Holy Place, allowing the smoking incense escaping from the censer to fill the Most Holy Place of the tabernacle. The cloud of incense was to cover the presence of God above the mercy seat so that Aaron would not die when he returned to sprinkle the bull's blood.

Following the sacrifice of the bull came two unique offerings: two goats. One goat was killed, and its blood was brought into the Holy Place. The second, the escape goat (or scapegoat), was driven away into the wilderness.

In the course of the Day of Atonement, Aaron went into the Most Holy Place four times: first with the censer, then with the offering for his own sin, again with the censer, and a final time with the great and unique sacrifice that stood for the sin of the people. Afterward, there was a final ceremony in which he performed burnt offerings for himself and the people as a sort of dedication once everything else was accomplished.

THE MEANING OF THE
DAY OF ATONEMENT

The two goats that were offered symbolized two important things that have to be done with our sin. Our sin makes us guilty before God, and we fall under the judgment of God because of our sin; the Judge of all the universe must do right. He has to punish sin; he can't ignore it. Like most sacrifices, the first goat symbolized the innocent dying for the guilty, just as Jesus Christ, wholly sinless, dies in the place of guilty sinners.

But the second goat, the one that was driven into the wilderness, symbolized something equally important. The death of Jesus does not just provide for the penalty of our sin but also removes from us the guilt and burden of our sin.

Let's examine this in more depth.

THE SIGNIFICANCE OF THE FIRST GOAT

In chapter 13, "The Ceremonial Law," I described the ark of the covenant in the Most Holy Place. It was a box containing (among other things) the Ten Commandments on stone tablets, with a cover, made of solid, beaten gold, called the mercy seat. This was the place of God's earthly dwelling among his people, his presence hidden but made visible by the descent of the glory cloud described at the end of Exodus. This was the very throne of God; no one could barge into his presence. Even Aaron had to be shrouded by the smoke of incense and needed to make atonement for his own sin before entering the Most Holy Place on the Day of Atonement once a year.

The picture is clear. Here is the thrice holy God—holy, holy, holy—looking down on the law that he has given and that everyone on the face of the earth has broken. The holy God of the universe must judge sin. We fall under his curse of spiritual death—being cut off from God's presence forever.

Now with that in mind, understand what happens on the Day of Atonement. The high priest confesses the sin of the people over the first goat, so that the goat represents the people as it dies for their sin. The high priest—Aaron, in the first instance, and then every successor who came after him for generation after generation—takes the blood of the animal and carefully, having filled the Most Holy Place with incense, goes in and sprinkles the blood with his finger on the covering of the ark. Now we understand why it is called the mercy seat. As God looks down, he sees not the broken law that condemns us, but rather the blood that testifies to the death of the victim that died in place of the sinner. The wages of sin is death. But judgment has been meted out. Since the animal has died, the love of God can go out to embrace and fully save the sinner.

Remember the Pharisee whom Jesus contrasted with the tax collector? Both men went to the temple to pray. Pharisees were highly regarded; Jesus' audience would have agreed that this Pharisee was not like other men. The tax collector, however, was a sinner, a bad man—yet he went home justified and the other man did not (see Luke 18:14). Jesus' audience had thought they understood him up until that point. Now they were taken aback. The good man was not saved, and the bad man was saved? Could it be that the Pharisee only *seemed* to be good? Did the tax collector secretly have a heart of gold?

That's not it at all. The two men were exactly alike in terms of their standing before God. Both were sinners. The only difference was that one knew it and the other did not. And because one knew it, he prayed rightly, asking for mercy. He came to God in faith, believing that God would save him from his sins. On the basis of this prayer, he went home justified.

What did the tax collector pray? "God be merciful to me a sinner" (v. 13 KJV). A good prayer always has two elements: *God* and *sinner*. If you are truly praying to God, you see yourself as a sinner; if you see yourself as righteous when you pray to God, you haven't the faintest idea of what God is like. Heaven is for sinners redeemed by the blood of Christ. Unless you recognize yourself as a sinner, you haven't even begun to know what God is like. You don't know what you're like, and you certainly don't see any need for a Savior. If you don't need a Savior, you don't trust him. You're not saved. This is why the Pharisee wasn't justified. True, he began his prayer by saying, "God," but he wasn't praying to God; he was praying to himself. Essentially he said, "God, I thank you that I'm not like everybody else. Look how wonderful I am."

The middle of the tax collector's short prayer is also important. The word in the Greek text within Jesus' story is the word *hilasterion*, which refers to the mercy seat. This man wasn't praying naively or in mere desperation. Sometimes we ask for God's mercy without the faintest idea of where that mercy can be found. But this man knew, because when he used that word (or its Aramaic equivalent), he was saying, "God, don't treat me on the basis of my works. I haven't got any chance of pleasing you by my works. The Pharisee thinks that he does, but I certainly don't. I can't please you that way. Deal with me on the basis of the blood sprinkled upon the mercy seat by the high priest on the Day of Atonement. That's what makes atonement for my sin."

And Jesus said that the tax collector went home justified.

THE SIGNIFICANCE OF THE SECOND GOAT

The second unique sacrifice was called the *scapegoat*. The word occurs several times in the chapter, and it is translated *scapegoat* based on the word *escape*—taking away or bearing away. The text makes very clear what was happening with the sin in this sacrifice. Aaron was to "lay both his hands on the head of the live goat, and confess over it all the iniquities of the people of Israel, and all their transgressions, all their sins. And he shall put them on the head of the goat" (Lev. 16:21). This is vivid language. God is saying:

Here are wicked, adulterous people. Put their sin on the goat's head.

Here are people who don't observe the Sabbath. Put their sin on the goat's head.

Here are people who are guilty of covetousness, people who live for material things, people who are selfish, people who lie. Put their sin on the goat's head.

That was what the priest did. Then the goat was given into the care of a man who took it outside the city, beyond the walls, where it was chased into the wilderness. Somewhere in the wilderness it died, bearing away the sin of the people.

This is psychologically profound. So many people are caught up in guilt, and this sending out of the scapegoat speaks to our need. We don't need merely to have the penalty of our sin removed and another to bear it in our place. We need to get out from under the guilt of our sin as well. Here, in a dramatic way, God shows what he does for us. Not only does he punish our sin through an innocent victim, but he also bears the sin away so that we don't have to worry about it anymore: "as far as the east is from the west, so far does he remove our transgressions from us" (Psalm 103:12).

Jesus did both of these things for us. He came at the end of the culmination of the revelation—one sacrifice for an individual, for a family, for a nation, and finally for the world. But not only that. He also, in himself, combined the meaning of all the sacrifices. He made only one sacrifice. He didn't have to make a sacrifice for his own sin. In himself in his death on the cross, he became both the propitiation, that is the sacrifice that satisfied the requirement of judgment for sin, and also the one who bore our sins away. That's why Hebrews says that he suffered for our sins outside the wall of the city, where Golgotha was located, bearing away our sin (see Heb. 13:12). Jesus does it all.

LEARNING FROM LEVITICUS 16

How do we apply this? As we compare Scripture with Scripture, and especially as we look to the New Testament for the light that it throws on the Old, we find that the New Testament not only gives us the right understanding of the Old Testament but also applies it for us. This is nowhere more apparent than with the Day of Atonement, which is interpreted and applied in the book of Hebrews. This epistle deals with all the Jewish types, and its point is that these types are all fulfilled in Jesus Christ.

Hebrews 9–10 deals with these sacrifices, and it is a helpful study to compare those two chapters to Leviticus 16. Hebrews itself makes many applications, but I want to give the four main ones.

Bloodshed is necessary. The writer of Hebrews makes the statement that "without the shedding of blood there is no forgiveness of sins" (Heb. 9:22). This means that there is no forgiveness of sins apart from death. If your sin is not covered by the blood of Jesus Christ, you have to pay for it yourself, dying spiritually for your sin as well as physically. This points to the unique importance of what Jesus Christ did.

Only one sacrifice is necessary. Hebrews 9:28 states clearly, "Christ was sacrificed once to take away the sins of many people" (NIV). In the Old Testament, sacrifices had to be repeated again and again. Although the Day of Atonement took place only once a year, it took place *every* year. Hour by hour, day by day, week by week, and year by year, sacrifices for sin were made by generation upon generation of Jewish priests.

But when the Lord Jesus Christ came to earth, he sacrificed himself once, thereby accomplishing for good all that needed to be done. The next chapter of Leviticus says that "the life of the flesh is in the blood . . . it is the blood that makes atonement by the life" (Lev. 17:11). Therefore, through the atoning blood of Christ we have everything we need. The blood of Jesus Christ gives us redemption (see 1 Peter 1:18–19), forgiveness (see Eph. 1:7), justification (see Rom. 5:9), spiritual peace (see Col. 1:20), and holiness (see Heb. 10:10). Jesus did it all. Nothing else needs to be accomplished.

Christ is necessary. For "it is impossible for the blood of bulls and goats to take away sins" (Heb. 10:4). Not only do we need to know that Jesus Christ fulfilled all the types and achieved salvation for us, but we also have to know that nothing else and nobody else could do that. The sacrifices were given by God and played their role, explaining in vivid imagery what Jesus Christ would do. This is why it is worthwhile to study and visualize the ark, the sacrifices, and the mercy seat. All of this gives us a way of understanding what Jesus Christ did. But none of it took away sin. You have to come by faith in Jesus, because it's Jesus or nothing.

Faith is necessary. Hebrews 10:21–22 urges, "Since we have a great priest over the house of God, let us draw near with a true heart in full assurance of faith." This verse might be used of prayer, but in the context of the book of Hebrews itself it is talking about faith in Jesus Christ as the Savior. Hebrews was written to Jewish people who had heard the gospel, who were even enamored of it, and who maybe believed it to a certain extent, but who were still trying to hang on to their Old Testament rituals. The author of Hebrews told them,

"Give that up. The fulfillment has come." No one would be saved by the blood of sheep and goats or by reenacting the Day of Atonement. Instead, all must draw near in full assurance of faith in the completed work of Jesus Christ.

In one of the strongest warnings in Scripture, the writer describes what will happen to those who know the way of salvation but do not fully embrace it—those who sin in unbelief, not just in outward actions.

> For if we go on sinning deliberately after receiving the knowledge of the truth, there no longer remains a sacrifice for sins, but a fearful expectation of judgment, and a fury of fire that will consume the adversaries. (Heb. 10:26–27)

The same book that presents the way of salvation in such vivid imagery, pointing us to Jesus Christ, also speaks very clearly of the holy God's judgment on unholy men and women's sin. If you're not trusting Christ, you have nothing to look forward to in the life to come but dreadful judgment.

Don't draw back. Don't continue in the sin of unbelief. Rather, press forward into the kingdom, believing in Jesus Christ and seizing the cross, knowing that through his death the veil has been torn and the way has been opened into God's presence forevermore. Let your prayer be that of the tax collector, who said, "God, be merciful to me, a sinner."

20

JUBILEE

Leviticus 25—27

A MOST AMAZING
PIECE OF LEGISLATION

For those of us who have been taught that the unlimited, unhindered accumulation of wealth is the ultimate good, Leviticus 25 is amazing. In fact, it is one of the most amazing pieces of legislation in the whole Old Testament. In the Year of Jubilee, all land holdings in Israel would revert to their original owners. This was one of the earliest processes and laws for land reform in all the history of the world, if not the first, and it was certainly one of the most unique.

Many schemes of utopianism have sought to bring prosperity to everybody through a redistribution of wealth by various means. One obvious form of this is communism, which denies the right of private ownership. Everything is in the hands of the state, so the state has the responsibility of owning everything and seeing that everyone is well cared for. We discovered, through a seventy-year experiment with communism, that it doesn't work very well. Socialism is philosophically quite different from communism—it doesn't deny all ownership, but there is an attitude that government should take over the responsibility of providing for everyone, in the name of egalitarianism. Finally, further down the scale, there is the idea of the simple lifestyle. This idea, which we sometimes talk about in Christian circles, is quite popular—and, I think, good. The idea is that we should live simply in order to have more money to give to other people—and, unlike communism and socialism, it is voluntary sharing.

Leviticus 25 is a little hard to follow, and people have misused the Jubilee principle. Often we come to something like this in Scripture and find it useful for supporting our preconceived ideas. We can easily draw out of the Jubilee principle all sorts of concepts that support our idea of a just way of handling an economy, but that is not the way to do things.

Therefore, I will look at the Jubilee very, very carefully, going through the chapter section by section and following the flow to see what it actually says. I will ask whether communism, socialism, and the simple lifestyle are supported by the Jubilee—and, if they are, to what extent.

THE JUBILEE AND THE SABBATH

Leviticus 25 is the only chapter in the whole Bible that deals with the Jubilee; it is also mentioned in passing in Numbers 36:4. The Jubilee was announced by the sounding of trumpets on the Day of Atonement (which came halfway through the year) in the Jubilee year (see Lev. 25:8–9). All the trumpets throughout the land sounded on that day as a proclamation of freedom.

Significantly, however, this unique chapter on the Year of Jubilee begins not with trumpets and the Jubilee but with the sabbatical year. The Sabbath was the seventh day, so the sabbatical year was the seventh year. Laws for the sabbatical year commanded that the land lie fallow during that year. In other words, the Israelites were not to plant or harvest. Of course, some plants would spring up, because seeds would remain in the field from the previous year. This was primarily a provision for the poor, who were free to go into the fields during the sabbath year and help themselves. But the principle was to allow the land to lie fallow, which was good land management—even though there is no indication in the text that the Hebrew people of that day understood the scientific principles of land conservation. Deuteronomy 15 also mentions the sabbatical year, adding that in that year all debts were to be cancelled (see v. 2) and slaves were to be set free (see v. 12).

The Jubilee, the special year that came twice a century, had the same elements as the sabbatical year. But it had an additional, unique feature: in that year, all the land that had passed from owner to owner in the course of the decades had to revert to the families that had originally owned it. The families remained established in this way.

Now, just as the seventh day of the week was the day of regular Sabbath rest, and just as the seventh year was to be a Sabbath year, so also the Year of Jubilee was to be a Sabbath of Sabbaths. This is the way it is introduced: "You shall count seven weeks of years, seven times seven years, so that the time of the seven weeks of years shall give you forty-nine years" (Lev. 25:8). Because the next verse says, "Then you shall sound the loud trumpet" (v. 9), people have assumed, with some justification, that the Jubilee year was the fiftieth year.

That may be. The word *fiftieth* is mentioned twice in the chapter. However, it may have been the forty-ninth year instead, for this reason: The Jubilee year was a year in which the land was to lie fallow, just as it was to lie fallow in the sabbath year. If a Jubilee year followed directly after a sabbath year, the land would have to lie fallow for two years in a row. It is hard to imagine an agricultural economy in which people could survive that way. It's true that God promised a hefty crop in the sixth year that would supply the people until the ninth year (see Lev. 25:21–22), but this is not explicitly promised for a special Jubilee year, which would mean two sabbath years in a row.

This has led some to suggest—I think probably rightly—that the Jubilee sabbath was the same as the seventh of the sabbath years, so that the last of seven sabbath years was a Jubilee year in which the reversion of the land took place.

The Israelites often counted numbers in an inclusive way. The first sabbath year is the first year. If you count off seven sabbath years after that, the final sabbath year is the fiftieth. Both the first sabbath and the last sabbath are counted. There is an extrabiblical book called The Book of Jubilees that gives a history of Israel dating everything in terms of the sabbath, the sabbatical years, and the Jubilee years. In the Book of Jubilees, the period between Jubilees is forty-nine years, not fifty years.

While I do want to clarify this, my main reason for emphasizing the time frame is to show that the Jubilee year is linked to the sabbath year in a very special way. The principles carry over and are broader and even more important than the Jubilee year itself.

THE REVERSION OF THE LAND

In this year, the land was to revert to the original families that owned it. But if you look at the text carefully, you will see that this is not the way that the chapter itself talks about what happened. The text speaks of the *people* returning to their own *land* (or *property*). This must be important, because it is said five times over (see vv. 10, 13, 27, 28, 41). We are glad to manipulate people or get rid of them as long as we can accumulate our holdings—not generally land, today, so much as bank accounts, stocks, and so forth. God says that the people are important, not the possessions. He is more concerned with the people than with the land.

God established the family as the foundation of society when he brought Adam and Eve together and told them to grow their family (see Gen. 2). Here was the beginning of human society. One of the great strengths of the Jewish people over the many, many centuries of their existence has been the solidarity of their families. This is one way in which they've been able to stand against all the persecutions they have endured. But in ancient Israel, during the course of the decades, a family could be scattered for various reasons, and through poverty their land would be sold and divided up. Here we're told that there was to be a time when families re-gathered—when they came back and were reestablished as families on their own land.

Was this Jubilee principle ever put into effect? We might say it was impractical. Could it ever be pulled off? This is an interesting question, because there is no indication anywhere in the Old Testament that it was. We do not find any reference to land being returned to the original families, or to families going back to their original land, so we do not know whether it was actually ever implemented.

THE FAIR RENT OF THE LAND

Sometimes people appeal to the Jubilee as justification for forcibly taking property or money from those who own it and redistributing it to people who are poor. But this is not what the Jubilee involved. If somebody owns something and you take it away forcibly and give it to someone else, that is stealing, and the Bible says, "Thou shalt not steal." People are to work, their earnings belong to them, and the Bible from beginning to end recognizes the right of private property. So verses 14–17 of this chapter tell us that the sale—actually the rent—of the land was to be proportional to the number of years remaining before the Jubilee. The principle is that God is the ultimate owner of the land and that he has given the land to the families of Israel to be tenants in perpetuity (see v. 23).

Therefore, in this particular case, the land could not actually be sold. It is true that sometimes the word *sale* is used for the transaction. An impoverished family might "sell" the land to a neighbor who had more money, in order to survive in hard times. But because the land couldn't actually be sold, it was to revert to the original families at the Jubilee year. The sale was actually a rental.

This is made very clear when the passage discusses the price. The price for the land was not determined by whether it had a nice view of the Mediterranean or whether it was located near a walled city where you would be safe. No, the land was valued in terms of the crops that it would produce, and the price was based on the number of years that remained until the Year of Jubilee. For example, if the Jubilee was twenty years off, you paid ten times as much for the land than if the Jubilee was only two years off.

This is far removed from justifying resentment against those who are well off. There is a great deal of resentment against those who prosper, which has been used by angry people—such as Karl Marx—to justify taking wealth away from the wealthy and giving it to somebody less well off. On the one hand, what we have in this chapter is not communism or socialism but something quite different, a restoration to the original owners and therefore a cancelation of their debt—"a fresh start." But on the other hand, this law does not justify a system in which the rich get richer and the poor get poorer. It is compassionate legislation designed to protect and prosper everybody, and to keep the poor from being endlessly trapped in poverty.

THE OWNER OF THE LAND

In verse 23 we come to the principle that lies at the basis of everything: the land is God's. Even the original families were not owners of the land. They only held it in trust; therefore they could not sell it, nor could anybody else buy it. The land had to be handled according to the laws of God, the ultimate owner.

A system like this can operate only in a theocracy—that is, a form of government in which God rules directly through prophets. In this case, Moses spoke the word of God about how things were to be done. We do not have this situation today. As a matter of fact, in all history no true theocracy has ever existed except the theocracy of Israel. Nevertheless, this principle does have bearing on Christians. Psalm 24:1 says, "The earth is the LORD's and the fullness thereof, the world and those who dwell therein." We recognize that God owns everything; therefore, everything that we personally hold from God we hold as his stewards. We are responsible to him for what we do with our possessions.

This is why we cannot make the accumulation of wealth an end in itself. There is nothing wrong with money, and if God prospers us that is wonderful. But we are stewards of the wealth. It is our responsibility to see that it is used in a responsible way to help other people and, above all, to advance the gospel of Jesus Christ.

Unfortunately, money tends to corrupt us. We sometimes think that the rich are generous, because from time to time they give large sums of money. If the most you can ever give at one time is a hundred dollars, and then there is a need in the church and somebody gives ten thousand dollars, he or she seems very, very generous. But if that person has millions, the ten thousand dollars might mean a whole lot less to him or her than your hundred means to you. Jesus expressed this when he talked about the widow and her offering (see Mark 12:41–44). Statistics show that the rich are not very generous.

I often say that God would give us more money if he could trust us with it, but he knows what it would do to us. Generally speaking, that is why many of us do not have more.

THE DUTY OF THE KINSMAN-REDEEMER

If a family was forced to sell its land because of poverty, the Year of Jubilee might seem a lifetime away. Suppose the Jubilee came in your youth—you'd be an old man before you receive your land back.

However, it was possible for the land to be bought back and restored to the original owner before the Year of Jubilee by a near relative called a *kinsman-redeemer* (see vv. 25–28). Or, if the original owner prospered, he had the right to buy back the land. The amount he would have to pay was the difference between what the buyer had originally paid for the land and the number of crops that the buyer had already harvested. For example, if the buyer had paid for what amounted to ten years of crops and only three harvests had gone by, the original owner would have to pay him for the remaining seven years of crops. We do not know whether the Jubilee was ever actually put into practice, but we do know, from the marvelous illustration in the book of Ruth, that the buying back of the land was practiced.

The book of Ruth tells the story of a poor family: because of poverty, a husband and wife sold their land and went with their two sons down to Moab to live. While they were there, the two sons married two Moabite women. The husband died. The sons died. The first widow, Naomi, was left with two widowed daughters-in-law, one of whom was Ruth. When Naomi decided to go back to her own land in Israel, Ruth went back with her. The land that had been sold should have gone back to Naomi, so there was a negotiation to see who, as the kinsman-redeemer, would buy it back.[1] A very near relative was willing to do it at first. His reasoning must have gone like this: "Naomi doesn't have any sons. Therefore, if I redeem the land for her, eventually it will come to me anyway. So I do not mind paying for

---

1. Redeeming something involves having relinquished its ownership, often under duress, and then buying it back.

it. I will be glad to get the land." Then Boaz pointed out that if this near relative redeemed the land, he also had to marry Ruth—because she was the daughter-in-law—and raise up an heir to Naomi from Ruth. The land would then belong to Naomi's heir, not to the man who had redeemed it. When the first man learned that, he decided he did not want to redeem the land, so Boaz did (see Ruth 4:1–10). Boaz was glad to play the role of the kinsman-redeemer, because he was in love with Ruth. In doing so, he established the line through which David came, and eventually the Lord Jesus Christ (see Ruth 4:18–22).

Most Bible scholars see in this a prefiguring of the work of Jesus Christ. Jesus is our Redeemer, but he is also our Kinsman-Redeemer. He became our relative through the incarnation; he became one of us. Then he redeemed us, he bought us back from slavery to sin, paying the price for our redemption in his death on the cross.

THE HOUSES IN THE CITIES

Leviticus 25:29–34 describes how houses in a city could be sold without the right of redemption. Why does this matter? Because it shows that there were cases of ownership to which the Jubilee principle did not apply, and this is one of them.

What makes this case different? Houses within a walled city had no land attached to them. Therefore, they did not fall under the provisions that were meant to keep land intact for the benefit of the Hebrew people and their families. If there was a field in the countryside with a house on it, and it was sold, then the house went back with the land in the Year of Jubilee—it was the farmhouse. But in the city this did not apply, because the principle had to do with the land, not with buildings.

This was a very balanced legislation. It doesn't lend itself to justification of forced redistribution of land, but neither does it lend itself to indifference toward the poor. It establishes, among other things, the right of private property, because a man who owned a house in the city really owned it. If he sold it, he really sold it, and the man who bought it really owned it. He could pass it on to his descendants without worrying about its being given up during the Year of Jubilee or any other time. The text says, "The house in the walled city shall belong permanently to the buyer and his descendants" (v. 30 NIV).

At the same time, there was a safeguard built in. The man who was forced to sell his house under adverse circumstances had the right to redeem it within a period of twelve months from the date of the sale. After that time, he no longer had the right to buy it back. This was eminently fair legislation because it protected the man who was forced to sell. Maybe he had a pressing financial need. His family was starving, but he did not want to give up his house. He needed his house. It protected him. If fortune changed, he could get it back. At the same time, the legislation protected the man who bought the house. He knew that for twelve months he did not possess absolute ownership of the property, but at the end of the twelve months he really owned it.

It strikes me that this principle of time might be worked into certain kinds of U.S. law. I'm not a lawyer, and lawyers would be far more helpful than I am when it comes to this. But I did notice in the newspapers a case of a little girl named Jessica, who had been raised for two years by foster parents who were well into the adoption process. Then, because the biological mother changed her mind and wanted her baby back, the laws of our country forced the family that had raised and loved the child to give her up to parents who did not even know her, although they wanted her.[2] Most people recognize that this is not just or right. Now, it would be possible to build in a time limit in laws like that. In other words, you could give up a child for adoption but have, for example, six months or a year in which you could reconsider. A family seeking to adopt a child would realize from the beginning that the mother might have a chance to reclaim the child, but at the end of that period, the adoptive family would really have the child. This is just one modern-day scenario in which this principle might be helpful.

---

2. See Bill Hewitt, "The Battle for Baby Jessica," *People*, May 31, 1993, http://www .people.com/people/archive/article/0,,20110512,00.html.

THE DUTIES TO THE POOR

The long concluding section of this chapter, verses 35–55, has to do with duties to the poor. You might say, at first glance, "Why are these duties to the poor here at all? Why is this in a chapter about the Jubilee?" This section emphasizes, through a number of examples, that the central concern of the chapter is to protect and help the poor.

THE HEBREW WHO NEEDS A LOAN

When a Hebrew, an Israelite, was in financial need, his fellow countrymen—especially his relatives—were to help him. They were to lend him whatever money was necessary or give him whatever else may have been necessary, whether money or food. This was a family obligation.

It didn't have to be outright charity, however. The money was not to be given with the thought of charging interest—in other words, they were not to profit from their poor family members because they were in need. However, because the verses say they were *not* to collect interest, they do imply that the money itself—the capital—was to be given back. The people were to help the poor, but not necessarily just by giving or by encouraging perpetual charity cases. What the passage emphasizes is that the rich were not to take advantage of the poor, especially if those in need were members of the family.

THE HEBREW INDENTURED TO ANOTHER HEBREW

In a case where the poor man, or poor family, couldn't get by with merely a loan or short-term borrowing, there was another opportunity. If the man was really in trouble, and the only way he could survive was by indenturing himself to a fellow Hebrew, he was not to become a permanent slave, nor was he to be a charity case. He was to work for the one who was paying him, and he was to use the money to satisfy his obligations and feed his family. Because he was not a slave, he had the right to redeem himself. In all cases, he was to be set free in the Year of Jubilee. This is because, when God purchased, or redeemed, his people out of Egypt, they were slaves and he set them free—and once free, they were not to become slaves again.

273

We have a carryover of this principle in the New Testament in the book of Galatians, which deals with the matter of slavery to the law. In the fifth chapter, which sums up Paul's arguments, he says this: "For freedom Christ has set us free; stand firm therefore, and do not submit again to a yoke of slavery" (Gal. 5:1). This is exactly the principle of the Jubilee, applied spiritually. Once free from the slavery of sin, do not return to that previous state of bondage by trying to keep the Old Testament law.

THE GENTILE SOLD TO A HEBREW

Gentile slaves, however, really were slaves, not indentured servants (see vv. 44–46). Is this a double standard? It is certainly a different standard: Hebrews were treated one way and Gentiles another way. Double standards are often a fact of life: you treat your own family differently than you do strangers. But the laws involving the Gentile slaves were no worse than the laws that prevailed in Gentile lands regarding slaves. They did not lose any rights. As a matter of fact, if you examine the whole picture, Gentile slaves were treated far better in Israel than they were ever treated in Greece or Rome.

THE HEBREW INDENTURED TO THE GENTILE

Finally, in the longest section, we have the example of a Hebrew who is indentured to a Gentile. This is the final case that is needed to round out the possibilities, and it establishes the rights of a Hebrew as a Hebrew in his own country. Even though the Gentiles have slaves who do not have any right to be free, a Hebrew in Israel who becomes the servant of a Gentile maintains his rights as a Hebrew. In other words, a Gentile living in the Israelites' country has to do things the Israelites' way. In Gentile countries they do what they want, but in Israel the Israelites protect their people.

The chapter ends by stating that the overriding factor is that the Israelites had become God's servants—"for it is to me that the people of Israel are servants" (Lev. 25:55)—having been purchased by him out of their Egyptian slavery, and hence they were always to be regarded as free men and women. And so are you and I, if Jesus Christ has purchased us from the slavery of sin.

REWARDS, PUNISHMENTS, MERCY, AND REDEMPTION

I want to touch very briefly on the last two chapters of Leviticus.

Leviticus 26 deals with rewards and punishments. Most ancient law codes were based on the famous law code of the Babylonian emperor Hammurabi. They would have a section on rewards and punishments or curses and blessings that would go like this: "I am the king. If you obey me, these are all the blessings that will come. If you disobey me, these are the curses that you'll get." This chapter follows the pattern of those law codes. This same pattern appears elsewhere in the Mosaic books. In fact, it is the basis of the structure of Deuteronomy, as can be clearly seen in Deuteronomy 28–30.

The rewards section is shorter than the punishments section. If the people follow God's decrees and are careful to obey all his laws, then God will (1) give rain in its season, (2) provide peace and victory over their enemies, and (3) assure them of his ongoing covenant presence with them. The longer curses section suggests that we're motivated more by fear of what we might lose than by promises of good things we might gain. If the Israelites fail to carry out all God's commands, and so violate his covenant, God will (1) bring sudden disasters upon them, (2) withhold rain, (3) allow wild animals to harass them, (4) send hostile enemies against them, (5) lay waste the land, and (6) cause those still alive, who have been carried away by their enemies, to waste away in fear and poverty.

This is exactly what happened in the latter years of Israel's history, after civil war had divided Judah from Israel. The Assyrians carried away the people of the northern kingdom, Israel. About a hundred years later, the Babylonians carried away the people of the southern kingdom of Judah. This is exactly what God had said would happen.

Yet the very end of chapter 26 emphasizes God's mercy. The books of the prophets, which were written later, do the same thing. There are terrible warnings of the judgment and disaster that will come on the people. However, almost every prophetic book ends not on that note but with an emphasis on the mercy of God. Because of his covenant with their fathers, God says that he will not abandon the people utterly. He will keep them, even when they're in the land of their enemies. Our God is a very gracious God. Mercy is his name.

Leviticus 27 has to do with redeeming things that are the Lord's. Although no one was required by the law to do so, the Israelites would often dedicate people, animals, or property to the Lord with a vow. Then their circumstances would change, and they would want the person or thing back. You might think that God would say, "No, you gave it to me; it's mine." But actually, God gave instructions to show how the thing could be brought back. The Levitical law was humane and flexible, and it allowed for the redemption of what had been vowed.

LEARNING FROM LEVITICUS 25-27

WHERE HAVE YOU SET YOUR HEART?

Nothing in the laws for the Year of Jubilee, the rest of the Pentateuch, or the whole of the Bible says that we can't prosper financially. As a matter of fact, there are promises that *generally*—although not in every circumstance—if we follow after God, we will prosper. God will bless us and take care of us. But the Jubilee was a curb on greed, and it was certainly a curb on massive land accumulation, especially at the expense of poorer families. It was a reminder that, although wealth can be a good, it can also be an evil, and can be used to oppress other people. The Jubilee was designed to restrain that abuse of wealth.

We live in a very materialistic culture. It tells us that the most important thing is to get rich. We have to remember that we are not to set our hearts on accumulating riches. If God is prospering you, are you using your money rightly? Are you using your resources in a way that honors him? Or, has money taken an improper and harmful place in your life? These are questions that demand an honest examination of our own hearts and motives.

WHERE DO YOUR POSSESSIONS COME FROM?

Everything that we have, we have as a trust from God. This was basic to all the Jubilee laws, because they were based on the fact that

God owned the land. If God owned the land and gave it in trust to Hebrew families, then they held it as a trust from him. They were stewards of what he had given.

We are stewards of what God has given us. We know this perfectly well. Everything that we have, whatever it may be—not just our wealth but our talents, time, opportunities, friendships, anything we can think of—we hold as a steward from God, because it all came from God and belongs to him. It is not ours. He gave it to us, and he can take it away whenever he chooses. Are we using all that we have for him and for his glory?

The day will come when we will stand before God and have to give an accounting. Will God disapprove of us in that day? Will he say, as the master did in one of Jesus' parables, "'You wicked and slothful servant'"? Or will he say instead, "'Well done, good and faithful servant. You have been faithful over a little; I will set you over much. Enter into the joy of your master'" (see Matt. 25:14–30)?

WHERE DO YOU RECEIVE YOUR NOURISHMENT?

It is not enough merely to put worldly goods in their proper perspective, or even to use them responsibly as God's steward. You could do that and still not grow in the Christian life. What you have to remember is that we are not just bodies occupying space that need food and raiment and housing and such things. We are also souls meant for eternal communion with God, and the soul is not nourished on material things. The soul is nourished on the Word of God.

When the devil was tempting Jesus in the wilderness, he said, "You're the Son of God. You're hungry. Here are these stones. Turn them into bread," and Jesus replied, quoting from Deuteronomy (that is, the Mosaic law), "Man shall not live by bread alone, but by every word that proceeds from the mouth of God" (Matt. 4:4 NKJV). This truth applies to us. We can accumulate great wealth. We can even use it wisely. We can become great philanthropists but still wither in our souls. The body, and all that is material, will one day fade and disappear. What will endure is our spirit, and to nourish it we must feed on the Word of God.

WHAT IS YOUR PERSPECTIVE?

Earlier in the chapter I mentioned that the Jubilee Year began with the sounding of trumpets. One day, according to the teaching of Paul, another trumpet will sound, the dead in Christ will be resurrected, and living believers will join the resurrected ones to meet Jesus and be with him for all eternity (see 1 Thess. 4:16–17). If you are cherishing this hope, waiting for the sounding of the trumpet and the day when you will be caught up to be with Jesus Christ forever, it will give you a right perspective on the things that you possess now, and you will live for God and his Word. Do you have that perspective? Do you want to live for God and his Word?

Do not wait. Life is short. It is passing away. Make it count, and make it count right now.

PART 4

THE LONG, HOT DESERT

21

NUMBERS: AN OVERVIEW

Numbers 1–10

WORSE THAN AN AUDIT?

Let's face it: Numbers is not the kind of book you naturally pick up to while away a few hours over the weekend. It is part of the Old Testament law, for one thing. That is bad enough. None of us likes law very much. But in addition, it is also called Numbers. Some people who score very high on achievement tests might be interested in numbers, but the rest of us think they are generally pretty irrelevant. The title is not an aberration either—the book really *is* about numbers, at least in the first section. Numbers is about the numbering of the tribes and the people of Israel, and the arrangement of their camp, and the purification of the people for their march. That is not terribly appealing. In fact, somebody suggested to me that a study of the book would be just about as appealing as an audit by the Internal Revenue Service.

Remember what Paul wrote to Timothy: "All Scripture is God-breathed and is useful for teaching, rebuking, correcting and training in righteousness" (2 Tim. 3:16 NIV). "All Scripture" includes Numbers. Therefore, when we approach the book, we want to ask God to make it useful and profitable to us, so that we will be trained, corrected if necessary, and established in righteousness.

THE TITLE AND PURPOSE OF NUMBERS

The title *Numbers* comes to us in an interesting way. In the Greek translation of the Old Testament, the Septuagint, the book is titled *Arithmoi*, which is the Greek word from which we get the word *arithmetic*. When St. Jerome translated the Greek and Hebrew Old Testament, he called the book *Numeri*, which was the Latin equivalent of the Greek name. From this word we get "numerical," and so we call the book *Numbers*.

But this was not the Hebrew title. The Israelites actually have a number of titles for this book. One is the *BeMidbar*. *BeMidbar* is the fifth word in the Hebrew text and is translated "in the wilderness." This is a good name for Numbers, because the book describes what happened to the people during the thirty-eight years or so that they wandered in the wilderness before finally standing on the very brink of the promised land. The Jews also call it *Vayedabbar*, meaning "And God spoke." These are the very opening words. *Vayedabbar* is not a bad title either, because the book emphasizes again and again how God spoke to Moses and the people, giving them instructions, and how the people responded to God's speaking. The phrase "God spoke," or its equivalent, occurs 150 times in the book.

It is helpful to come to Numbers after having studied Leviticus. The five books of the Pentateuch all flow in a sequence—and with the exception of Deuteronomy, the last of the five, every book after Genesis begins with "and."[1] They are all tied together in a narrative. However, as we have seen, there is very little narrative material in Leviticus, which is essentially a manual for the priests: how they were to conduct themselves, what kind of sacrifices they were to perform, and how they were to conduct the worship activities. But when we come to Numbers, the narrative picks up again as the people prepare to march. Then the people move forward, and we get the incidents that we know so well. The great hymn "Guide Me, O Thou Great Jehovah"[2] is full of imagery based on the journey through the desert to the promised land, as described in Numbers.

---

1. The KJV's "Now," "And," and "And" retain this sense of continuity (see Exod. 1:1; Lev. 1:1; and Num. 1:1).
2. William Williams, 1745.

In his excellent study of Numbers, Gordon Wenham writes, "Nowhere is the general biblical principle that the people of God should imitate God so well illustrated as in the book of Numbers."[3] This is significant. Here is a book that we do not think of very often, but an Old Testament scholar says that, better than any other book in the entire Bible, Numbers illustrates the principle that we should imitate God. If we study this book with empathy and understanding, we will begin to learn this lesson.

OUTLINE OF NUMBERS 1–10

The first ten chapters of Numbers can be roughly divided into four sections. The first four chapters describe the census of the people. Following this, a number of chapters deal with the purification of the people, or the ceremonial setting aside of the people to God. The third section deals with the offerings of the tribes. Finally, at the end of the introductory section, the people actually start out for Canaan.

THE NUMBERING OF THE PEOPLE (NUM. 1–4)

In the first four chapters, the people themselves are counted, the tribes are ordered, and the Levites are numbered and assigned their duty as a body within the greater whole.

THE CENSUS OF THE PEOPLE (NUM. 1)

The number of men of Israel who were of fighting age—that is, from the age of twenty upward—was 603,550. I've been using the rough figure 600,000 because it is given in another place, but this is the exact numbering. On that basis we surmise that the total number of the people was at least two million, if we include the wives, children, and others who joined the Israelites at the time of the exodus. Some people say it was probably three million.

---

3. Gordon J. Wenham, *Numbers*, Tyndale Old Testament Commentaries (Downers Grove, IL: IVP Academic, 1981), 44.

It is a great puzzle to imagine how three million people could have survived in the desert. Of course, apart from the miraculous provision of God on their behalf, survival would have been impossible. If God had not provided manna from heaven for them to eat and water from the rock for them to drink, and if he had not overshadowed them with the cloud to protect them from the sun, they would all have died in the desert.

This teaches us that, apart from God, we are all equally on the verge of death, of physical death, because our life could end at any time, but especially of spiritual death. We do not think this way, of course, because we think in physical terms about physical things rather than in spiritual terms. But if God did not feed us and care for us, we would not have a prayer in the world. God does this through Jesus Christ, who described himself as the Living Water and the Bread of Life. He sent the Holy Spirit, who does for us what the cloud did for the Israelites—leading us and directing us in the way we should go. We need to learn to think more in these terms.

Note that all the fighting men were counted. Every one of them was important. This is true today in the church as well. The Bible says in several places that God has a scroll on which our names are recorded before God (see, for example, Ps. 139:16; Rev. 20:12). Every single one of us is important. Although we do not have a census on earth that corresponds with the very literal census of Israel, there is a heavenly census that is far more important.

Also notice that it was the fighting men who were counted. In other words, they were being numbered for battle, if there were battles to be fought. This is exactly the case today. Paul writes in Ephesians that we are engaged in a great battle that is not against flesh and blood (see Eph. 6:12). You and I are not hitting people with swords or shooting them with guns, because we fight a spiritual battle, a battle against powers in the heavenly places—the spiritual forces that stand behind the evil of this world. If we're fighting, we have to be trained and armed, and we must be armed with the weapons and armor that God has provided. Paul spells out the nature of our spiritual weapons in Ephesians 6:14–18 (see also II Cor. 10:4). If God was so serious about Israel's earthly battles that he numbered the fighting men and recorded these numbers in a portion of his Word, we should be serious about the fact that we ourselves are called to fight spiritual battles.

THE ARRANGEMENT OF THE TRIBES (NUM. 2)

How many tribes of Israel were there?

We all know the answer to that: twelve, of course! But this is actually incorrect. There were thirteen tribes. Joseph was one of the twelve sons of his father, but there was no tribe of Joseph. That makes eleven tribes. But Joseph had two sons, Ephraim and Manasseh, and each became the father of a tribe. That makes thirteen. However, when Numbers 2 describes the arranging of the tribes around the camp, there are twelve again.

You may be saying at this point, "I thought I just learned something I didn't know before—that there were thirteen tribes. Now I find out that there are only twelve. How can that be?" The answer is that the tribe of Levi had a special position that didn't quite fit in with the rest. The tribe of Levi was the tribe of the priests and their helpers, and their position was around the Tent of Meeting—the tabernacle placed in the very center of the camp. So when the description is given for the layout of the camp and the position of the various tribes, we're told that three of them were to the north, three to the east, three to the west, and three to the south. Those are the twelve tribes, but Levi is not included in the list.

Their camp was in the form of a square, with the tabernacle in the center. When the march set out, six of the tribes went first—with Judah, the largest tribe of all, leading the way. After these six came the tabernacle, carried by the Levites, and the last six tribes followed. When they went into battle, the cloud and the ark went before them.

Numbers 2 is thus all about God's being in the very midst of his people. Do we experience less of God's presence today? Of course not. We have with us the very presence of God, the Holy Spirit. As Jesus promised, when he was about to leave his disciples, his Father would give the believers "another Helper, to be with you forever . . . for he dwells with you and will be in you" (John 14:16–17). But more even than the Spirit just indwelling individual believers, there is a promise of his presence when believers gather as the people of God. Where two or three of us come together in God's name, he is in our very midst (see Matt. 18:20). Jesus Christ is present with the power of his Spirit when we meet together, when the Word is preached, when we testify about his grace. The Israelites had God's presence in a visible way. They could look up and see the cloud, and they could look back and see the tabernacle in their midst. We cannot see the Holy Spirit, but he is with us. We have to recognize that this arrangement of the people in Numbers is a visual manifestation of what has become for us a spiritual reality.

There must have been something particularly beautiful about this arrangement. When every tribe was in its place, each one important, the people must have looked around and rejoiced. Even the pagans saw the beauty and order. Later, when the pagan prophet Balaam looked down from the mountains on the tribes of Israel arranged around the ark of the covenant and the tabernacle, he said, "How lovely are your tents, O Jacob, your encampments, O Israel!" (Num. 24:5). You have to pause over these chapters to feel what it must have been like for this ancient people as they dwelt with God's presence in their midst.

THE CENSUS OF THE LEVITES (NUM. 3–4)

The census of the Levites recorded in chapters 3–4 is a little bit different from the census in chapter 1. For one thing, there are two listings of the Levites. In chapter 3 there is a census of every male from the age of one month[4] and upward, for a total of twenty-two thousand. In chapter 4:34–49, there is a listing of those who were of the right age to serve in the Tent of Meeting: a total of 8,580.

There are a couple of interesting things about the first listing. First, the census in chapter 1 was a numbering of the fighting men. The Levites were not counted in that census because they did not fight. They were to protect and carry the ark of the covenant. The women were not counted, because they did not fight either. But when the Levites are numbered, they are counted from a very early age: one month and upward.

---

4. That is, those who were likely to live. They couldn't be sure about newborn infants.

The second thing is that the number in the third chapter is compared to the total number of firstborn males in Israel. Directly before the exodus, God had killed the firstborn of all the Egyptians when the angel of death had passed through the land. The firstborn had been spared of all the Israelites who had put blood on the doorposts of their houses. But God had said that those firstborn children nevertheless belonged to him. They were saved only by the blood. They were sinners just like everybody else, and their salvation was by the shed blood that pointed forward to Jesus Christ.

Now, the Levites are not numbered like the rest of the people. They were the priests, and all those who served with the priests, each one set aside for God's work. Instead of taking the firstborn from all the tribes, God took the Levites in their place. Each Levite represented a firstborn Israelite. But when everyone was numbered, there were twenty-two thousand Levites and 22,273 firstborn males in Israel.[5] What were they going to do about the 273 extra? They had to be redeemed, too. So instructions were given that five shekels were to be collected for each one (see Num. 3:46–47). We're not told who paid it or where the sum was paid, but this was a vivid way of showing that these were a people separated unto God. A price was paid; the firstborn were redeemed as a sign that this people belonged, not to themselves, but to the Lord.

All this seems so distant to us. It is about another culture in another time with another people. But one principle can be taken and carried over into the church of Jesus Christ: every believer is separated unto God. We do not have to be redeemed by five shekels, or even ten, a hundred, or a thousand shekels. We have been redeemed from our sin by the blood of Jesus Christ (see 1 Peter 1:18–19).The price of redemption has been paid in full by Jesus.

When we begin to think about these things and to see them in the whole scope of the Word of God, we understand that each of these chapters in Numbers points to a vital spiritual truth.

---

5. This number seems to be consistent with an estimate of the firstborn males born after the departure from Egypt.

PURIFICATIONS (NUM. 5:1–6:21)

Numbers 5 introduces a section dealing in one way or another with purification. Once the people were numbered, they knew who they were. Then they had to be, as a people, set apart to God. This happened in several ways. First, those who were ritually defiled were expelled from the camp (see vv. 1–4). Restitution was commanded for outstanding offenses against other people within the camp (see vv. 5–10). Then a procedure was given for resolving problems of marital distrust or jealousy (see vv. 11–31). This suggests that, as God's people, we have to be right with both God and one another. John gives us a similar picture of fellowship, writing that if we have true fellowship with God, we will be in fellowship with one another (see 1 John 1:7). Only when both levels of fellowship are a reality are we able to go and do what God would have us do.

Numbers 6 describes the role of the Nazirites. The English word *Nazirite* comes from the Hebrew word *nazar*, which means "to be set apart." All the people were set apart by belonging to God, but it was possible for a person to set himself apart in a special way for a special purpose for a set length of time through the taking of a special vow. As far as we know, the Nazirites were able to do this for any length of time they wanted. They could, for example, have taken a special vow to give the next ten years of their lives to God's service. Their function in Israel was like a monk's or a nun's in the Catholic system, only it had nothing to do with celibacy. They could be married. But they had to let their hair grow and abstain from alcohol. And they couldn't touch a dead body. This is spelled out in chapter 6. The significant thing is that they set themselves apart to God.

Sometimes people wonder whether Christians should take vows today. I think it is very dangerous to take vows, for this simple reason: we take vows, but we often do not or cannot keep them. Some years ago I was at a ministers' conference in London that the Rev. Dick Lucas was leading. At the end, there was a time when it was natural to call for dedication and commitment from the people, and I was somewhat startled to hear Dick say, "Now, don't make vows to God that you won't keep." A wise word of caution.

Nevertheless, vows are mentioned in the Bible, and people have taken them. Significantly, in this chapter there are provisions for people to get out of their vows if their situation changes. It was a serious business to get out of a vow you had made to God. It involved sacrifices and expense, but it could be done. God was saying, "I know your frame; I know that you're weak. I know you can't always do the things you promised to do."

THE AARONIC BLESSING (NUM. 6:22–27)

Right at the very heart of instructions that may seem strange to us, we come to something that is at once clear, relevant, and beautiful: the Aaronic blessing at the very end of chapter 6.

> The LORD bless you
>   and keep you;
> the LORD make his face shine upon you
>   and be gracious to you;
> the LORD turn his face toward you
>   and give you peace. (Num. 6:24–26 NIV)

This comes at a very suitable place in these early chapters. The section before the blessing dealt with the Nazirites, a special people who set themselves apart to God in a special way. We might think they would receive a special blessing for doing that, and maybe they did. But at the end of the chapter is a blessing for all the people of God. You do not have to be a Nazirite, and you do not have to take a special vow to be blessed by God. This blessing is for all of us.

This is a very beautiful benediction—perhaps more so in Hebrew than it appears to be in English, although it is beautiful in English as well. In Hebrew there are three lines, broken down to six in our Bibles, and each one begins with the name of Yahweh, the LORD. Each line has two elements of benediction arranged in a typical parallel fashion. The lines become progressively longer. In Hebrew, the first line has three words, the second line has five words, and the third line has seven words. It is as if the blessing of God is unfolding and pouring out upon the people.

The first section refers to God's graciousness to us in this life. The word for "keep" can mean "guard" or "protect." The middle section ("The LORD make his face shine upon you") and the last section ("The LORD turn his face toward you") refer to God's graciousness but also reveal the longing for God's abiding presence with his people. The great desire of the Hebrew people, the saints of the Old Testament, was to see the face of God. Remember when Moses prevailed on God to continue with the Israelites and bless them. He then asked God to show him his glory (see Ex. 33:18). That was the great desire of the people, and yet God told Moses, "You cannot see my face, for man shall not see me and live" (Ex. 33:20). Moses was only granted a glance of the back of God after the Lord had passed by where his servant was hidden.

However, when Philip said to Jesus, "Lord, show us the Father," Jesus answered him, "Whoever has seen me has seen the Father" (John 14:8–9). To see the face of Jesus was to see the face of God. The time is coming for all believers that "when [Jesus] appears we shall be like him, because we shall see him as he is" (1 John 3:2). Then indeed the face of God will shine upon us. Because we have this hope, John urges us to purify ourselves "as [Jesus] is pure" (v. 3).

OFFERINGS (NUM. 7)

Numbers 7 deals with the offerings. Chronologically, it is misplaced. These offerings occurred earlier, at the very end of Exodus, when over the space of twelve days each of the tribes came to present their offerings (see Ex. 40). Why is it described here?

Often the Bible orders things theologically rather than chronologically. Think of the Gospels. There is a general sequence, but the details do not follow the exact chronological sequence we would expect. Instead, they are grouped to make theological points. This happens here as well. It is important that the offerings follow the purification. We present offerings when our hearts are right with God, not the other way around.

What strikes us here is the repetition. Beginning in verse 12, we are told what each one of the tribes brought. Then, for paragraph after paragraph, the wording is virtually identical. The single exception is the names of the different people who brought the offerings and the names of the tribes for which they brought them. This strikes us as a boring way to write. Why didn't Moses just say that every tribe brought an offering over a sequence of twelve days?

We do not appreciate this detailed account because we are swamped with books and movies and television—more information and more trivia than anyone can absorb. The Israelites didn't have television. Moses' writings may have been the only book they had. It was significant to these people that in the book of God, inspired by the Holy Spirit, written down by Moses, each tribe and offering was recorded. Some of these tribes were big. Some were small. But the same language recorded each one in the book of God. God noticed what they gave to him, and each gift was important.

Be encouraged by that. You may have done something very sacrificially for the Lord on behalf of other people—perhaps directly, perhaps indirectly—and nobody knows it. People may even think poorly of you because they think that you haven't done enough. God notices what we do. He appreciates it. Anything that is done for God, out of love for God, is recorded by God in his book and will never be blotted from his mind. Isn't that wonderful? What we do in his name really does matter.

FINAL PREPARATIONS (NUM. 8:1–9:14)

Numbers 8 tells us about the dedication of the Levites. This had to do with the setting up of the lamps and with the dedication and purification of the Levites. The Levites were to be a light to the people just as the lamps were to be a light within the tabernacle.

In the ninth chapter we have a second observance of the Passover. The Passover had been observed initially at the time when the people left Egypt. A year later they observed it again. This section introduces provision for those who were unable to observe the Passover at the right time, perhaps because they were away or ceremonially unclean. They would be able to observe it at a later period.

THE CLOUD MOVES (NUM. 9:15-23)

At the end of the ninth chapter, the cloud moves. In Exodus, the moving of the cloud was the climax of the book. But this reference to the cloud shows us important things about God. It reveals his grace to his people, shown in the very fact that he condescended to be with them, to dwell in the middle of their camp in the middle of the desert. It reminds the people about his sovereignty. When God expected them to move, they had to move; when God expected them to stop, they had to stop. If we read Numbers 9 with any kind of feeling at all, we will understand the problems they must have had. Sometimes the cloud stayed in one place for a long time, but other times it stayed only overnight. They never knew what the cloud would do. God was teaching them, training them in discipline and obedience.

It is often that way with us. When we look at our lives, sometimes God seems to be moving and sometimes he doesn't seem to be doing anything at all. During these blank periods, we wish God would do something. We pray, but we do not seem to get an answer to our prayers. But these times of waiting, or seeming inactivity, are as important as the other times. God is sovereign, and he will do with us what he will do. The important thing is to follow the leading of the cloud. If the cloud doesn't move, stay where you are; and if the cloud moves, be sure that you're ready to move. It is as simple as that.

LEAVE-TAKING (NUM. 10)

By the tenth chapter, the Israelites were ready to go. They had made trumpets that were to be sounded when they began their march. This section probably also belongs earlier chronologically. The trumpets were perhaps made when all the other articles were made, as described especially in Exodus. But their description is held until here, because the trumpets signaled the march.

When the trumpets sounded, the Israelites went. It must have been a splendid moment. They had come out of Egypt as a bunch of rabble. Now they were disciplined, formed into tribal units, counted, and arranged. They had a law, and they had a portable temple where

God condescended to dwell. Moses must have been excited. As the cloud rose and started out, we find Moses exclaiming his battle hymn: "Rise up, O LORD! May your enemies be scattered; may your foes flee before you" (v. 35 NIV). When that cloud stopped and settled down on the tabernacle again, Moses said, "Return, O LORD, to the countless thousands of Israel" (v. 36 NIV). What a wonderful time. They were marching as God's people toward Zion, the promised land.

Yet shortly after this, when the Israelites were at the very edge of the promised land, ready to go in and take it, they fell once more into disbelief and disobedience. They assumed that God was impotent, and they failed to advance. All the glory and excitement of their initial triumphs evaporated with their sin.

LEARNING FROM NUMBERS 1–10

THE IMPORTANCE OF PREPARATION

Numbers has thirty-six chapters. Ten of these—nearly one-third of the book—are spent on preparation. How long are you going to live? Sixty years? If the percentages in Numbers mean anything, you should expect to spend a good twenty of those years in preparation. And if you're going to live to be ninety, you'll need thirty years of preparation to do something worthwhile.

I'm sure the percentages are not a hard-and-fast rule. Still, you do not become trained for God's service without time and effort. Do you want to be used by God? Then get ready to be used. Spend time in preparation. Learn the Word of God; acquire the skills that are necessary to serve him. The church exists for worship, praise of God, fellowship, and witness, but also to train God's people for works of service. Take the time to get prepared. There is work for you to do.

WHAT FOLLOWS PREPARATION

Preparation is important, but, as important as it is, it has to be followed by a deliberate setting out at God's command. You have to put into operation what you have learned.

What are we to do? A lot of this depends on our gifts, but one thing we all are to do is to take the gospel to other people. Do you know anybody who is not a Christian? That is somebody you ought to teach about the gospel. Do you know the gospel? Do you understand why Jesus Christ died and what happened on the cross? Why he endured the agony of the crucifixion? Can you describe that in any terms at all to an unbeliever? If not, you had better go back and study more. But if you understand in some measure the gospel, you need to teach other people. Are you teaching, or sharing with anyone, the great truths of salvation?

WE EACH HAVE A PLACE

Numbers contains the numbering of the people, the arranging of the tribes, the numbering of the Levites, the setting apart of the people. In all the details, in all the various breakdowns of the people into groups, everyone has his place. Each of us has a place in this advance. Each of us is important. That means that you are important. What you do for the Lord Jesus Christ counts—and not only does it count, it counts forever, because you and I are engaged in spiritual work. We're not building up a secular company; we're not constructing buildings that will one day fall down. We're building for eternity.

When Jesus was calling the disciples, he told them to follow him and he would make them "fishers of men" (Matt. 4:19). It is good to fish for fish, because people have to eat. But fish will be eaten, and the eaters will still die. If you fish for men with the gospel, those who are saved will live forever, and so your works will live forever.

WE CAN ALWAYS FAIL

Let me give you a sober thought related to that first census. Although what we do counts, we can fail to do anything. Failure is inevitable if we do not really trust and obey God. With the exception of Joshua and Caleb, every single individual whose name is recorded in the first census in Numbers died in the desert and never reached Canaan. Joshua and Caleb were the two faithful spies who came back with the good report, and God allowed them to go into the land. They fought and did a marvelous job later, but everybody else died. A second census, found in Numbers 26, gives an entirely different list of names.

With this in mind, think of Hebrews 3–4. The author of the book of Hebrews refers to these events, warning the people in his day that they must press on in belief and obedience to God and not fall by the wayside as those did who perished in the desert. This is a sober warning. You can hear these things, understand the gospel, and even agree with it to a certain extent, and yet refuse to go on with Jesus Christ and so perish in your sin. The book of Numbers says that God doesn't want you to do that. Believe the gospel—the good news, the offer of eternal life—when you hear it, so that you can go on in service to Jesus Christ that will produce fruit which will last forever and ever.

22

COMPLAINTS AND OPPOSITION

Numbers 11–12

THE PROBLEMS BEGIN

In the first ten chapters of Numbers, everything seems to be going well. The people are commended for obeying God, and we read again and again that they did as the Lord commanded (see, for example, 1:19, 54; 2:33–34). Yet when we come to the eleventh chapter, suddenly the tone is different: the people are complaining. This begins a series of complaints that will continue throughout the whole book.

Isn't it remarkable that we can move so quickly from a time of joy and obedience to the Lord to a time of disobedience and complaint? This should not be. Our God is faithful. He gives us even the hard times for his own purposes, and he sees us through them. But as soon as the hard times come, we think something has gone wrong—that God should not be allowing this to happen. Then we often begin to murmur and complain against him the way that the people of Israel did.

The complaining begins about three days after the people set out from Sinai, starting with the rabble mentioned in Numbers 11:4 but quickly spreading. Pretty soon, everybody is complaining. Eventually even Aaron and Moses sin, and in consequence even Moses doesn't get to enter the promised land. This is pretty grim, but it is an illustration of what our lives are like. We are looking forward to the land that Jesus has gone to prepare for us. But are we often defeated, often complaining? There is, unfortunately, a great deal of defeat and complaining. But that is not the whole story.

As we look at these chapters, we see the character of Moses. He emerges as a great and humble leader who is strong under opposition and who responds in the right way most of the time. Additionally, we see the mercy and grace of God. We see that God is a God who judges sin, but even in the midst of his judgment he remembers mercy. His mercy emerges again and again.

TWO COMPLAINTS (NUM. 11:1–9)

The problems begin with two separate complaints at the very beginning of Numbers 11. The first is a general murmuring. The people have just started out from where they had camped at Sinai. I would not regard *living in* the desert as particularly desirable or nice, but it was a lot better than *traveling through* the desert. After they've traveled for about three days, the Israelites decide they do not like it and begin to murmur. Their second complaint is about food (see v. 4). They've been given food that they do not like.

The complaint about food had occurred before. In Exodus 16 we find an incident that almost directly parallels the one here. The people did not like what they were eating. They wished they had meat. God sent quail. Because a similar story occurs at two points, the higher critics of the Old Testament say that these are two parallel, independent accounts of only one incident. Actually, there are some differences, and the differences point out some lessons.

Both complaints occur in the springtime, about a year apart. People who study the region tell us that at this time quail migrate from the south in Ethiopia, north across the desert to the Mediterranean Sea, and then to southern Europe. As far as we know, the facts of the story fit exactly what is known today of these migrations.

When the people complained earlier, God heard them and provided the quail. This time, when they complain, God judges them. The general complaint in the first three verses is judged by "fire of the LORD" (Num. 11:1) that breaks out on the edge of the camp. Only by the intercession of Moses is its destruction halted. Later, when they complain about food, God sends quail again, but this time it makes them sick. God says that he will give them more than they want, and some begin to die because of what they've eaten.

What's the difference? During the past year, God had revealed a great deal about himself. When the Israelites came out of Egypt, they did not know much about God at all. They were a nation of slaves. But God taught them about himself at Sinai. He taught them that he is a holy and powerful God. He showed them miracles. As the Israelites went through the desert, they knew that God was preserving them through the manna they ate and the water they drank. A great cloud overshadowed the camp to protect them from the hot desert sun in the daytime and then turned into a pillar of fire at night to provide both warmth and light. They had perfectly adequate evidence of the power and grace of God. They should not have been complaining.

Do you have any evidences of the power and grace of God in your life? Have you been a Christian for any length of time? Whether you've been a Christian for one year or for twenty years, you've seen many evidences of the grace of God. Isn't it more serious for you to complain about God now than it was for you to complain within a day or two of your conversion? You see how it works. This story begins to tell us how very serious it is to complain about God.

The Israelites had been in the wilderness for a year, and God had fed them throughout that entire time with manna. But when they complain about having only manna to eat, it is very easy for us to sympathize. We would feel exactly the same way. After all, we're used to supermarkets. We would want a little variety—maybe a little meat in our diet. Meat is good for you, after all. And if we *did* want manna, we would expect a whole row of it to choose from—new and improved manna, *new* new and improved manna, strawberry-flavored manna, manna in powder form, bottled manna, manna that you could buy in bulk, and so forth.

This story tells us that it is very serious to complain to God about anything that he has provided, and especially about food. After all, when Jesus taught his disciples to pray, he had them pray, "Give us this day our daily bread" (Matt. 6:11). We ask God for our daily bread, and if we receive it, it comes from him. If we complain about it, we are complaining about God, saying that God doesn't know what he's doing—or at least saying that we do not like what he's doing and that he should be doing it another way instead.

We ought to remember that it was, in part, a problem with food that led to the sin of our first parents. Of course, there was much more involved than that; they were rebelling against any kind of restriction that God would put on them, which is the very nature of sin. But their sin did have to do with food. Adam and Eve had been given all the abundance of the garden except for the fruit of one forbidden tree, and that was the one thing that they wanted. We ought to learn from this and be careful. We ought to be satisfied with God's day-by-day provision. This doesn't mean that we shouldn't expand our diet; but it means we should be thankful for what God provides for our needs. That is why we offer prayers before meals (and, in some traditions, after meals as well). This is not just a senseless religious rite that Christians go through. It is exceedingly proper, because we are acknowledging that God provides all the necessities of life for us, including the food which nourishes us daily. We do not acquire or achieve these things by ourselves; God provides them—therefore, we're thankful to him for his care and provision.

A LONG, ANGRY PRAYER (NUM. 11:10–35)

What follows is not a very attractive moment in Moses' life. Starting in verse 10, Moses gives vent to his frustration in a long, angry prayer. It is surprising to find this here, because in the very next chapter Moses will be described as the meekest man who ever lived (see Num. 12:3 KJV). Meek, yes, but in this prayer he expresses his frustration, complaining bitterly to God.

> Why have you dealt ill with your servant? And why have I not found favor in your sight, that you lay the burden of all this people on me? Did I conceive all this people? Did I give them birth, that you should say to me, "Carry them in your bosom, as a nurse carries a nursing child," to the land that you swore to give their fathers? Where am I to get meat to give to all this people? For they weep before me and

say, "Give us meat, that we may eat." I am not able to carry all this people alone; the burden is too heavy for me. If you will treat me like this, kill me at once, if I find favor in your sight, that I may not see my wretchedness. (Num. 11:11–15)

We might have issues with this prayer. We might say, quite rightly, "That's no way to talk to God!" After all, Moses is complaining about how the people are complaining. This is not the kind of prayer a Presbyterian would pray—at least not in church on Sunday morning.

But God doesn't criticize Moses. God understands exactly what Moses is going through. Moses truly is trying to carry the burden of all the people on his shoulders. Ask any pastor how easy it is to deal with a church of a hundred, and he'll tell you that there are lots of problems. There are always problems, even with those who follow God—and Moses was trying to deal with two million, not one hundred. No wonder he said to the Lord, "I can't handle this anymore. I would rather die. As a matter of fact, if you like me, take me home to glory right now."

Think of Elijah under the broom tree: "I have had enough, LORD. . . . Take my life; I am no better than my ancestors" (1 Kings 19:4 NIV). What he meant was that he was no stronger than anybody else. He was just a human being. He couldn't handle this. He'd done the best he could but had been driven out and was being hunted down to be killed.

What did God do in Elijah's case? He gave him a helper, Elisha. Similarly, what does he do with Moses? He gives Moses helpers (see Num. 11:16–17).

When the burden seems too great, bring it to God, because God understands our burdens and takes them on himself. Jesus Christ lived on earth and knows the burdens that we bear. You'll find that if you aren't able to bear your burden, God will provide helpers. Now, sometimes we *are* able, and God wants us to be strengthened by what we go through. But if we have an intolerable burden that is producing this kind of frustration, God will provide a helper.

This is what he does for Moses. He provides seventy elders and sends his Spirit on them so that they begin to prophesy. Not only does he do that, but he also promises to provide quail—the meat that the people are requesting. At this point, in doubt and disbelief, Moses demands how God can possibly promise to give meat to that many people: "'Shall flocks and herds . . . be enough for them? Or shall all the fish of the sea . . . be enough for them?'" (Num. 11:22).

Think of the disciples. They'd been listening to Jesus' teaching all day, along with thousands of people. When it came time for dinner, they had five loaves and a couple of little fish. "Here is what we have," they said, "but what is it with so many to feed?" (see John 6:9). They had no appreciation of the Lord Jesus Christ's ability to multiply the loaves and fish.

In spite of his great faith and his leadership ability, it seems that Moses really did question whether God could provide the quail. God could and did, but his provision turned out to be a judgment on the people, because God was angry with them for complaining, for forgetting his faithful provision thus far, and for doubting his ability to provide for them in the next days and months. The Israelites got what they wanted, but they got more of what they wanted *than* they wanted, and they found out that getting their cravings satisfied was not a good thing: "While the meat was yet between their teeth, before it was consumed, the anger of the LORD was kindled against the people, and the LORD struck down the people with a very great plague" (Num. 11:33).

AARON AND MIRIAM'S OPPOSITION TO MOSES (NUM. 12)

Starting in Numbers 12, the story becomes one of opposition, hard hearts, and divisions within the camp. The opposition that Moses faced now comes from within his own family circle—from his brother Aaron and his sister, Miriam, who seems to have been the ringleader.

The ground for their attack is Moses' wife, whom the Bible describes as being a Cushite (see v. 1). Because Zipporah, his first wife, was from Midian, it seems that she had died and that Moses had taken a second wife—an Ethiopian.[1] If that is the case, then Miriam

1. Cush was located in the region of Ethiopia.

was saying, "I don't like this black woman in my family." This is not only sibling rivalry but also the worst kind of racial prejudice.

MOSES' RESPONSE

Miriam was upset with Moses' wife, but she attacked Moses himself, saying that he had claimed too much authority. She and Aaron asked, "Has the LORD indeed spoken only through Moses? Has he not spoken through us also?" (v. 2). What did Moses do as his siblings attacked him and his wife? Instead of lashing back, he said nothing. Verse 3 says something very revealing about Moses: "Now the man Moses was very meek, more than all people who were on the face of the earth." Moses remained silent when he was accused.

Moses was not always silent. When God was attacked, Moses spoke up. When the people did wrong, Moses interceded. But when Moses himself was attacked, he was silent. This is the way to respond to personal attacks. You and I do the opposite, don't we? When the honor of God is attacked, we are silent. When people attack us personally, we get very defensive. Moses had it the right way round.

GOD'S VINDICATION

Seldom in history has God's vindication of one of his servants been more rapid and more direct than his vindication of Moses on this occasion. The impression of the story is that while Aaron and Miriam were voicing their complaint to Moses, God called the two brothers and their sister to come forward before the Tent of Meeting, the place where God spoke with Moses. When the three came forward, God called for Aaron and Miriam to come forward, and he spoke these words.

When a prophet of the LORD is among you,
I reveal myself to him in visions,
I speak to him in dreams.
But this is not true of my servant Moses;
he is faithful in all my house.
With him I speak face to face,
clearly and not in riddles;

he sees the form of the LORD.
Why then were you not afraid
    to speak against my servant Moses? (vv. 6–8 NIV)

"Why then were you not afraid to speak against my servant Moses?" This is a word that evangelicals need to take very, very seriously. No one today quite corresponds to Moses. Moses was above even the prophets in his own day, as these verses make clear. Yet there is a principle here. When God has chosen somebody to speak and teach in his name, as he does with those who are ordained to gospel ministry, it is with fear and trepidation that we should dare to say a word against such a messenger. Those who speak in the name of God are sinners. All of us are. Many err greatly. Some fall into grievous sin. But we should be very, very careful before we accuse them; and, should we accuse them, we ought to do so carefully and judiciously, praying that they might be restored and blessed even more than previously in the days to come.

I know stories of those who have gotten rid of a church's minister because they did not like this or that about him. God does not take that lightly. We should pray for pastors and other church leaders rather than belittle them or demean their efforts to serve God.

When God gives judgments, he gives significant judgments. His judgment is not arbitrary. Here God judged Miriam with leprosy,[2] so that when the cloud was removed her skin was white as snow (see v. 10). In attacking Moses' wife, Miriam had been saying that she did not want any black person in her family. In his judgment of Miriam, God is saying, "Do you think your lighter skin makes you better than the woman Moses married? You want to be white? I'll give you white."

God doesn't take racial prejudice lightly. We are all made in his image. We're all sinners in need of his grace, and God does not discriminate. He will use those who give their lives to him and serve him, no matter what color their skin is, and he will reject those who do not—no matter how high or privileged they seem to be.

---

2. The word refers generally to some kind of skin disease.

TWO INTERCESSIONS

The story wraps up with two examples of intercession. First, Aaron looked at Miriam and was aghast at what he saw. He turned to Moses and begged him to do something. As he interceded on her behalf with Moses, he confessed his own sin, linking himself with Miriam: "Oh, my lord, do not punish us because we have done foolishly and have sinned" (v. 11). Maybe he was afraid that something would happen to him next. Regardless, he did intercede for his sister. Second, Moses interceded with God, and God said he would graciously heal her.

Still, Miriam's sin was serious. God asked Moses a question: if Miriam's father had been offended by her and had shown his disapproval by merely spitting on her, would she not have had to remain outside the camp for seven days in disgrace? So they sent Miriam outside the camp for seven days. It was a greatly chastened woman, a greatly humbled woman, who came back into the camp a week later.

LEARNING FROM NUMBERS 11–12

Moses is quite often used as a typology of Jesus Christ. We see in Moses the character of Christ, and, because we are supposed to imitate Jesus Christ, we can learn from Moses and imitate him. Gordon Wenham says this:

> Jesus is the prophet like Moses (Acts 7:37). Like Moses, Jesus is meek and lowly in heart (Mt. 11:29), and kept silent before his accusers (1 Pet. 2:23ff.). But whereas Moses was but a servant in God's house, our Lord was the son of the house (Heb. 3:1–6); Moses saw God's form and heard his word, but Jesus was the Word and in the form of God (Jn. 1:14–18; Phil. 2:6).[3]

What can we learn from Moses' example? Commentator William Taylor gives us three ways that we can learn from Moses' conduct in this particular incident.[4]

---

3. Gordon J. Wenham, *Numbers*, Tyndale Old Testament Commentaries (Downers Grove, IL: IVP Academic, 1981), 113–14.

4. See William M. Taylor, *Moses the Law-Giver* (New York: Harper & Brothers, 1879), 316–21.

1. *"The noblest disinterestedness will not preserve us from the shafts of envy."* Moses' conduct in these chapters was utterly above reproach. Although he complained to God, he did not misbehave in any way. If there was ever a model leader, it was Moses—and yet the people rose up against him, even his own brother and sister. This will happen if you take any kind of leadership in the church of Jesus Christ. You can be utterly disinterested, not pursuing your own glory in any way. You can be serving in an utterly selfless and even costly manner, and there will be criticism. There will always be people who are envious of what God is doing through you. Do not be surprised when attacks come. Be ready for them and handle them humbly.

2. *"Envy of disinterested greatness may show itself in the most unexpected quarters."* We can sometimes handle attacks when they come from without. It is much harder when suddenly someone right next to us is complaining. Jesus warned us about this when he said that even people within a man's household will be his enemies (see Matt. 10:36). How do we handle that? We should be ready for such things, not unduly crushed by them when they come. In addition, we should be sure that we do not do this very thing ourselves. Do you find yourself envying the success of others in your family—that brother who has done better than you have; a sister who seems to be closer to the Lord? Do you become critical of them? Are you poking away at their faults because you think they are doing better than you are? You mustn't do that. Moses did not think that way. And when his siblings got in trouble, he did what a Christian should do. He interceded for them before God.

3. *"The assaults of envy are always best met by a silent appeal to Heaven."* There are many fine moments in the life of Moses. Back in Exodus 32, when God was ready to destroy the people for making the golden calf, Moses interceded for them. God had said he was going to destroy the people and start again with Moses, but Moses said, "No—destroy me and save them" (see Ex. 32:32). I'd call that the finest hour in the life of Moses, but this is a fine moment too. Moses doesn't defend himself; rather,

305

he leaves the defense of himself to God. God has said, "Vengeance is mine, and recompense" (Deut. 32:35). God will be just. Our task is to live humbly before God and serve him and intercede for other people, especially for those who criticize or attack us. What Paul says in Romans 12:21 is exactly to the point: "Do not be overcome by evil, but overcome evil with good."

23

THE TWELVE SPIES

Numbers 13–14

FAILURE TO BELIEVE

The vivid style of narrative that began in Numbers 11 is especially noticeable in chapters 13 and 14. Here we meet the twelve spies, who emerge as real, lifelike people, passionately concerned about the things they believe in. Their story is told with great drama. It is also filled with lessons, which is one reason why it is referenced so many other times in the Bible (see Num. 32:8–13; Deut. 1:19–46; Ps. 95:10–11; 1 Cor. 10:5). At the end of this chapter, we'll look at a great passage on this episode from the book of Hebrews.

After all that the people had gone through and seen over the past year—their deliverance from Egypt by the mighty hand of God; the miracles; the frightening, awe-inspiring revelation of God at Sinai; God's provision of manna and water in their wandering; the cloud that went before them day and night—one would think they would have been ready to possess the land that God had promised to them. Yet they did not do it. We can learn from them because we are exactly the same. We have seen the power of God in Jesus Christ. We have his promises. Yet we are afraid to act on them. Like the Israelites, we too suffer the consequences of our unbelief.

What was the Israelites' failure? Their failure was a failure to believe the Word of God. Ours is the same. We've seen great demonstrations of God's power. No promise of God has failed. Augustus M. Toplady puts this well in his hymn "A Debtor to Mercy Alone": "His promise is Yea and Amen, and never was forfeited yet."[1] Yet when we come up against the giants of this world, we think, "God may have done it in the past, but he can't do it now." We disbelieve him.

Are the people who are standing on the very edge of the promised land going to believe God, go in, and possess it? We know the answer. They did not, and they suffered the consequences.

The same question is before us. We have our battles to face. Are we going to believe God, fight as his soldiers, and possess the land that he has given us to possess? Or are we going to believe that the enemies are too great, the giants too tall, the war too strenuous, and allow the victory to go by?

THE SPIES' MISSION (NUM. 13:1–25)

When Moses tells this story again in Deuteronomy 1, there is a seeming contradiction with Numbers 13. In Deuteronomy, Moses writes that the people suggested they send in spies and that Moses thought it was a good idea. Numbers says that *God* told Moses to send in the twelve spies. But you can imagine how something like this happened. The people had come to the very edge of the land. Their anticipation had been building for a long time. They were a bit anxious and were tired from their desert wandering. In a situation like this, they were probably glad to have an excuse to delay the conquest just a little. They wanted to spy out the land before they plunged in.

Moses knew that they did not need to send spies. They did not have to know what was there, because God knew and would lead them in the right way. But the people were anxious, so Moses probably thought that spies wouldn't hurt. When they came back with a good report, that would encourage the people. So he agreed to the plan.

Moses would not have agreed to this without consulting God. This is what Numbers tells us. Moses must have talked to God about the people's suggestion and asked what they should do. At that point,

---

1. Augustus M. Toplady, "A Debtor to Mercy Alone," n.d.

God told him to pick twelve spies, representative of each of the twelve tribes, and to send them into the land to spy it out carefully.

Thus Numbers 13 begins with a long list of the names of the men who represented the twelve tribes. Note that Joshua's name is written as "Hoshea the son of Nun" (v. 8). *Hoshea* means "God is salvation" or "salvation is of God," which has virtually the same meaning as *Joshua*, the name that Moses gives him in verse 16. But there is one significant difference: *Hoshea* is based on the more general name for God, *Elohim*, while *Joshua* is based on the name *Jehovah*. Thus Joshua's new name specifically meant "Jehovah is salvation" or "Jehovah saves." This is significant because Jesus' name is *Yeshua* or *Joshua*, meaning "Jehovah is salvation" (see Matt. 1:21).

Once selected, the twelve spies were sent into the land. They were to investigate an area of about 250 miles, and they investigated it thoroughly. They went from the desert in the south—known as Zin, or the Negev—to the furthest reaches in the north. Exploring the land took about forty days. On the way back, they traveled through a valley filled with enormous grapes. They took a huge cluster of grapes that was so big that one man couldn't carry it. They had to put it over a pole for two men to carry.[2] Think what that must have meant to people who had just spent a year in the desert eating manna. You would think that that would have led to a great report. But it did not.

The spies also investigated the city of Hebron. Abraham had lived at Hebron, and it was where God had promised to give him and his offspring forever all the land that he could see—everywhere he could plant his foot would belong to him and his descendants (see Gen. 13:14–18). Later, Abraham went out from Hebron to chase the kings who had carried off his nephew Lot and the people of Sodom and Gomorrah. Still later, Abraham bought the cave Machpelah, by Hebron, where he buried his wife, Sarah. He himself was buried there, and so were some of the other patriarchs. If there had ever been a shrine for Israel, it was at Hebron. This is why, when Joseph was dying in Egypt long before the Israelites' years of slavery, he made the people swear that when God took them

---

2. Today, the logo of Israel's Ministry of Tourism is two men carrying a branch supporting a cluster of giant grapes.

up out of Egypt and into their own land they would take his bones with them and bury them at Hebron with the other fathers of the people. As the Israelites stood at the very border of the land, they had with them the bones of Joseph. All they had to do was move forward, and God would give them Hebron. We know, of course, that this is not what happened.

THE SPIES' REPORTS (NUM. 13:26-33)

The heart of the story is found in the two reports of the spies, which begin in verse 26. The majority report is given first. It is told very well, with great dramatic writing. Then the minority report is voiced by Caleb. Joshua's report is held for later, probably for dramatic effect, and perhaps, some also suggest, because he was Moses' right hand and so we can guess what he would say.

In one respect, all twelve spies were in agreement: the land really was a good land. It was a prosperous, fruitful land—as proof they had brought back with them "a branch with a single cluster of grapes" which took two men to carry (13:23). It was extensive. It had wonderful, walled cities, so they would not even have to build their own cities for their defense. And it was filled with people, which is where the problems began. The land was filled with Amalekites, Hittites, Jebusites, Amorites, and Canaanites. However, this should not have surprised them; God had told Abraham that he would send them into a land possessed by all these peoples (see Gen. 15:18–21).

Ten spies said that the Israelites would never be able to drive the Canaanites out of their strong cities. They reported, "All the people that we saw in it are of great height" (Num. 13:32). The people they found in Palestine couldn't have been much bigger than they were—probably no bigger at all—so to say such a thing was probably an exaggeration. But there was a germ of truth in their report. They had seen something that frightened them: the descendants of Anak—Ahiman, Sheshai, and Talmai (see v. 22)—who were said to have come from the Nephilim (see vv. 28, 33) and were presumably giants.[3] It

---

3. There is some debate about what the word *Nephilim* means. It also occurs in Genesis 6:4, where the Nephilim are said to be "heroes of old, men of renown" (NIV).

was like seeing three Goliaths all in one place, and it scared the spies so much that they reported, "We are not able to go up against the people, for they are stronger than we are" (v. 31).

It is too bad that the ten spies did not have the faith of young David when he faced Goliath. He was just one young man, but when he spoke to King Saul he said, "Your servant killed a lion and a bear, and this uncircumcised Philistine is going to be like one of them, because the Lord's going to give him into my hand" (see 1 Sam. 17:36). He confronted Goliath with the words "You come against me with sword and spear and javelin, but I come against you in the name of the LORD Almighty, the God of the armies of Israel, whom you have defied" (1 Sam. 17:45 NIV). The unbelieving spies should have had that same spirit. They should have come back saying, "Giants are in the land, but in the name of the Lord we're going to overthrow them." Sadly, they did not.

In the midst of the negative reports, Caleb's recommendation was short and simple: "Let us go up at once and occupy it, for we are well able to overcome it" (Num. 13:30). He was a soldier type, not given to long speeches, but he had faith that God would give them the land.

CALEB

Caleb is a fascinating man. He was the representative of the tribe of Judah (see v. 6) and also a son of Jephunneh, a Kenizzite (see Josh. 14:6, 14). The Kenizzites were not Israelite, but were descendants of Kenaz, a grandson of Esau, and thus descendants of Abraham but not through the line of the patriarch Jacob. Thus Caleb was not by birth a member of one of the twelve tribes of Israel, but with his extended family or clan, at some point, perhaps during their sojourn in Egypt, had become attached to the tribe of Judah, and was now chosen to represent that tribe as one of the twelve spies (see 13:6). Caleb's loyalty and commitment to Israel and the God of Israel never wavered. And that first view of the promised land, and in particular of the city of Hebron and its environs in the south, made a lasting impression on him. He seems to have been overcome with a desire to conquer it and put it in Hebrew hands, and he was sure that it could be done. It must have been a bitter disappointment, when he came back with his good report, to find that ten of the spies were against him and then to watch the rest of the people agree with the nonbelievers.

Caleb was forty years old when he went into the land, and it would be thirty-eight years before he saw Canaan again. Furthermore, the battle to take the land took seven more years, meaning that Caleb was eighty-five years old at the end of the campaign. All this while, for forty-five years, he remembered Hebron. When the fighting was nearly at an end and Caleb had an opportunity to take a portion of the land for himself, he asked Joshua, his friend and commander-in-chief, for permission to conquer Hebron. He had said that they could take it, and he was determined to show that it could be done. He might not have been eloquent in his report in Numbers, but he made a great speech to Joshua.

> You know what the LORD said to Moses the man of God in Kadesh-barnea concerning you and me. I was forty years old when Moses the servant of the LORD sent me from Kadesh-barnea to spy out the land, and I brought him word again as it was in my heart. . . . And Moses swore on that day, saying, "Surely the land on which your foot has trodden shall be an inheritance for you and your children forever, because you have wholly followed the LORD my God." And now, behold, the LORD has kept me alive, just as he said, these forty-five years since the time that the LORD spoke this word to Moses, while Israel walked in the wilderness. And now, behold, I am this day eighty-five years old. I am still as strong today as I was in the day that Moses sent me; my strength now is as my strength was then, for war and for going and coming. So now give me this hill country of which the LORD spoke on that day, for you heard on that day how the Anakim were there, with great fortified cities. It may be that the LORD will be with me, and I shall drive them out just as the LORD said. (Josh. 14:6–7, 9–12)

And he did it. Caleb's speech wasn't braggadocio. He did what he did because he trusted God.

Caleb was given two main cities in the hill country: Hebron, the city he had remembered all those years, and Debir. He wanted to take Hebron for himself, so he attacked it and drove out the three descendants of Anak: Sheshai, Ahiman, and Talmai. They were a good bit older by this time as well, but he drove them out, because he knew it could be done. Then he offered his daughter to the man who conquered Debir. A man named Othniel did it; he and Caleb's daughter were married, and they all settled down together in the hill country (see Josh. 15:13–19).

A MATTER OF PERSPECTIVE

This great story of belief and perseverance is set against the unbelief of the people, and the unbelief is tragic. In the midst of the tragedy of their unbelief, however, there is something quite humorous. After the ten spies described the Nephilim, they said, "We seemed to ourselves like grasshoppers, and so we seemed to them" (Num. 13:33). None of the twelve spies disagreed about what they had seen. Where they differed was in their awareness, or lack of awareness, of God. Ten spies looked at the giants, compared themselves to the giants, and felt like grasshoppers. Caleb and Joshua had their eyes fixed on God, not on themselves or their circumstances, and from that perspective the giants looked small. They said, "Don't be afraid of the people of the land, because we'll swallow them up." The ten spies said, "The land swallows up the people who are in it." Caleb and Joshua said, "Their protection is gone, but the Lord is with us. Don't be afraid of them." Alan Redpath writes, "The majority measured the giants against their own strength; Caleb and Joshua measured the giants against God. The majority trembled; the two triumphed. The majority had great giants but a little God. Caleb had a great God and little giants."[4]

It might be a turning point in your life if you decide to stand with Caleb and Joshua and take their approach to life. If you look at the problems in life, you are always going to believe (unless you are absolutely arrogant) that the problems are greater than you are, because the problems *are* great—probably greater than you are. How can you possibly overcome them? You can't. But if you put your eyes

---

4. Alan Redpath, *Victorious Christian Living: Studies in the Book of Joshua* (Westwood, NJ: Fleming H. Revell, 1955), 197–98; quoted in James Montgomery Boice, *Joshua*, Boice Commentary Series (Westwood, NJ: Fleming H. Revell, 1989; repr. Grand Rapids: Baker, 2005), 104.

on God, the situation is altogether different. You can't overcome your problems, but God can.

Do you have a big God and little giants? Or do you have big giants and a little God? How we answer these questions marks a fork in the road for many, many Christians.

CONTEMPT FOR GOD (NUM. 14:1-12)

At the beginning, the people seemed undecided. They gathered around to hear the spies. Ten spies gave their report. Caleb gave a contrary report. The first ten exaggerated in order to carry the day. The people followed along with the ten. Finally, Joshua spoke up, and pleaded with the people of Israel to fear the Lord, and not the people of the land, but he could not sway the mob either. Tensions were high. The people were ready to elect a new leader to take them back to Egypt.

"Then all the congregation said to stone [Moses and Aaron] with stones" (Num. 14:10). In my Bible I put two lines between this sentence and the next, because something abrupt happened at this point. The people were buzzing; they did not know what to do. But when they decided to believe the negative spies, Moses and Aaron fell down on their faces in prayer before God. They were in this position often—they had assumed it when God had been on the verge of destroying the people.

And suddenly, the Lord appeared.

God appeared "at the Tent of Meeting to all the Israelites" and said, "How long will these people treat me with contempt? How long will they refuse to believe in me, in spite of all the miraculous signs I have performed among them? I will strike them down with a plague and destroy them, but I will make you into a nation greater and stronger than they" (vv. 10–12 NIV). This should sound familiar. The same scene played out in Exodus 32, when the people made the golden calf and God told Moses he would blot them out and start again with him, Moses. Moses did now exactly what he had done then. He interceded for them, asking God to forgive their sin and to spare them.

What brought out God's anger on this occasion? This was not

obvious idolatry, as in Exodus 32, yet the wrath of God was the same. The threatened judgment was identical. What had made God so angry? He explained it when he said, "You have contempt for me."

Refusing to believe God shows contempt for him. God says that hell is a real threat and that Jesus Christ has provided the way of salvation. If we do not believe that, we are showing contempt for God—in God's eyes, if not our own (and God is the one with whom you have to deal!). Someday we will stand before him. Will he say, "You have shown contempt for me and for my Son, when I gave my Son to die in your place, and you didn't believe"? This is not just a warning for unbelievers. If you are a Christian but are not willing to trust him with your life, you are showing contempt for God as well.

What does God most want from us? He needs nothing that we have to offer, but he wants to be believed. Do you believe him? Are you willing to believe his Word and act on it?

ANOTHER INTERCESSION (NUM. 14:13–19)

As Moses interceded for the people, he rejected God's offer once more. He pleaded with God to spare the Israelites, presenting arguments to God that are very similar to the ones he had given before.

GOD'S REPUTATION

In Exodus 32 Moses said to God, "Why should the Egyptians say, 'With evil intent did he bring [the people] out, to kill them in the mountains and to consume them from the face of the earth'?" (v. 12). Here he says virtually the same thing.

> Then the Egyptians will hear of it . . . and they will tell the inhabitants of this land. They have heard that you, O Lord, are in the midst of this people. For you, O Lord, are seen face to face, and your cloud stands over them and you go before them, in a pillar of cloud by day and in a pillar of fire by night. Now if you kill this people as one man, then the nations who have heard your fame will say, "It is because the Lord was not able to bring this people into the land that he swore to give to them that he has killed them in the wilderness." (Num. 14:13–16)

This was no small matter. Who is the God who is able to do what he promises? That was the issue then, and it is the issue today. When Moses said that the nations would hear about it, he was making a very forceful argument. The nations *did* hear about it. When God brought the people into the land, the citizens of Jericho and the other major cities already knew what God had done. And yet the majority of the nations still did not believe in God as a result of these reports. Belief has to come from God himself; unbelief is very deeply entrenched.

But some did believe. One example is Rahab of Jericho. When she was with the spies, she told them, "We've heard about all the things that God has done for you" (see Josh. 2:9–10). She believed because of what she'd heard; the others didn't believe but trembled nonetheless. And Jericho fell.

GOD'S GRACE

Moses' second argument concerned God's grace. This argument was not so much a part of his prayer in Exodus 32; perhaps Moses did not know as much about the grace of God at that time. But after interceding for the people following the golden calf disaster, Moses had asked God to show him his glory. God explained that this was not possible; a human being who looks on the face of God will die. But God put Moses in a cave in the rock, covered it with his hand, and passed by. As he did, Moses heard God say, "The LORD, the LORD, a God merciful and gracious, slow to anger, and abounding in steadfast love and faithfulness, keeping steadfast love for thousands, forgiving iniquity and transgression and sin" (Ex. 34:6–7). In other words, when Moses asked to see God's face, the "face" that God showed Moses was a revelation that he was a faithful and merciful God.

Moses appealed to that mercy here: You have said that you're merciful. You have revealed yourself as gracious. And he pleaded, "Please pardon the iniquity of this people, according to the greatness of your steadfast love, just as you have forgiven this people, from Egypt until now" (Num. 14:19).

How many people want to approach God on the basis of his justice? They say they want God to treat them fairly, to give them a fair shake. But if you ask for justice from God, the justice of God will send you to hell. That is no way to approach God. Instead, the Bible teaches us that we can only approach God on the basis of his mercy, which is found in Jesus Christ. If you say, as the tax collector did, "God be merciful to me a sinner" (Luke 18:13 KJV), God will hear you and save you through the work of Christ.

GOD LISTENS (NUM. 14:20–45)

God listened to Moses, as he had listened previously, and spared the people.[5] Yet there is a sad irony: sometimes God deals with disbelief by letting us have what we want. The people had said, "Would that we had died in the land of Egypt! Or would that we had died in this wilderness!" (Num. 14:2). All right, God told them—in that case, they would wander in the desert for thirty-eight more years, until everyone over the age of twenty who had grumbled against the Lord had died (see 14:29). God would wait for a new generation.

God gave the Israelites what they wanted, and a generation perished. Years later, when the actual invasion of the land took place, there is a new listing of the people. It is an entirely different list from the one at the beginning of Numbers, except for Caleb and Joshua.

The people realized they had made a mistake. They decided to press on, but without God's blessing the result was a foregone conclusion. They were defeated in battle, and many, many died (see vv. 44–45).

LEARNING FROM NUMBERS 13–14

The story of the spies is a watershed event that is referred to throughout the rest of the Bible. Paul writes, "Now these things occurred as examples to keep us from setting our hearts on evil things as they did" (1 Cor. 10:6 NIV). The writer of Hebrews gives the best biblical interpretation and application of the story, showing that the people were not able to enter the land because of their unbelief. He concludes,

5. Although he does consume the ten unbelieving spies with a plague.

317

See to it, brothers, that none of you has a sinful, unbelieving heart that turns away from the living God. But encourage one another daily, as long as it is called Today, so that none of you may be hardened by sin's deceitfulness. (Heb. 3:12–13 NIV)

There are several things we can focus on as we learn from this failure and its consequences.

THE TRAGEDY OF UNBELIEF

Unbelief is no small matter. We think of other sins being great and hardly think of unbelief at all. But unbelief is the tragedy of this story. It is tragic because it brings judgment, but also because it spreads. Twelve men went to see the land. Ten made a bad report. The bad report spread to the people. Soon the entire nation was denied the conquest. Eventually more than a million people perished in the desert.

However, belief spreads too. Belief is blessed by God so that it spreads as someone talks about the grace of God out of his or her faith in him and, by the grace of God, as others come to believe and experience that grace in their lives.

Are you contributing to the advance and victory of faith by your belief? Or are you standing against it because you do not trust God?

THE BATTLES AHEAD

In this spiritual warfare of ours, there are always battles to be fought. We may not like them. We may want our lives to be lives of ease, but we're given warfare instead. We are not to lay down our armor until we get to heaven. A great hymn by Isaac Watts says,

Sure I must fight if I would reign:
Increase my courage, Lord;
I'll bear the toil, endure the pain,
Supported by thy Word.[6]

This is the life of faith we are called to pursue.

6. Isaac Watts, "Am I a Soldier of the Cross?", 1724.

THE NECESSITY OF GOD'S PRESENCE

An obvious point is that without God you can do nothing. When the people did decide to enter Canaan, they went in without the presence or the blessing of the Lord, and they were defeated. Jesus said, "apart from me you can do nothing" (John 15:5). Do you believe that? If you do, why do you attempt so much without consulting God or seeking to walk in his way? Why are you so timorous about doing the things that you know you ought to do?

THE CHARACTER OF MOSES

We do not see Moses much in this episode, since its focus is on Caleb, Joshua, and the unbelieving spies. But we nonetheless learn about Moses' character. At the end of Numbers 10, as the people started out, Moses went with what must have been great joy and anticipation. The cloud started forward, and Moses said, "Arise, O LORD, and let your enemies be scattered" (v. 35). When the cloud rested he said, "Return, O LORD, to the ten thousand thousands of Israel" (v. 36). He believed that after all the preparation and all the struggle, they really were going to the promised land and were going to conquer and possess it. He must have thought that the conquest would be quick and that he himself would settle down and live for years before he died in the land.

But this was not to be. Moses too was obliged to wander with the people for thirty-eight years. Later we learn that he didn't even get to enter the land. Yet there is not a single word of complaint from Moses. Instead of thinking of himself, he thinks of the people. They were almost destroyed, but he interceded for them, and God spared them. Moreover, Moses was willing to be their leader for another four decades.

What a difference it would make if you and I thought less of ourselves, more of God, and sacrificially of other people. That is the way Jesus Christ our Lord has told us to think.

24

THE KORAHITE REBELLION

Numbers 16–17

THE HEART OF REBELLION

Before Jesus returned to heaven, he told his disciples that as long as they were in the world they were going to have trouble and tribulation (see John 16:33). If that is true of disciples in general, it is certainly true of leaders. His point is illustrated very dramatically in the case of Moses. Again and again in Numbers, opposition, rebellion, criticism, and grumbling were directed against Moses as the leader of the people. The theme of opposition has come up many times since Numbers 11. Complaints came from the rabble, from the people as a whole, and from Moses' own intimate family circle: his brother and sister. Opposition then arose as the result of a negative report from ten of the twelve spies who were sent into the promised land. Two spies, Joshua and Caleb, had faith that God would give them the land, but the people listened to the unbelieving spies and were ready to stone Moses and Aaron and elect another leader who would take them back to Egypt.

In Numbers 16–17, opposition now came from the leaders of the people. The general spirit of rebellion that began with the rabble and infused the people was now focused within a group of leaders: a man named Korah, three leaders from the tribe of Reuben—Dathan, Abiram, and On—and 250 other leaders, presumably elders or men of distinction from the other twelve tribes. It was a formidable, significant opposition.

But although the rebellion was partly against Moses, and Moses had to deal with it, the true focal point was Aaron. Aaron was the high priest; Korah, and perhaps some others, wanted to take over the priesthood. The issue in these chapters, therefore, was the priesthood, and by extension, the sacrifices appointed by God for the priesthood to carry out and so, ultimately, the way of salvation. Are human beings able to decide how to approach God, or is this something that God must determine? Here this issue was raised and dramatically settled. These chapters show the priesthood's divine origin, sacred character, cultic role, and, above all, expiatory function.

THE REBELLION OF KORAH (NUM. 16:1–40)

The events in these chapters may have taken place relatively early in the forty years of wandering, or they may have come relatively late. We aren't told the time. The reason the story is placed here seems to be because of the verses that come immediately beforehand. Numbers 15:37–40 tell us that the people were all to have tassels on their garments, with a blue thread in the tassel to symbolize the fact that they were set apart to God—blue being a color that symbolized purity or holiness.

Like most errors, Korah's had some truth to it. He picked up on the idea and said, "Look, God has been showing us that all we Hebrew people are holy. Since that's the case, Moses and Aaron, you've gone too far in taking on special leadership of the people." It was true that the people were appointed to be holy. The entire book of Leviticus is meant to teach us that; after all, its theme is "You shall be holy, because I the Lord your God am holy." But one truth doesn't undermine another. God had determined who would be the high priest, who would assist him, and how the sacrifices were to be made and by whom. When Korah and the others who rebelled intruded on those offices, God judged them so severely that the people cried out for a mediator: "Everyone who comes near, who comes near to the tabernacle of the

LORD, shall die. Are we all to perish?" (Num. 17:13). The answer is yes, unless God provides a mediator. His mediator is symbolized by the choice of Aaron.

Of the men who are introduced in Numbers 16:1–2, one of the Reubenites—On, the son of Peleth—is not mentioned again. This may suggest that somewhere along the line he realized what was going on and how dangerous it was and pulled back from the very brink of destruction. If that is the case, we have a lesson of the mercy of God and the possibility of repentance right at the very beginning of the story.

We see God's mercy elsewhere. Korah is judged, but his sons are spared. They seem to have disassociated themselves from his sin and lived to continue his line (see Num. 26:10–11). In fact, they became very prominent in the history of Israel, and several of the Psalms (42, 45–49, 84–85, 87–88) are attributed to them. Though the consequences of sin often continue in families and the sins of the fathers are often visited on their children, this is not always the case. Here we have an example to the contrary.

KORAH'S COMPLAINT (VV. 1–3)

Korah's complaint wasn't honestly expressed. He began by suggesting that he was quite a democratic individual. All the Israelites were set apart as holy; all he wanted to do was preserve their rights. Most rebellions begin with revolutionaries saying that they're on the side of the people and want everybody to be free, when what they really want is to assume power for themselves. That was precisely what Korah wanted, and that was what Moses was responding to. Korah wanted to get rid of Aaron and be the priest in his place.

The tribes were laid out with both the Korahites (a particular branch of the Levites) and the tribe of Reuben on the south side of the tabernacle. As Korah associated closely with the Reubenites, apparently he began to insinuate his rebellious thoughts on them: "You know I'm not interested in this for myself. But you Reubenites are descended from Reuben, the first of all the tribes. I can't stand by when I see that you are being pushed aside in favor of some other tribe." What he really wanted was to stir up a rebellion that would put him at the top of the pyramid.

MOSES' RESPONSE (VV. 4-11)

When Korah expressed his complaint to Moses, Moses fell face-down before the Lord. This position of submission to the Lord also indicates that when Moses told Korah and his followers what to do, Moses was not speaking on his own. Instead, Moses was speaking as the prophet of the Lord with the word of God, and God answered in a powerful way.

When Moses finally rose up, he told the Korahites and Korah's 250 followers to take fire in their censers (bronze trays that contained fire) and stand before the Lord. We ought to know where this is heading. When two sons of Aaron had presented unauthorized, or unholy, fire before the Lord, God had judged them (see Lev. 10:1–2). Aaron's sons were in the priestly family and would have succeeded Aaron, but they did not follow the rules that God had laid down for acceptable worship, and they were judged for it. Moses told the people who wanted to take over the priesthood to go ahead and do it—try it out, see what happens. He pointed out that God would judge them. They should have been afraid. They should have remembered what happened to Aaron's sons. But sin has a short memory. The rebels conveniently left all that in the past, thinking that they could get away with such an action now.

Note two particular points in Moses' response.

1. Moses said to the Levites, "You have gone too far, sons of Levi!" (Num. 16:7), turning back on them the very accusation they had made to him. When they argued that all the people of God were holy and Moses was thus taking too much on himself, the rebels were telling Moses that he had gone too far. But when they tried to take over Aaron's priesthood, *they* went too far. God had appointed Aaron as the priest, not them.

2. Moses pointed out that by challenging him and Aaron for leadership, they were actually challenging God. God had appointed Moses and Aaron. This is the problem with attacking those in leadership. If God sets them in that position, then attacking them opposes what God is doing.

DATHAN AND ABIRAM'S COMPLAINT (VV. 12–14)

The complaint that came next, this time from Dathan and Abiram, was somewhat different from Korah's, and also ruder and more self-important. When Moses summoned them to appear before him, they refused to come, explaining their arrogance by saying, "You have not delivered on your promise to give us land flowing with milk and honey" (see v. 14). They even applied their point in a very strange way: "Is it a small thing that you have brought us up *out* of a land flowing with milk and honey, to kill us in the wilderness . . . ?" (v. 13).

This was a strange twisting of the facts. One could hardly have called Egypt a land of milk and honey, and certainly as slaves they had not had much to enjoy there. More than that, Moses had indeed brought them to the land of milk and honey. It was the people who, standing on the very verge of the land, had refused to enter. They, not Moses, had listened to the negative report from the spies. Besides all that, it wasn't Moses who was leading them but God. God had brought them to the border of the land, and the fact that they hadn't entered was God's judgment of their rebellion and unbelief.

It must have been very painful for Moses to listen to that kind of rebellion. Although the people had been slaves in Egypt, Moses had been a very favored individual when he was younger. If there had been milk and honey to be had in Egypt, Moses would have had it. But he had turned his back on luxurious living in order to help the people, and he had identified with the Israelites in their slavery, their struggles, and their wandering (see Heb. 11:24–27). Now they were saying he had failed to deliver on his promise.

GOD'S RESPONSE (VV. 15–34)

Moses became very angry (see v. 15). But his anger was not violent or vituperative. It was actually very magnanimous. First, he protested his innocence—not to Korah and his followers, but to God. He asked God to reject their offering, but not to destroy them.

Later, when God said that he was going to destroy the people, Moses and Aaron did what they had done again and again: they interceded for the people, and because of their intercession the people as a whole were spared. "O God, the God of the spirits of all flesh, shall one man sin, and will you be angry with all the congregation?" (v. 22). The answer is no. God doesn't judge everybody for the sin of one. When God was going to destroy Sodom and Gomorrah and Abraham prayed a similar prayer (see Gen. 18:23–32), God spared Lot and his two daughters—the righteous ones in Sodom—although he went on to destroy the city.

God hears the same kind of appeal here. He agrees not to destroy the people, but he does destroy the leaders. His judgment is swift and utterly unexpected: the ground opens up and swallows the rebels, their households, and their possessions, and "they and all that belonged to them went down alive into Sheol" (Num. 16:33).

This is very grim, and intentionally so. Through it, God shows what will happen if you try to set up a religion of your own instead of coming to him in the way he has provided. This act of physical destruction is symbolic of the destruction of our souls in hell if we do not come to him by the way of the one Mediator whom he has provided—namely, Jesus Christ.

THE CONCLUSION TO THE REBELLION (VV. 35–40)

Korah and his household were taken down alive into the earth. The 250 men with their censers were still standing before the tabernacle, and the fire of the Lord went out and consumed them. Afterward, God told the people to go into the charred remains and gather up the censers. Although the men were unholy and had been consumed, the censers, which had been set aside for use in worship, were holy.

The people gathered up the censers and hammered them into a covering for the altar, where the sacrifices were made. Whenever the people came to the altar, they would see the metal that had once formed the censers of the men who had been consumed. It is a very interesting combination of ideas—unholy men but holy objects, the wrath of God poured out in judgment, and a reminder of this where the animals were consumed on the altar as a substitute for sin. This all came together in a very dramatic way, obviously so that the people would remember and learn to avoid such rebellion and its terrible consequences.

AARON AND THE PLAGUE (NUM. 16:41–50)

Moses and Aaron had interceded for the people, but the following day they grumbled against Moses and Aaron all over again, so God sent a plague to judge them. Moses recognized what was happening and told Aaron, "Quick! Make atonement for the people. Stand between them and the judgment of the Lord" (see v. 46). And that is what Aaron did—he ran. He was more than eighty years old, a man whom the younger men wanted to push aside, and yet he ran to intercede for the people.

Aaron offered the incense and made atonement for them. "He stood between the dead and the living, and the plague was stopped" (v. 48). An intercessor does exactly this; he stands between the living and the judgment of God. Aaron is a picture of Jesus Christ. He was the high priest of Israel, but the Great High Priest is Jesus Christ. By his death, he stands between us and judgment.

THE BUDDING OF AARON'S STAFF (NUM. 17)

In the next chapter, God demonstrated whom he had chosen to be high priest, lest there be any more doubt about it. Each of the tribes elected a leader. Each leader came forward with his staff—the rod that he used to walk with or direct sheep. The leaders marked their names on their staffs and laid them before the Lord overnight. Whichever staff sprouted, Moses explained, belonged to the man whom God had chosen. In the morning when they returned, not only had Aaron's rod produced leaves, but it had gone on to bud, blossom, and produce almonds.

This is very instructive. The staffs laid out before the Lord were all dead wood. Humanly speaking, there was not a chance in the world that any one of them was going to show any signs of life. When one of the staffs was fruitful, it was obviously so because God had blessed it. In the same way, Aaron was not any different from the others. He was not more holy than they were. All God's servants are sinners. But God chose to bless his particular ministry, pointing forward to

326

the coming of Jesus Christ. That is the way it is. If God chooses you to fill a position of leadership, teach a class or Bible study, or witness to a neighbor, he will bless your work—not because of who you are but because it pleases him to do so. In the case of Aaron, we see that God was very much pleased.

Interestingly, Aaron's rod was not returned to him but was instead put in the ark (see Heb. 9:4), along with the stone tables of the law containing the Ten Commandments and a little golden jar containing some manna. These things were a testimony—a reminder.

It strikes me as significant, however, that these objects were not laid before the people. After all, the ark was in the Most Holy Place, where nobody went except the high priest, who himself went only once a year, and he never looked in the ark. These objects were not so much a reminder to the people as a reminder to God. They were a reminder that we have broken the holy standard of the law, but at the same time they are a reminder that God has appointed a priesthood through whom sacrifices are to be made and sin is to be forgiven. This is a wonderful way of saying that God remembers the work that Jesus Christ has done for us. That reminder is laid before him forever. If you've come to God through faith in Jesus Christ and on the basis of his work, God doesn't forget that. You may have periods in your life when you forget him, but God doesn't forget. He remembers.

LEARNING FROM NUMBERS 16–17

Aaron's priesthood was important—so important that God judged those who challenged it—but its most significant purpose was to point forward to Jesus Christ. The New Testament provides commentary on Numbers 16–17 in Hebrews 4:14–10:39, a very extensive section that is somewhat difficult to understand. The discussion in Hebrews is far removed from what most people are acquainted with today, and the Old Testament is even farther removed. But these concepts and realities are so important that they appear not only in the Old Testament but also in the New. They are at the very heart of what we mean when we talk about salvation.

Jesus has been appointed as our High Priest. Just as Aaron was appointed by God to be the Hebrew high priest, instead of taking that honor on himself, so God's Son, Jesus Christ, was appointed by God to be our High Priest and Savior.

No one takes this honor for himself, but only when called by God, just as Aaron was.
So also Christ did not exalt himself to be made a high priest, but was appointed by him who said to him,

"You are my Son,
today I have begotten you";

as he says also in another place,

"You are a priest forever,
after the order of Melchizedek." (Heb. 5:4–6, quoting from Pss. 2:7; 110:4)

The book of Hebrews reinforces the fact that God is the one who determines how atonement is made and how we should approach him. This is not for us to do. God chooses the one who will be the priest, the mediator, between our most holy God and sinful human beings.

Jesus is the perfect priest. Although it was necessary and important, the priesthood of Aaron was embodied in imperfect, sinful men. The superior priesthood of Jesus Christ is embodied in one who is utterly perfect and holy. Under the Levitical system, when the high priest offered a sacrifice on the Day of Atonement—the most important sacrifice of all—he had first to offer a sacrifice for himself and his family, because he was a sinful man. Only after doing that could he approach God in the Most Holy Place to offer a sacrifice for the sins of the people. But Jesus did not have to offer a sacrifice for himself, as the author of Hebrews points out:

For it was indeed fitting that we should have such a high priest, holy, innocent, unstained, separated from sinners, and exalted above the heavens. He has no need, like those high priests, to offer sacrifices daily, first for his own sins and then for those of the people, since he did this once for all when he offered up himself. (Heb. 7:26)

Jesus Christ is the perfect priest.

Jesus' sacrifice is the perfect offering. The offerings of the Jewish priests were types that pointed to the way of salvation, but only types or foreshadowings. Jesus Christ's offering of himself was the one, true, and only sufficient way of salvation. The author of Hebrews makes very clear that the sacrifices under the Old Testament system were inadequate: they had to be repeated again and again because the blood of sheep and goats could never take away sin (see Heb. 10:4). How can killing an animal possibly atone for the sin of human beings? But when Jesus Christ, the holy Lamb of God, offered himself and died in our place, his was a true and sufficient sacrifice. By that one sacrifice, he takes away forever the sins of those who trust him, "because by one sacrifice he has made perfect forever those who are being made holy" (Heb. 10:14 NIV).

Jesus' sacrifice was once and for all. Unlike the sacrifices of the ancient priests, which had to be repeated daily, the sacrifice of Jesus Christ was once for all and eternal. The author of Hebrews points out that there were no chairs in the tabernacle (see Heb. 10:11). Priests couldn't sit down; they had to keep working. Their work wasn't complete. But after Jesus offered himself up as a sacrifice, he was seated at the right hand of the almighty God in heaven. His work was finished and finished forever (see 10:12).

Salvation is only through Jesus. These chapters in the Old and New Testaments also teach that there is salvation in no one other than in Jesus Christ. God has established the way for how we can approach him. There must be atonement for our sin and the means of atonement is by sacrifice; God has appointed Jesus Christ to be both the sacrifice and the Mediator. As the perfect sacrifice he takes on himself the penalty for our sin, and as the Mediator he intercedes for us before our heavenly Father on the basis of that sacrifice (see Heb 7:25). Aaron occupied that role of mediator for a short time and stayed the plague. The Lord Jesus Christ is the one perfect Mediator, and not just for a short time. The apostle Paul writes, "There is one God, and there is one mediator between God and men, the man Christ Jesus" (1 Tim. 2:5). There is no salvation apart from him.

Jesus' priesthood must not be rejected. Anyone who would detract from Christ's priesthood or glory, discounting his atoning work, is in deadly peril. The failure of Korah, Dathan, Abiram, and their followers was not only a failure to come to God in the way he had appointed. They were trying to insinuate themselves into the holy office, trying to set up another way of approaching God, another religion. On the outside, it looked similar. There were to be sacrifices, and the priests were to wear the robes and observe the holy days and so on. But theirs was not the religion that God had appointed. When they did these things on their own, they were trying to work out a way of salvation apart from the shed blood of Jesus Christ. This is exactly what people are doing today, working out ways to come to God apart from the way God has revealed we must come. This despises the work of the very Son of God—it is an affront to the God who has determined how we shall approach him.

William Taylor wrote, "If you repudiate Christ's death as a sacrifice for sin, if you fritter away the crucifixion into a martyrdom, if you deny the necessity for atonement of any sort, then are you kindred spirits with Dathan and Abiram, who maintained that all priesthood was unnecessary."[1]

What does God think of a man or a woman who says, in effect, "It's not necessary that Jesus Christ die; I can get to heaven on my own"? This story answers that. God takes such rebellion very seriously, and anyone who stubbornly engages in it is going to be judged and will perish hopelessly.

---

1. William M. Taylor, *Moses the Law-Giver* (New York: Harper & Brothers, 1879), 355.

Hebrews provides commentary on this point as well.

> Anyone who has set aside the law of Moses dies without mercy on the evidence of two or three witnesses. How much worse punishment, do you think, will be deserved by the one who has trampled underfoot the Son of God, and has profaned the blood of the covenant by which he was sanctified, and has outraged the Spirit of grace? For we know him who said, "Vengeance is mine; I will repay." And again, "The Lord will judge his people." It is a fearful thing to fall into the hands of the living God. (Heb. 10:28–31)

Korah found that out the hard way. Do not wait and find it out yourself someday, but come instead to God the way he has appointed, through Jesus Christ, our great, eternal, High Priest.

25

MOSES' SIN AND THE DEATH OF AARON

Numbers 20

A SAD CHAPTER

Moses' sister, Miriam, is introduced at the beginning of Exodus when Moses is born, and throughout Exodus and Numbers several incidents in her life are recorded for us. Now, at the start of Numbers 20, she dies. Moses' brother, Aaron, has also been a recurring character in this story—in fact, in the last chapter we saw God defending him in his priesthood. Now, at the end of Numbers 20, he dies as well, as a judgment from God. Aaron's death anticipates the death of Moses, which is also in judgment, for even Moses will not enter the promised land.

This sad chapter is best studied in conjunction with Psalm 90, the only psalm in the Bible that was composed by Moses. The psalm begins by reflecting on the grandeur of the eternal God. It then contrasts God's grandeur with the weakness and mortality of man, tracing that mortality to man's sin. Finally, it ends with a great appeal to the grace of God to bless us in this life and to establish the work of our hands after we are gone. In my judgment, Moses must have composed this psalm after the events of Numbers 20, providing us with his own thoughts on the meaning of the events here.

The chapter begins the final of three travel sections in Exodus and Numbers. The first, found in Exodus 13–19, describes the journey the people made when they left Egypt and traveled to Sinai. The second, in Numbers 10–11, records their journey from Sinai to Kadesh, when they were anticipating their entrance into the promised land. The final travel section, in Numbers 20–21, traces their journey from Kadesh to Transjordan, which is on the very border of the promised land, where the Jordan River separates them from Jericho.

This final travel section is different from the other two. The others begin on a high note and then end in discouragement and defeat. When the people leave Egypt, they start out singing songs with voices of triumph and end up complaining about the lack of bread and water. When the people leave Sinai, they go out accompanied by the presence and power of God, thinking that at last they're on the way to Canaan. Yet they prefer the report of the ten unbelieving spies, then try to go into the land on their own when God says that they cannot, and finally are defeated in the great battle. But the journey from Kadesh to Transjordan begins sadly with the deaths of Miriam and Aaron and then goes uphill from there. We see that the pattern of God's people is to get into sin and do many terrible things in this life, but the pattern of God in dealing with his people is one of perseverance. Despite two false starts, God brings the people into the promised land at last, with great victory and great rejoicing.

THE DEATH OF MIRIAM (NUM. 20:1)

The death of Miriam is reported very briefly in just six words, at least in the English text. It must have been a terrible loss for Moses. Miriam was his older sister. She wasn't perfect—at one point she and Aaron had become jealous of Moses because of his unique position and had challenged his authority. God had judged her for this, though in the end he was merciful. But Miriam must have had a kind of proprietary interest in Moses throughout his life. When he had been born and his mother had put him in the little ark and stuck him in the bulrushes, Miriam had stood on the hill to watch what would become of him. She must have shared some of her mother's faith. She wanted to see how God would deliver the child. When Pharaoh's daughter found the baby there, Miriam, with real strength and power of imagination, went and asked if Pharaoh's daughter wanted her to find a wet nurse to take care of the baby for her—and then, very cleverly, she fetched Moses' mother. By and large Miriam had been a great support to Moses. Moses, almost 120 years old now, had had her and Aaron to talk to all these long years, even as many others who had come out of Egypt had died along the way. He must have thought back to the years long ago when their mother and father had raised them with godly counsel.

Miriam's death was a reminder of God's judgment on the people: no one of that generation would enter the promised land. Her death reminds us of our own deaths as well. Death is an inescapable reality. As God declares, "It is appointed for man to die once, and after that comes judgment" (Heb. 9:27). At the very start of the chapter we are reminded of the importance of preparing for death.

THE SIN OF MOSES (NUM. 20:2–13)

We usually think of the people of Israel spending their time in the wilderness massed together in an encampment like the one described at the beginning of Numbers. When they were on the march, it is probable that they did move that way. But over their decades-long period of wandering, the people must have scattered around. They lived by their flocks and herds, so they ended up moving to find water and grazing land, perhaps over a very wide area of the Sinai. But now, after thirty-eight or forty years, the advance is about to begin, and the people have returned to the very border of the promised land.

Once they were back together again, water became a problem, and they began a very vehement complaint: "Would that we had perished when our brothers perished before the LORD!" (Num. 20:3). They were saying that they were sorry they had lived as long as this. They complained to Moses,

> Why have you brought the assembly of the LORD into this wilderness, that we should die here, both we and our cattle? And why have you made us come up out of Egypt to bring us to this evil place? It is no place for grain or figs or vines or pomegranates, and there is no water to drink. (vv. 4–5)

Reading this, we get the impression that they had not learned anything in thirty-eight years. They actually had, though, because they eventually showed some repentance—earlier, they had not always repented of their complaining. Still, they do not seem to have learned very much.

But in response to their complaining, Moses did not do exactly what God had told him to do in order to bring water from the rock. He spoke to the people instead of to the rock. And he spoke in anger. Then he struck the rock—not once but twice. He involved both himself and Aaron in the miracle by saying, "Shall *we* bring water for you out of this rock?" (v. 10), instead of giving all the glory to God. Moses sinned, and God judged him for it.

I am very sympathetic with Moses. He had been doing his job for at least forty years in the wilderness. He was an old man. He had waited an awfully long time to enter the promised land. And the people had been extremely difficult. Nowhere do we read that they came to Moses and said, "Moses, you're doing a great job. Keep up the good work." Instead, all they did was complain, complain, complain when things weren't going well. If you have a job that is not going well and you last twelve months, you think that you're doing pretty well. Moses had been doing his job for thirty-eight years! Now, at the end, his patience has worn a little thin. He was angry, and he moved on his own. It seemed like a very small thing. It *was* a small thing. But with God, small things matter, whether they are good or bad. If you do something small for God, he takes note of it and blesses. But God also takes note of small bad things, as in the case of Moses.

Three things were wrong with what Moses did, and together they add up to quite a significant failure on his part.

He did not follow instructions. Moses did not follow the instructions of God exactly. God said, "Take the staff, and assemble the congregation, you and Aaron your brother, and tell the rock before their eyes to yield its water. So you shall bring water out of the rock for them and give drink to the congregation and their cattle" (v. 8). Moses took the staff, just as God had commanded him, and gathered the people in front of the rock. So far, so good. But then, "Moses lifted up his hand and struck the rock with his staff twice" (v. 11). God said to *speak*, but Moses *struck*. Even though the water came out of the rock, his action greatly displeased God.

He did not fully glorify God. Moses' most obvious failure was to take some of the credit for the miracle for himself instead of giving the glory fully to God. He said, "Must we do it?"—implying that he and Aaron were going to bring water out of the rock.

If we want to avoid repeating this particular failure of Moses in our own lives, we will have to work hard in giving glory to God. This is one of the hardest things for us to do, because when God does something, he does it through secondary causes. If, for example, God wants to reach someone with the gospel, God sends a Christian to him or her to explain the gospel. The secondary cause—the witness of the Christian—is as important as the fact that God is sending that person and doing the work of conversion. God worked through Moses to do miracles. God is involved in everything we do for him, but it is very easy for us to think that we deserve the credit, or at least some of the credit. We have to realize that even though we may be called by God to do something, and even though God may bless what we do, God is the one who is doing the work through us and who is bringing the blessing. For, as Paul states, "it is God who works in you, both to will and to work for his good pleasure" (Phil. 2:13).

Since God does the work, we must get in the habit of giving glory to him always. One of my friends, the head of an important theological seminary, does this remarkably well. I've said to him on many occasions, "Boy, you're doing a great job there," and he always says that it is God who is doing the work. He is only the instrument, the tool.

The world never says such things. It cannot. The world always takes credit itself. The answer in the Westminster Shorter Catechism to the first question—"What is the chief end of man?"—states that "Man's chief end is to glorify God, and to enjoy him forever." The world glorifies itself and tries to enjoy itself forever. We have to follow a different pattern.

He did not fully trust God. Moses did not fully trust God. We know this because God accuses him of this particular sin: "Because you did not believe in me, to uphold me as holy in the eyes of the people of Israel, therefore you shall not bring this assembly into the land that I have given them" (Num. 20:12). We do not know exactly how Moses failed to trust God—but we are not responsible for Moses; we are responsible for ourselves. We ought to be very concerned about the many ways in which we ourselves fail to trust God. F. B. Meyer writes, "Let us watch and pray, lest there be in any of us an evil heart of unbelief; lest we depart in our most secret thought from simple faith in the living God; lest beneath a fair exterior we yield our jewel of faith to the solicitation of some unholy passion."[1]

THE EDOMITES (NUM. 20:14–21)

The best way to move north from the Sinai into Canaan was to go straight through Edom, a mountainous area about thirty miles wide that extends about a hundred miles into the desert south of the Dead Sea. There was a highway through the country, the main passageway from Egypt to Syria, so the Edomites collected tribute from any who passed that way. After the sin of Moses, the people contacted the Edomites and asked for permission to take the highway. They promised to stay on the road and to pay for the water that they and their flocks would drink. With a surly response, the Edomites not only refused to let them go but also came out against them in force with an army.

Moses decided not to contest the Edomites but to go around their country. Undoubtedly, God led him in this decision. Greater explanation comes in Deuteronomy 23:7, which says, "You shall not abhor an Edomite, for he is your brother." The Edomites can be traced back to Esau, the brother of Jacob and a descendant of Abraham. God told the people that their request had been right and that the Edomites ought to have let them go through. But they were not to fight them. So the Israelites had to make a very lengthy detour all the way around Edom, finally coming up against the Jordan from the east, out of the desert.

The Old Testament book Obadiah, one of the Minor Prophets,

---

1. F. B. Meyer, *Moses: The Servant of God* (New York: Fleming H. Revell Company, n.d.), 177.

is a prophecy entirely against Edom. It condemns Edom for its pride. The people of Edom sat in their strongholds, thinking that nobody would ever bring them down, but in the end they were destroyed. Today the land is utterly uninhabited, a barren area where jackals roam. Obadiah criticized the people of Edom for not treating their Hebrew brothers in a brotherly way (see Obad. 10). Such relationships should be established and kept holy, but the Edomites failed to do so.

THE DEATH OF AARON (NUM. 20:22–29)

The death of Aaron is recorded at the very end of the chapter. His death is significant. Aaron was so important that when his position as the high priest had been challenged by Korah and his followers, God had judged them with one of the harshest judgments and in the most sudden manner that we can imagine—the earth literally opened up and swallowed them. Now Aaron himself passes from the scene, and his garments are taken and placed on his son Eleazar.

A phrase is used here that is worth thinking about: he was "gathered to his people" (vv. 24, 26). This means more than that he had merely died. Such a phrase is an Old Testament expression of faith in the afterlife, equivalent to what David said when his son who was born to Bathsheba died: "I shall go to him, but he will not return to me" (2 Sam. 12:23). Although they did not understand much about the afterlife (we do not understand a lot about it either), nevertheless they believed that when people died their souls still existed and that the souls of the righteous went to join the souls of their believing ancestors.

The death of Aaron in the wilderness was a judgment, as was the death of Moses. Neither entered the promised land. But for the righteous, redeemed people, physical death is the end of judgment. When Aaron died, he was gathered to the saints before him, joining the presence of Abraham, Isaac, and Jacob. When Moses died, he was gathered to the saints as well. God is indeed gracious, and Moses was aware of that.

The account describes the transfer of power and authority from Aaron to his son Eleazar. This was done in a very formal way: they went up the mountain, and Moses took from Aaron the garments symbolizing the office of high priest and put them on Eleazar. Through this transfer of garments, Aaron's important role as high priest passed from one man to another individual, his son.

Significantly, this points forward to the one Man who alone could be the perfect High Priest—namely, Jesus Christ. When Jesus Christ fulfilled his priestly function, interceding for us by his death and continuing to do so by his prayers, the priesthood ceased among the people of God. We no longer need a human priest to come into the presence of God or to make intercession for us. Jesus Christ is that priest.

LEARNING FROM NUMBERS 20

As I mentioned earlier in this chapter, Numbers 20 gives us the background to appreciate Psalm 90, which I believe Moses wrote in response to these events. Moses had lost his sister and brother. He was the last survivor of his family, soon to face his own death. Caleb and Joshua were the only two others living of those who had come out of Egypt forty years before.

THE GRANDEUR OF GOD

Reflecting on this, Moses begins his psalm by writing of the grandeur of God.

> Lord, you have been our dwelling place
>> in all generations.
> Before the mountains were brought forth,
>> or ever you had formed the earth and the world,
>> from everlasting to everlasting you are God. (Ps. 90:1–2)

Moses was surely more aware than most of us that life is short and uncertain at its best. He was also aware, however—undoubtedly more than most of us—of the greatness of God, because he had stood on the mountain with God and conversed with him face-to-face. He knew the greatness of the God who had called his people to himself. Moses tells us, through his own example, that if we are going to reflect on life and death with any wisdom, our view of both must begin with God, the eternal one.

Those who trust in God have an eternal, secure dwelling place in him. We do not have a secure dwelling place on earth; the earth will pass away (see Luke 21:33). But if we are anchored in God, our dwelling place with him is secure. This is why Abraham did not build a mansion on earth but rather "looked for a city . . . whose builder and maker is God" (Heb. 11:10 KJV).

Are you anchoring your life in God, or are you putting your hope and earthly efforts into perishable things that will pass away? Paul gave his own testimony in these words: "We fix our eyes not on what is seen, but on what is unseen. For what is seen is temporary, but what is unseen is eternal" (2 Cor. 4:18 NIV). This is the same perspective Moses reflects in this psalm.

THE FRAILTY OF MAN

Next, Moses reflects on the frailty of man in contrast with the stability and grandeur of the eternal God.

> You return man to dust
>   and say, "Return, O children of man!"
> For a thousand years in your sight
>   are but as yesterday when it is past,
>   or as a watch in the night.
>
> You sweep them away as with a flood; they are like a dream,
>   like grass that is renewed in the morning:
> in the morning it flourishes and is renewed;
>   in the evening it fades and withers.
>
> For we are brought to an end by your anger;
>   by your wrath we are dismayed.
> You have set our iniquities before you,
>   our secret sins in the light of your presence.
>
> For all our days pass away under your wrath;
>   we bring our years to an end like a sigh.
>
> . . . .

> Who considers the power of your anger,
>> and your wrath according to the fear of you? (Ps. 90:3–9, 11)

These statements are profound, because Moses links the mortality and weakness of man to sin. This is appropriate and particularly significant coming from the one who recorded the events of the fall in Genesis 3. Right at the start of the first book of the Bible, sin and death enter the world. God connects them when he says, "When you disobey and eat of the tree you will surely die" (see Gen. 2:17), and now Moses understands the connection. Sin always leads to death. If you're aware of this, you won't treat sin as lightly as many of us do. You'll say with David, "Who can discern his errors? Declare me innocent from hidden faults" (Ps. 19:12). You'll pray, as he does, "Keep back your servant also from presumptuous sins; let them not have dominion over me" (Ps. 19:13).

THE GRACE OF GOD

The final verses point us to our need for God's grace. Moses was very aware of this. He has brought before our eyes the grandeur of God. He has considered the frailty and sin of man, which brings the wrath of God on him. In a world like this, with people like this, with sin like ours, we need the grace of God. We need the grace of God that provides forgiveness so that we may stand and live before him. But we also need the grace of God to make valuable anything we do, because unless God establishes our works, everything we do will pass away.

> Return, O LORD! How long?
>> Have pity on your servants!
> Satisfy us in the morning with your steadfast love,
>> that we may rejoice and be glad all our days.
> Make us glad for as many days as you have afflicted us,
>> and for as many years as we have seen evil.
> Let your work be shown to your servants,
>> and your glorious power to their children.
> Let the favor of the Lord our God be upon us,

and establish the work of our hands upon us;
yes, establish the work of our hands! (Ps. 90:13–17)

Unless God establishes the work of our hands, nothing that we do will matter. But if God places us on earth to do something, it *will* matter. Even though a generation is passing away, even though Miriam and Aaron have died—even though Moses himself is about to die—Moses asks that God establish, by his grace, the work that they have done for him. And God does just that.

Moses did the work that God had given him to do, and God established it. We have our proof right in the Bible. We have not only the history of Israel, which led eventually to the coming of Jesus Christ, but also the record of what Moses had done, in words inspired by the Holy Spirit for our benefit.

Has God established your work? *Will* he establish your work? Are you looking to him to establish your work? You should want what you do to be so blessed by God that those who come after you will say that God was in it, God was glorified by it, and they are blessed. Then, when you get to heaven, God will say to you, "Well done, good and faithful servant."

26

THE SERPENT IN
THE WILDERNESS

Numbers 21

A TURNING POINT

Numbers 20, with the deaths of Miriam and Aaron and the sin of Moses, was a chapter of almost unremitting gloom; but in the next chapter the tone begins to change. Numbers 21 marks an important turning point in the affairs of the people: the beginning of the march on Canaan and the first victory, pointing to the full conquest of the promised land.

THE FIRST BATTLE (NUM. 21:1-3)

As an indication of this turning point, Numbers 21 begins with a reference to the Canaanite king. So far in their wanderings, the Israelites had only run up against Edom, but Edom was a brother nation, and God had explicitly commanded them to treat the Edomites well. Now, for the first time, they were in conflict with the Canaanites—the people who possessed the land. A battle ensued, and the Israelites completely destroyed the people and their towns (see v. 3). The destruction of the Canaanite king of Arad who lived in the south of Palestine was the beginning of battles that would lead in time to the full possession of the land.

After this battle, the people called the name of the place *Hormah*. *Hormah* means "destruction," which is an appropriate name for any place where there has been a great battle such as this one. What makes that word particularly significant, however, is that thirty-eight years beforehand, when the people had tried to go into the land without God's blessing, they had experienced a great defeat at a place called Hormah. This may or may not have been the same place, but it was in the same area of the country. Now the tide had turned. Thirty-eight years before, the Israelites had been destroyed. Now the Canaanites were beginning to be destroyed.

This theme holds throughout the chapter. Beginning at verse 10, we read that the people started to move out from Moab—located in Transjordan on the eastern side of the Jordan River. As they moved northward, they battled Sihon and the Amorites, and then they destroyed Og, the king of Bashan—striking down him and his sons, leaving no survivors, and taking possession of his land (see v. 35). Bashan was part of Transjordan, but Reuben and Gad, and half of Manasseh, would settle there. The land is being conquered now; the conquest has begun in this chapter.

THE BRONZE SNAKE (NUM. 21:4-9)

While these battles are important, the most interesting part of this chapter concerns the strange story of the bronze snake. Jesus himself refers to this in one of the best-known chapters of the New Testament. In John 3 Jesus unfolds to Nicodemus, a ruler of the Jews, some of the most important doctrines in the entire Bible, doctrines that center on himself: his incarnation, the need for the new birth, the work of the Holy Spirit, and the revelation of the love of God through the lifting up of the Son. Then he says,

> And as Moses lifted up the serpent in the wilderness, so must the Son of Man be lifted up, that whoever believes in him may have eternal life. (John 3:14–15)

Jesus thus singles out this incident as teaching something of great importance about the incarnation and the love of God. The bronze serpent is the great example of how God saves sinners. When Moses

344

lifted up the snake, people who were perishing because of venomous snakebites looked to it and were saved. In the same way, people today who are perishing because of sin can be saved by looking in faith to Jesus Christ, who was lifted up on the cross for our sin.

The incident began with the complaints of the people—some of the most outspoken complaints of all. For the first time, the people were marching on Canaan. They had had their first victories over the Canaanites and were beginning to possess the land, but, despite this turning point, they were still the same people, still complaining about food!

I can understand complaining about food in general, but their reasoning here is particularly clear because of the route they had to take. They had come up from the south into the Negev, but now they have had to go back, take the road from the Red Sea to go around Edom, come up on the far side of the mountains, and then enter the promised land from the east. This is an enormous, very difficult detour. To people who felt that they were on the verge of conquest, this must have seemed like a terrible regression. Instead of going forward, they would have to go back into the desert, where so many of them perished during the thirty-eight years of wandering. Furthermore, they would have to eat the same "worthless food," as they called it (Num. 21:5). The people had complained before, but nowhere else have they spoken so badly of the food.

Here we learn where a pattern of complaining leads. You may begin by complaining in a mild way, but there is a tendency, once you start, to get into a complaining frame of mind. Once you do that, you exaggerate difficulties so that they get worse and worse every time you talk about them. The more you complain, the more and more vehement you become. (This is a bad way to pray, by the way.)

In response to the complaints, the Lord sent judgment on the people in the form of "fiery serpents" (v. 6), or venomous snakes. The word in the Hebrew does in fact mean "burning and fiery," referring to what happened when they bit someone. The venom got into the blood and began to burn, and many of those who were bitten died.

345

The people had learned, by this point, that it is always good to acknowledge that you have done something wrong. So they confessed that they had sinned, and Moses did what he always did and prayed for them.

God told Moses to make a snake out of bronze and to put it up on a pole. He promised that if a snake bit anybody, that person would be cured if he or she looked to the bronze snake on the pole. Of all the things that God might have told Moses to do, this was certainly one of the most bizarre. Examining what snakes symbolized in ancient cultures, commentator Ronald B. Allen points out that this is the last remedy you would expect, for three reasons.[1]

1. *God had told the people not to make images*, especially ones that could be associated with worshipping gods. Although the bronze snake did not represent God, it had religious overtones and could easily become a talisman of some sort. In fact, years later King Hezekiah had the bronze snake destroyed because it was worshipped as something that was holy and miraculous in itself (see 2 Kings 18:4). The people had been told not to make images precisely in order to safeguard against this temptation, yet in this instance God told Moses to do so.
2. *Snakes are feared and detested by most people in a wide variety of cultures.* To put something that you fear and detest on a pole is a very strange thing to do.
3. *Snakes are frequently associated with Satan in biblical literature.* In Genesis, when our first parents were tempted by the devil, he came to them in the form of a serpent. At the very end of the Bible, the book of Revelation references the great serpent who is Satan (see Rev. 12:9). Although the snake on the pole did not symbolize Satan, it was nonetheless a bizarre image to use for this particular cure.

Allen writes,

---

1. See Ronald B. Allen, "Numbers," in *The Expositor's Bible Commentary*, gen. ed. Frank E. Gaebelein, vol. 2, *Genesis–Numbers* (Grand Rapids: Zondervan, 1990), 877.

With all these factors in view, now we think again of the enormity of what Moses was asked to do, of the taboos he was asked to break. This is not unlike Peter being told to kill and eat food that he regarded as unclean (Acts 10). The people had called the bread of heaven detestable. Moses is commanded of God to make an image of something truly detestable in their culture and to hold that high on a pole as their only means of deliverance from disease. Only those who looked at the image of the snake would survive the venom that coursed through their bodies. This is an extraordinary act of cultural shock.[2]

This is an exceptionally daring use of potent symbolism. Yet the healing wasn't from the serpent itself. The bronze serpent was just a way of getting through to the people that their state was absolutely desperate; if they were going to be saved, it would be by the grace of God.

When Jesus refers to the snake being lifted up on the pole, he uses it as an image of himself. He is saying, "When I am lifted up on the cross to die for sinners, I will be the one source of salvation, just as people were only saved in Moses' day by looking at the snake." When we think of the cross from a perspective outside Christianity, it seems absurd. How can the crucifixion of one man two thousand years ago possibly be God's means of saving the world? To an unsaved person, this sounds ridiculous—one might even say detestable. What could be attractive about a naked man hanging on a cross, bleeding and dying? That is a revolting sight, yet it is the very power of God unto salvation.

Paul recognized the difficulty when he wrote to the Corinthians, "The word of the cross is folly to those who are perishing" (1 Cor. 1:18). He recognized that according to human wisdom the cross was an offense but he knew too that Christ crucified is still the power and the wisdom of God (see 1 Cor. 1:24). This episode in Numbers 21 illustrates that truth.

2. Ibid.

WHAT DOES THE BRONZE
SNAKE TEACH US?

Donald Grey Barnhouse once wrote a good study on this incident, in which he imagined all the ways the dying people might have tried to cure themselves.[3] The things that we might imagine them doing parallel the things that people do today regarding the matter of their salvation. They do not want to trust Christ—to do something so absurd and unattractive—so they try to help themselves. But what does this story teach us?

There is no human remedy for sin. When we are faced with a problem, we generally feel good if we can try to do something about it. It would have been natural for the people to attempt to make a medicine to cure their snakebites. Barnhouse says that brewing potions and making salves would have given them all something to do—would have satisfied every natural instinct of the heart to work out its own cure. But nothing of the kind is mentioned. The people were to cease from human remedies and turn to a divine remedy.

If we preach a religion that tells others that good deeds will make us right with God, or how to do certain things to achieve prosperity, we flatter the human mind and heart. We want to hear that it all comes down to us. "We will tackle anything," we say. "Whatever it is, we will do it." We feel good about that. But when it comes to sin, no human cure is adequate, just as no human cure would have saved the people from the deadly snakebites.

Salvation cannot come through self-reformation. The people might have concluded that they had gotten into a bad area of the desert. They had made a mistake, but, well, you learn from experience. They could simply mark the snake territory on their charts and never go back there again.

---

3. All of Barnhouse's material referred to throughout this section is taken from Donald Grey Barnhouse, *Romans*, vol. 3, *God's Remedy* (Wheaton, IL: Van Kampen, 1954), 219–21.

Of course, the problem with this solution is that it does nothing to help the people who have already been bitten by the snakes. It is the same way with people today. We talk about spiritual things and decide that we just have to avoid certain problems or not do certain things again. Well enough, but the problem of sin is that it is within us and has to be dealt with at a deeper level than by a list of do's and don'ts.

Sin cannot be fought by human effort. Barnhouse says, humorously now, that if the incident had been handled after the fashion of our day, there would have been a rush to incorporate the Society for the Extermination of the Fiery Serpents (SEFS). There would have been badges, district workers, secretaries, organization branches, pledge cards, mass rallies, and a publication office with a weekly journal to update others on the progress. Faithful workers would kill heaps of serpents, but even all that would not have solved the problem.

This is not to say that there is something wrong with social work. Social work is helpful, and Christians have generally led the way in that field, but it doesn't cure sin. Social work attempts to mop up the effects of sin. We ought to help people the best we can. Jesus cared for the poor, the fallen, the outcast. Government programs can pour more and more money into the problems of the day without solving them. The programs may patch up some of the effects of the sin problem, but they certainly do not solve the underlying problem of sin.

Salvation is not earned by prayer. The people who were bitten by the serpents weren't told to pray to the serpent on the pole; they were told to look at it. I am not saying that prayer is bad—we are told to pray, after all—but praying for salvation saves no one. Salvation is not produced by prayer but is received by faith. If we think that prayer can save us, salvation has become a work again, something that we ourselves are able to do—if we pray enough, maybe God will save us. The way of salvation is given in Christ. You do not have to ask for it; you have to believe it and receive it.

Relics are useless. The people weren't commanded to buy a relic of the serpent or possess a fragment of the pole on which the snake had been erected. One of the most bizarre ideas in all the history of the Christian church is that people are saved by relics. In the Middle Ages, selling relics of the cross and other items associated with Christ was big business. But the people of Israel were to believe that God would save them if they just looked to the snake as God had told them to do. When they did, they were saved.

THE THREE ELEMENTS OF FAITH

In his book *All of Grace*, Charles Haddon Spurgeon writes that faith is "*the eye* which looks," "*the hand* which grasps," and "*the mouth* which feeds upon Christ."[4] It really is as simple as that.

It is important to understand what faith is so that people do not mistakenly believe that they are saved when they are not. When classical theologians used to talk about faith, they said that faith had three elements: content, assent, and trust. Faith is based on the promise of God, so we teach and preach the gospel so that others are informed of his promise. Once the content is understood, there must be agreement that it is true, followed by commitment to Jesus Christ.

CONTENT

John Calvin may have been the strongest of all the Reformation writers on this first point, because he was opposing a pernicious error that had entered the church in the Middle Ages. The church had been derelict in teaching doctrine to the people. Instead of founding schools to teach people to be able to read the Bible and understand it, the church had retreated into traditions and a sort of showmanship that dazzled without engaging the mind. As a result, the question arose: how are people to be saved if they do not know anything about the basic teachings of the Bible?

In the years before Calvin, the church's answer was that people are saved by *implicit* faith. This meant that they had to have implicit trust in the *church's* knowledge of the Christian faith. If they trusted the

---

4. Charles Spurgeon, *All of Grace: An Earnest Word With Those Who Are Seeking Salvation* (1886; repr. Apollo, PA: Ichthus Publications, 2014), 37.

church, they did not have to actually know anything about Christian doctrine; they just had to believe and do what the church told them.

Calvin said that this was not good enough: "Faith rests upon knowledge, not upon pious ignorance." He continued,

> We do not obtain salvation either because we are prepared to embrace as true whatever the church has prescribed, or because we turn over to it the task of inquiring and knowing. But we do so when we know that God is our merciful Father, because of reconciliation effected through Christ . . . and that Christ has been given to us as righteousness, sanctification, and life. By this knowledge, I say, not by submission of our feeling, do we obtain entry into the Kingdom of Heaven.[5]

The lack of knowledge of biblical content was a huge problem in the Middle Ages, but it still continues to be an issue today. In many sectors of the evangelical church, preaching and teaching have taken on the overtones of entertainment—people are simply told funny stories and sent away without understanding much about the Bible or theology.

Some time ago I heard of a man who was being received into church membership. The elders were examining him and asked, "What do you believe?"

The man said, "I believe what the church believes."

The elders weren't quite satisfied with that, so they pressed him: "Well, what does the church believe?"

"The church believes what I believe."

The elders pressed him again. "What do you and the church believe?"

"We believe the same thing," the man said resourcefully.

This is why Calvin insisted that we teach content.

ASSENT

It is possible to know the content of Christian theology and not agree with it. When I was studying English literature in college, my

---

5. John Calvin, *Institutes of the Christian Religion*, ed. John T. McNeill, Tran. Ford Lewis Battles (Philadelphia: Westminster, 1960), 3.2.2.

professors knew theology very well—English literature is filled with Christian doctrine—but they did not believe it. Saving faith requires not just knowledge; it requires agreement.

I like the picturesque way that Calvin puts it: "It now remains to pour into the heart itself what the mind has absorbed. For the Word of God is not received by faith if it flits about in the top of the brain, but when it takes root in the depth of the heart that it may be an invincible defense to withstand and drive off all the stratagems of temptation."[6] In other words, although you can understand the basic doctrines of Christianity perfectly well, you will perish unless you also, by the grace of God, come to agree that Christianity describes your need and God's way of salvation through the work of Jesus.

COMMITMENT

The third element, commitment to Jesus Christ, may be the most important element of all, at least in the evangelical church. Today, some people view faith as simply an intellectual agreement with what is preached. As long as I can say, "I believe that Jesus is the Savior and that he died for my sins," then it doesn't make any difference whether I actually follow after Jesus Christ. But if Christ is not my Lord, then he is not my Savior. If I am trusting a Christ who is not the Lord, then I am not trusting the true Christ. Only the Lord can save me, so I must commit myself and follow after him.

Writing about true faith versus superficial faith, James points out that the devils have faith—if what we mean by *faith* is intellectual agreement. They know perfectly well that Jesus Christ is the Son of God and that he died to be the world's Savior, but they are not trusting him for their salvation (see James 2:19). That is where the difference comes in.

A good example of this difference appears at the very end of John's gospel. Jesus had been raised from the dead and had appeared to all the disciples except Thomas, who wasn't present. When the other disciples told Thomas that Jesus had risen, he refused to believe it. Then Jesus himself appeared to him, and Thomas fell at his feet in worship, saying,

6. Ibid., 3.2.36.

"My Lord and my God!" (John 20:28). Those five words are the climax of the gospel. John holds out these truths before us: Jesus Christ has come in the flesh, been lifted up on the cross, and been raised from the dead, and we must fall down before him and say, "My Lord and my God." When we do that, we are demonstrating faith that saves.

LEARNING FROM NUMBERS 21

THE NATURE OF SIN

The story of the bronze snake teaches us about the nature of sin. Sin is like the serpent's bite. It is a deadly venom within us—not an external, basically harmless blemish that can be cured by human remedies. Unless a cure beyond our own ability is found, we are destined to perish miserably and forever. Any genuine cure must come from God, and it must deal with the sin problem radically.

THE HEALING POWER OF THE UPLIFTED CHRIST

We can't save ourselves, but God can—and he has done so through Jesus Christ. Is there another way? No, there is no other way. Jesus said, "For even the Son of Man came not to be served but to serve, and to give his life as a ransom for many" (Mark 10:45). He also said, "And I, when I am lifted up from the earth, will draw all people to myself" (John 12:32). Christ lifted up is the focal point of the Bible and indeed the focal point of all history. We can never speak of him enough.

Do you tell other people about the uplifted Christ, or do you spend all your time talking about things that do not matter to people who will perish without him?

THE NECESSITY AND SIMPLICITY OF FAITH

Although the classical theologians stressed the importance of content, assent, and commitment in faith, we must not get bogged down by making faith complex. Faith contains these elements, but ultimately faith is as simple as looking to the snake on the pole.

Charles Haddon Spurgeon was a young boy when he was saved. God had been working in his heart, and he was restless. One day he went into a small Primitive Methodist Chapel during a snowstorm. Hardly anybody was there, and a layman was asked to preach because the pastor had not been able to make it through the storm. The man did the best he could; he was uneducated and couldn't even pronounce the words properly. He picked a text from Isaiah: "Look unto me, and be ye saved, all the ends of the earth: for I am God, and there is none else" (Isa. 45:22 KJV). The lay preacher began to preach, very simply, but he hammered his points home: "My dear friends, this is a very simple text indeed. It says, 'Look.' Now lookin' don't take a deal of pains. It ain't liftin' your foot or your finger; it is just, 'Look.'" He went on as long as he could, and then he noticed Spurgeon sitting under the balcony on his right. He turned to him, fixing his eyes on him, and said, "Young man, you look very miserable. . . . and you always will be miserable—miserable in life, and miserable in death—if you don't obey my text. . . . Young man, look to Jesus Christ. Look! Look! Look! You have nothin' to do but to look and live."[7] Spurgeon did. He was converted and became the greatest evangelist of his age.

Have you looked to Jesus Christ to cure you from the serpent's bite of sin? If not, why not? No one has ever looked to Jesus Christ for salvation and been turned away.

---

7. C. H. Spurgeon, *Autobiography*, vol. 1, *1834–1859* (repr.; Carlisle, PA: Banner of Truth Trust, 1973), 87–88.

27

OPPOSITION FROM WITHOUT

Numbers 22–25

TROUBLE AHEAD

One of the mistakes we often make as Christians—especially when we are young Christians—is to think that if we are on the right path with God, everything will be smooth sailing. Not only is this *not* the case, but it is almost always the opposite. The more we follow after Jesus Christ, the more opposition we will face, because the world and the devil are opposed to him. Therefore, to the extent that we are on Jesus' side, the world and the devil will be opposed to us, too. We ought to expect this, because there was never anybody who was more on the right path than Jesus Christ. Yet the author of Hebrews writes, "Consider him who endured from sinners such hostility against himself, so that you may not grow weary or faint-hearted" (Heb. 12:3).

The people of Israel had not been perfect, as we have seen, nor was their leader perfect; but they were on the right track, moving in the right direction. They were trying to follow the leading of the Lord, and so the whole book of Numbers has been filled with various stories of opposition. Until this point, all the opposition had been internal. Now it became external.

BALAAM

In Numbers 22 we learn that the Israelites had reached Moab, and were "camped along the Jordan across from Jericho" (22:1 NIV). However, before they could cross the Jordan River and enter Canaan, the land of promise, they had more challenges to face and more words of instruction to hear from Moses.

The first challenge involved Balaam, a pagan prophet hired by Balak, the king of Moab, to curse the people. Balak's plan strikes the reader as humorous. The idea of a pagan king hiring a pagan prophet to stand against the people that God had blessed is simply ludicrous. God had called his people out of Egypt with mighty miracles; he had led them, two million in number, through the desert; he had kept them alive in the wilderness for nearly forty years, giving them food and drink and defeating their enemies; and he had brought them to the very border of the promised land. Now a petty king is hiring a petty prophet to try to resist God's work.

This is humorous, although such a situation might not seem all that funny if we are going through a battle ourselves. We can see the humor only if we realize that Satan and the world are just as ludicrous, when the Almighty God of the Jews is on your side. We will persevere to the end because God perseveres with us—no one can ultimately stand against the church of Jesus Christ. This doesn't mean, however, that the world and Satan won't achieve seeming victories at times. God's people can stumble, can still fall into sin, as we see here.

It is easy to understand what was going on in the mind of King Balak. The Amorites had defeated him earlier and had taken away his cities. Now the Israelites had come out of the desert and defeated the Amorites. Putting two and two together, Balak realized that if he wasn't strong enough to stand against the Amorites, and if the Amorites weren't strong enough to stand against this horde from the desert, then obviously Balak was not strong enough to stand against them either. Furthermore, Balak had received reports that two of his northern neighbors, Sihon and Og, had also been defeated by the Israelites.

Balak did not know—and neither do we, since we do not learn of this until Deuteronomy 2:9—that God had forbidden the Israelites from attacking Moab. He assumed that these two million people were going to overwhelm him and his kingdom, and all he could think to do was to appeal for supernatural aid. He remembered that there was a prophet named Balaam, who lived near the Euphrates River—quite a distance away—but who, if the reports were right, was really successful in his blessings and curses. When Balaam blessed somebody, that person seemed to be truly blessed, and if he cursed somebody, that person seemed to be truly cursed. This man struck Balak as exactly what he needed, so he sent for him with this request:

> Behold, a people has come out of Egypt. They cover the face of the earth, and they are dwelling opposite me. Come now, curse this people for me, since they are too mighty for me. Perhaps I shall be able to defeat them and drive them from the land, for I know that he whom you bless is blessed, and he whom you curse is cursed. (Num. 22:5–6)

This ought to make us think back to something that God told Abraham when he first called him: "I will bless those who bless you, and him who dishonors you I will curse, and in you all the families of the earth shall be blessed" (Gen. 12:3). Similar language is used here by this pagan king as he hires a prophet to curse the Israelites.

What kind of person was Balaam? At first glance, he seems to be quite a noble character. He uses the name *Jehovah*, for one thing. For another, although he is hired to curse Israel, he maintains what we would call professional integrity, saying, "Though Balak were to give me his house full of silver and gold, I could not go beyond the command of the LORD my God to do less or more" (Num. 22:18) and "The word that God puts in my mouth, that must I speak" (v. 38). Some scholars have studied this story and said very commendable things about Balaam. Was Balaam intent from the outset on doing the right thing?

Our first clue that this may not be the right assessment of his character is that every reference to him in the Bible is unfavorable. For example, Numbers 31:8–16 tells of his death as an incident in the war against the Midianites. Judgment is pronounced against the Canaanites, who are to be exterminated in holy war, and Balaam is also killed.

That passage also makes clear that it was Balaam's idea to have the Israelite men enticed to "indulge in sexual immorality with Moabite women, who [in an earlier incident] invited them to the sacrifices to their gods," bringing about sin and ensuing judgment (Num. 25:1–2 NIV). Furthermore, Deuteronomy 23:4–5 describes Balaam as wanting to curse Israel even though he was not allowed to do so.

There is ambiguity in this story. God was angry with Balaam for going, but he told Balaam to go nevertheless and to say what God would have him say. Why was God angry with him for going when he had given him permission to go? We must ask ourselves why Balaam wanted to curse the Israelites in the first place, and the obvious answer is: he wanted the money. The king of Moab promised to reward Balaam handsomely if he would come and curse the people (see Num. 22:17). This is how the New Testament handles the story: Peter writes of Balaam as one who "loved the wages of wickedness" (2 Peter 2:15 NIV). Jude talks about those who have "rushed for profit into Balaam's error" (Jude 11 NIV). Revelation 2:14 talks about the evil counsel of Balaam, "who taught Balak to entice the Israelites to sin by eating food sacrificed to idols and by committing sexual immorality" (NIV).

With these clues in mind, we see Balaam in quite a different light as we return to Numbers. Balaam is introduced first of all as a pagan. This is not a favorable description in the context of the Old Testament. Pagans did not know the true God, and the Israelites did; pagans worshipped false gods, while the Israelites worshipped God as he had revealed himself to them. Moreover, Balaam was a prophet who was paid for his services. In other words, he was a court priest whose job it was to say whatever the king wanted him to say. His harping on money, which comes up again and again throughout the story, was probably just his ploy to get more money for what he is called on to do. If you say to your employer, "I couldn't do that even if you gave me a house filled with gold and silver," you are saying, "If you give me a house filled with gold and silver, I just might consider it."

Above all, the incident with the donkey is meant to clue us in. Balaam was a seer—a prophet who saw into the future—but he could not even see the angel who was standing with a drawn sword to oppose him. He was supposed to be able to speak the words of God; but the donkey, who was incapable of speech by nature, spoke the words of God, and Balaam did not understand a word. The story is a typical Semitic polemic against paganism, saying that heathen prophets are dumber than the donkeys, because a donkey spoke the truth and Balaam didn't.

A sound evaluation of Balaam comes from Joseph Butler: "The object we have now before us is the most astonishing in the world: a very wicked man, under a deep sense of God and religion, persisting still in his wickedness, and preferring the wages of unrighteousness, even when he had before him a lively view of death."[1]

BALAAM AND THE DONKEY (NUM. 22:21-35)

A lot was happening in the story of Balaam and the donkey. First, Balaam pushed the donkey onward until God's angel brought him up short; in exactly the same way, King Balak kept pushing Balaam to curse Israel until God brought him up short. Second, just as God opened the donkey's mouth to speak to Balaam, so God opened the prophet's mouth to speak God's words of blessing on Israel. Even though the donkey spoke, she was not a true prophet; likewise, Balaam's speaking did not make him a true prophet either. But he did speak the words of God, because God came on him. Third, the donkey's dilemma mirrored Balaam's. The donkey was caught between Balaam with his stick and the angel of God with his drawn sword. Balaam was caught between pressure from the king of Moab, who wanted him to curse the people, and pressure from God, who stood against him.

This is one of the most amusing stories in the Bible. When the donkey spoke to him, it is humorous in itself that Balaam did not consider this an unusual phenomenon. He talked back to the donkey as if it was the most natural thing in the world. He told the donkey, "Because you have made a fool of me . . . I wish I had a sword in my hand, for then I would kill you" (v. 29), but it was not the donkey who

---

1. Joseph Butler, *Human Nature, and Other Sermons*, ed. Henry Morley (London: Cassell & Company, 1887), 107.

was the fool—the fool was Balaam. There *was* a sword present, but the sword was the sword of the angel, and it was not directed against the donkey but against Balaam. The angel said, "I have come out to stop you, and the donkey saw me. If she had not turned away, I would have killed you and spared her" (see vv. 32–33). The speaking donkey was a miracle, but she was not the point of the story. The point was that Balaam was opposing God.

BALAAM'S SEVEN ORACLES (NUM. 22:36–24:25)

The story begins to get serious, at least in terms of the oracles that Balaam was given to deliver. It was not entirely serious, however, because the king of Moab was trying to get Balaam to curse the Jewish people. Instead, Balaam blessed them every time, and the poor king was fit to be tied. He wrung his hands; he jumped up and down; he wanted Balaam to leave—but the oracles kept coming, and the king couldn't do anything about it.

Balaam's seven oracles began by dealing with the past (focusing in particular on God's blessing to the patriarchs) before speaking about the future and—if we understand them rightly—the coming of the Messiah. We get a picture of the frantic king of Moab trying to make it all stop, but there was no stopping it. Balak wanted curses, but he got blessings (and by this point he would rather have had nothing at all).

THE FIRST ORACLE (NUM. 23:1–12)

The theme of the first oracle is the unique position of the people of Israel. God had blessed them irrevocably; they were not like any other people. They did not fit in with the other nations of the earth. Already throughout their history the Hebrew people had been a people to themselves, surviving many hundreds of years while other nations perished along the way.

Balaam also refers to the great number of the people: "Who can count the dust of Jacob . . . ?" (v. 10). This in itself refers back to what God told Abraham—that his offspring were going to be as numerous as the stars in heaven or the sand of the seashore (see Gen. 22:17). In a sense, Balaam is acknowledging the truth that God has fulfilled the promises he made to Abraham. God has blessed the people, and they are very numerous. This is an encouragement, because God also said that he would lead them into a land of their own—and they are now on the border of that territory.

At the end of the oracle, Balak is angry and alarmed. "What have you done to me?" he asks. "I took you to curse my enemies, and behold, you have done nothing but bless them!" (Num. 23:11). The reader should chuckle at the frustration of this ignorant pagan king.

THE SECOND ORACLE (NUM. 23:13–26)

Kings do not give up easily, so Balak tries another tactic. Maybe he has got Balaam in the wrong place; maybe a different site with a different view will produce a different result. So Balak takes Balaam to the top of Mount Pisgah, where he can see a part of the Hebrew people. As they did before the first oracle, they go through various sacrifices. But in spite of the change of location, the sacrifices, and the king's wishful thinking, the result is unchanged.

The oracle itself points this out from the start: "God is not man, that he should lie, or a son of man, that he should change his mind" (v. 19). Balak has called Balaam to curse the people, but God has determined that they will be blessed, so they are going to be blessed. Nothing that Balak or Balaam can do will get God to change his mind.

The second oracle goes beyond the first in two ways. First, the initial oracle says that God has blessed his people; the second says that God is dwelling in their midst. This was an important aspect of what had happened at Sinai. The people built the tabernacle, and God, present in the great shekinah cloud of glory, came and dwelt within their camp.

Second, this new oracle extends into the future. The first oracle says that God has blessed his people; the second says that he is going to keep on blessing them. Not armies nor sorcery nor divination will be able to stand against the Hebrew people. To put this in theological language, the first oracle concerns *divine election*: God has set his favor on the Israelites and called them. The second oracle has to do with *perseverance*: God, who has begun a good work in them, is going to keep on perfecting it until the end (see Phil. 1:6).

To the reader's amusement, the king's dismay seems to be growing. He calls Balaam to curse Israel, but Balaam has blessed them twice. It would be best at this point for him to say nothing. Balak tells Balaam, "Do not curse them at all, and do not bless them at all" (Num. 23:25). But the fat is in the fire, and poor Balak can't do anything about it.

THE THIRD ORACLE (NUM. 23:27–24:14)

Balaam follows the king's instructions, building altars and offering sacrifices, but he is beginning to see that Balak's cause is absolutely hopeless; and, in a certain sense, he gives himself up to the Hebrew God. For the first time in the story, we read that the Spirit of the Lord came upon him (see Num. 24:2). Although God had guided him in his observations up to this point, when the Spirit of the Lord comes on him, the result is a truly prophetic utterance as he talks about future events.

Balaam's most specific prophecy is that the Israelite king will be greater than Agag (see v. 7). Agag, a ruler of the Amalekites, is defeated by King Saul several hundred years in the future. Some scholars speculate that there was another king by that name, but since Saul was the first king of Israel, this is surely a genuine prophecy of an event in the distant future.

Once again, Balak is furious to the point of banging his hands together. In wild exasperation, he tells Balaam to get out and go home—and there will be no reward or payment (see v. 11). If Balaam had done what Balak asked him to do, Balak would have given him lots of gold and silver, but now he refuses to pay him a cent. He wants him to leave before he makes matters even worse.

But Balaam won't go.

THE FOURTH ORACLE (NUM. 24:15–19)

Balaam's fourth oracle is a much more distant prophecy, as the language makes clear. His prophecy about Saul refers to an event about three hundred years away. Now he says, "I see him, but not now; I behold him, but not near" (v. 17). He is looking far down the road.

The language he uses is messianic: "A star shall come out of Jacob, and a scepter shall rise out of Israel. . . . And one from Jacob shall exercise dominion" (vv. 17, 19). There will be lots of rulers, of course: Joshua, judges, kings. But this ruler is *the* ruler—the one who will reign on the throne of David forever. Many commentators have understood these verses as a messianic prophecy, referring not just to future conquests of Israel's enemies, but to the final, ideal king of David's royal line. As one of the early church fathers, Justin Martyr, said, the shining star that is risen is none other than Jesus Christ.

THE FINAL THREE ORACLES (NUM. 24:20–25)

From our point of view, Balaam's last three oracles are a bit anti-climactic after the prophecy about the coming of the messianic king. They have to do with battles in the immediate future. The Israelites are going to defeat the Amalekites (see v. 20), then the Kenites (see vv. 21–22). The final oracle regarding Kittim, Asshur, and Eber (v. 24) is harder to understand.

Given the context, this must have been an encouragement to the people. A prophecy about a huge triumph a thousand years in the future is great, but the people had immediate battles to fight. It was true that the Messiah was coming and that he would be a great blessing to God's people. But in the meantime, God is still working and enabling them to defeat their enemies.

THE SEDUCTION OF ISRAEL AND THE RESPONSE OF PHINEHAS (NUM. 25)

Until this point, these chapters have been somewhat humorous, and the prophecies have been promising. But Revelation 2:14 tells us that, having failed to curse the people, Balaam then advised the king of Moab to work from within to undermine the Israelites' religion.

Then came a terrible event. Typically people must have gone outside the camp to associate with the Moabites and their religion, but in this instance, one Israelite man brought a Midianite woman into the camp. In delicate language, the passage describes the couple having sexual intercourse right alongside or virtually in the precincts of the tabernacle. Phinehas, the son of Eleazar, a grandson of Aaron, rose up to judge them, plunging a spear through the man's back so that it went through him into the woman. With that, a great plague that God had pronounced on the people was stayed.

The people had fallen into sin many times before, but this sin was more serious than any of the previous ones had been. This was apostasy, not just a sexual matter. It had to do with the worship of Baal, a pagan fertility god, and it would plague the people throughout their history.

Phinehas, the grandson of Israel's first high priest, is praised for his intervention. God honors him, saying, "it shall be to him and to his descendants after him the covenant of a perpetual priesthood, because he was jealous for his God and made atonement for the people of Israel" (v. 13). This is a pivotal section in the book of Numbers.

LEARNING FROM NUMBERS 22–25

There are several lessons we can learn from this story.

The sovereignty of God. We have seen the sovereignty of God taught many times before this. It is the most dominant, pervasive doctrine in the Bible. Here it becomes evident as Balaam and Balak attempt to manipulate God to fit their desires. They want to get God to curse the people, but God is not manipulated. What God determines to do, God does. Do you believe this? Do you believe it enough to fit in with what God is doing? Or do you, like the people in this story, try to oppose God in his actions?

The faithfulness of God. Balak wanted God to abandon or curse Israel, but God had set his love on that nation and would not forsake his covenants. This does not mean that God would ignore sin among his people, as his judgment by the plague shows—but it does mean that God perseveres with us, even when we do not steadfastly pursue or obey him. Philippians 1:6 says, "He who began a good work in you will bring it to completion at the day of Jesus Christ." Aren't you glad that our God is like that? If God were not faithful, he would have given up on us long ago. But God is faithful to his covenants and this truth should be a great encouragement to his people.

The sin of loving money. While this lesson is not made explicit in these chapters, it emerges in references to this episode later on in the Bible. There is nothing wrong with money in itself, but Balaam was a man who loved money and allowed his love of money to determine what he did. He "loved the wages of wickedness" (2 Peter 2:15 NIV); and people are condemned who, like him, rush for profit into error (see Jude 11). As Jesus said, you cannot serve both God and money (see Matt. 6:24).

One of the great problems with American evangelical Christianity is that we are so wrapped up in our material possessions that we do not set God or spiritual things first. The more money we have, the more danger we are in of depending on it rather than on God. Many of us have plenty of money—certainly enough to ruin us. Is your love of money holding you back from something that God would have you do? Is this something for which you should repent?

God's use of unlikely people. God is able to use the most unlikely means to bring his Word to other people. Sometimes we marvel at the fact that God could use a donkey, but the donkey is not the surprise in this passage. It is an innocent animal. Balaam was opposed to God, yet God used him to deliver seven oracles—even one pointing forward to the coming of Jesus Christ.

You are no donkey. You are not even a false prophet if you belong to Jesus Christ. You are one of his. If God could use Balaam, he can certainly use you. Are you willing to have him use you? If you are, isn't it about time that you get busy telling other people about the Lord Jesus Christ?

28

FINAL PREPARATIONS
FOR ENTERING CANAAN

Numbers 26–36

FINAL MATTERS

The story of Balaam is the last significant narrative in the book of Numbers. The chapters that follow prepare the people to enter Canaan and conquer the land. Numbers 26:3 sets the stage: All of this happened on the plains of Moab, by the Jordan River, across from Jericho. However, the Israelites needed to take care of some smaller matters before they crossed the river and attacked Jericho.

These smaller matters are important, too. We know that they mattered to Moses, the author of Numbers, because they fill eleven of the book's thirty-six chapters. If nothing else, they give us a picture of the 120-year-old Moses, the great leader of the people. Although God had told him that he was going to die, he didn't wash his hands of the whole business and tell somebody else to carry on in his place. Instead, as long as the Lord led him, he faithfully pursued his responsibility to lead the people to the very end.

This last section takes up almost a third of Numbers. We have already studied some of these matters in previous chapters, and were I to examine them again in intricate detail, it would take many hundreds of pages to do so carefully. I will give an overview here, emphasizing the lessons that apply to us.

A SECOND CENSUS (NUM. 26)

There are two censuses in Numbers: one at the very beginning of the book (Num. 1–4) and the other in Numbers 26. The objective of both is to determine how many men were fit for war so that the soldiers could be organized for battle. After the initial census, however, there was a hiatus of thirty-eight years. By the time the second generation was ready to go into the land, the people had to be counted all over again.

A different emphasis emerges in the second census: the people were being numbered not only for the sake of the conquest, but also for the apportionment of the land. In the first census, "All the Israelites twenty years old or more who were able to serve in Israel's army were counted according to their families" (Num. 1:45 NIV). Similar wording is used in the second census, but only at the beginning of the instructions (see Num. 26:2). After the list of all eligible fighting men and their combined number is given, the Lord gives Moses additional instructions: "Among these the land shall be divided for inheritance according to the number of names" (26:53). We also see the different focus when the clans as well as the tribes are introduced, because the apportionment of the land will be according to these various tribal groupings.

Note that the final numbers of the men of fighting age are almost the same as in the first census. Most of the tribes had increased slightly in size, although four had declined—the total is 601,750 instead of 603,550, a difference of less than two thousand. In spite of the people's wanderings, their sin, and God's judgments on them, they still numbered almost as many as they did at the beginning of these thirty-eight years of desert wandering. Although sin has consequences, God's purposes are not thwarted. God is not frustrated by our shortcomings. His plans are set in history and carried out perfectly.

It should also be noted that, with the exception of Caleb and Joshua, all the names in the second census are different. God had told the first generation that because they had refused to go into the land with the faith that God would give it to them, they would die in the desert (see Num. 14:20–23). And so they did. The people in the second census are entirely different. Are we standing with men like Caleb and Joshua, believing that our great Lord can accomplish his purposes? Or do we disbelieve him, fearing to move forward in service and ministry?

THE APPOINTMENT OF JOSHUA (NUM. 27:12–23)

Aaron and Miriam had died, and God had told Moses that he would merely go up the mountain and look out to see the land before he was gathered to his fathers, just as his brother Aaron had been (see Num. 27:13). Moses was terribly disappointed at being forbidden to enter the promised land. He had been in the desert for eighty of the 120 years of his life; he had been on the very border of the land thirty-eight years earlier, ready to go in, when the people had lost their opportunity. He wanted to put his foot over the river so that he could at least stand in the promised land, even if he died immediately afterward. We see elsewhere that he had pleaded with the Lord, begging to be allowed to cross over the Jordan. God had said no (see Deut. 3:23–26).

However, in the brief narrative in Numbers 27, we see that although Moses was disappointed that he would not enter the land, he did not seem shocked, rebellious, or unhappy at the fact that he would soon die. His concern in this passage was not for himself, but for the people.[1] They needed a leader to direct their going out and coming in after he was gone, because they were, as he says, "like sheep without a shepherd" (v. 17 NIV). This phrase is picked up by Jesus himself, when he looks out at the masses and has compassion on them, because "they were . . . like sheep without a shepherd" (Matt. 9:36; see also Mark 6:34).

This remains true today. Masses of people, even Christians, are without a shepherd. They have no good leaders to direct, teach, challenge, or inspire them. As a good leader, Moses was very concerned about this issue. He knew what the situation had been while he had been present and what it would be like when he was gone, so he asked God to appoint a leader to replace him.

---

1. See A. A. MacRae, "Numbers," in *The New Bible Commentary*, ed. F. Davidson (repr., Grand Rapids: Erdmans, 1960), p. 191.

God appointed Joshua, the ideal man for the job. Joshua had been Moses' understudy for the forty years in the desert and had seen how Moses operated. Something of the spirit of this great leader had been passed on to Joshua. When God told Moses to appoint Joshua, he commended him, saying Joshua was "a man in whom is the Spirit" (Num. 27:18)—referring to the Holy Spirit. Joshua was a godly man as well as a strong one.

We can learn several things about the transfer of leadership from this example.

NEW LEADERS HAVE DIFFERENT GIFTS

When God appoints a new leader, the new leader is never exactly like the old. People grow accustomed to the old leader and want to get the same kind of leader all over again. It never works that way.

Joshua was not like Moses. Moses was a charismatic, bold leader. He had stood before Pharaoh and said, "Let my people go." He had the kind of strength necessary to keep the people on track in the wilderness for many years. Joshua was a faithful man but a stolid one—a soldier type. A whole book in the Old Testament goes by his name. He served brilliantly as a general, but he does not *personally* perform miracles as Moses had. Yet this was the man whom God had chosen to be Moses' successor.

Whenever one pastor, parachurch leader, or Bible teacher succeeds another, the one who follows is never like the one before. We shouldn't expect that. God appoints both, but each has different gifts. We must learn to appreciate those various, God-given gifts.

NEW LEADERS CONTINUE THE SAME WORK

In spite of changes in leadership, and in spite of the different gifts and abilities of the individuals involved, the work itself continues. We see this in the ceremony of the laying on of hands (see vv. 18–23). God told Moses to take Joshua, bring the high priest, and lay his hands on the younger man to commission him for his new role. This ceremony symbolically transferred something of the spirit and authority of Moses to the man who would take his place.

The work is always the Lord's. The Lord may do his work through different individuals, and individuals differ widely, but the work is the Lord's. That means that there is continuity. When a transition takes place, we can be confident that God is at work, thank him for that, and rally behind the new leader whom he has chosen.

OFFERINGS, FEASTS, AND VOWS (NUM. 28–30)

Numbers 28–30 deal with offerings, feasts, and vows—topics that have already appeared in Exodus and Leviticus. These chapters give some more details about the offerings before moving on to discuss feasts, since offerings were made at the feasts. The offerings are listed in an escalating pattern. Every day of the year, two lambs were sacrificed. On the Sabbath, two lambs were sacrificed as well as seven others, and grain and drink offerings were also made. On the first of each month, there were additional sacrifices. There were special sacrifices at the various feasts, leading up to the great Feast of Tabernacles, at which a very large number of animals was offered. In a year's time, the offerings amounted to 32 rams, 113 bulls, 1,086 lambs, more than a ton of flour, and thousands of vessels of oil and wine.

These numbers give us a greater appreciation for what the author of Hebrews is talking about when he marvels at the many repeated offerings throughout the many, many years of Jewish history. He says, in effect, "Aren't you glad that all these sacrifices have been fulfilled in Jesus Christ?" As important as the sacrifices were, they were just foreshadowings, and were all fulfilled in Christ, because he is our one perfect, all-sufficient sacrifice forever and ever.

WAR WITH THE MIDIANITES (NUM. 31)

The final narrative section in Numbers tells of a fierce war against the Midianites, in which all the Midianites were killed. Since the Midianites were not in Canaan, this may seem like a bit of a digression amid the preparations to cross into the promised land. Our first question might be, why is this section here? There are a few reasons. This narrative is part of the ongoing story of the advance of the people toward Canaan, and it is a foretaste of the conquest itself, which will involve divinely commanded, though incomplete, extermination of the Canaanite people. The account also concludes the story of Balaam. When we left him back in Numbers 24, he was alive and well, either back home at the edge of the Euphrates or lingering near the Midianite encampments. Now he is executed in connection with the Midianite war because he had caused the people of Israel to sin by taking pagan wives and lovers.

The real question regarding the Midianite war is the moral question. God told his people to kill all the people of Midian—not just the men or the soldiers, but the women, children, and animals as well. This is only the beginning. He instructed the people to do the same thing to the Canaanites when they moved into the promised land. They did not always complete the destruction of the Canaanite settlements, and God warned them that they would have much trouble if they did not obey him in this matter. This command rightly disturbs people. How could God tell the Israelites to slaughter an entire people?

Part of the answer is that this warfare was a judicial act of God, not something that the Israelites thought up themselves. If the Israelites had decided to slaughter all the Canaanites, this would have been no different from the Egyptians' decision to kill all male Hebrew babies. But here God appears as the Judge of all the universe, executing judgment on human beings for their sin. He chose to use human agents to bring judgment on the Midianites as he used fire and brimstone to judge Sodom and Gomorrah.

This is spelled out in Genesis 15 when God promised the land to Abraham. He explained that the Israelites would not get the land for another four hundred years, because "the sin of the Amorites has not yet reached its full measure" (Gen. 15:16 NIV), meaning that God would allow the people of Canaan to go on sinning for another four centuries before he judged them—using the Hebrew people as his instrument.

This pattern is how God works in history. When nations come to the pinnacle of their power and consider themselves to be better than other peoples, their pride, exhibited in their idolatrous and violent culture, destroys them, and God, who brings them down, often uses the armies of another nation to bring about that downfall. God has done this throughout history, and he will judge the United States, perhaps in the same way, if we fall into the same kind of prideful, idolatrous behavior.

People assume that the Canaanites were innocent or no worse than any other people group. The Canaanites were far from innocent. Whenever we assume innocence, we forget that we should be asking not why some are judged by God for their sin, but why some are spared. We should be marveling at the mercy of God, not complaining about his justice.

Jesus deals with this issue in a very short passage in the gospel of Luke. In a recent tragedy, soldiers of Herod had fallen on some unsuspecting Galileans when they were offering sacrifices in Jerusalem. Moreover, a tower in Jerusalem, the tower of Siloam, had collapsed, killing eighteen people who seemingly were not more sinful than any other group of people in that city. How could God allow such things to happen? Either he is not all-powerful and can't prevent tragedies such as those, the argument runs, or else he is not all loving.

But Jesus' answer, the answer of God himself, is very profound.

> Do you think that these Galileans were worse sinners than all the other Galileans, because they suffered in this way? No, I tell you; but unless you repent, you will all likewise perish. Or those eighteen on whom the tower in Siloam fell and killed them: do you think that they were worse offenders than all the others who lived in Jerusalem? No, I tell you; but unless you repent, you will all likewise perish. (Luke 13:2–5)

Whenever we question the morality of God's decisions, we are asking the wrong questions. We are on dangerous ground. We should be asking why a fate such as this *hasn't* happened to us. Aren't we all guilty of sin against the holy God? Aren't we all deserving of his judgment in this life and in the life to come? If God is moral, he must punish sin. Why are we *not* now in hell? Our problem is that we have forgotten how sinful we are. We do not realize that it is not justice we need from God, but mercy.

If his judgment of sin is delayed, that is evidence of his mercy, as Peter reminds those who were dismissing the promise of Christ's return because it hadn't happened yet. Peter declares that the delay was a sign of that mercy, for "the Lord is not slow to fulfill his promise as some count slowness, but is patient toward you, not wishing that any should perish, but that all should reach repentance" (2 Peter 3:9).

The Lord had given the Canaanites another four hundred years to turn from their wickedness and repent before he brought judgment and destruction on their corrupt culture. His patience with sinful men and women is great, but we are not to forget that "now is the day of salvation" (2 Cor. 6:2).

Now is the time to turn from our sin and come to the Savior, before the day of judgment comes.

WRAPPING UP (NUM. 32–33)

In Numbers 32, the tribes of Reuben and Gad had asked if they could settle down on the eastern side of the Jordan River. This came as a shock to Moses, which explains some of his initial harsh language. In a seeming repeat of Numbers 13–14, it sounds as though they were opting out of the conquest instead of helping their brothers. Moses did not like that. But no, this was not what the two tribes had in mind. They intended to fight alongside their brothers to the end of the war, but they wanted permission to come back afterward and settle in Transjordan. When this was explained, Moses agreed to the request.

Numbers 33 records the stages in Israel's journey from Egypt to the Jordan. Since many of these places were associated with great events in Moses' life, and since this comes toward the end of his life, the passage may well be a sort of obituary.

BLESSING OUT OF JUDGMENT (NUM. 35:1–5)

After Numbers 34 reports the boundaries of the land to be divided, Numbers 35 provides towns for the Levites and establishes six cities of refuge for those who are guilty of manslaughter.

While the other tribes each received a portion of the land, neither the Levites nor the Simeonites were given a tribal territory. Hundreds of years beforehand, when Jacob had pronounced his final words on his sons, he had passed a judgment on Simeon and Levi: they would not inherit land in the conquest because they had been guilty of an atrocity—the massacre of the Shechemites (see Gen. 34:25–31). Jacob had spoken prophetically about the descendants of these two sons: "I will divide them in Jacob and scatter them in Israel" (Gen. 49:7).

This scattering indeed happened, and it happened in a very interesting way.

Without a land of their own, the descendants of Simeon settled in Judah's territory. Because Judah was a strong tribe, and because Jerusalem was in Judah, the worship of God remained purest in that territory. Because of this association, the tribe of Simeon was more or less kept faithful to God. Although the judgment didn't cease to be a judgment, in the hands of God it turned into a blessing.

This happened also with Levi, only in a more striking manner. The people of Levi did not receive a tribal territory, but they were appointed priests and keepers of the tabernacle. Although scattered throughout the land, they had the great honor of being the ones appointed to keep the memory of the true God alive and to lead public worship. Moreover, the tribe of Levi produced some of the nation's greatest leaders: Moses, Aaron, Phinehas, Eli, Ezra, and John the Baptist.

What an encouragement, especially if you have suffered as a result of someone else's sin. The descendants of Simeon and Levi did not receive the land because of what their forefathers had done. The sins of the fathers are visited on the children frequently, as God says, even to the third and fourth generation (see Num. 14:18). Sin has consequences. But if you have suffered because of someone else's sin, particularly the sin of a parent, know that God is able to bring blessings out of judgment. The very thing that seems so hard to you—and that might be entirely destructive to a non-Christian—can be turned into a blessing in God's hands. Do not think that you are excluded from God's favor. We are told that God sees a contrite heart and brings blessings.

Even if you are suffering for your own sins, there is still hope. Do not draw away from God. Repent of your sins and seek God's face, and you will find that God is able, not only to forgive, but also to bring great blessing and restoration into the life of his repentant child.

THE CITIES OF REFUGE (NUM. 35:6–34)

In this ancient time, most communities had very rudimentary justice, if they had any justice at all. According to custom, if someone was killed, the victim's relatives appointed an avenger of blood to seek out the one responsible and put him to death. In a situation of premeditated murder, this provided a kind of frontier justice to deal with a genuine crime. But if the death was accidental, this *lex talionis*—"an eye for an eye" approach—amounted to a great injustice. For example, a man is chopping wood with an axe when his axehead flies off and kills his friend. He is guilty of manslaughter, and he knows that the friend's relatives are going to send someone to get him. What can he do? Wait around for his killer to come? Flee the country? Where is the justice in those alternatives?

When the Levites were given forty-eight cities (see Numbers 35), Moses, at the direction of God, appointed six of these as "cities of refuge" (v. 6). Three were on one side of the Jordan, and three on the other. If somebody was guilty of manslaughter—accidental killing, not premeditated murder—he could run to one of these cities and be safe inside it. This was not meant to excuse murder. The person had to explain to the elders what had happened, and if the elders decided that the death really was an accident, the man was allowed to stay in the city. He was protected until the reigning high priest died, at which point he was free to go. Nobody could touch him. If the death was a murder, not an accident, then the killer was not allowed inside the city. Instead he was turned back, so that vengeance could take place.

The cities of refuge are an illustration of, and a contrast with, how we find salvation in Jesus Christ. But the illustration is imperfect for a couple of reasons. For one, the cities of refuge were for people who were innocent of any real crime. We are not innocent but are guilty of sin. Furthermore, although the cities were spaced throughout the land at convenient intervals, a person who had accidentally killed somebody had to scramble to get to one. There was a possibility that he would be overtaken on the way. Salvation is never like that. We do not have to scramble to find Jesus Christ; he is waiting with open arms, inviting us to come (see Matt. 11:28). Not only that, but he actually pursues us—we do not have to pursue him. Despite these flaws, however, the spiritual lessons in the illustration of the cities of refuge are important, particularly in the following ways.

The way must be well indicated. The Israelites had a duty to indicate the way to the cities of refuge. Deuteronomy 19:3 commanded roads to be built so that the cities would be easily accessible. Extra-biblical Jewish sources tell us that they also built bridges over any ravines along the way, so that the fugitive would not be slowed down. They had to repair the roads every year. They had to have a sign at any crossroads that indicated the way to refuge.

We have a responsibility to do this as well. People are perishing in sin. Apart from Jesus Christ, a sinner is a dead man or dead woman. Who will help these people? Our duty as Christians is to point the way. We are to say, "There is refuge: Jesus Christ is the refuge. Don't hesitate. Flee to him."

The way is open. The cities of refuge were always to be unlocked. This was unusual in the ancient world, because city walls were for protection. City gates were locked at night and during times of war, but the cities of refuge were to have gates that were always open. In the same way, the arms of Jesus are always open to anyone who will come.

It is the only way. If an accidental manslayer did not flee to a city of refuge, he had no hope. There was no other provision in the law of Moses by which he could be saved. The same is true of us. If we in our sin do not flee to Jesus Christ, the Savior, there is no hope for us, because there is no other way of salvation. "For there is one God, and there is one mediator between God and men, the man Christ Jesus" (1 Tim. 2:5). If we are to find salvation, it must be in him.

A deadly enemy, an avenger of blood, pursues the person who is not in Christ. That enemy is death. You may live a long, long time, but sooner or later the avenger will catch up with you and you will die. Your only hope in death is that you have found life in Jesus Christ before your death. The author of Hebrews may have been thinking of the cities of refuge when he wrote of those "who have fled for refuge to lay hold upon the hope set before us" in Jesus Christ (Heb. 6:18 KJV). That is the challenge for you. Flee to Jesus and find salvation in him. He is the only place where salvation can be found.

LEARNING FROM NUMBERS 26–36

My study is not just of Exodus, Leviticus, Numbers, and Deuteronomy, but of Moses himself, and my applications have reflected this. We can hardly end this chapter without going back to what I wrote at the beginning: Moses was faithful. He persevered in his work to the very end. He had been told that he was about to die, but he had not given up. Rather, he kept on working, knowing that he had work to do until God finally took him to himself.

It is the same with you and me. We can retire from our secular work, but we can never retire from our spiritual work. The best Christian workers I have known are people who have been retired from their secular work. They give themselves to the Lord, and they carry on to the very end. That is the challenge for you and me as well.

When he was dying from tuberculosis, the great American pioneer missionary David Brainerd, a friend of Jonathan Edwards, was trying to teach a small Indian boy to read and write. He said it was a blessing that, even though he did not have enough strength to go out and preach, there was still one small thing he could do for his Master.

We are not retired from serving Jesus Christ on earth until God himself retires us permanently by taking us to be with him.

PART 5

A Covenant to Keep

29

DEUTERONOMY:
AN INTRODUCTION

Deuteronomy 1–26

This is a book about Moses; therefore I want to keep our focus on him, rather than going into the book of Deuteronomy in great detail. In this chapter I will introduce the last book of the Pentateuch—this further testimony from Moses—before covering the heart of Deuteronomy in chapter 30, the second song of Moses in chapter 31, and the account of Moses' death in chapter 32. As we take a quick look at Deuteronomy, I want you to see how chapters 1–26 fit in with what follows.

WHAT IS DEUTERONOMY?

Deuteronomy marks a new beginning. The books preceding it—Exodus, Leviticus, and Numbers—each begins with the word "and" in the Hebrew text. This may sound like a very strange way to begin a book, but in the context of the Pentateuch the opening "and" links each book to the one before it: Genesis, *and* Exodus, *and* Leviticus, *and* Numbers. Deuteronomy breaks from this pattern; it begins without the initial connective "and." In fact, some scholars think that Deuteronomy begins a new block of material that extends through Judges to the end of 2 Kings, because those books are also linked by "and."

The people were poised on the very banks of the Jordan, ready to cross and enter the promised land. Joshua had been commissioned as

Moses' successor, and Moses was very soon to die, although we have a whole book to read and study before his death takes place. What exactly is this last book about?

Essentially, Deuteronomy is a sermon or a series of sermons, given in a particular place within a very short space of time: "the words that Moses spoke to all Israel beyond the Jordan in the wilderness" (Deut. 1:1). The book contains Moses' passionate last words to the people as he pleaded with them—on the basis of God's law—not to forget what God had done for them in the past, and to remain faithful to him, that they and the land might be blessed.

Deuteronomy could even be considered a second sermon. Its very name indicates this. *Deuteronomy* is a Latin term composed of two separate parts: *deutero*, meaning "second," and *nomos*, meaning "law." The book of Deuteronomy is a restatement of the law. But it is more than this. As a sermon, it is also a vigorous homiletical application of the law.

The main theme of Deuteronomy is found in chapter 6:

> You shall do what is right and good in the sight of the LORD, that it may go well with you, and that you may go in and take possession of the good land that the LORD swore to give to your fathers by thrusting out all your enemies from before you, as the LORD has promised. (vv. 18–19)

I might summarize this theme as: *Remember; don't forget. Obey the Lord your God.*

Deuteronomy is quoted eighty times in the New Testament, in all but six of the New Testament books. Notably, when Satan was tempting Jesus, Jesus replied with quotations from this book (see Matt. 4:1–11; Luke 4:1–13; cf. Deut. 6:13, 16; 8:3).

Moses' addresses were given in a relatively short space of time. He began them on the first day of the eleventh month of the fortieth year of the people's desert wanderings (see Deut. 1:3). The people crossed the Jordan on the tenth day of the first month of the following year (see Josh. 4:19). That gives us a period of two months and ten days. It took the people three days to make preparations to cross the Jordan, and they mourned the death of Moses for thirty days. If we subtract these periods, we have a month and seven days left for Moses to deliver the addresses that are found in this book. At one hundred twenty years of age, that is a remarkable achievement. Speaking as a pastor, I think he was working on these messages in advance. He knew that the day was coming. At the proper time and in the right place, he gave the sermons he had prepared.

AN OUTLINE OF DEUTERONOMY

An outline will help.

The first five verses are a preamble (Deut. 1:1–5).

Next come three addresses by Moses. Scholars break them up differently, but generally they can be divided this way: Moses' first address (Deut. 1:6–4:43), which reviews the people's travels from Mount Sinai to the borders of Canaan; Moses' second address (Deut. 4:44–26:19), which summarizes, restates, and applies God's law and urges it on the people; and Moses' third address (Deut. 27–30), which gives instructions for a ceremony to be enacted, after the people have entered the land, reaffirming the covenant between God and the people. According to this covenant, the people will be blessed for their obedience and cursed for their disobedience. I will cover this third address in more depth in the next chapter.

Following is a short historical section, and then what I call the second song of Moses (Deut. 31–32).

In the final chapters, Moses blesses the tribes, and his death is described (Deut. 33–34).

THE FIRST ADDRESS (DEUT. 1:6–4:43)

Seminaries teach that a sermon ought to have one clear point that can be stated in a short sentence. Moses' basic message (though it is not a short sentence) is this: Look at your past, and see from experience what your dealings with God have been—when you obeyed God, he blessed you; when you disobeyed God, you have suffered for it.

The sermon has four parts. First, Moses starts with a section on disobedience (see Deut. 1:6–2:23). Disobedience resulted in thirty-eight years of desert wandering; when the people did not trust God enough to go into the land, they suffered for their unbelief. Second, Moses deals with obedience that leads to victory (see Deut. 2:24–3:20). When the people did obey God, he gave them victory over Sihon and Og, two pagan kings, in preparation for their invasion of the land of promise. A third section (see Deut. 3:21–29) recounts Moses' personal disobedience, when he dishonored God and was punished by not being allowed to go into the land. What had happened to the people as a nation had happened to Moses himself as well.

The only unique aspect of the review of past history in the first three parts is that we now have Moses' own personal and emotional perspective on what had happened. When we read the original narratives in Exodus through Numbers, which Moses himself wrote, we do not necessarily learn how Moses felt. But sometimes when a person preaches, he becomes personal, and here Moses starts to express how he himself had felt in those long years. He describes the burden he carried in having to govern so many people, and his frustration over the people's unbelief. The people were weary, but so was Moses. But on the other hand, he had been glad when Og and Sihon were defeated. Finally, he recounts how he had pleaded painfully with the Lord to be allowed to enter the land of promise. He had asked the Lord again and again, until God got tired of his asking and had told him not to ask any more. The Lord had made his decision—Moses could not enter the land. And Moses accepted that hard decision (see Deut 3:23–26).

Finally, in the fourth part, Moses exhorts the people to obedience based on these experiences (Deut. 4:1–40). This is the most important section of this address. Over and over again, Moses admonishes the people to obey God.

And now, O Israel, listen to the statutes and the rules that I am teaching you, and do them, that you may live, and go in and take possession of the land that the LORD, the God of your fathers, is giving you. (v. 1)

Keep them and do them. (v. 6)

Only take care, and keep your soul diligently, lest you forget the things that your eyes have seen, and lest they depart from your heart all the days of your life. Make them known to your children and your children's children. (v. 9)

Therefore watch yourselves very carefully. (v. 15)

Take care, lest you forget the covenant of the LORD your God, which he made with you. (v. 23)

Know therefore today, and lay it to your heart, that the LORD is God in heaven above and on the earth beneath; there is no other. Therefore you shall keep his statutes and his commandments. (vv. 39–40)

A particularly significant verse in this section is the warning in 4:2 not to change or tamper with the Word of God. The language is similar to the verses at the very end of the book of Revelation (see Rev. 22:18–19). Moses says here, "You shall not add to the word that I command you, nor take from it, that you may keep the commandments of the LORD your God that I command you." The Word of God, the Bible, is God's great gift to us. We must not add to it, and we had better not take anything from it—there is a curse in Revelation for anyone who does either. The Bible is sufficient for what we need, and it is as relevant today as it was in Moses' day.

THE SECOND ADDRESS (DEUT. 4:44–26:19)

More than 22 chapters long, the second address makes up the substance of Deuteronomy. The first part (Deut. 5–11) reiterates the law of God as it bears on the people's relationship to God. The second part (Deut. 12–26) reiterates the law of God as it bears on the people's relationship to the land and to other people. This kind of division ought to ring a bell, because it is the same as in the Ten Commandments. The first table of the Ten Commandments has to do with our relationship to God: we are to remember him, worship him only, have no other gods before him, and remember the Sabbath day to keep it holy. The second table begins with the family—honor your father and mother—and concludes with the commandment not to covet. The two parts of the Ten Commandments are reflected in a dynamic way in Moses' second address.

DEUTERONOMY 5: THE TEN COMMANDMENTS

Deuteronomy 5 repeats the Ten Commandments. There are some slight variations (but not many) between this iteration and the first giving of the commandments in Exodus 20. The Ten Commandments are the great moral code of the human race. They are cited again and again throughout the Old Testament, Jesus refers to them on various occasions, and they lie behind many of the ethical admonitions in the New Testament, particularly in Paul's writings.

DEUTERONOMY 6: A KEY CHAPTER

This chapter is extremely important for several reasons.

When Jesus was tempted by Satan in the wilderness, he quoted three times from the book of Deuteronomy, and two of the three quotations came from this chapter. Jesus knew Deuteronomy 6 well, and because it was in his mind and heart it quickly came to his tongue when he was tempted. We ought to know this chapter, too.

Furthermore, when the Pharisees asked Jesus which commandment was the greatest (a popular question in that day), Jesus had a ready answer, and it came from this chapter. He quoted verse 5: the greatest commandment is to love the Lord your God with all your heart, with all your soul, and with all your strength. Then he brought in a verse from Leviticus: "You shall love your neighbor as yourself" (Lev. 19:18). Jesus' response encapsulates the first and second tables of the law, showing *how* we are to love the Lord our God and *how* we are love to our neighbors as ourselves.

Deuteronomy 6 also contains the well-known *Shema*, meaning "hear," so called because *hear* is the first word of the verse: "Hear, O Israel: The LORD our God, the LORD is one" (v. 4). This is a strong, magnificent early statement of monotheism. The people of Israel were surrounded by polytheistic cultures. Again and again they would be tempted to worship other gods, but a monotheistic creed would always lie at the very heart of their religion.

In Deuteronomy 6 we find two new and distinctive encouragements:

The people are encouraged to love God. All the people were to fear their great, holy, and sovereign God. When God came down on Mount Sinai in thunder and fire, the noise was so loud that they were afraid to come near the place. They were in awe of God, but they weren't told to love him until Deuteronomy 6, when they were told not just to love God but to love him with all their heart, soul, and strength (see v. 5). Jesus called this the first and greatest of all the commandments. The greatest duty and the greatest privilege of any human being is to know and love God.

This love of God does not come naturally. As a matter of fact, the exact opposite comes naturally to us in our sin. We hate God. We hate him for many reasons, although we often pretend that we do not. We hate God because he is sovereign when we want to be sovereign ourselves. We do not want anybody telling us what to do—least of all a God whom we cannot even see. We hate God because he is holy, and his holiness condemns our sin. We hate God for his omniscience—we can't even hide from him, because he knows us, and knows where we are when we flee from him (see Psalm 139). And we hate God for his changelessness.

The only way we can ever love God is by receiving a new nature from him. In other words, we must be born again. We must be made spiritually alive by the Holy Spirit who comes to dwell in us and transform us into the image of Jesus Christ (see Rom. 8:29).

This is what the people of Israel needed. In Deuteronomy 6, Moses tells them to love God, but they do not love him. The prophets will come to tell them that they do not love God because they are in rebellion against him. Eventually one prophet, Jeremiah, will say that a new covenant is necessary, a covenant written not on stone tablets, but written by the Lord on their hearts (see Jer. 31:31–33).

The people are encouraged to impress these laws—and, above all, the duty to love God wholly—on their children. After stating the ultimate expression of the whole law of God—"You shall love the LORD your God with all your heart and with all your soul and with all your might"—Moses immediately urges,

And these words that I command you today shall be on your heart. You shall teach them diligently to your children, and shall talk of them when you sit in your house, and when you walk by the way, and when you lie down, and when you rise. You shall bind them as a sign on your hand, and they shall be as frontlets between your eyes. You shall write them on the doorposts of your house and on your gates. (Deut. 6:6–9)

When we Gentiles look at these commands today, we find it strange that the people took them so literally. The Jews wrote down these verses on bits of paper, put them in little boxes, and bound them to their foreheads and arms, just as the verses command. Were they taking the commands too literally? It seems strange, but it is much stranger for us who have come to know something of the love of God through Jesus Christ—how wide and long and high and deep it is, according to Ephesians 3:18—not to speak to our children more often about the love of God or tell our neighbors about it. Why should we remain so silent?

These verses are a great challenge to us, to share the love of God in every way possible with our children, our neighbors, with the strangers at our gates—or those sitting next to us in airport boarding areas.

DEUTERONOMY 7: GOD'S ELECTING LOVE

Why did God love Israel? Was it because they were more numerous than other people? The answer is no. Nor was it because they were better, nicer, kinder, or wiser. According to the text in Deuteronomy 7, God set his love on them because he set his love on them: it was "because the LORD loves you and is keeping the oath that he swore to your fathers, that the LORD has brought you out with a mighty hand and redeemed you from the house of slavery, from the hand of Pharaoh king of Egypt" (v. 8).

This applies to you as well. Why did God save you? Not because you are brighter, better looking, more energetic, or more moral than anyone else. No, he saved you because he loves you. That is all. God set his love on you—that is what electing love means. His love is utterly unconditional, not drawn forth by anything good in you. We see this teaching in Deuteronomy and all the way through the Bible. If it were not for God's unconditional love, none of us would be saved. If God wanted to find something in you or me that would make it possible for him to love us, what could that possibly be? We can't produce anything in ourselves that would cause the holy God of the universe to love us. No, he set his love on us in an electing way. As Paul states simply and clearly, salvation "does not, therefore, depend on man's desire or effort, but on God's mercy" (Rom. 9:16 NIV).

DEUTERONOMY 8–10: DANGERS TO COME

Deuteronomy 8–10 foresees two dangers that will come when the people begin to prosper in the land. First, there is the danger that they will begin to forget God. In difficult times we cry out to God for his help, and God hears us, but then our situation improves and we forget him. Moses warns the people to watch out for that danger.

Second, when the people prosper in the land, they might begin to think that it is because of their own righteousness. But this is not so, because the people do not have any. At this point, Deuteronomy begins to sound like the book of Romans. As soon as we do well, we think it is because we are living moral lives and serving God, causing God to bless us. But as soon as we begin to think that way, we get into trouble. We prosper not because of our righteousness but because of the love and mercy of God.

DEUTERONOMY 13: DISCERNING FALSE PROPHETS

The next part of this address, which bears on the people's relationship to the land and to other people, can be dealt with quickly. But one key point relates to detecting and rejecting a false prophet.

If somebody pronounces a prophecy that does not come to pass, he is a false prophet—you should not listen to anything else he says. That is self-evident. But sometimes a false prophet may prophesy something that *does* come true. After all, Balaam prophesied the future when the Spirit of God came on him. What do you do when a person seems to be vindicated by historical events? Deuteronomy 13 tells us that even if a prophet's words come true, he is not to be listened to, believed, or followed unless he is a follower of the Lord God. If he is a pagan prophet who follows another god, you shouldn't listen to him regardless of anything he might be able to do, no matter if it is supernatural, insightful, or anything else. He has "taught rebellion against the LORD your God, who brought you out of the land of Egypt and redeemed you out of the house of slavery" (v. 5).

This has great application to our situation today. In the United States, even in our evangelical churches, we have a tendency to say that words are backed up by the miraculous. If somebody can do a miracle, or claims to have done a miracle, we think that we ought to listen to that person. But Deuteronomy 13 tells us that a miracle doesn't mean anything at all. The demons themselves can produce apparent miracles!

Biblical teaching is measured by whether it teaches about God according to his Word. When you hear teaching on television, do not be impressed with it because it is flashy and entertaining, or because of what the preacher claims, or because of the stories that he tells. Forget about those things. When the apostle Paul taught the Bereans, the book of Acts says that they were noble because they searched the Scriptures to see whether the things he said were true (see Acts 17:11). They tested the words that they heard, even from the apostle Paul, by the teaching of Scripture. We are to evaluate human teaching the same way, testing it against the inerrant teaching of the Word of God.

DEUTERONOMY 18: A COMING PROPHET

Deuteronomy 18 twice prophesies the coming of a prophet who will be like Moses (see vv. 15, 18). After a severe warning about avoiding the abominable practices of the pagans in the land, Moses delivers a great promise: "the LORD your God will raise up for you a prophet like me from among you, from your brothers—it is to him you shall listen" (Deut. 18:15). He goes on to repeat words the Lord gave him at Mount Horeb concerning this prophet: "And I will put my words in his mouth, and he shall speak to them all that I command him" (v. 18). This successor to Moses will be the prophet above all other prophets—the Messiah.

This is the way first-century Jews understood these references. When John the Baptist came as a forerunner to Jesus Christ, one of the questions the Jewish leaders asked him was, "Are you the Prophet?"

(John 1:21), referring to the Messiah described in Deuteronomy 18. John replied that he was not that prophet, nor Elijah, but a voice crying in the wilderness to prepare the way of the Lord (see vv. 21–23). The prophet was coming, John said; and when he comes, the people must listen to him. Later on, when Jesus did appear publicly, the voice from heaven said, "This is my beloved Son; listen to him" (Mark 9:7).

Do you want to know the truth? The truth is Jesus Christ. Do you want to know the truth in propositional form? That truth is Jesus' teaching. Jesus tells us what we need to know. The Word of God is sufficient, and Jesus is the fulfillment of the Deuteronomy 18 prophecy. He is the prophet whom Moses foretold, speaking God's words, and we need to listen to him.

LEARNING FROM DEUTERONOMY

In Deuteronomy we have a repetition of the law. Why is that important? It is important for the obvious reason that we need to hear these things again and again. We need to hear them not only taught analytically and didactically, but also urged on our minds, hearts, and consciences in order that we might obey them. This is what Moses is doing. I encourage you in your devotions this week to read these chapters and pay attention to the tone in which Moses is speaking. He is about to die; he knows how willful the people are; he knows how serious the matter is, and so he admonishes the people: If you obey God, you are blessed; if you disobey God, you bring down curses on yourself. He is passionately pleading with the people whom he loves to remember what has happened, to remember especially the terrible consequences of disobedience, and to choose the way of blessing by determining to obey the law of God.

If you have an opportunity to teach—whether at home or at church, whether to children or adults—do not be afraid to repeat, repeat, repeat the teachings of the Word of God. People need to hear the law, they need to hear the gospel, and they need to hear both again and again and again.

Significantly, in the middle of this repeated law, we find the greatest of all the commandments: love the Lord your God with all your heart, mind, soul, and strength. As we learn to love him, by the grace of God, we also learn to obey.

30

CURSINGS AND BLESSINGS

Deuteronomy 27–30

THE VERY HEART OF THE
OLD TESTAMENT

Some scholars call Deuteronomy the heart of the Old Testament, and some call chapters 27–30 the heart of Deuteronomy. In these chapters, Moses forcefully urges on the people the kind of life that is based on what God has done. In chapters 4–26, he has given the chief substance of his teaching. Now, like the preacher he is, he presses his point home. He is about to be parted from the people whom he has led for decades. In light of this, he implores them, one last time, to choose righteousness and obey God, because this is the way of blessing. The only other way is the way of death.

Incidentally, Joshua will go on to do the same thing. At the very end of the book of Joshua, after Joshua has led the people for years, he gives a sermon and ends it with the same message: "Now therefore fear the LORD and serve him in sincerity and in faithfulness. Put away the gods that your fathers served beyond the River and in Egypt, and serve the LORD" (Josh. 24:14). If the people want to serve false gods, then by all means serve them, he says. "But as for me and my house, we will serve the LORD" (Josh 24:15).

PREPARING FOR THE RENEWAL OF THE COVENANT (DEUT. 27:1–8)

The conclusion to Moses' sermon covers four points. The first is the matter of preparing to renew the covenant. Deuteronomy 27:1–8 describes two preparatory acts. First, the people were to take large stones and set them up on a mountain they will find in the promised land, Mount Ebal. They were to whitewash the stones and write on them all the words of the law. Second, they were to construct an altar of unhewn stone—natural stones from the field—and make sacrifices on it.

We do not know how much of the law Moses wrote on the stones. It is unlikely that "all the words of this law" (v. 8) would include the entire Pentateuch. Perhaps not even all the law codes of the five books were included; the law may have been limited to the law code in Deuteronomy. However much was written, the important point is that the law was to be set up in the land that the people were entering, showing that God's law was not just the law of desert wanderings but also the law by which the land was to be governed. It is also important to note that if the people had any question at any time about the way they were to live, they could simply go to the stones and read them to find out. Today, we do not even have to walk up to Mount Ebal—all we have to do is read the Bible.

When God instructed Moses to write the law on the stones, placing them where all could read them, he also instructed Moses to set up an altar. At Mount Sinai God had given the law and had commanded the people not to break the law, but he knew that they *would* break it, and so he provided an escape from the penalty of their sin through the sacrifices performed by the high priest, Aaron. That is why the altar on Mount Ebal was so significant. If the law was stated clearly and the people read and understood it, they would come to the inevitable conclusion that they were sinners, they were lawbreakers. What could they do to escape the just penalty for their sin? God's answer from the beginning was that they were to come to him by means of sacrifice, and—as the New Testament makes clear—the death of an innocent animal in the place of the sinner pointed forward to Jesus Christ.

The two mountains were set against each other; the priests would speak blessings from one and curses from the other (see Deut. 11:29).

It is interesting that the altar was set, not in the valley between the mountains or even on Mount Gerizim, the mountain of blessing, but on Mount Ebal, the mountain of curses. If, standing on Gerizim, an Israelite could say, "I am righteous and obey the law," he would not need the altar. Of course, the problem is that we are all sinners who belong on Mount Ebal; we all need the altar. We must come to God as sinners, because none of us is righteous.

It is also interesting that that altar was made of fieldstone. The tabernacle and later the temple were made beautifully, with the Holy Spirit coming on the workmen to inspire them to do great work. Not so with the altar. All that the people were told to do was to pull stones out of the field and pile them up. This is a visual reminder that nothing human can go into our salvation. We do not have anything to offer; we must take salvation the way God gives it in his grace. Our temptation is always to embellish our altar so that we can be proud of it. But here the people must pile together uncut fieldstones and kill an animal on the heap, because God says that is the way he will save sinners, without our additions or embellishments.

BLESSINGS AND CURSES
(DEUT. 27:9–28:68)

Moses' instructions continue. Once in the land, when the stones with the law written on them had been set up and the altar and the sacrifices had been made, the people were to take their places on Ebal and Gerizim, in the area now known as Samaria, about 3,000 feet above sea level. At one point the two mountains come close together. Half of the tribes were to stand on Mount Gerizim and half on Mount Ebal and the Levites were to recite in the hearing of all a list of curses for disobedience and a list of blessings for obedience. And after each curse and each blessing the people were to say "Amen."

CURSES (DEUT. 27:9–26; 28:15–68)
The curses begin in Deuteronomy 27:15, in a section listing the sins that will lead to curses. After a section of blessings (see Deut. 28:1–14), the sermon goes back to more curses (see vv. 15–68). I wish it were

the other way around. But perhaps this is saying that people disobey the law more than they obey it, or that people hear curses better than they hear blessings.

Sins that bring curses. The first section explains that the curses will judge particular sins. The list is representative, as we can see from the first two offenses mentioned: (1) carving an image or casting an idol for worship (see v. 15) and (2) dishonoring one's father or mother (see v. 16). The first has to do with the first table of the law, and the second has to do with the second table of the law. The curses come on those who break God's commandments—and all the commandments are involved.

The third sin listed has to do with the land that the people are entering. They are not to move a neighbor's boundary stone—that is, to steal his land by falsifying the records. Today, we would call a sin by means of false documentation "white-collar crime."

The next two sins involve taking advantage of the poor and the unfortunate by (1) leading the blind astray and (2) withholding justice from the alien, the fatherless, or the widow. Then come four curses for sexual offenses, particularly incest, and then two that concern murder. Finally, there is a blanket curse for those who do not keep and practice the words of the law: "Cursed be anyone who does not confirm the words of this law by doing them" (v. 26).

As the list of sins was read, the people were supposed to say, "Amen," acknowledging their agreement: "This is what morality should be, and we agree to be bound by it." This is the essence of entering into the covenant.

The curses themselves. Nowhere else in the Bible is there anything quite like what follows. Having explained that curses will come if the people break the law of God, Moses now elaborates. The comprehensive scope of the curses in Deuteronomy 28:16–19 sets the stage for the curses that follow in the rest of the chapter:

> Cursed shall you be in the city, and cursed shall you be in the field. Cursed shall be your basket and your kneading bowl. Cursed shall be the fruit of your womb and the fruit of your ground, the increase

of your herds and the young of your flock. Cursed shall you be when you come in, and cursed shall you be when you go out.

It will make no difference what the people do or where they go. If they do not obey the law of God, their lives will become one continuous, overwhelming, devastating curse.

Can it get any worse? It can, because Moses goes on to explain in more detail. Nothing that the people do will ever prosper. They will lose their health, their homes, their vineyards, their cattle, their wives, their children. Even their land will be overrun by their enemies. Why? "Because you did not serve the LORD your God with joyfulness and gladness of heart, because of the abundance of all things" (v. 47). They will be carried into exile, away from the land that God has given them. In the time of siege, particularly the siege of Jerusalem, the people will resort to cannibalism and even worse (v. 53; cf. 2 Kings 6:24–31; Lam. 2:20; 4:10). It seems to me that some things described in this passage shouldn't even be talked about openly today, but God says it is what will happen if the people go their own way.

This is bad news, but none of it *needs* to happen. The curses do not *have* to come on the people. The people can go God's way and be blessed just as abundantly—or more abundantly—as they would have been cursed if they had disobeyed him.

BLESSINGS (DEUT. 28:1-14)

In the Hebrew text, both the blessings and the curses in this passage are written as poetry—very short, very terse, and very easily memorized. Moses wanted to give this to the people in a form that wouldn't escape their minds. These blessings were intended to be the exact opposite of the curses that we looked at in the last section. They are almost an exact parallel. The people will be blessed wherever they are; their families, livestock, and crops will prosper; their enemies will be defeated (see Deut. 28:1–7).

How you live really does matter. Believers are saved by grace, and God is very gracious to us, even when we sin. Nevertheless, God holds the way of obedience before us, and he says that obedience is the way of blessing and that disobedience is the way of judgment.

URGING TO OBEY (DEUT. 29-30)

Moses was a great preacher, and he rose to heights of eloquence here. Even after spelling things out as sharply as he does in Deuteronomy 27–28, he goes on to urge his applications on the people at greater length. He reminds them of the past, describes what entering into the covenant means, gives an additional specific warning of disasters to come, and finally promises prosperity in the future if, after falling away, the people repent of their sin and come back to the Lord they have deserted.

A REMINDER OF THE PAST (DEUT. 29:1-8)

In the first three chapters of Deuteronomy, Moses had reviewed the history of the people. The point of his lesson was that when the people obeyed God, they had victory over their enemies, and when they disobeyed God, they did *not* have victory over their enemies. Blessing followed obedience, and defeat followed disobedience. Deuteronomy 9 made the same point. Now it is being made again. While taking only eight verses, Moses is nonetheless comprehensive. Beginning with when the people were in Egypt and Pharaoh was defeated, he takes them all the way to the division of the Transjordan territories.

Why is Moses saying all this again? He explains that although the people saw these things, they did not really see what they should have seen. It did not get through. The people were blind to the implications of the work of God (see Duet. 29:3–4). We, too, need spiritual healing, because we also are spiritually blind. We need the sight, the understanding of the ways of God, that comes only from God himself. Let us pray with David, "Teach me your way, O LORD, and lead me on a level path" (Ps. 27:11).

THE MEANING OF THE COVENANT (DEUT. 29:9-21)

Next, Moses makes the point that God's covenant is not something to be entered into lightly, nor is it something that lasts for only a moment. The people were not to think, "I will be safe, even though I persist in going my own way" (v. 19 NIV). Such a line of thinking would be disastrous. Moreover, as the people entered into the covenant, they needed to realize that they were entering into it not only for themselves but for their children as well. The covenant would be binding, not only for their generation but also for generations to come.

LATER DISASTERS (DEUT. 29:22-29)

Moses also warns of specific disasters to come, looking beyond the sieges to the exile. Enemies will encircle their cities and wall them up; they will breach their defenses and carry the people away, leaving the land desolate. Everything will be destroyed. Their houses and olive groves will be gone; all the vines will be uprooted and destroyed; all the city walls will be cast down. Strangers will come into the land, look around, and ask themselves, "What in the world did the people do to cause their God to destroy their land like this?" Moses provides the answer that will be given: "It is because they abandoned the covenant of the LORD, the God of their fathers, which he made with them when he brought them out of the land of Egypt" (v. 25). God's response to covenant breaking is furious punishment and exile.

This is exactly what ends up happening. The people are given their first warnings here, but they will nonetheless go their own way. They will follow the gods of the land, worshipping them at the high places of Canaan. God will send his prophets, warning the people again and again. The people will return to God during brief times of repentance, but then they will plunge into apostasy once more. Finally, everything that Moses prophesied will come true. The northern kingdom would be overthrown in 721 BC. Nearly one hundred fifty years later, in 586 BC, Judah and Jerusalem would likewise be conquered.

A verse at the end of Deuteronomy 29 has assumed unusual importance in people's thinking: "The secret things belong to the LORD our God, but the things that are revealed belong to us and to our children forever, that we may do all the words of this law" (v. 29). In context, the verse means that the people have not been told what will happen: whether they will receive blessings or curses. From their perspective, this is contingent on what they will do; God himself knows, but he is not revealing it to them. It is just exceedingly important that they obey.

Commentators have drawn out of this verse a great principle that, I think correctly, applies at all times to all God's people—including us. A lot of Christians have a great interest in finding out things that we have no business or need to find out. We want to know what will happen, what we can expect for our lives, or what God will do with somebody else. We wish that God would unfold his secret things for us. We rush around, trying to find out God's will in areas that simply are not revealed in Scripture and will not be revealed.

The secret things are none of our business. This is not to say that God does not have a will for our lives or that he won't lead us in accordance with that will. He *does* have a plan, and he *will* lead us in a lot of ways. But the only things we can know for sure are spelled out in Scripture. Knowing anything more might boost our pride, but it will not help us to live the Christian life. We have the Word of God, and that is all we need to follow in order to live the Christian life. We have the Word of God, and that is all we need in order to know and obey what God has revealed as his will for his people.

THE FINAL PROPHECY (DEUT. 30:1–10)

Finally, Moses looks beyond the exile. Speaking as a prophet, he tells Israel, "I know you're going to go your own way; I know judgment is going to come; I know you're going to be carried off to another land. And yet, if you repent, God is faithful to his promises—he will bring you back. You will prosper in the latter days if you follow his will." This also is what happened, at least in part. At the end of the seventy-year captivity in Babylon, many thousands returned to the land. However, Moses' words point to a greater fulfillment than the partial return of the Jewish exiles who were led by Ezra, Nehemiah, and others. Moses speaks of a restoration that will be marked by circumcised hearts: a restoration of the people of Israel to the land, when they will fully keep the law—because, as Jeremiah states, the law will be written on their hearts (see Jer. 31:33). That day has not yet come—but one day "the Deliverer will come from Zion, he will banish ungodliness from Jacob" (Rom. 11:26), and the blessed restoration of which Moses speaks will be accomplished.

LEARNING FROM DEUTERONOMY 27–30

When we read these sections of blessings and curses, it may seem as though there is something almost mechanical about them—as though they operate independently of the living God who stands behind them. They might seem like the law of gravity: if you jump off a building, you fall; if you do not jump, you're all right.

But Moses is saying that they are not a question of natural law. These blessings and curses fit a spiritual law that flows from the character of God. What is important is our relationship with God. This is not just a matter of temporal blessings and curses but a matter of life and death. God alone is the source of life, and the way to be in relationship with him is to believe and obey him. Moses has been challenging the people to do this all along. If they believe and obey God, they will not merely be blessed—they will live. But if they will not believe and obey but instead go their own way, they will die—spiritually as well as physically. The choice that Moses sets before the people is a choice between life and death.

In Romans 10, Paul picks up on this choice as he presents the way of salvation apart from works. The Jewish people in his day thought that they could get to heaven by doing good deeds, by keeping the law. You can't, Paul says, none of us can keep the law: "none is righteous, no, not one" (Rom. 3:10). We get to heaven only by the grace of God, as revealed in the gospel. Quoting Moses' words in Deuteronomy 30:12–14, Paul argues that it is not necessary to go up to heaven in order to bring Christ down with good works, or to go down to hell to bring him up (see Rom. 10:5–7). There is nothing we can do; salvation is by grace and comes from God alone. All we need to do is believe what God has done for our salvation. Then, having received salvation as a free gift, we are to walk in the way that he has set before us.

If you know you are a sinner, turn to Jesus Christ. Go to Christ, confess your sin, and find salvation in him. Then, by his grace and the power of the Holy Spirit, get on with living the Christian life. "If you confess with your mouth that Jesus is Lord and believe in your heart that God raised him from the dead, you will be saved" (Rom. 10:9).

Is salvation that simple? It is. But despite its simplicity, it is of eternal importance. Whether we believe and act on our belief is a matter of spiritual life or spiritual death.

400

31

THE SECOND SONG OF MOSES

Deuteronomy 31–32

NO RETIREMENT PARTY

We mustn't get into the habit of thinking we can retire in the Christian life. We may retire from our jobs and from particular aspects of our labor, but as long as we live, we have work to do and a testimony to bear. This was true for Moses as well. His life was drawing to a close, but as long as he lived, he did his work. We see this in the last four chapters of Deuteronomy, the first two of which we will look at in this chapter.

MOSES' FINAL CHARGES (DEUT. 31)

The first of these four chapters has four charges in it: three from Moses—to the people, to Joshua, and to the priests—and then one from God to Joshua, in which God prophesies that the time is coming when the people will prove unfaithful to him. Throughout these four charges the same three themes recur, so, instead of moving through Deuteronomy 31 section by section, I will instead examine its main points. These recurring themes are very important and must be taken into consideration as they relate to our own lives and walk of faith.

REMEMBER THAT GOD IS GOING BEFORE YOU

Moses started this final part of his last address to the people by acknowledging that he was now advanced in age (see vv. 1–3). At 120 years old, he did not have the strength that he once had, and he is unable to go out before the people and bring them into the land that God was giving them. We are later told that Moses' strength was not abated and that even his eyes were still keen (see Deut. 34:7)—but in Deuteronomy 31 he acknowledged that the days of rigorous leadership were over for him. He could not lead them, but God himself would. Moses told the people not to forget that God was with them and would be with them until the very end.

This theme is repeated more than once. Moses began with these words:

> I am 120 years old today. I am no longer able to go out and come in. The LORD has said to me, "You shall not go over this Jordan." The LORD your God himself will go over before you. He will destroy these nations before you, so that you shall dispossess them. (vv. 2–3)

In his charge to Joshua, Moses made this point again: "It is the LORD who goes before you. He will be with you; he will not leave you or forsake you" (v. 8). Finally, when God himself gave a charge to Joshua, he told him, "Be strong and courageous, for you shall bring the people of Israel into the land that I swore to give them. I will be with you" (v. 23).

It is hard to read these verses without recalling an earlier incident. In Exodus 33, God told Moses that he would *not* go with the people himself—he would send an angel, but he himself would not go with them, because they were an unruly people who would rebel against him, causing him to destroy them in his anger (see vv. 2–3). In a great example of impassioned and fervent prayer, Moses responded by pleading with God to go with them nevertheless. If God would not go with them, then Moses did not want to go (see vv. 15–16). He would rather stay in the desert for the rest of his life and die in the wilderness at the base of Sinai than go to the promised land without the presence of God. If God would not go with the people, Moses asked, how would anybody know that God favored them? The Israelites would be just like any other people. Sure, they might succeed—or they might not—but only if God went with them would people see that God was their God and come to know him.

Now, at the very end of his life, Moses was able to remind the people of God's promise. God *will* go with them; he will be with them throughout the conquest. God had told Moses that he will do this, and so Moses tells the people that they can count on it.

This guarantee applies to us as well. Shortly before his ascension into heaven, the Lord Jesus Christ made this promise: "I am with you always, to the end of the age" (Matt. 28:20). Just as Moses assured the people that the great God of the nation would go with them, so the Lord Jesus assures us that he will go with us.

I wish we would think, speak, believe, and act the way Moses did in Exodus 33. Moses did not want to go anywhere unless God went with him. Christians are very wise if they learn this lesson. We must always follow the Lord and go where he goes, always desiring his presence and seeking his blessing. If God goes with you, you will prosper; but if you go your own way, you will not.

BE STRONG AND COURAGEOUS

Both God and Moses encouraged the people in general—and Joshua in particular—to be strong and very courageous. This admonition was and is very important. Throughout Scripture, God's presence and our courage always go together. God is with us—and for that very reason we can be courageous.

This command is expressed again and again. It first is heard in Moses' charge to the people: "Be strong and courageous. Do not fear or be in dread of them [the people of the land]" (Deut. 31:6). In Moses' charge to Joshua, he urges, "Be strong and courageous, for you shall go with this people into the land that the LORD has sworn to their fathers to give them. . . . Do not fear or be dismayed" (vv. 7–8). When God charges Joshua, he says the same thing: "Be strong and courageous, for you shall bring the people of Israel into the land that I swore to give them. I will be with you" (v. 23). This theme continues in the book of Joshua, directly following Deuteronomy. God speaks to Joshua in the first chapter, saying, "Be strong and courageous, for you shall cause this people to inherit the land that I swore to their fathers to give them. Only be strong and very courageous" (vv. 6–7); and "Be strong and courageous. Do not be frightened, and do not be dismayed, for the LORD your God is with you wherever you go" (v. 9). The people give this charge to Joshua themselves: "Only be strong and courageous" (v. 18). Later on, Joshua says it back to them: "Do not be afraid or dismayed; be strong and courageous" (Josh. 10:25). It is worth noting that David seems explicitly and consciously to pick up on these words when he charges his son Solomon not to be afraid but to have courage (see 1 Chron. 28:20).

Why this emphasis on courage? The obvious answer is that we tend to be so fearful. On the one hand, while God may be with us, he is an invisible God; we can't see him. It is very hard for us to believe in the things we cannot see. On the other hand, we can see our enemies, and they are all around us. We see them, we do not see God, and we tremble.

Joshua must have been very worried as he stood on the brink of the conquest. The people were ready to fight, but they were untried. What would happen when they got into the land and came up against fortified cities? He needed God to tell him to be strong and courageous. Moreover, God told him not to be afraid because God himself would be with him and would give him the victory.

Even the apostle Paul must have been afraid on some occasions, because he told the Ephesians, "Pray also for me, that whenever I open my mouth, words may be given me so that I will *fearlessly* make known the mystery of the gospel" (Eph. 6:19 NIV). If Paul recognized a temptation to be fearful, then we should pay attention because these words of encouragement need to be spoken to us as well.

We are fighting spiritual battles in a hostile environment, and there are citadels of unbelief we must throw down. We need courage, and we get it from reading the Bible, from praying, and from being encouraged by one another. Moses encouraged Joshua, God encouraged Joshua, Joshua encouraged the people, and the people encouraged Joshua. We, too, need to practice this kind of mutual encouragement. Sometimes life seems relatively easy, but when difficulties come into our lives, we need Christian friends to tell us, "Don't be afraid. God will be with you and will bless you." Here is a great ministry. Ask the Lord whom you can encourage to press on, and to keep pressing on.

GOD'S WRITTEN REVELATION IS VERY IMPORTANT

Although subtler, a third significant theme comes through in Deuteronomy 31: the importance of God's written revelation.

Moses is the author, through God's inspiration. Many times in this chapter, Moses is said or implied to have written these things down (see vv. 9, 19, 22, 24). We know that Moses authored the first five books of the Bible because when other biblical writers—especially New Testament writers—quote from them, they refer to them as the books of Moses. Yet up to this point, except for one or two rare incidents, Moses has not been declared to be the author. As he wrote the books, he did not see much need to mention that he was writing them; but now, toward the end of his life, he writes several times that he is the one recording these things. He is a prophet of God, writing the Pentateuch at the command of God, and these last chapters state that clearly: "when Moses had finished writing the words of this law in a book to the very end . . ." (v. 24).

God's written revelation is part of Israel's religious ceremonies. Part of the emphasis on the written revelation of God comes when the priest is charged to preserve the law and to read it in its entirety to the people at least once every seven years at the Feast of Tabernacles. In the course of a year, all able men and their families were to go to Jerusalem for three feasts, and of these the Feast of Tabernacles was a high feast. More sacrifices were performed at this feast than on any other occasion. The reading of the law on this occasion would represent a renewal of the covenant. It is especially emphasized that the children had to hear it—everybody in Israel would experience this impressive ceremony at least once, and perhaps twice, in his or her childhood (see vv. 9–13).

God's written word is to be preserved. A third indication of the importance of the written law is Moses' command to preserve it by laying it in the tabernacle in the Most Holy Place. Now, the ark of the covenant already contained the stone tables of the law—the Ten Commandments, the very heart of the law. But Moses told the people to take the law that he had written down during their years of wandering in the wilderness and to lay it beside the ark. It would be a testimony to God that the people had been given the law and had promised to obey it. It would also be a testimony to them of God's requirements. If there were ever a question about what should be done or how they were to live, the law was there. All they had to do was consult it. We can see that the people were to have a very special relationship with the written law of God (see vv. 24–26).

Do not miss the fact that even at this early stage in Israel's history, the people had a written revelation. Although their canon consisted of only the first five books of the Bible—not yet the entire Scriptures—they had their code in writing, from God, and it was binding. Liberal theologians neither like nor believe this. According to them, no law existed at this time. Yet the books themselves tell us that the people not only had a written revelation from God but also *recognized* it as a written revelation from God. Joshua, in particular, received God's Word and was told by God to meditate on it day and night and not turn from it to the right or to the left (see Josh. 1:7–8). Francis Schaeffer says,

> Joshua knew Moses, the writer of the Pentateuch, personally. Joshua knew his strengths and weaknesses as a man; he knew that Moses was a sinner, that Moses made mistakes, that Moses was just a man. Nonetheless, immediately after Moses' death Joshua accepted the Pentateuch as more than the writing of Moses. He accepted it as the writing of God. Two or three hundred years were not required for the book to become sacred. As far as Joshua was concerned, the Pentateuch was the canon, and the canon was the Word of God. The biblical view of the growth and acceptance of the canon is as simple as this: When it was given, God's people understood that it was his Word. Right away it had authority.[1]

---

1. Francis A. Schaeffer, *Joshua and the Flow of Biblical History*, 2nd ed. (Downers Grove, IL: InterVarsity Press, 1975; repr. Wheaton, IL: Crossway, 2004), 40.

We must have that same conviction. We must respond to the Bible in the same way the Israelites did, saying, "God has given us the Word. We receive it and believe it." This links us not only to Joshua and Moses, but also to God. We know God through his written revelation, through which he has spoken. It is on this great truth that Deuteronomy 31 ends.

THE SECOND SONG OF MOSES (DEUT. 32)

In Deuteronomy 32 God gives Moses a second song to record. This does not necessarily mean that God dictated it and that Moses heard the words and wrote them down. Just as the whole Pentateuch is from God even though Moses composed it, so Moses composed this hymn under the guidance and inspiration of God's Spirit.

I call this a "second song" because there is an obvious parallel between this song, written just before the people enter the promised land, and the song that the people sang after they were delivered from Egypt forty years beforehand (see Ex. 15:1–18). The song at the beginning was filled with joy; the song at the end is filled with warnings. Yet at both the beginning and at the end of the journey there was a song.

THE PURPOSE OF HYMNS

The people of God have always been a singing people. Jews have their songs of faith, and Christians have their hymns. Hymns often fulfill at least one of two purposes.

Praise. A very important purpose of a hymn is to praise God and express our joy in him and in his works. Some of our hymns do this very well. The first song of Moses fits this pattern. It was an outburst of joy and praise to God at the time of the people's deliverance, recounting his great deeds.

Instruction. Another purpose of a hymn is to teach. Hymns put into verse form—a form that can be memorized and retained—truths that we need to learn and remember for our souls' good. Falling into this category, Moses' second song is meant to teach us about God, God's ways, and the propensity of our hearts to go astray from those ways. It also reminds us of the danger of going astray and of the blessing to be found in trusting in a God who is faithful even to a disobedient people, a God who makes atonement for their sins.

Many of our hymns were written for instruction. The hymns of Ambrose of Milan (c. 340–397), for example, were meant to teach basic Christian theology to people who did not have access to Scripture or were unable to read.[2] The familiar Christmas carol "O Come, All Ye Faithful" is very didactic: the phrases "God of God, light of light" and "very God, begotten, not created" are taken from the Nicene Creed, written in response to the heretical teaching of the Arians in the fourth century (who believed that Jesus did not exist from the beginning, but was created by the Father). Luther's great Reformation hymn of the sixteenth century, "A Mighty Fortress Is Our God," is intended to strengthen a persecuted people who had lost property or even been threatened with death at the stake:

> That Word above all earthly powers, no thanks to them, abideth;
> The Spirit and the gifts are ours through him who with us sideth.
> Let goods and kindred go, this mortal life also;
> The body they may kill: God's truth abideth still;
> His kingdom is forever.[3]

God's truth abides in those who will stand with God, and they will stand forever because his kingdom is forever. Singing these great hymns anchors our hearts and minds in the eternal truths of the Word of God.

THE SONG ITSELF

Moses' song has a number of parts, which I will discuss briefly. As you will see, the whole song is about God and about the people's relationship with him. It is a panoramic picture, for, as G.T. Manley states, "It recounts the birth and childhood of the nation, their ingratitude

---

2. See his "O Splendor of God's Glory Bright" (trans. compiled by Louis F. Benson, 1910) in which he teaches the full deity of Christ: "the Word in God the Father one, the Father imaged in the Son."

3. Martin Luther, "A Mighty Fortress Is Our God," 1529; trans. Frederick H. Hedge, 1853.

and apostasy, their punishment and restoration. Seen otherwise, its theme is the name of the Lord, His loving care for His people, His righteousness and His mercy. It carries us from the creation to the final judgment, and begins and ends with praise."[4]

A Call to the People (vv. 1–2). First, Moses calls on heaven and earth to listen to what he has to say. He is calling on the whole created order to hear these words giving praise to God and warnings to his people.

God's people should listen to him, Moses says, because if they do, his words will be to them like rain, dew, showers, and abundant rain—symbols of blessing and fruitfulness. This should make us think of what God says elsewhere of his Word: it never returns to him empty but always accomplishes what he pleases; it is like the showers and the snow that come down from heaven to water the earth and make it fruitful (see Isa. 55:10–11).

Praise to God (vv. 3–4). Moses wants the people to be thinking about God, so, having gotten their attention, he praises God in these opening verses. He calls God "the Rock," a description that he repeats throughout the song (see vv. 4, 15, 18, 30, 31, 37) and that we see throughout the Bible, particularly in the Psalms. David loved this image of God as the unshakable, unchanging, utterly secure One in whom he could trust:

> The LORD is my rock and my fortress and my deliverer,
>   my God, my rock, in whom I take refuge. (Psalm 18:2)

> For you are my rock and my fortress. (Psalm 31:3)

> Lead me to the rock
>   that is higher than I,
> for you have been my refuge,
>   a strong tower against the enemy. (Psalm 61:2–3)

---

4. See G. T. Manley, "Deuteronomy," in *The New Bible Commentary*, ed. F. Davidson (repr., Grand Rapids: Erdmans, 1960), 220.

The image also makes us think of Jesus' words at the end of the Sermon on the Mount, when he says that the man who hears his words and keeps them is building his life on the rock: the totally secure foundation of his word (see Matt. 7:24–25).

Rebuke (vv. 5–6). Having praised God, Moses rebukes the people for their rebellious behavior. The contrast he introduces between the goodness and faithfulness of God and the evil and faithlessness of the people carries on throughout the entire song. God is the Rock of the people, but the people are a "crooked and twisted generation" (v. 5) and have acted corruptly toward him though he is their father and the one who created them. Moses asks them, is this a reasonable way to respond to such a God? The answer, of course, is no.

Reminder of God's Goodness (vv. 7–14). Moses has asked the people if their behavior is wise. Now he takes them through a pattern of sanctified thinking as he reminds them of God's goodness toward them, spelling it out at some length. This is poetry of a high order. He pictures God as finding Israel in a barren and howling waste, stirring her up, protecting her as an eagle protects and instructs her young, and providing for her with honey from the rock, oil from the flinty crag, curds and milk from the herd, and fattened lambs and goats. Should not these reminders of God's goodness and provision for his people make all of us consider our ways?

In verse 8 of this section, a universal note is struck when Moses pictures God as the Most High God who gives to every nation the territory it is supposed to occupy. In a very nice turn of phrase, Moses says,

> When the Most High gave to the nations their inheritance,
> when he divided mankind,
> he fixed the borders of the peoples
> according to the number of the sons of God [Israel].
> But the LORD's portion is his people,
> Jacob his allotted heritage. (vv. 8–9)

Paul refers to this statement about the territorial apportionment of the peoples of the earth in his sermon to the pagan Greeks on Mars Hill (see Acts 17:26).

Israel's Rejection of God (vv. 15–18). After speaking of God's goodness, the people's evil, and God's blessing, Moses points out that Israel has turned away from God to follow after foreign gods, which are no gods at all: "they sacrificed to demons that were no gods, to gods they had never known" (v. 17)

God's Rejection of the People (vv. 19–27). The consequences of turning from the true God to false gods are made clear. Terrible calamities will come on the people. They have rejected God, so God will reject them. The Hebrew says that they have rejected the true God for a "no god," so God will reject them for a "no people." In this play on words, he refers to the people as a people who are nothing in his sight. Indeed, God will reject them in favor of the Assyrians, who, centuries later, overthrew the northern kingdom, and then in favor of the Babylonians, who overthrew the kingdom in the south.

God's Assessment of the People (vv. 28–33). What are we to think of a nation that does something like this? God had called these people, led them out of Egypt with a mighty hand, preserved them in the desert, brought them to their own land, and soon would give them cities that they did not build and vineyards that they did not plant. What are we to think of a people who went their own way, chasing after false gods, after the Lord their God had protected and prospered them?

The kindest thing we can say about such people is that they lack common sense, and this section says exactly that: they lack spiritual discernment. There is a great parallel between what Moses says in this chapter and what Paul says in Romans 1. When people go their own way, God gives them up to a depraved mind—a mind totally mixed up in its thinking, that sets itself in opposition to God and actually approves evil.

A number of famous sermons have been preached on texts from this chapter of Deuteronomy. One is a sermon preached around the world by D. L. Moody based on (and titled after) verse 31: "Their rock is not like our Rock."[5] Moody points out that in the crises of life, the gods of the unbeliever are no help, because they are "no gods." But the God of the Bible is a sure foundation, a Rock, for those who build on him.

Sinners in the Hands of an Angry God (vv. 34–38). The next few verses contain another text that led to a great sermon, probably the best-known sermon ever preached in North America. The sermon was based on the verse "Their foot shall slide in due time" (v. 35 KJV) and was preached by Jonathan Edwards in Enfield, Connecticut, on July 8, 1741, under the title "Sinners in the Hands of an Angry God." God blessed that sermon so effectively that, although Edwards delivered it in almost a monotone, people began to moan as he described the terrors that await those who do not find salvation in Jesus Christ.

Puritan sermons always had three parts: (1) exegesis, (2) theology, and (3) application. Edwards skipped over the first part, exegesis, quickly, not because it was not important, but because his audience knew the Bible well enough to know the context of the passage. He developed a theology from the passage very clearly, point after point. Then, for more than half the sermon, he pressed home the application. The foot of the sinner will slide in due time, he reminded them; judgment is certain. The only thing that kept them out of hell right then, he said, was the sheer mercy of God—who nevertheless was infinitely angry with them. Yet there is an escape from God's judgment of sin, for "this is a day of mercy; . . . a day wherein Christ has thrown the door of mercy wide open . . . calling and crying with a loud voice to poor sinners."[6] Edwards made the wrath of God so terrifying, and the mercy of God so compelling, that by the blessing of God, revival came to that town in Connecticut.

5. See Dwight L. Moody, "Their Rock Is Not Our Rock," available in *Dwight Lyman Moody's Life Work and Gospel Sermons*, ed. Richard S. Rhodes (Chicago: Rhodes & McClure, 1907), 116–35.
6. Jonathan Edwards, "Sinners in the Hands of an Angry God" (sermon, Enfield, CT, July 8, 1741); repr. (Phillipsburg, NJ: P&R, 1992), 26, 30.

Moses' points for the people of Israel are exactly the same. First, judgment is being prepared for the wicked. Second, this judgment is close at hand—indeed, their day of disaster is near and their doom rushes on them. Third, there will be no one to help them when that terrible, inevitable day of judgment comes. The gods they took refuge in will be nowhere to be found.

This is a very unpopular message today. I do not hear many ministers preaching about hell, the wrath of God, or the damnation awaiting the wicked. I do not hear preachers stressing that nothing but the sheer good pleasure of God is keeping us from hell this very instant if we are not in Christ. But this message of coming judgment has been forcefully preached to the saving of souls in days past, and it is the message that explains why Jesus had to die.

The Nature of God and the Final Victory (vv. 39–43). The song of Moses does not end on a note of judgment. At the very end, the word *atonement* appears suddenly, almost surprisingly. God will "make atonement for his land and people" (v. 43 NIV). The word surely made the people think of the Day of Atonement, which we know points forward to the coming of Jesus Christ. It is only through Jesus that we can escape the judgment that hangs over us because Jesus took that judgment on himself. Christ shields us from all wrath; outside of Christ, we are exposed to all wrath. Moses' conclusion to this great song is that certain judgment is coming but God provides escape from judgment by making atonement for his people. The people need to find refuge in their God.

THE FINAL CHARGE (DEUT. 32:44–47)

At the end of the chapter, Moses charges the people one more time: "Take to heart all the words by which I am warning you today, that you may command them to your children, that they may be careful to do all the words of this law. For it is no empty word for you, but your very life, and by this word you shall live long in the land that you are going over the Jordan to possess" (vv. 46–47).

Moses' final assessment is very important. Deuteronomy is not just a law book. It is true that if you follow the legal maxims in the book of Deuteronomy, you will have an ordered society, you will

413

keep violence under control, and people will be encouraged to do the right things. But this is a matter of life and death—not just physical life and death, but spiritual life and death. Jesus said, quoting from this very book, "Man shall not live by bread alone, but by every word that comes from the mouth of God" (Matt. 4:4; cf. Deut. 8:3). You can have plenty to eat, a lovely house to live in, the high regard of people in this world—and yet die and go to hell. But the Word of God, blessed by the Holy Spirit, gives spiritual life, which is for eternity. You may go hungry or homeless, but the time will come when you will spend eternity with God. Jesus himself says that he has gone to prepare a mansion for you (see John 14:2–3).

Moses ends this way: "Take to heart all the words by which I am warning you today, that you may command them to your children, that they may be careful to do all the words of this law. For it is no empty word for you, but your very life" (Deut. 32:46–47). Whatever may come, remember that the words that come to you from God are your life; by them you must live. All other ways lead to eternal death. So give great attention to these life-giving words.

LEARNING FROM DEUTERONOMY 31–32

At the end of his life, Moses was focused on God. We have learned a number of things about God from Moses in these chapters from Deuteronomy.

God is sovereign. Moses had a great sense of the sovereignty of God. God is the eternal Creator and sustainer of his people, and of all people. He determines the boundaries of the earth's nations—in fact, he determines all things. Nothing ever surprises God, because he controls everything.

Do you have a God like that? Are you aware that your God is in charge of all things, including all the little details of your life? When you have begun to grasp this truth, you will learn to trust him more and more. If the Lord God is truly sovereign, even clothing the grass of the field, we can stop worrying about tomorrow, leaving all our cares in the hands of this all-powerful God (see Matt. 6:34).

God is faithful. The faithfulness of God demands faithfulness from his people. God had entered into a covenant with the people of Israel and he has entered into a covenant with us. He will not abandon us, nor will he allow us to abandon him. As Paul writes to his beloved Timothy, "If we are faithless, he remains faithful—for he cannot deny himself" (2 Tim. 2:13). He is faithful and he expects faithfulness from us.

How can we not seek to be faithful, praying for the Holy Spirit's help to do so, to the One who has been utterly faithful to us?

God is gracious. God had been gracious to the people even though they had gone their own way, at times even preferring false gods—turning their backs on the very God who created, redeemed, and preserved them.

The grace of God has saved you and me. The grace of God has kept you and me. The grace of God takes us back even when we persist in going our own way. John Newton called it "amazing grace," and it truly is amazing, "grace that is greater than all our sin."[7]

God's words create and sustain life. Moses emphasizes nothing in these final words more than he emphasizes the power of God's words: "They are not just idle words for you—they are your life" (Deut. 32:47 NIV).

Do you really believe that God's words are more important than your daily food? If you do, God's Word will become your meditation day and night. Like godly Ezra, you will give attention to the Word, make time for it, study it, and then strive to obey it (see Ezra 7:10).

---

7. Julia H. Johnston, "Marvelous Grace of Our Loving Lord", 1910.

32

THE DEATH OF MOSES

Deuteronomy 33–34

THE BELIEVER'S DEATHBED

Charles Haddon Spurgeon once preached a sermon called "Sermons from Saintly Deathbeds," in which he studied some of the final testimonies of believers.[1] It is fascinating to do this. For example, Matthew Henry, a great commentator and godly man, said when he was dying, "A life spent in the service of God and communion with Him is the most comfortable and pleasant life that any one can live in this world."[2] As a more obscure example, Thomas Halyburton, a great Scottish preacher born in the 1600s, said, "You may . . . believe a man venturing on eternity. . . . I have weighed eternity this last night. I have looked on death as stript of all things pleasant to nature . . . and under the view of all these, I found that in the way of God that gave satisfaction; not only a rational satisfaction, but a heart-engaging power attending it, that makes me rejoice."[3]

Moses, the servant of God, had many dying words. In a sense, they make up the entire book of Deuteronomy. We have studied two

1. Charles Haddon Spurgeon, "Sermons from Saintly Deathbeds" (sermon no. 783, Metropolitan Tabernacle, Newington, London, December 1, 1867).
2. Quoted in C. Palmer, "Matthew Henry," in *The Sunday Magazine*, ed. Thomas Guthrie (London: Strahan & Co., 1872), 333.
3. *Memoirs of the Rev. Thomas Halyburton* (Edinburgh: John Johnstone, 1848), 258.

of his three addresses: the first urged godliness on the people, and the second dealt with the challenge to the people. Now, in Deuteronomy 33, Moses delivers his final address: a blessing on the tribes. Moses' last words are in praise of God, and the final words of God in this book—the last three verses—are in praise of Moses.

THE FINAL BLESSING (DEUT. 33)

The first five books of the Bible give us the dying words of only one other man, Jacob, recorded by Moses at the end of Genesis. His series of blessings on the tribes is very similar to Moses' words at the end of Deuteronomy, making an interesting parallel. The blessings of Jacob can also be compared with Moses' second song, which came only the chapter before (ch. 32). Both Moses' song and the final blessing anticipate the future, Charles Erdman points out, but they are strikingly contrasted.[4] The song talks about apostasy and failure, while the blessing is bright with expectation of divine favor.

Moses has every reason to be honest. He has experienced the people's waywardness for forty years in the wilderness. He has told them that they will eventually fall away and that, when they fall away, the judgment of God will come on them. He has warned them so that they will stay close to God for as long as possible. Yet when he comes to the end, Moses' very last words are words of blessing.

The Christian life is the same. Failures flow from us throughout our lives, but when everything is drawn together, our final thoughts and observations should focus on the grace and the glory of God and on his faithfulness to the end.

PREAMBLE TO THE BLESSING (DEUT. 33:2–5)

The preamble begins with God—"The Lord" (v. 2)—and we will see that it also ends with God. This is the most significant aspect of the biblical world- and life-view. Consider Romans 11 when Paul gets to the end of the most difficult section of perhaps the most difficult

---

4. See Charles Rosenbury Erdman, *The Book of Deuteronomy: An Exposition* (Grand Rapids: Fleming H. Revell, 1953; repr., Grand Rapids: Baker, 1982).

book in the Bible. Having written about election, reprobation, and God's purposes in history, Paul breaks into praise of this great, transcendent, all-powerful God. His last words are, "For from him and through him and to him are all things. To him be glory forever. Amen" (Rom. 11:36). Paul follows exactly the same pattern as Moses when he wraps up by saying that it starts with God, is from God, and ends with God. To him be the glory.

When Moses starts with God, he starts with his coming down on Mount Sinai to give the people the law, rather than with his calling of the patriarchs or with Jacob's twelve sons. He has a very good reason for that. His blessing on the people is a blessing on the *nation*. In a sense, that nation began at Sinai. God had called a race of people to himself beginning with Abraham, that people had multiplied in Egypt, and they had come out of Egypt as a great people, but they were not a nation until Sinai. At Sinai, they were organized: they were given the law and instructed in the right way of approaching God.

This blessing, and particularly its opening (see Deut. 33:2), must have meant a great deal to the people because it is quoted at other points in the Old Testament. We find it in the song of Deborah (see Judg. 5:4–5) and in the minor prophet Habakkuk's great prayer of blessing (see Hab. 3:3). There may be other, subtler references throughout the Bible as well.

REUBEN'S BLESSING (DEUT. 33:6)

After the preamble, Moses pronounces blessings on the tribes by calling them by the names of the sons of Jacob, their forefathers. Without any special introduction, he starts with the tribe of Reuben. Reuben was the oldest son of Jacob and had forfeited his birthright because of his sin with Bilhah, his father's concubine (see Gen. 35:22; 1 Chron. 5:1). But even though he had lost his birthright, he had not lost his place among the tribes of Israel. In fact, Moses says that the tribe will continue, and will produce sufficient offspring to preserve the identity of Reuben's line. "Let Reuben live, and not die, but let his men be few." This is not a promise of great things to be accomplished, but it shows that even when there has been deplorable sin, God is very gracious.

JUDAH'S BLESSING (DEUT. 33:7)

The kings of Israel would eventually come from the tribe of Judah, so it is appropriate that when Moses speaks of Judah in his second blessing, he speaks of it as the tribe that would lead the people in their battles. He speaks of Judah defending Israel's cause, and he asks God to be Judah's help against his foes.

Given that Judah will go on to become the dominant, most important tribe, it is perhaps surprising that so little space is given to it in the series of blessings. Nonetheless, what is said about Judah is important, and the brevity of the blessing is understandable at this stage in Israel's history. The people have not yet entered the land and do not yet have a king, so Judah has not yet become the kingly tribe.[5]

LEVI'S BLESSING (DEUT. 33:8–11)

The dominant tribe at this time, in Moses' view, is Levi, the tribe of the priests. Three things are granted to Levi in this blessing: (1) the Thummim and Urim, which were used to discern the will of God; (2) the privilege of teaching people about God, a tremendous privilege that all Christians have today; and (3) the duties pertaining to offering up sacrifices and incense.

Moses praises Levi for the conduct of its people at Massah and Meribah, the two places where water had been produced from rock to meet the Israelites' needs. On the second occasion of his bringing forth water from the rock, Moses had sinned by not properly honoring God. In his blessing here, Moses graciously says that the Levites will be blessed by God at the very point where he himself had failed.

Moses also praises the Levites for their conduct at Sinai, when the rest of the people were worshipping the golden calf. Moses had tried to reclaim their allegiance, calling for any who were loyal to come forward, and the tribe of Levi had responded. At Moses' command, they had taken their swords and killed the ringleaders. The Levites are commended here for putting God's word and his covenant above all else, even before family.

---

5. The absence of reference to Judah as the kingly tribe is one evidence for an early date for the composition of Deuteronomy (i.e., during Moses' lifetime).

BENJAMIN'S BLESSING (DEUT. 33:12)

Benjamin, the second child of Rachel, was the son whom Jacob especially loved; therefore Moses calls him "the beloved." But what is most important is that Benjamin was beloved not just by Jacob but by the Lord. Everybody wants to be loved. To be greatly loved by another human is a wonderful thing, but the most important thing of all is to be loved by God, which is what Moses says of Benjamin in this blessing: "Let the beloved of the LORD rest secure in him" (v. 12 NIV). God's perfect love will never change or fade away. If God loves us through Jesus Christ, nothing in all heaven or earth will ever separate us from that love (see Rom. 8:38–39).

JOSEPH'S BLESSING (DEUT. 33:13-17)

Joseph had married Asenath, the daughter of Potiphera, a priest of On, an Egyptian, and had two sons—Ephraim and Manasseh—who went on to become two tribes of Israel. When Moses blesses Joseph, his blessing falls on these two half-tribes. They have experienced prosperity and will be greatly blessed in the future. Moses uses very poetic language: "May the LORD bless his land with the precious dew from heaven above and with the deep waters that lie below; with the best the sun brings forth . . . with the best gifts of the earth and its fullness" (vv. 13–14, 16 NIV); all these blessings will be given to Joseph's posterity.

This is an appropriate blessing, because Egypt had been blessed through Joseph in his day. When famine had been about to come on the whole Mediterranean world, God, through the dream of Pharaoh, had revealed to Joseph what would happen and Joseph had saved grain so that Egypt prospered during that time. Just as Egypt had prospered under Joseph, the territories of Ephraim and Manasseh would prosper under Joseph's descendants.

ZEBULUN AND ISSACHAR'S BLESSINGS (DEUT. 33:18-19)

Zebulun and Issachar will be blessed in their "going out" and in their remaining in their tents (see v. 18) These two phrases may refer to times of war and peace, but may instead mean that the people will be blessed at *all* times; no matter what they do, at home or away from their homes, they will be blessed. In addition, they will encourage the people in their worship and they will prosper through commerce (see v. 19).

GAD'S BLESSING (DEUT. 33:20-21)

Gad was one of the two and a half tribes that settled in Transjordan, the land east of the Jordan river, and Moses says, "He chose the best of the land for himself" (v. 21). This sounds like a pejorative statement, because, put that way, Gad's decision sounds selfish, as though the tribe grabbed the best land and left the rest for other people. Actually, this criticism is not what is expressed here. Moses *commends* Gad for possessing the leader's portion, adding that Gad "executed the justice of the LORD" (v. 21) and Moses blesses God as the one who enlarges Gad's domain.

Why is this a blessing and not a criticism? I believe the reason is that Gad, situated in the desert in Transjordan, would bear the brunt of any attack that came from the east. The people of Israel, when settled in Canaan, were largely attacked by the kings from the east or by robbers from the desert. The Israelites probably thought very highly of Gad's lion-like qualities as that tribe protected their eastern flank.

FURTHER BLESSINGS AND POSTSCRIPT (DEUT. 33:22-29)

After rapidly blessing Dan (see v. 22), Naphtali (see v. 23), and Asher (see vv. 24–25), Moses praises "the God of Jeshurun" (v. 26 NIV). *Jeshurun* probably means the "upright one" or the "righteous one." The name refers to Israel—what Israel is or should be—so this statement is in praise of Israel's God. Who is like the God of Israel, the God of Jeshurun? There is no God like him; he is a marvelous God and always to be praised. He is faithful; we can trust him. Under the shadow of his wings, we can abide in safety.

This is worth reading in full.

> There is none like God, O Jeshurun,
>> who rides through the heavens to your help,
>> through the skies in his majesty.
> The eternal God is your dwelling place,

and underneath are the everlasting arms.
And he thrust out the enemy before you
   and said, "Destroy."
So Israel lived in safety,
   Jacob lived alone,
in a land of grain and wine,
   whose heavens drop down dew.
Happy are you, O Israel! Who is like you,
   a people saved by the LORD,
the shield of your help,
   and the sword of your triumph!
Your enemies shall come fawning to you,
   and you shall tread upon their backs. (Deut. 33:26–29)

These are the very last words of Moses, the author of more biblical material than any other single human being, and in these final words he confesses that there is no god like God. This is wonderful. If Moses could praise God like that, shouldn't we do it too? We say, "O for a thousand tongues to sing my great Redeemer's praise,"[6] but the one tongue that we have is so often silent. Moses spoke of the glory of God; may we do so as well, and do so more and more as we go on in life and experience more and more of his mercy and his grace. If we do this throughout our lives, when our time comes to die, we will be able to testify to his grace and mercy even then.

MOUNT NEBO (DEUT. 34)

The end has come, and Moses ascends Mount Nebo to be gathered to his people. Yet before he dies, God comes to stand behind him, as it were, and points out all the features of the land that he promised to Abraham, Isaac, and Jacob and to which he has led the people at last:

Gilead as far as Dan, all Naphtali, the land of Ephraim and Manasseh,
   all the land of Judah as far as the western sea, the Negeb, and the

---

6. Charles Wesley, "O for a Thousand Tongues to Sing," 1739.

Plain, that is, the Valley of Jericho the city of palm trees, as far as Zoar. (Deut. 34:1–3)

There is a measure of sadness here. Moses has brought the people to the threshold of the land, yet, as God says once more, Moses himself will not enter it. But there is joy and satisfaction in this moment as well. Moses has led the people for forty years, he has brought them to the land, and he has been faithful to the end. He has done all the things that God gave him to do. Having completed his work and transitioned his leadership to Joshua, he lies down to rest.

Like the apostle Paul, Moses could have said,

> I have fought the good fight, I have finished the race, I have kept the faith. Henceforth there is laid up for me the crown of righteousness, which the Lord, the righteous judge, will award to me on that day, and not only to me but also to all who have loved his appearing. (2 Tim. 4:7–8)

Will we be able to say this as well, when we come to our own last days? Now is the time to prepare.

Deuteronomy 34:7 states, "Moses was 120 years old when he died. His eye was undimmed, and his vigor unabated." This may be a passing reference, but it strikes me that it has special meaning. God had taken him up the mountain to show him the land, and God had preserved his eyesight so that he could see it. It would be natural for a man of 120 years to have failing eyesight, but God was gracious to him to the very end. Although Moses would not enter the land, he would be able to see it.

The land of Canaan was never going to be the final home of God's people, as the writer of Hebrews says so eloquently. As with all the redeemed, Moses "looked for a city which hath foundations, whose builder and maker is God" (Heb. 11:10 KJV).

LEARNING FROM MOSES

Now, at the end of Moses' life, I must try to evaluate him as a leader. We have seen him in all kinds of situations: alone with God on the mountain, before Pharaoh, before the masses of the people. We have watched him face down angry people; we have observed him speaking to the mighty and to the lowly; we have seen him angry, and bowed in fervent prayer. He was a man with the sinful nature of men, yet a great man too.

What most stands out about him? How should we remember him, his achievements, the character that God developed in him? He was a man of faith and of prayer; he was humble and courageous. I discussed these four categories in my first chapter; throughout this book our appreciation of him in those areas has been deepened. We have seen Moses exercise faith in God in the most trying circumstances. He prayed effectively and at all times. But even though he was a great man, he remained humble right to the end, and nowhere did he show greater courage than when he delivered his final charges to the people and then, with firm step and upward glance, ascended Mount Nebo where he was to die.

Moses wrote the Pentateuch, and under difficult circumstances. Has any written work been more influential in the long history of the world than the first five books of the Bible? Christians have the Gospels, and we love the Pauline epistles, but Genesis, Exodus, Leviticus, Numbers, and Deuteronomy are an achievement of monumental order, even just from a literary or historical point of view—and one man wrote them all.

But how I evaluate Moses is not important. What matters is how God sees him, and we are given this at the very end:

> And there has not arisen a prophet since in Israel like Moses, whom the LORD knew face to face, none like him for all the signs and the wonders that the LORD sent him to do in the land of Egypt, to Pharaoh and to all his servants and to all his land, and for all the mighty power and all the great deeds of terror that Moses did in the sight of all Israel. (Deut. 34:10–12)

Moses was the greatest spokesman for God, as well as the greatest worker of miracles, in the entire Old Testament period. What was the secret of his success? He knew God face-to-face. *He knew God.* He spent time with God, he loved God, God was always in his mind and in his heart. F. B. Meyer wrote,

> All that he wrought on earth was the outcome of the secret abiding of his soul in God. God was his home, his help, his stay. He was nothing: God was all. And all that he accomplished on the earth was due to that Mighty One indwelling, fulfilling, and working out through him, as his organ and instrument, his own consummate plans.[7]

God was Moses' focus, his first true and only love, his constant companion, and the subject of his most exalted meditation through-out his many long years. God was his life's goal and desire, and he is with God today. In this deeply settled attitude Moses rightly makes us think of Jesus Christ. Christ lives with the Father; everything he does, he does for the Father; and everything he does pleases the Father (see John 5:19–21). Although Jesus came after Moses, Moses learned to follow this pattern.

This is what you and I are called to do. How do we show forth the power of God to a world that doesn't have the faintest idea what God is like? There is only one way. We must live for God; we must have God so much in our minds and our hearts that he is at the center of our thoughts. We must do our work, earn our living, make our meals, and so on, within the framework of the presence, blessing, and glory of our God.

This does not happen naturally. If it is to happen to us, we must spend time with God. I cannot emphasize this enough. Spend time with God. There is no substitute. Then, because we are spending time with God, we must obey God. Moses was the great lawgiver, and he stressed this again and again. We can't just get in a pious mood and spend time with God; we must also seek to do what God commands. Moses did that. We must also trust God. Moses went through very difficult experiences. At times it seemed that almost everyone had turned against him, including members of his own family. Through it

---

7. F. B. Meyer, *Moses: The Servant of God* (New York: Fleming H. Revell Company, n.d.), 184.

all, this great man turned to God and trusted God. That was because he knew the Lord, the Holy One who keeps covenant with his people, and he trusted him.

Moses didn't have a greater God than we do. We worship exactly the same God, and by his grace we know even more about him than Moses did. In the New Testament as well as the Old, God's attributes, glory, and grace are unfolded for those who will read and study his Word.

I do not know what will come into your life this year. You may experience grievous things, as God does allow trials and severe experiences to come into the lives of his people. But in these hard times, the people of God triumph and show forth his grace, because they have their eyes on God, knowing that he is working out his good and pleasing purposes in and for his people.

May our Father grant that we might be what he intends us to be—his people—in the midst of a world that is alienated from him and hostile toward him. May we set our eyes on God and serve him as long as he gives us breath, so that when we come to the end, whether it is true in the physical sense or not, our *spiritual* eyes will be undimmed and our *spiritual* strength unabated, forever and ever.

Index of Scripture

Index of Subjects and Names